"The volume brings together a wealth of experience with impediments and successes in institutionalizing inter- and transdisciplinary research (ITDR) through case studies that uniquely cover the regions of the globe. Epistemic and organizational cultures matter and so do the different communities involved in building cross-border collaborations. As the world re-emerges from the devastating effects of the COVID-19 pandemic, facing a global sustainability crisis, it is of utmost relevance to pursue the institutionalization of ITDR while enabling and empowering younger researchers to explore the new spaces thus created".

Helga Nowotny, Former President of the European Research Council, ERC

"This important volume offers fresh perspectives on how inter- and transdisciplinarity have been conceptualised and institutionalized around the world. Grounded in the latest empirical research, the volume bristles with practical insights, examples of best practice, suggestions about how best to support researchers, and the opportunities inter- and transdisciplinarity afford".

Jane Ohlmeyer, Erasmus Smith's Professor of History (1762), Trinity College Dublin, Ireland, and Chair of the Irish Research Council.

"As interdisciplinarity and transdisciplinarity continue to expand in their global influence, it is imperative that we understand how to institutionalize them so that we can take full advantage of their insights and accomplishments. Edited by two leaders in the field, this book is required reading for anyone interested in building, stabilizing, and sustaining interdisciplinary and transdisciplinary programs".

Michael O'Rourke, Professor of Philosophy and faculty member in AgBioResearch and Environmental Science and Policy at Michigan State University, USA

INSTITUTIONALIZING INTERDISCIPLINARITY AND TRANSDISCIPLINARITY

Institutionalizing Interdisciplinarity and Transdisciplinarity fills a gap in the current literature by systematizing and comparing a wide international scope of case studies illustrating varied ways of institutionalizing theory and practice.

This collection comprises three parts. After an introduction of overall themes, Part I presents case studies on institutionalizing. Part II focuses on transdisciplinary examples, while Part III includes cross-cutting themes, such as funding, evaluation, and intersections between epistemic cultures. With expert contributions from authors representing projects and programs in Asia, Africa, Australia, Europe, Russia and South Caucuses, and Latin and North America, this book brings together comparative perspectives on theory and practice, while also describing strategies and models of change. Each chapter identifies dimensions inherent in fostering effective and sustainable practices. Together, they advance both analysis and action-related challenges. The proposed conceptual framework that emerges supports innovative practices that are alternatives to dominant academic cultures and approaches in pertinent disciplines, fields, professionals and members of government, industry, and communities.

Applying a comparative perspective throughout, the contributors reflect on aspects of institutionalizing interdisciplinarity and transdisciplinarity as well as insights applicable to further contexts. This innovative volume will be of great interest to students, scholars, practitioners, and members of organizations promoting and facilitating inter-disciplinary and trans-disciplinary research.

Bianca Vienni Baptista, Senior Researcher at the Transdisciplinarity Lab of the Department of Environmental Systems Science (USYS-TdLab), ETH Zurich, Switzerland.

Julie Thompson Klein, Professor of Humanities Emerita at Wayne State University and International Research Affiliate in the Transdisciplinarity Lab at ETH Zurich, Switzerland.

Research and Teaching in Environmental Studies

This series brings together international educators and researchers working from a variety of perspectives to explore and present best practice for research and teaching in environmental studies.

Given the urgency of environmental problems, our approach to the research and teaching of environmental studies is crucial. Reflecting on examples of success and failure within the field, this collection showcases authors from a diverse range of environmental disciplines including climate change, environmental communication and sustainable development. Lessons learned from interdisciplinary and transdisciplinary research are presented, as well as teaching and classroom methodology for specific countries and disciplines.

Interdisciplinary and Transdisciplinary Failures
Lessons Learned from Cautionary Tales
Edited by Dena Fam and Michael O'Rourke

Environmental Consciousness, Nature and the Philosophy of Education
Ecologizing Education
Michael Bonnett

Theatre Pedagogy in the Era of Climate Crisis
Edited by Conrad Alexandrowicz and David Fancy

Institutionalizing Interdisciplinarity and Transdisciplinarity
Collaboration across Cultures and Communities
Edited by Bianca Vienni Baptista and Julie Thompson Klein

For more information about this series, please visit: www.routledge.com/Research-and-Teaching-in-Environmental-Studies/book-series/RTES

INSTITUTIONALIZING INTERDISCIPLINARITY AND TRANSDISCIPLINARITY

Collaboration across Cultures and Communities

Edited by Bianca Vienni Baptista and Julie Thompson Klein

First published 2022
by Routledge
4 Park Square, Milton Park, Abingdon, Oxon OX14 4RN

and by Routledge
605 Third Avenue, New York, NY 10158

Routledge is an imprint of the Taylor & Francis Group, an informa business

© 2022 selection and editorial matter, Bianca Vienni Baptista and Julie Thompson Klein; individual chapters, the contributors

The right of Bianca Vienni Baptista and Julie Thompson Klein to be identified as the authors of the editorial material, and of the authors for their individual chapters, has been asserted in accordance with sections 77 and 78 of the Copyright, Designs and Patents Act 1988.

All rights reserved. No part of this book may be reprinted or reproduced or utilised in any form or by any electronic, mechanical, or other means, now known or hereafter invented, including photocopying and recording, or in any information storage or retrieval system, without permission in writing from the publishers.

Trademark notice: Product or corporate names may be trademarks or registered trademarks, and are used only for identification and explanation without intent to infringe.

British Library Cataloguing-in-Publication Data
A catalogue record for this book is available from the British Library

Library of Congress Cataloging-in-Publication Data
A catalog record has been requested for this book

ISBN: 978-0-367-65435-1 (hbk)
ISBN: 978-0-367-65434-4 (pbk)
ISBN: 978-1-003-12942-4 (ebk)

DOI: 10.4324/9781003129424

Typeset in Bembo
by Deanta Global Publishing Services, Chennai, India

CONTENTS

List of figures x
List of tables xii
List of contributors xiii
Acknowledgments xvii
Foreword by Christian Pohl xx

1 Introduction: Institutionalizing interdisciplinarity and transdisciplinarity: Cultures and communities, timeframes and spaces 1
  Julie Thompson Klein, Bianca Vienni Baptista, and Danilo Streck

PART I
Interdisciplinary institutional spaces and timeframes **11**

2 Excellence with impact: Why UK research policy discourages "transdisciplinarity" 13
  Catherine Lyall

3 Taking interdisciplinarity and transdisciplinarity to eye level with scientific disciplines: Teaching and learning in Complementary Studies at Leuphana College, Lüneburg, Germany 27
  Maik Adomßent

4 Interdisciplinary projects and science policies in Mexico: Divergences and convergences 43
Juan Carlos Villa-Soto, Mónica Ribeiro Palacios, and Norma Blazquez Graf

5 A long and winding road toward institutionalizing interdisciplinarity: Lessons from environmental and sustainability science programs in Brazil 57
Gabriela Litre, Diego Pereira Lindoso, and Marcel Bursztyn

6 Interdisciplinary education and research in North America 72
Karri A. Holley and Rick Szostak

PART II
Transdisciplinary institutional spaces and timeframes 87

7 The rise of transdisciplinary "boundary organisations" within the Australian tertiary education sector: Beyond the disciplined university 89
Isabel Sebastian, Dena Fam, and Jason Prior

8 A contextual approach to institutional change: Transdisciplinarity in Ghanaian higher education 107
Beatrice Akua-Sakyiwah

9 The development of interdisciplinarity and transdisciplinarity in modern Russian science and higher education 124
Vladimir Mokiy and Tatyana Lukyanova

10 "Leaping over" disciplines: Historical context and future potential for interdisciplinarity and transdisciplinarity in Chinese higher education 139
BinBin J. Pearce

11 Challenges and opportunities for implementing transdisciplinary case study approaches in post-Soviet academic systems: Experiences from Armenia and Georgia 152
Tigran Keryan, Andreas Muhar, Tamara Mitrofanenko, Kristine Tanajyan, and Lela Khartishvili

12 Research Institute for Humanity and Nature: A Japanese center for inter- and trans-disciplinary consilience of socio-cultural dimensions of environmental sustainability 168
Yasuhisa Kondo, Terukazu Kumazawa, Naoki Kikuchi, Kaoru Kamatani, Satoe Nakahara, Natsuko Yasutomi, Yuta Uchiyama, Kengo Hayashi, Satoko Hashimoto, Akihiro Miyata, and Shin Muramatsu

PART III
Intersections between cultures and communities **185**

13 Epistemic cultures in European intersections of art–science 187
Paulo Nuno Vicente and Margarida Lucas

14 Making and taking time: Work, funding, and assessment infrastructures in inter- and trans-disciplinary research 204
Ulrike Felt

15 Co-productive evaluation of inter- and trans-disciplinary research and innovation projects 218
Jack Spaapen

16 Conclusion: A comparative framework for institutionalizing inter- and trans-disciplinary research and teaching in higher education 232
Bianca Vienni Baptista, Julie Thompson Klein, and Danilo Streck

Index *249*

FIGURES

3.1 Study structure of the bachelor's model at Leuphana College. Students acquire 90 CP in their major and 30 CP in their minor. Leuphana Semester and Complementary Studies (30 CP each) together comprise one-third of the entire program   28

3.2 Structure and modules of Complementary Studies at Leuphana College   29

3.3 Localization of Leuphana's holistic approach in implementing inter- and trans-disciplinary teaching in sustainability (the lower-right quadrant) in Rusinko's (2010, p. 253) generic matrix to integrate sustainability in higher education   34

3.4 Aligning institutional facilities at Leuphana University: interplay of the Center for Methods, Teaching Service, and Course evaluations   36

5.1 The "star model". The modes of engagement of faculty members in an interdisciplinary program offered at a major university. **D:** disciplinary faculty; **In:** interdisciplinary program/center   59

5.2 Evolution of the graduate programs in CAPES' interdisciplinary and environmental assessment areas. The year 2019 had no updated data at the time of publication of this chapter for interdisciplinary courses, so the chart replicates results from the year 2018   61

5.3	Proportion of graduate programs classified in CAPES' interdisciplinary (until 2018) and environmental science (until 2019) areas. **MSc:** master's; **PhD:** doctorate; **MSc/PhD:** master's and doctorate; **MP:** professional master's; **DP:** professional doctorate; **MP/DP:** professional master's/professional doctorate	63
5.4	Distribution of the postgraduate courses/programs evaluated as interdisciplinary and environmental sciences by CAPES according to Brazilian regions	65
7.1	The evolution of ISF within the University of Technology Sydney 1997–2021	92
7.2	Characteristics of a transdisciplinary boundary organisation (TD-BO)	95
11.1	Dimensions for investigating the implementation of transdisciplinarity into academic systems	155
12.1	Ideal timeline of a research project of the Research Institute for Humanity and Nature	169
12.2	External affiliates of Research Institute for Humanity and Nature in March 2020	171
12.3	Number of full research (FR) projects per year (bars) and the gross annual expenditure of Research Institute for Humanity and Nature (broken curves)	172
13.1	Boxplot of the perceptions of "two cultures" problem	196
13.2	Boxplot on the impact of educational specialization	197
13.3	Boxplot on the impact of academic department structure	198
13.4	Boxplot on the integrated approach to addressing contemporary societal challenges	199
16.1	A heuristic and comparative framework for institutionalizing inter- and trans-disciplinary research and teaching: dimensions for institutionalizing	237
16.2	Factors for institutionalizing inter- and trans-disciplinary research and teaching	238

TABLES

2.1	Results from the Economic and Social Research Council website showing significant disparity between highlighted search terms	15
3.1	Queries of the optional question block on interdisciplinarity in the component system of Leuphana's teaching evaluation	37
3.2	Contrasting characteristics of teaching and learning in communities-of-interest with those of communities-of-practice (after Fischer and Ostwald, 2005)	39
7.1	Characteristics of a transdisciplinary boundary organisation	96
12.1	Major characteristics of inter- and trans-disciplinary research	173
12.2	Checkpoints for management and intellectual development of collaborative research projects	175
12.3	List of the interviewed projects (anonymized)	176
12.4	Guidelines for semi-structured interviews	177
12.5	Key factors of intellectual development extracted from the interviews	177
13.1	Demographic characteristics of survey respondents	194
13.2	Countries represented by survey respondents	195

CONTRIBUTORS

Maik Adomßent, Coordinator of Complementary Studies at Leuphana College, Leuphana University, Germany.

Beatrice Akua-Sakyiwah, Head and Senior Lecturer at the Gender Development and Resource Centre, GIMPA School of Liberal Arts and Social Sciences, Ghana.

Norma Blazquez Graf, Research Professor at the Center for Interdisciplinary Research in Sciences and Humanities of the National Autonomous University of Mexico, Mexico.

Marcel Bursztyn, Full Professor at the Center for Sustainable Development, University of Brasília, Brazil.

Dena Fam, Associate Professor and Sustainable Design Scholar engaged in inter- and trans-disciplinary, design-led research and practice, Australia.

Ulrike Felt, Professor and Head of the Department of Science and Technology Studies at the University of Vienna, Austria.

Satoko Hashimoto, Project Specialist at the Institute of Social Science, University of Tokyo, Japan.

Kengo Hayashi, Associate Professor at the Institute of Industrial Science, University of Tokyo, Japan.

Karri A. Holley, Professor of Higher Education, University of Alabama, USA.

Kaoru Kamatani, Associate Professor at the School of Food Management, Ritsumeikan University, Japan.

Tigran Keryan, Doctor of Social and Economic Sciences at the BOKU University of Natural Resources and Life Sciences, Austria.

Lela Khartishvili, Doctor of Social and Economic Sciences at the BOKU University of Natural Resources and Life Sciences, Austria.

Naoki Kikuchi, Associate Professor at the Center for Advanced Tourism Sciences, Institute of Human and Social Sciences, Kanazawa University, Japan.

Yasuhisa Kondo, Associate Professor at the Research Institute for Humanity and Nature (RIHN), Japan.

Terukazu Kumazawa, Associate Professor at the Research Institute for Humanity and Nature (RIHN), Japan.

Gabriela Litre, Full Researcher at the Center for Sustainable Development, University of Brasília (CDS-UnB) and the Observatory of Social and Environmental Dynamics, INCT Odisseia, Brazil.

Margarida Lucas, Researcher at the Research Centre for Didactics and Technology in the Education of Trainers (CIDTFF), University of Aveiro, Portugal.

Tatyana Lukyanova, Main Expert at the Russian School of Transdisciplinarity, Russia.

Catherine Lyall, Professor of Science and Public Policy at the University of Edinburgh, UK.

Tamara Mitrofanenko, Project Coordinator at the Institute of Landscape Development, Recreation and Conservation Planning, BOKU University of Natural Resources and Life Sciences, Austria.

Akihiro Miyata, PhD Student at the Graduate School of Arts and Sciences, The University of Tokyo, Japan.

Vladimir Mokiy, Head of the Russian School of Transdisciplinarity and Director of the Institute of Transdisciplinary Technologies, Russia.

Andreas Muhar, Professor in Sustainable Landscape Development, Transdisciplinarity and Knowledge Integration, at the BOKU University of Natural Resources and Life Sciences, Vienna, Austria.

Shin Muramatsu, Professor at the Graduate School of Business Design, Josai International University, and Emeritus Professor at The University of Tokyo, Japan.

Satoe Nakahara, Cultural Anthropologist and former Researcher of the Open Team Science Project of the Research Institute for Humanity and Nature (RIHN), Japan.

BinBin J. Pearce, Senior Researcher at the Transdisciplinarity Lab of the Department of Environmental Systems Science (USYS-TdLab), ETH Zurich, Switzerland.

Diego Pereira Lindoso, Research Fellow in the INCT Odisseia project, University of Brasília, Brazil, and the PONDERFUL project, University of Girona, Spain.

Christian Pohl, Senior Lecturer and Co-director of the Transdisciplinarity Lab of the Department of Environmental Systems Science (USYS-TdLab), ETH Zurich, Switzerland.

Jason Prior, Professor at the Institute for Sustainable Futures, University of Technology Sydney, Australia.

Mónica Ribeiro Palacios, Researcher at the Interdisciplinary Research Center of the Autonomous University of Querétaro, Mexico.

Isabel Sebastian, Researcher at the Institute for Sustainable Futures (ISF), University of Technology Sydney, and Marie Skłodowska-Curie Fellow at Cardiff University, UK.

Jack Spaapen, Independent Expert on Research and Innovation Policy and Senior Policy Advisor at the Royal Netherlands Academy of Arts and Sciences, The Netherlands.

Danilo Streck, Professor at the Graduate School of Education of the University of Caxias do Sul, Brazil.

Rick Szostak, Professor and Chair of Economics at the University of Alberta, Canada.

Kristine Tanajyan, Lecturer at the Department of Education, Psychology and Sociology, and Researcher at the Chess Education Institute at the Armenian State Pedagogical University, Armenia.

Julie Thompson Klein, Professor of Humanities Emerita at Wayne State University and International Research Affiliate in the Transdisciplinarity Lab at ETH Zurich, Switzerland.

Yuta Uchiyama, Assistant Professor at Kobe University, Japan.

Paulo Nuno Vicente, Assistant Professor at Universidade Nova de Lisboa, Portugal.

Bianca Vienni Baptista, Senior Researcher at the Transdisciplinarity Lab of the Department of Environmental Systems Science (USYS-TdLab), ETH Zurich, Switzerland.

Juan Carlos Villa-Soto, Academic Technician of the Center for Interdisciplinary Research in Sciences and Humanities of the National Autonomous University of Mexico, Mexico.

Natsuko Yasutomi, Research Associate of the Aakash Project of the Research Institute for Humanity and Nature (RIHN), Japan.

ACKNOWLEDGMENTS

This book, like many challenging projects, is the outcome of a shared process of reflection, discussion, and elaboration. We envisioned it several years ago when we started exchanging ideas on common interests. Bianca, in particular, still recalls the moment when approaching Julie at the 2015 International Transdisciplinarity Conference, hosted in Basel (Switzerland) by the Network for Transdisciplinary Research (td-net) to share her thoughts. One of the future projects we contemplated included rethinking institutionalizing processes and how to foster them. After that first conversation, and subsequent publications and conferences, we began designing this volume.

This brief recollection shows that informal conversations and academic generosity are forces that can make a difference in striving for change. Over these years, other deeply generous colleagues contributed as well. Special thanks go to Christian Pohl, Co-director of the Transdisciplinarity Lab (TdLab, ETH Zurich), and to Ulli Vilsmaier (Leuphana University) for collaborations that inspired this book in profound ways. In addition, we acknowledge other colleagues at the TdLab including Sandro Bösch, who helped us design the figures in Chapter 16.

We are deeply grateful to the authors as well, whose chapters are essential contributions to this book and the prospect of replicating their vision and experiences in the future while opening further spaces for comparative analysis. Together, they constitute an amazing group of scholars who invested their time in this project while sharing their expertise and perspectives. They imprinted a unique vision of institutionalizing interdisciplinarity and transdisciplinarity on this book that we consider its main asset. Danilo Streck (University of Caxias do Sul) has also collaborated with us in writing the Introduction and Conclusions, sharing his experience and knowledge of comparative studies, and Catherine

xviii Acknowledgments

Lyall (University of Edinburgh) supported this project from the start with positive feedback.

We are further grateful to scholars who served as anonymous peer reviewers of chapters, enriching them with their insightful feedback. They include (in alphabetical order):

- Tateo Arimoto, Professor at National Graduate Institute for Policy Studies (GRIPS) and Principal Fellow, Japan Science and Technology Agency (JST/CRDS) (Japan).
- Felicity Callard, Professor in Human Geography, University of Glasgow (UK).
- Luis Carrizo, Advisor to the UNESCO Regional Office of Sciences for Latin America and the Caribbean (Uruguay).
- Frédéric Darbellay, Head of the Inter- and Transdisciplinarity Unit at the Centre for Children's Rights Studies (CIDE), University of Ginebra (Switzerland).
- Deborah DeZure, Assistant Provost for Faculty and Organizational Development Emerita, Michigan State University, East Lansing, Michigan (USA).
- Olivier Ejderyan, Research Associate at the Chair of International Political Economy and Energy Policy, University of Basel (Switzerland).
- Maria Helena Guimarães, Researcher at the Mediterranean Institute for Agricultural, Environment and Development (MED), University of Évora (Portugal).
- Jeremias Herberg, Assistant Professor at the Institute for Science in Society, Radboud University (The Netherlands).
- Andi Hess, Director of the Interdisciplinary Translation and Integration Sciences Initiative, Arizona State University (USA).
- Katri Huutoniemi, Senior Advisor at the Helsinki Institute for Social Sciences and Humanities (HSSH), University of Helsinki (Finland).
- Machiel Keestra, Assistant Professor of Philosophy at the Institute for Interdisciplinary Studies, University of Amsterdam (The Netherlands).
- Roderick J. Lawrence, Honorary Professor, University of Geneva (Switzerland).
- Yves Lenoir, Professor Emeritus at the Faculty of Education, University of Sherbrooke (Canada).
- Stephanie Pfirman, Professor at the School of Sustainability, College of Global Futures, Arizona State University (USA).
- Melissa Robson-Williams, Research Priority Area Leader for integrated land and water management, Manaaki Whenua Landcare Research (New Zealand).
- Giulia Sonetti, Assistant Professor at Interuniversity Department of Regional & Urban Studies and Planning, Politecnico di Torino and Università di Torino (Italy).

Acknowledgments **xix**

- John Van Breda, Research Fellow at the Centre for Sustainability Transitions (CST), Stellenbosch University (South Africa).
- Marta Varanda, Assistant Professor at the Lisbon School of Economics and Management (ISEG), University of Lisboa (Portugal).
- Federico Vasen, CONICET Research Fellow at the Institute of Educational Research, University of Buenos Aires, and Assistant Professor at the National Technological University (Argentina).
- Jakob Zinsstag, Professor, Department of Epidemiology and Public Health, Swiss Tropical and Public Health Institute (Switzerland).

The Introduction and Conclusion were also inspired and enriched by the EU-funded project "Shaping interdisciplinary research practices in Europe" (SHAPE-ID) (Grant Agreement No. 822705). Discussions and exchanges held at the td-net and the Nodo de Estudios sobre Interdisciplina and Transdisciplina (Nodo ESIT), allowed us to re-define the boundaries of successful institutionalizing processes.

We also acknowledge Annabelle Harris and Matthew Shobbrook, editors at Routledge, for offering invaluable support for completing the publication process of this book. We are grateful, as well, to the five anonymous reviewers of our original publishing proposal for comments and suggestions.

Finally, our special thanks to Max, for his endless support.

FOREWORD

Christian Pohl

Institutionalizing interdisciplinarity (ID) and transdisciplinarity (TD) requires that these ways of research and teaching obtain a place of their own within the academic system where they can be sustained and thrive. Not for a short-term period of one or two decades to address a particular societal issue, but for at least a century, like established disciplines. Institutionalization is necessary to build "transactive memory" of all experiences in successful and failed interdisciplinary and transdisciplinary projects. Otherwise, these experiences – and the theories, methods, and practices behind them – will remain within project participants' minds, and the wheel of ID and TD will be reinvented with every new project. This institutionalization should happen in diverse contexts and sites in parallel and be driven by different schools of ID and TD. Otherwise, a dominant conception and form of institutionalization would end the currently vibrant and inspiring debate and development process.

The context in which ID and TD persist and prosper has manifold dimensions: including research and teaching projects; courses for newcomers to experience particular challenges of ID and TD; and positions for scholars to further develop theories, methods, and practices and to impart their knowledge with newcomers. These dimensions require institutionally powerful individuals able to anchor ID and TD for a long period of time in academic institutions as well as institutions that welcome and support such initiatives. They require reviewers who are familiar with the state of art and are able to see and judge particular interdisciplinary and transdisciplinary qualities of proposals or manuscripts. Not least, they require networks and events that connect scholars across countries and diverse thematic fields such as research for gender equality, peace, justice, health, and sustainable development.

The editors and authors of this book provide a rich bouquet of exciting insights about institutionalizing ID and TD in many of these dimensions across

14 countries from the South, the North, the East, and the West. Among other insights, I learned, for instance, to think of ID's and TD's institutionalization in relation to a country's history in collective political decision-making. Thematic or methodical centers that complement the disciplinary structures seem the standard approach in universities to keep alive the excellence (disciplinary structures) first and grand challenges (centers) second approach. In rare cases, centers are the primary academic home of interdisciplinarians and transdisciplinarians and universities dedicate major parts of the curriculum to complementary ID and TD studies. I further realized how omnipresent "the stigma of generality and shallowness" of ID and TD is. In countries with a strong top-down government, ID and TD should not be too encompassing, either focus on technological innovation and leave aside social innovation or risk being labeled as pseudoscience. Strict hierarchical relationships between university leaders, lectures, and students also hinder ID and TD institutionalization. Finally, I became aware of established scholars' responsibility. We must find influential means to protect younger scholars who dare to take the risky path of ID and TD.

The overarching insight of the book is how deeply ID and TD and their institutionalization are related to a country's history, culture, political system, socio-ecological situation, and role of its respective universities. Consequently, interpretation of ID and TD and their purpose differs and comes with particular challenges. In some countries, ID and TD initiatives are rooted in critical thinking, liberal arts education, and autonomous universities, while some aim to educate critical thinkers in order to transform currently unsustainable development paths. The challenge for these initiatives is not to end in a niche. In other countries, ID and TD explicitly aim to better connect universities with industry and economy, presenting the challenge of being instrumentalized for simple technological progress or economic profit. Yet again, in other countries with authoritarian governments not open to bottom-up initiatives of civil society, ID and TD initiatives have to navigate between critique and empowering ideas along with the government's demand that universities should primarily serve the state in its current form.

Fortunately, ID and TD are multi-dimensional concepts with several aims: to develop a comprehensive understanding of societal issues; to include various societal groups in the process of understanding and addressing an issue; to criticize the current way of handling an issue that often entails criticism of those in power; and to look for ways of unifying many dimensions and perspectives in order to come to a balanced or systemic view. These dimensions allow, in principle, adapting institutionalization to a country's specific context by foregrounding less critical dimensions without losing more critical ones. Individual chapters of this book affirm the importance of exploring and foregrounding context along with other dimensions of ID and TD, including inclusion of different societal groups in countries familiar with bottom-up initiatives, dedicated searches for unity, comprehensiveness, and bridging of disciplinary viewpoints in more top-down governed countries. This degree of complexity also means, depending on the dimension of ID and TD and its institutionalization a reader is interested in, (s)he must read other chapters of the book and engage in comparative analysis.

This book is a key first step in experience-based discussion of how to advance institutionalizing ID and TD. It is not a cookbook with a set of recipes or formulas, rather sources of insight and inspiration. It provides case studies and reflections on what worked well and what did not in particular socio-historical contexts. In the course of doing so, it also provides sophisticated concepts for how to think about ID and TD and their institutionalization. Moreover, it includes as well as cites other dedicated scholars from around the world who are exploring, studying, and reflecting on the institutionalization of ID and TD. Finally, the book itself is a sign of the ongoing institutionalization of the two concepts, making it yet another step on a longer pathway to obtain a place of their own within the academic system where they can be sustained and thrive.

1
INTRODUCTION

Institutionalizing interdisciplinarity and transdisciplinarity: Cultures and communities, timeframes and spaces

Julie Thompson Klein, Bianca Vienni Baptista, and Danilo Streck

Increased interest in interdisciplinarity (ID) and transdisciplinarity (TD) has heightened calls for institutionalizing structures and strategies that cross boundaries of expertise. A state-of-the-art account of *Facilitating Interdisciplinary Research* reported interest is being driven today by four major factors: "the inherent complexity of nature and society, the desire to explore problems and questions that are not confined to a single discipline, the need to solve societal problems, and the power of new technologies" (NASEM, 2005, p. 40). Interest in transdisciplinarity, in turn, stems from not only traditional focus on unity of knowledge but also new synthetic paradigms and theories in addition to trans-sector co-production of knowledge with stakeholders aimed at solving complex problems (Klein, 2021). The 1972 volume entitled *Limits to Growth* (Meadows et al., 1972), Machiel Keestra recalled, was one of the earliest reports highlighting the need to prioritize complex and wicked problems requiring both inter- and trans-disciplinary solutions (pers. comm., 5 June 2021). That same year results of the first international seminar on interdisciplinary teaching and research in universities, co-sponsored by the Organization for Economic Cooperation and Development (OECD), drew insights from challenges of institutionalizing in universities across OECD countries (Apostel et al., 1972). Seminar participants predicted research contexts and societal problems would become increasingly complex, requiring greater institutional synergy. Yet, shortfalls in support curbed prospects for transformative change. As scholars of both ID and TD, we are keenly aware of both mounting momentum for change and continuing limits in not only our own countries but across the world, leading us to invite other researchers and educators engaged in reform efforts to advance understanding dynamics of institutionalizing (Clark, 1995). By the early 21st century, interest in both interdisciplinarity and transdisciplinarity had spawned a burgeoning literature spanning organizational, epistemological, conceptual, and

DOI: 10.4324/9781003129424-1

methodological approaches (Frodeman et al., 2017; Klein, 2010; Holley, 2009). However, possibilities and limits in particular contexts are not fully understood.

All parties in this book's audience – including educators and researchers, administrators and funders, as well as educational and science-policy bodies – will benefit from informed awareness of dynamics and structures elsewhere. Given the heterogeneity of practices, we do not impose a universal definition, though recognize consensus on core traits. Interdisciplinarity is conventionally defined as integration of approaches from two or more existing disciplines or bodies of knowledge with the aim of advancing a new understanding of or solution to a complex problem, question, or topic that cannot be handled from a single perspective. In contrast, transdisciplinarity connotes an overarching synthesis and a trans-sector collaboration, with the aim of transcending and even transgressing traditional boundaries. Both ID and TD, then, interrogate the existing structure of knowledge and education, but they are confronted by a gap between widespread endorsements and continuing impediments. Nothing less than a culture change is needed to elevate both interdisciplinarity and transdisciplinarity to a norm within the academic system (after Klein, 2010). The importance of doing so is reinforced by a growing belief that they are essential for tackling complex societal problems, including the COVID pandemic and other diseases, climate change, and social and political inequalities, as well as conflict and war. Talk of transformation rings hollow, however, when the regulatory power of established rules, procedures, policies, and protocols continues to narrow prospects for transformative change (Gardner, 2004). Furthermore, institutionalizing both interdisciplinarity and transdisciplinarity are not without risks.

Programs dedicated to both forms of research and education are often marginalized in the discipline-dominated system of higher education and, following suit, individuals often face obstacles to career advancement. Russell et al. (2008) further cautioned that consolidation around selected strengths and priorities runs the risk of creating "mega-silos" that marginalize other areas. As a result, attempts to institutionalize transdisciplinarity, and we add interdisciplinarity, can actually inhibit flexibility and openness while diminishing values often associated with boundary crossing, such as creativity, interconnection, complexity, and systems thinking. Nevertheless, as this volume demonstrates, prospects for change depend in no small part on institutionalizing new and alternative practices into systems of higher education. Otherwise, they remain marginal and even ephemeral. Since embedding is a process, not a pre-determined formula, we treat institutionalizing as a verb rather than the static connotation of a noun associated with buildings, organizational charts, and fixed objectifications of ideas and goals. In doing so, we adopt Davidson and Goldberg's (2009) definition of institutions as mobilizing networks. Their focus was the future of learning in the digital age, but the concept can extend to inter- and trans-disciplinary research and education. The metaphor of mobilizing heightens awareness of dynamic processes of change, not fixed structures and policies and protocols that reinforce them. For that reason, case studies in this book address both temporal and spatial dynamics of institutionalizing, accounting for history and context. By focusing on the concept as a verb, not a static noun, the book also considers challenges of capitalizing on strategies aimed at improving research and teaching across higher education. A dynamic view of institutionalizing across countries calls, as well, for understanding the nature of a comparative approach.

Comparative study

Comparative study examines phenomena in two or more entities of the same type (after Morlino, 2018). It is key to comprehending similarities and differences across contexts, including the countries featured in this book. It also fosters a richer and more nuanced understanding of ID and TD, mutual learning in collaborative work, and decision- and policy-making. As a social science methodology, Schriewer (2018, p. 51) explained, comparative study entails establishing interconnectedness in "relations of relations" or "systems of relations", rather than differentiation of isolated facts. In contrast to constitutive, causal, or etiological explanations, Keestra also noted, comparative explanation aims to explain and predict a phenomenon by comparing different stages or varieties of the phenomenon (pers. comm., 5 June 2021). Moreover, following Simon et al. (2018), interdisciplinarity, transdisciplinarity, and comparative studies are all intellectual projects and scientific-political programs that require dialogue across academic disciplines and institutions. ID and TD cannot be dissociated, either, from policies and practices across the global landscape of higher education. Hence, interculturality is an added focus of comparative studies, as well as micro, meso, and macro levels of organization (per Morlino, 2018). And finally, comparative analysis can build on while contributing to Phillips and Schweisfurth's (2014) tri-part framework of purpose:

(a) Providing an adequate morphology for global description and classification of various forms of institutionalization,
(b) Determining relationships and interactions between different factors within and among institutions and between institutions and society in their practices,
(c) Identifying underlying conditions and conceptual developments for institutionalizing.

To further aid in comparing individual experiences with institutionalization we gathered insights from a questionnaire sent to all authors in this volume, based on four dimensions:

a) Personal and professional: including cultural factors (e.g., kind of commitment, focus, and origin, as well as personal abilities in the form of professional/technical competencies).

b) Academic and epistemological: intellectual factors (e.g., conceptual frameworks, fields of knowledge such as sciences or humanities) and pertinent themes (e.g., ecology/sustainability/organizational development).
c) Institutional (e.g., national policies, university/research structures, organizational cultures, budgets, and funding).
d) Socio-political: values and actions (e.g., responses to societal needs and interests as well as policy considerations).

With particular regard to the first personal and professional dimension, most contributing authors acknowledged the relevance of self-learning and learning-by-doing while conducting research projects and designing programs that were subsequently institutionalized. These traits also intersect, Keestra added, with the academic and epistemological dimension (pers. comm., 5 June 2021). In a few cases, authors were able to learn how to perform collaborative research and teaching from their workplace experiences. Yet, researchers, lecturers, and practitioners all invest a great deal of effort in "reinventing" successful organizational structures that are usually supported only in the short term due to lack of long-term funding, other forms of support, legitimation, and narrow criteria of evaluation. Even successful initiatives are not systematized or their lessons shared through publications reaching wider communities. We also found some researchers became interested in inter- and trans-disciplinary research and teaching because they had a mentor or supervisor who motivated them to do so. However, in a recent book, Catherine Lyall (2019) reported their influence is not always sufficient. Many early career researchers confront strong obstacles to embarking on an inter- or trans-disciplinary career path, even though new generations have possibilities to participate in capacity-building opportunities such as inter- or trans-disciplinary degrees, summer or winter schools, and PhD programs.

Chapters in this book document these and other opportunities. Maik Adomßent (Chapter 3), for example, presented an undergraduate and graduate program in Germany. Sebastian et al. (Chapter 7) cited an example of students invited to work together with representatives from industry in Australia. Keryan et al. (Chapter 11) reported an effort is underway in Armenia and Georgia aimed at a more transdisciplinary approach to research and teaching. And Villa-Soto et al. (Chapter 4) identified institutional policies catalyzing interdisciplinary graduate programs in Mexico. Furthermore, despite constraints, responses to the questionnaire revealed the academic and epistemological dimension incentivizes researchers to participate (see also Boix Mansilla et al., 2016; Callard and Fitzgerald, 2015). Personal and professional motivations also appear in chapters by Ulrike Felt (Chapter 14), Jack Spaapen (Chapter 15), and Paulo Nuno Vicente and Margarida Lucas (Chapter 13). And, beyond individual sites, networks and communities of practice illustrate institutional and socio-political dimensions, ranging from informal to formal associations and communities of practice, including the Network for Transdisciplinary Research, the Association for

Interdisciplinary Studies, the International Network for the Science of Team Science, and the Global Alliance for Inter- and Transdisciplinary Research and Education. In addition, they include regional efforts such as Nodo de Estudios Sobre Interdisciplina and Transdisciplina (Nodo ESIT) representing eight Latin American countries, the Leading Integrated Research for Agenda 2030 (International Research Council), and Oceania's Global Leaders of Interdisciplinary and Transdisciplinary Research Organisations.

Together, the chapters and aforementioned examples question traditional structures that have unsuccessfully institutionalized ID and TD. The challenge then becomes how to inspire and to support newcomers and early career researchers, especially to promote and foster transformative inter- and trans-disciplinary initiatives. One respondent to the questionnaire commented:

> The reason I developed a scholarly interest in "ID" as an object of study in its own right was because we used the term to describe our work but did not reflect on what that meant and – importantly – did not consider what that meant for the academic careers of the several young researchers who had been employed by the centre.
>
> *(Questionnaire N°3, 2020)*

Paradigmatic examples and best practices also have implications for the sociopolitical dimension. It highlights values and actions in relation to societal needs and interests as well as policy considerations.

Furthermore, successful means of consolidating organizational structures include actions, values, and social commitments such as resolving social problems afflicting vulnerable populations and promoting emancipation of hegemonic discourses. See, especially, chapters by Litre et al. (Chapter 5), Vladimir Mokiy and Tatiana Lukyanova (Chapter 9), and Beatrice Akua-Sakyiwah (Chaper 8). A comparative approach also reveals actions do not promote ID and TD in isolation. One researcher emphasized "Interdisciplinarity and transdisciplinarity allow us to understand the pliability and transversality that keeps disciplinarity moving; it helps protect disciplinarity from isolation, division, separation and fixity" (Questionnaire N° 8, 2020). Yet, as another informant put it, individualistic and self-centered postures persist in a competitive rather than collaborative spirit (Questionnaire N° 11, 2020).

Subthemes and guiding questions

Institutionalizing operates on multiple levels and across local, regional, national, and international scales. Based on literature reviews and insights from conference presentations on institutionalizing, this book's co-editors defined five cross-cutting subthemes translated into guiding questions for authors. Instead of imposing all of them on every chapter, we let authors select the most relevant ones for their particular cases:

1. Historical and geographical contexts that shape institutional possibilities and limits in different countries, including potentials and advantages for the future: translated into "How have historical and geographical contexts conditions shaped institutional possibilities and limits in your country?"
2. Inter- and trans-disciplinary research and teaching organization in time and space, including communities to accomplish national and regional goals: translated into "How are inter- and trans-disciplinary research and teaching organized temporally and spatially in your context?"
3. Transformations or modifications and/or integrations fitting into an existing structure: translated into "Are changes in your context transformative or modifications and/or integrations aimed at accommodation to fit into an existing structure?"
4. Theories of institutional change, including a robust portfolio that combines strategic targeting and loosening barriers across bottom-up, mid-tier, and top-down efforts: translated into "Are changes part of a systematic plan based on a philosophy of change and how extensive are they?"
5. Factors that help or hinder institutionalizing processes and dynamics for ID and TD in different contexts: translated into "Given the prior subthemes, what future prospects emerge from for inter- or trans-disciplinary research and teaching in your country?"

The first subtheme and its guiding question point to the influence of historical and geographical contexts that bridge past, present, and future. By combining spatial and temporal dimensions, the second subtheme and question focus attention on how institutions, cultures, and communities are embedded in specific spaces and timeframes for both research and education. The third, fourth, and fifth subthemes and accompanying questions focus on theory and practice, factoring in how change is imagined and realized pragmatically while recognizing catalysts for and hindrances to new ways of knowing, thinking, acting, and living in the world. Culture, in particular, shapes theory and practice by building on traditions, customs, beliefs, values, and conventions. Together, they constitute a praxis in which the four multiple dimensions introduced above are embedded: personal and professional, academic/epistemological, and institutional as well as socio-political. Thus, the way knowledge is conceived and produced influences and is determined by cultural and temporal organizations of work and its landscapes (echoing Felt, 2017; Nowotny, 2017). The composite set of subthemes and guiding questions also incorporates multiple dimensions of institutionalizing identified in Klein's (2010) earlier framework for creating interdisciplinary campus cultures. This book, though, updates the earlier framework with new examples and lessons from a wider range of geographical and cultural contexts.

Following Keestra's suggested foci, the features of past and updated insights counter universalizing generalizations, build on communal efforts of researchers and educators, aim for change in education and research, and vary by degree of change and purpose (pers. comm., 5 June 2021). This book also accounts for increased interactions with stakeholders beyond the academy, aligned with the connotation of transdisciplinary co-production of knowledge with them in government, industry, and communities. Moreover, prospects for institutionalizing are shaped by conditions within particular countries. Yet, this update still asks, as did the prior volume (Klein, 2010), a general question. Where do particular structures and strategies sit on a generic spectrum of change? The spectrum ranges from isolated and ad hoc reforms to robust portfolios of strategies that combine both targeting of specific agendas and general loosening of barriers. It also recognizes that initiatives emanate from and take root at bottom-up, mid-tier, and top-down levels. In addition, it acknowledges change remains partial when not legitimized or funded long-term. Even with exemplary models then, to echo Peter Weingart (2014), there is a paradoxical gap between widespread promotion and continuing impediments, conferring Vienni Baptista and Rojas's (2019) notion of a double identity upon individuals and communities of practice. Interdisciplinarity and transdisciplinarity are endorsed as part of academic culture, but many efforts still struggle. Closing this gap requires not only an epistemic reflection on how knowledge production is being reimagined but also pragmatics for institutionalization.

The chapters

This book emanated from panels the co-editors organized for the 2017 and 2019 international conferences of the Network for Transdisciplinary Research (known as td-net). Comparable to this volume, panel discussions were based on historical and geographical conditions that have shaped efforts to institutionalize ID and TD, modifications and transformations over time, and related challenges and opportunities. In expanding the original roster of potential authors for the book, the co-editors identified additional individuals from other countries and communities of inter- and trans-disciplinary practice, in order to move beyond the dominant focus in English-language literature on Europe and North America. As a result, chapters in this volume span Asia, Africa, Australia, Europe and the UK, and Latin and North America. Furthermore, in contrast to many prior collections, this book aimed for greater gender and cultural inclusion as well as individuals at different stages of their careers from emerging to established scholars. The resulting diversity of authors and geographical contexts brought a more detailed understanding of multiple levels of institutionalizing, including macro (administration, strategic planning, and policy), meso (centers, projects, and programs), and micro (small groups and individual researchers). Even while recognizing all three levels, though, the book pays special attention to micropractices because more research is needed on characteristics of individuals and small groups. And, finally, the authors span not only sciences and technologies but also social sciences, humanities, and arts.

The chapters that follow are divided into three parts. Part I presents case studies of interdisciplinary institutional spaces and timeframes. Macro-level examples appear first, followed by meso- and micro-level cases in order to represent the three levels of analysis in the book. A few points stand out in the way of preview, aligned with relevant subthemes and their guiding questions. In Chapter 2, Catherine Lyall situates interdisciplinarity within the context of the UK's top-down Research Assessment Framework. Its logic of measuring academic performance undermines prospects for co-production of knowledge with stakeholders, underscoring the political impact of national policy. In Chapter 3, Maik Adomßent places developments in Complementary Studies at Leuphana University College within contexts of both local commitments to expanding opportunities for interdisciplinary study and international momentum for addressing complex societal problems. In Chapter 4, Villa-Soto et al. also illustrate the dual impact of national imperatives and local initiatives in Mexico, while pointing to both top-down strategies and bottom-up methods for institutional change. Chapter 5 by Litre et al. recounts limits to reforming institutional structures in Brazil shaped by both political history and centralized top-down government regulations. They also describe local and regional efforts to address socio-environmental problems in response to larger international momentum. Karri A. Holley and Rick Szostak close Part I by comparing experiences in the United States and Canada in Chapter 6; even though they address similar challenges to institutionalization while developing interdisciplinary fields, the greater role of General Education requirements in the United States reminds us that patterns of practice are shaped by traditions in particular countries.

Part II has a similar grouping of cases as Part I, moving from macro to micro levels, though focusing on transdisciplinary initiatives in research and teaching. In Chapter 7, Sebastian et al. present both a historical perspective on the rise of transdisciplinary boundary organizations within Australian higher education and contemporary limits due to dominance of traditional discipline-based structures, though here too deepening understanding of possibilities for alternative structure and organization, practices and functions, and strategies in the case of one institute. In Chapter 8, Beatrice Akua-Sakyiwah situates possibilities and limits within Ghana's national economic agenda and environmental challenges that are heightening knowledge, despite urgency of universities to expand access to transdisciplinary knowledge, despite concept not being well established there. In presenting prospects for interdisciplinarity and transdisciplinarity in Modern Russia, in Chapter 9, Vladimir Mokiy and Tatyana Lukyanov also located them within a political context, the legacy of a top-down centralized hierarchy during the Soviet regime. BinBin J. Pearce's Chapter 10 sharpens awareness of cultural differences with the example of Chinese higher education, where Western conceptions of academic structure and practice are not shared and here too were shaped by a political regime, in this case the Chinese Communist Party. In Chapter 11, Keryan et al. also place reform efforts in Armenia and Georgia within conditions of post-Soviet countries, further illustrating the dual impact of societal conditions of governance and internal academic structure. Part II ends with Chapter 12, where Kondo et al. present a Japanese research institute focused on social-environmental problems, in this case, advancing the concept of consilience of differing approaches through reporting more on the individual than the institutional levels.

Part III shifts the thematic focus to intersections between cultures and communities in a short set of final chapters thinking across inter- and trans-disciplinary contexts. Paulo Nuno Vicente and Margarida Lucas' Chapter 13 deepens understanding of epistemic cultures and living spaces in the case of the art-science movement in Europe, treating it as an example of the widespread challenge of bridging the concept of a two-cultures divide of science and art reinforced by specialized education and academic structure. Ulrike Felt also casts a conceptual lens on inter- and trans-disciplinary research by drawing insights from interviews and discussion groups in Austria that illuminate temporal dimensions of academic work lives, socialization, and identity that appear across projects, institutions, and countries. Jack Spaapen's Chapter 15 draws insights from the Netherlands that illustrate widely faced challenges of instituting co-productive evaluation of inter- and trans-disciplinary projects addressing societal challenges, due to limits of academic culture, structures, and research and funding policies. In closing Part III and the book with Chapter 16, Vienni Baptista et al. present a framework for thinking broadly about institutional and cultural conditions for inter- and trans-disciplinary research and teaching in higher education. This heuristic framework for understanding and responding to challenges at intersections of cultures, institutions, and communities provides a closing synthesis of insights from both literature and the preceding chapters.

Acknowledgments

We thank Machiel Keestra of the University of Amsterdam for extensive comments and suggestions on an earlier draft of this chapter.

References

Apostel, L., Berger, G., & Briggs, A. (1972). *Interdisciplinarity: Problems of teaching and research in universities*. Paris: Organization for Economic Cooperation and Development.

Boix Mansilla, V., Lamont, M., & Sato, K. (2016). Shared cognitive–emotional–interactional platforms: Markers and conditions for successful interdisciplinary collaborations. *Science, Technology, & Human Values, 41*(4), 571–612. https://doi.org/10.1177/0162243915614103

Callard, F., & Fitzgerald, D. (2015). *Rethinking interdisciplinarity across the social sciences and neurosciences*. London: Palgrave Macmillan.

Clark, B. R. (1995). *Places of inquiry: Research and advanced education in modern universities*. Berkeley, CA: University of California Press.

Davidson, C. N., & Goldberg, D. T. (2009). *The future of learning institutions in the digital age*. Cambridge, MA: MIT Press.

Felt, U. (2009). Knowing and living in academic research. In U. Felt (Ed.), *Knowing and living in academic research. Convergence and heterogeneity in research cultures in the European context* (pp. 17–39). Prague: Institute of Sociology of the Academy of Sciences of the Czech Republic.

Fisher, D. (1988). Boundary work: A model of the relation between power and knowledge. *Knowledge, 10*(2), 156–176. https://doi.org/10.1177/0164025988010002004

Frodeman, R., Klein, J.T., and Pachecho, R. (Eds.). (2017). *The Oxford handbook of interdisciplinarity*. Oxford and New York: Oxford University Press.

Gardner, H. (2004). *Changing minds: The art and science of changing our own and other people's minds*. Boston, MA: Harvard Business School Press.

Holley, K. (2009). Understanding interdisciplinary challenges and opportunities in higher education. In *ASHE Higher Education Report*, vol. 35. San Francisco, CA: Jossey-Bass.

Klein, J. T. (2010). *Creating campus cultures. A model for strength and sustainability*. Washington, DC: Jossey Bass and Association of American Colleges and Universities.

Klein, J. T. (2021). *Beyond interdisciplinarity: Boundary work, communication, and collaboration*. Oxford: Oxford University Press.

Lyall, C. (2019). *Being an interdisciplinary academic. How institutions shape university careers*. London: Palgrave Pivot.

Meadows, D. H., Meadows, D. L., Randers, J., & Behrens III, W. W. (1972). *The limits to growth: A report for the club of Rome's project on the predicament of mankind*. New York: Universe Books.

Morlino, L. (2018). *Comparison: A methodological introduction for the social sciences*. Berlin: Barbara Budrich.

NASEM [National Academies of Science, Engineering, and Medicine]. (2005). *Facilitating interdisciplinary research*. Washington, DC: The National Academies Press. https://doi.org/10.17226/11153

Nowotny, H. (2017). Prologue: The messiness of real-world solutions. In S. Frickel, M. Albert, & B. Prainsack (Eds.), *Investigating interdisciplinary collaboration* (pp. 148–170). New York: Rutgers University Press.

Phillips, D., & Schweisfurth, M. (2014). *Comparative and international education: An introduction to theory, method, and practice*. London: Bloomsbury.

Russell, A. W., Wickson, F., & Carew, A. L. (2008). Transdisciplinarity: Context, contradictions and capacity. *Futures, 40*(5), 460–472. doi:10.1016/j.futures.2007.10.005

Simon, D., Palmer, H., Riise, J., Smit, W., & Valencia, S. (2018). The challenges of transdisciplinary knowledge production: From unilocal to comparative research. *Environment & Urbanization, 30*(2), 481–500. https://doi.org/10.1177/0956247818787177

Schriewer, J. (2018). *Pesquisa em educação comparada sob condições de interconectividade global*. São Leopoldo (Brazil): Oikos.

Vienni Baptista, B., & Rojas, S. (2019). Transdisciplinary institutionalization in higher education: A two-level analysis. *Studies in Higher Education*. https://doi.org/10.1080/03075079.2019.1593347

Weingart, P. (2014). Interdisciplinarity and the new governance of universities. In P. Weingart & B. Padberg (Eds.), *University experiments in interdisciplinarity: Obstacles and opportunities* (pp. 151–174). Bielefeld: Transcript.

PART I
Interdisciplinary institutional spaces and timeframes

2
EXCELLENCE WITH IMPACT

Why UK research policy discourages "transdisciplinarity"

Catherine Lyall

Introduction

As I was writing this chapter, the final submission date for the current round of the Research Excellence Framework (REF2021) in the UK was approaching, although this deadline and many activities worldwide were extended as a result of disruption due to the COVID-19 pandemic. The REF looms large in the lives of British academics, especially those who adopt a cross-disciplinary approach (Lyall, 2019, pp. 42–45). Taking place on a roughly six-year cycle, the REF is a national assessment of research quality across all UK universities. Structured around 34 subject-based "units of assessment", it assesses three distinct elements of "research excellence": the quality of outputs (primarily publications[1]), their impact beyond academia, and the research environment that supports submitted outputs. An independent review of the REF underlined "the essential role of interdisciplinary research in addressing complex problems and research questions posed by global social, economic, ecological and political challenges" (Stern, 2016, p. 28). However, this mechanism (and its precursor, the Research Assessment Exercise) have always presented problems for those whose work does not fit within a single discipline domain (Tait, 1999). Following a previous evaluation, REF2014, a series of process reviews led to the establishment of an Interdisciplinary Research Advisory Panel. Its subpanels will now have members with "a specific role to oversee and participate in the assessment of interdisciplinary research submitted (…) to ensure its equitable assessment", including "research users" who will participate in assessing impact.[2]

This chapter follows a broad and inclusive meaning of the term "interdisciplinary", adopting the National Academies of Sciences' (2005) definition, which illustrates the integrative and multifaceted nature of such research as individual or team based, basic or applied. While there are multiple understandings of the

DOI: 10.4324/9781003129424-3

term "transdisciplinary", this chapter follows the dominant definition of the Network for Transdisciplinary Research (td-net). This connotation of transdisciplinary describes research that crosses both disciplinary and institutional boundaries, involves societal partners (often local communities), and draws on different forms of knowledge in the co-production of research. Resulting benefits of interaction may derive as much from the process of engagement as from its outcome. In contrast, the REF is output oriented, so "excellent research" is the starting point of a predominantly linear narrative leading to "impact". Moreover, a "hierarchy of impact prestige" exists with many universities holding that international (rather than local) impact has a better chance of achieving a high REF score (Smith et al., 2020, p. 202). The chapter explores the twin foci of "research excellence" and "impact" and implications the relationship between the two has for interdisciplinary and transdisciplinary research in the UK.[3] By focusing on policy considerations and organisational factors related to national policies, university/research structures, and institutional culture, it explores the editors' underlying assumption that the way knowledge is constructed is determined by the overall temporal organisation of academic work and its policy and political landscapes. Politicisation of "research excellence" and "impact" combines with a traditional lack of participative government in the UK to the detriment of the more egalitarian co-produced, "transdisciplinary" research seen elsewhere in Europe.

Mise en scène

The UK has a long history of government interest in and periodic reviews of its research funding landscape. In the introduction to his own 2016 review, which led to current institutional arrangements described in more detail later, Paul Nurse referenced the Haldane report in 1918, those of Lords Dainton and Rothschild in 1971, and Lord Waldegrave in 1993. In particular, Waldegrave's *Realising Our Potential: A Strategy for Science, Engineering and Technology* (OST, 1993), significantly changed the relationship between government and research councils (Lyall, 1993). Lowe and Phillipson (2009) described how the Conservative government's move to harness the science base to a governmental agenda of improving wealth creation and quality of life required cross-council collaboration to stimulate interdisciplinary research and thus became "a key device in the increasing effort by government to steer the science base" (Lowe and Phillipson, ibid.). As national governments increasingly sought return on their investments in research, research funding bodies in the UK have been progressively expected to demonstrate their economic impact (with "economic" defined broadly to include policy, practice, and other dimensions of importance to society; see Meagher et al., 2008 for a more detailed account). While not unique in promoting incentives for research relevance, this trend is very apparent in the UK. "Research impact" now accounts for 25% of the final "score" for the REF, which correlates with public funding allocated to a submitting university.[4]

TABLE 2.1 Results from the Economic and Social Research Council website showing significant disparity between highlighted search terms (conducted 15 November 2020)

Your search for "impact" returned 779 results
Your search for "interdisciplinary" returned 99 results
Your search for "transdisciplinary" returned 3 results

Seventy per cent of ESRC grants are "in some sense multidisciplinary" and "more than a quarter of ESRC grants extend into disciplines outside ESRC's remit" (ESRC, n.d.; Hulkes, 2018).

This priority results in tensions between academic excellence and social relevance (Bandola-Gill, 2019).

Some 20 years after the 1993 white paper, Sir Paul Nurse was asked to review the structure of the research councils, in order "to explore how they can support research most effectively" and "ensure that the UK (...) invests public money in the best possible way".[5] Nurse's terms of reference included asking how research councils should take account of "the local and national economic impact of applied research"[6] and whether the right arrangements were in place to ensure optimal funding for research that crosses disciplinary boundaries. This latest review resulted in the establishment of UK Research and Innovation (UKRI), launched in April 2018 and responsible for a budget of £8 billion (financial year 2019–2020) in a new configuration that merges the seven disciplinary research councils, Research England,[7] and the UK's innovation agency (Innovate UK[8]). In making the case for UKRI, the Department for Business, Innovation, and Skills sought to establish a "funding system that rewards excellent and impactful research".[9]

Against this historical backdrop of research policy that underscores research excellence, interdisciplinarity, and impact, there is virtually no mention of "transdisciplinarity", illustrated in Table 2.1. A similar keyword search of the UKRI's larger database of all UK publicly funded research revealed a similar disparity, returning 3,666 grant-funded projects labelled as "interdisciplinary" and only 99 as "transdisciplinary".[10]

Influences on research and teaching

In the UK, virtually all leading research-intensive universities mention "interdisciplinarity" in their strategic plans (Bandola and Lyall, 2015), whether in the context of research, teaching, or infrastructure. Nevertheless, UK higher education largely remains structured on a conventional, disciplinary basis and is still grappling with the complexity of how to manage institutional structures unsuited for interdisciplinary teaching (Thew, 2007). Our evaluation of interdisciplinary teaching in the UK reflected these aspects (Lyall et al., 2015a). It recognised a dynamic range of experiments in interdisciplinary learning and teaching, suggesting potential for institutional change. More recently, this interest has been further evidenced by the development of a series of conferences sharing practice related to interdisciplinary learning and teaching activities.[11] Nevertheless, both Lyall et al. (2015a) and Lindvig et al. (2017) identified telling mismatches between rationales offered for interdisciplinary education and comparatively poor institutional structures and commitments.

UK universities may offer thematic teaching programmes, such as public health, policy studies, or global studies but do not necessarily brand them as "interdisciplinary". Others may be increasingly attracted by the perceived marketability of topical interdisciplinary courses. Yet, while interdisciplinary education activities are occurring within the walls of even traditional and monodisciplinary universities in the UK,[12] the dominant mode of knowledge production is still one of disciplines controlling content, pedagogy, and organisation of higher learning (Henry, 2005). Hence, well-recognised tensions within institutions appear, ranging from ontological debate on the "validity" of interdisciplinary courses to disruption of well-established administrative procedures not designed for accommodating interdisciplinary working across faculties. In this sense, the UK higher education sector as a whole has certainly not yet achieved the editors' designation of Level 3 curriculum change and is arguably somewhere between Toombs and Tierney's (1991) initial "modification" and "integration" stages depending on the institution. Turning to research, many national incentive schemes in the UK have intended to foster interdisciplinary research.

To elaborate, a 2009 presentation listing Research Council UK (the forerunner of UKRI) investments in interdisciplinary research for the period 2008–2011 detailed nearly £1.4 billion in programme funding across five programmes: for example, "Ageing: Life-long Health & Wellbeing" and "Living with Environmental Change Energy" (see Lyall et al., 2011, p. 111). Today, the UKRI Strategic Priorities Fund replaces these funding programmes with an £830 million investment in multi- and inter-disciplinary research across 34 subthemes grouped as eight overarching themes. Notably, the UKRI website[13] emphasises that "A key element of funded programmes is that many bring together people from different disciplines *to work on finding solutions*" [emphasis mine]. The other main components of the UK's public research funding are currently delivered through UKRI's Industrial Strategy Challenge Fund, which combines public money with industrial sponsorship to support innovation, and their Global Challenges Research Fund (GCRF), which responds to the government's overseas development agenda to address challenges faced by low- and middle-income countries. The GCRF fund supports "challenge-led disciplinary and interdisciplinary research"[14] but often from a technical rather than a social starting point.

Even so, there have been success stories: the Rural Economy and Land Use (RELU) programme required social and natural scientists to work together in all funded research projects and was arguably "transdisciplinary" in all but name (see Lyall et al., 2015b). During its lifetime, RELU was a highly self-reflexive research community that explored stakeholder involvement in interdisciplinary research (RELU, 2011) and left a legacy of publications for researchers and practitioners, a cadre of experienced transdisciplinary researchers, and shared learning in accessible briefing notes and evaluation reports.[15] The UK has also led in the area of "research use": for example, through the Research Unit for Research Utilisation (RURU) established in 2001 by initial funding from the Economic and Social Research Council (ESRC) as part of its investment in evidence-based policy and practice (Bandola-Gill and Smith, 2021). As political language around "evidence-based policy" has waned, RURU has pursued cross-institutional research collaboration that investigates knowledge mobilisation across a range of public policy and service delivery settings.

Nevertheless, as Barry (2007) notes, interdisciplinary research institutions "often have a fragile existence, dependent on political circumstances, or on the patronage and energies of key individuals". Moreover, the short-term, grant-funded nature of many interdisciplinary research investments is not conducive for long-term culture change required to develop and sustain new institutional governance structures necessary for interdisciplinary research and teaching to flourish (Lyall and Fletcher, 2013). The EU's recent SHAPE-ID project[16] affirmed such learning is hard won and the pace of change frustratingly slow. As a result, the "paradox of interdisciplinarity" (Weingart, 2000) persists: interdisciplinary research is often encouraged at a policy level but poorly rewarded by funding instruments and academic structures. Bruce et al.'s (2004) analysis of the EU's Fifth Framework programme conveys a similar sense of déjà vu. Arts and humanities disciplines are where the social sciences were some 30 years ago when Tait (1987) reported on attempts to integrate social and natural sciences within the UK's national research funding programmes. Recent interviews with British academics (Lyall, 2019) further indicate that the reality of interdisciplinary researchers' experiences still does not live up to the current promotional rhetoric of interdisciplinary research policy. Relatedly, over the past 20 years, many national incentive schemes in the UK have intended to foster academic research that yields "impact" (see Smith et al.'s 2020 account of the "impact agenda" in the UK).

The latter emphasis on an impact agenda has led to structural changes within universities that now dedicate significant (even disproportionate) amounts of academic and administrative time to generating and recording specific forms of research impact, to the detriment of other forms of knowledge generation and exchange such as consultancy or public engagement through science festivals. Here too British academics receive mixed messages. Over the past two decades, the policy language of research councils' communications has evolved from "technology transfer" through "knowledge transfer" to "knowledge exchange" with an accompanying, though sometimes begrudging, acknowledgement that this mobilisation of knowledge is no longer solely for economic gain or only in one direction, viz. from universities as "producers" of knowledge to the wider society as "users" often mediated through some form of "knowledge brokerage". Smith et al. (2020, pp. 141–142) reflect this shift in strategic priorities of the UK research councils from a translational role, required to impart knowledge to stakeholder groups, to now highlight "partnership working", "co-production", and "co-creation". This trend reveals one of the misalignments in UK research policy: in order to be considered for inclusion as a REF impact case study, "impact" only counts if it derives from "excellent research" undertaken by a submitting unit within a prescribed period.[17] This requirement cultivates a sense that economic and policy impacts may be privileged over more "amorphous" forms of societal engagement (Smith et al. 2020, pp. 102–103).

Plus ça change

During 2018, I interviewed British interdisciplinary academics about their careers. They indicated that they had "always been interdisciplinary" by virtue of their doctoral training and ranged in seniority from postdoc to professor (see Lyall, 2019, Appendix B for research design). These semi-structured career history interviews aimed in part at learning how attitudes towards interdisciplinarity might have changed over the course of their careers. Growth of performance metrics has been one of the widespread changes within the higher education sector so, unsurprisingly, informants often spontaneously raised "the REF" during these conversations. This reaction raises two questions. First, what is the potential for a mutually reinforcing link between skills that interdisciplinarians offer and types of research that might lead to the notion of "impact" venerated by "the REF"? Second, given that interdisciplinary researchers often struggle to establish themselves in academic careers (Klein, 2010; Lyall, 2019), might they now be appreciated more by universities keen to perform well in REF impact case studies?

While noting that interdisciplinary research does not have to be applied research, Quentin[18] (a professor) acknowledged the logic of this line of questioning:

> I think the sequence is: people want impact, that means applied research, applied research tends to be better if it involves more than one discipline. So yeah, I guess that would suggest that people who can work interdisciplinarily have got something to contribute to the impact agenda.
>
> *(Quentin)*

However, staff not yet in established university posts ("tenured" in the United States) sensed the REF "is something that happens elsewhere" (Belinda). REF rules demand only "independent" researchers' work is submitted for assessment, leading Carina to observe:

> Even though we're told to think about impact and you put impact on your funding applications ... it almost feels like it doesn't matter until you're a professor.
>
> *(Carina)*

While some of the interviewees indicated more ambivalence, Carina did explicitly see the connection between interdisciplinarity and impact:

> [university managers are] making a big deal of the fact that they view interdisciplinarity as a tool for getting research that has bigger impact.
>
> *(Carina)*

Significantly, she described these impacts as something that "tends to be reconstructed looking back, rather than a planned approach". Others, too, described their institutions as still in a learning phase in the process of turning "stakeholder engagement" into "impact" (for example, Vera). Helena described a situation where, with the advent of REF impact assessment, stakeholders with whom she worked were now being asked to join advisory boards for research projects already conceived by academic researchers. She saw this development as potentially a tentative step towards a future co-production model, observing "you have to start somewhere". Further conversations with interdisciplinary researchers also indicated that the impact agenda permeating British academia has not significantly changed the way interdisciplinary academics are valued within their institutions. The focus on impact is, in many cases, still retrospective and not engendering a turn towards a transdisciplinary model of co-production with societal partners who could demonstrate user demand for research outputs. Indeed, these performance metrics overlook many experienced interdisciplinary researchers who are on fixed-term contracts and therefore "don't count" for the REF.

More broadly, these interviews with British academics indicated that any changes within UK higher education are much less shaped by theories of institutional change but rather driven by the imperatives of policy and funding. Interviewees (for example, Gina, Iona, and Julia) expressed concerns about their institutions just "following the money" (Lyall, 2019, pp. 39–41):

> I think they're just pressured by money, they're influenced by where they can get the money from, it's not necessarily a belief in the good that interdisciplinary research can do, which a lot of interdisciplinary researchers have.
>
> *(Gina)*

University leaders voiced similar concerns about the resilience of universities undertaking problem-focused research that was "à la mode" and motivated by external funding drivers. This view implies a lack of any defining institutional strategy. Instead, echoing van der Zwaan (2017), this is a pragmatic response to a changing higher education funding landscape where any changes in practice are ad hoc and piecemeal modifications to the traditional, discipline-focused existing structure.

Right ingredients, wrong recipe?

In the UK, emphasis on research impact derives from the national government's concern with competitiveness and ensuring "value for money" from research supported through public funding in a country that has an international reputation for excellent science but poor application (Lyall et al., 2004). Indicative of this gap, many contradictions about the status of interdisciplinarity arose in my conversations with UK university leaders within "research-led" institutions.[19] Despite the prevalence of institutional rhetoric from universities and their research funders about interdisciplinarity, when research leaders spoke about "research excellence", it was predominantly a synonym for excellence within a single discipline. Smith et al. (2020, p. 155) report that one of the most common critiques of the REF model of impact discussed by interviewed British academics was its narrow view of what counted as research evidence to support impact. Comparably, while a number of my interviewees pointed to the importance of interdisciplinary work, they saw the UK's current approach to research impact as drawing primarily on academic research produced in monodisciplinary contexts. This finding prompted Smith et al. (2020, pp. 184–185) to also conclude that:

> impact in the REF appears to represent a reversion to, and veneration of, a paradigm of Mode-1 knowledge production, in which academics are positioned as the active research "experts", while potential beneficiaries … are demoted to the status of "users".

Thus, the REF changes the role of research partners:

> from being an active and essential cog in the machinery of scientific discovery to a passive receiver or beneficiary of academic triumphs.
> (Smith et al., ibid.)

The overriding lesson that emerged from interviews with researchers (Lyall, 2019, chapter 6), is that we need to rethink "excellence" in the context of interdisciplinary research. Doing so obliges institutions that aspire to succeed as interdisciplinary centres of excellence to adopt a more encompassing understanding of the qualities that make a "good" researcher and a "good" academic career.

Others have also spoken out against the "fetishisation of excellence" within universities, noting that this priority "impedes rather than promotes scientific and scholarly activity" (Moore et al., 2017). Referencing Kuhn (1970), Moore et al. (ibid.) admonish that this focus on excellence both discourages risk-taking (and hence advances in "paradigm-shifting research") and the careful "Normal Science" that tests and replicates work to allow knowledge to become established. These authors instead call for a research evaluation culture built on "soundness" and "capacity" with an emphasis on processes and the practice of "productive research". UK research leaders (notably senior women) are beginning to comment publicly on problems with the way universities define success and reward certain types of behaviours, decrying the shift from being driven by a sense of societal responsibility to becoming "too focused on the prize of a top spot in the global rankings" (Buitendijk, 2020). Buitendijk further notes that these rankings are primarily based on research production and reputation and are known to encourage competitive rather than collaborative behaviours.

Buitendijk is not alone in this assessment. Dame Ottoline Leyser, the new head of UKRI, has also called for more collaborative research environments with less emphasis placed on "individual brilliance" and "headline-grabbing results" at the expense of fostering a culture "where good science happens" (Gove, 2020). Prior to this call, she urged the REF to "shift its emphasis from the work of individual researchers to a portfolio approach" (Gove, 2020). Other representatives of research funding bodies are also expressing similar views. Science Europe, for example, has cautioned about unintended consequences of using terms such as "excellence", echoing others above, by contending individualism is promoted over team science, putting pressure on researchers to rush findings and discouraging "low-key but vital work on reproducing other's results" (Science Europe, 2020, p. x; Matthews, 2020). Thus, the problem lies not with the concept of research assessment but with narrow ideals of what constitutes "excellence" (Stilgoe, 2014). Similarly, the current conception of "impact" in the REF is representative of a culture of "competitive accountability" that is "endemic in UK higher education" (Watermeyer, 2019). Of added note, the UK lacks a tradition of participative governance in contrast to other European countries such as Germany or Switzerland.

Instead, the UK participative governance approach promotes an increasing role for non-governmental actors and stakeholders in policy and decision making as a means to mitigate public controversy over new technology developments (Lyall and Tait, 2005, p. 182). Interaction with stakeholders, including the public, has traditionally occurred through ad hoc policy consultations rather than ongoing interaction or dialogue. UK government departments tend to equate "consultation" with "engagement" (Laurie et al., 2009), rather than adopting a genuine commitment to user involvement that goes beyond simply an opportunity to "participate in participation" (de la Mothe, 2001, p. 8). Significantly, the UK discourse of participation has its roots in crisis management, stemming from a series of controversies in the UK during the 1990s that undermined public confidence in science, including bovine spongiform encephalopathy (BSE, "mad cow" disease) and the prospect of genetically modified food. In this "consultation" model, a largely pre-determined range of remedial or damage-limitation options are presented as a means of resolution (Rayner, 2003) rather than more "grassroots" debate. From a governance perspective, the process of governing at national, regional, or local levels is an interactive one because no single actor has the knowledge and resource capacity to tackle problems unilaterally (Kooiman, 1993).

As a result, cooperation replaces hierarchy and legislative competences are shared among several levels (Sloat, 2002). An earlier study of the rise of new modes of governance in science and innovation policy (Lyall, 2005) demonstrated that although the associative governance model of thinking about state-society relations is relatively pervasive in the European literature, British policy scholars tended to regard the policy network paradigm as a form of "interest group intermediation" often associated with the pejorative term "lobbying". In contrast, German and Dutch scholars viewed policy networks as a new form of governance, based on non-hierarchical interaction. What I infer from this is that other European countries have greater familiarity with a co-production model – be it in production of government policy or research knowledge – than has historically been the case in the UK. Bearing in mind these national differences, the question of "research excellence" resurfaces.

In order to be considered for inclusion as a REF impact case study, the impact/s being demonstrated must derive from excellent, original research.[20] This requirement excludes many other forms of interaction with partners outside the academy. These research users may not always be seeking "cutting edge" state-of-the-art, rather adapting existing research-derived knowledge to their worlds. Therefore, the knowledge produced may not be original in an academic context but nevertheless has a new and beneficial effect on that particular external audience. As we have seen, in the UK, the focus is still predominantly unidirectional: academics do something *to* the public in order to achieve impact rather than genuine co-production typical of td-net's transdisciplinary research approach. Spaapen and van Drooge (2011) use the term "productive interactions" to describe such exchanges between researchers and stakeholders, while Meagher and Lyall (2013) wrote about "enduring connectivity". The latter occurs when researchers and prospective users stay in contact even after a funded project ends. In each case, more process-oriented terms "shift the focus from attribution and impact to the contribution of specific actors" and the interactions and exchanges that take place among them (Spaapen and van Drooge, 2011).

Conclusion

The bottom line is that promotion of interdisciplinarity and transdisciplinarity can be undermined if we fail to appreciate its contingent and institutionally dependent existence (Lyall et al., 2011, p. 10). Yet, despite advocacy and funding for interdisciplinary research and impact in the UK, funding, management, support, and evaluation are still conducted predominantly by people whose values and ideals of research excellence are grounded in their disciplinary backgrounds. This reality is coupled with the fact that UK research policy commodifies impact rather than treating it as a social good. Most importantly, the UK's preoccupation with "excellence with impact" discourages other worthwhile forms of knowledge production and exchange, resulting in over-emphasis on generating new knowledge while not making better use of existing knowledge (see also Frodeman, 2014). A post-COVID-19 recession only underscores the urgency of re-evaluating and making more of what we currently have. The editors also asserted that inter- and transdisciplinary institutions have a double identity akin to Weingart's notion of a paradox. Such inter- and trans-disciplinary institutions are increasingly legitimised as part of academic culture but continue to struggle to implement successful environments for working across boundaries. A UK perspective on this double identity affirms progress will depend on rethinking the twin drivers of "excellence" and "impact" within research policy cultures. Only then will interdisciplinary research, and in particular teaching, be mainstreamed within British universities.

Furthermore, while the UK ostensibly has the right ingredients to develop meaningful transdisciplinary research, this term barely features in current research policy discourse. Combined with the UK's uneasy relationship with participative governance (Lyall and Tait, 2019), "transdisciplinary" research of the type seen in other European countries is effectively discouraged by prevailing institutional structures. Is it possible to break the deadlocks of "disciplinary excellence" and "impact" and propose a bold vision for the way forward? UK research development could embrace a more transdisciplinary approach to tackle wicked global challenges the world faces, now more than ever. This would introduce other forms of knowledge, different ways of knowing, and broader perspectives into research process. Doing so, however, would require not only rethinking research policy frameworks to support interdisciplinary or transdisciplinary work but also addressing deep-seated political norms that conventionally have not supported participative governance. Political traditions are even harder to change than research metrics. Yet, in response to the economic downturn caused by COVID-19, the UK government has announced budget cuts that will limit UK universities' ability to combat pressing global challenges via research funding mechanisms such as the Global Challenges Research Fund (Universities UK, 2021). Paradoxically, this cut in funding may drive researchers to adjust their habits once again, encouraging them to capitalise on their existing knowledge and look closer to home for their research partners.

Notes

1 The majority of submissions consist of peer-reviewed journal articles and monographs, performances, and exhibitions may also be submitted as evidence of research outputs.
2 www.ref.ac.uk/panels/what-is-the-role-of-expert-panels/ (accessed 15 November 2020). See also www.ref.ac.uk/media/1447/ref-2019_01-guidance-on-submissions.pdf.
3 The chapter title "excellence with impact" derives from a competition run by the Biotechnology and Biological Sciences Research Council (2013-2015) https://bbsrc.ukri.org/innovation/maximising-impact/fostering-innovation/excellence-impact/. The author was a member of the judging panel.
4 UK universities are funded via the "dual support" mechanism: an annual grant from funding councils to support research and teaching infrastructure and specific research project grants from research councils.
5 www.gov.uk/government/collections/nurse-review-of-research-councils.
6 https://assets.publishing.service.gov.uk/government/uploads/system/uploads/attachment_data/file/388069/Terms_of_Reference_for_the_Nurse_Review.pdf.

7 Research England supports research and knowledge exchange at higher education institutions in England but not the other three devolved administrations of the UK. Research England does, however, administer REF for the whole of the UK.
 8 www.ukri.org/about-us/who-we-are/.
 9 https://assets.publishing.service.gov.uk/government/uploads/system/uploads/attachment_data/file/527803/bis-16-291-ukri-case-for-creation.pdf.
10 https://gtr.ukri.org, accessed 15 November 2020.
11 https://interdisciplinaryuk.net/pastconferences/.
12 For example, University College London's Arts and Sciences undergraduate degree programme (Gombrich and Hogan, 2017).
13 www.ukri.org/our-work/our-main-funds/strategic-priorities-fund/.
14 www.ukri.org/our-work/collaborating-internationally/global-challenges-research-fund/.
15 See www.relu.ac.uk.
16 www.shapeid.eu.
17 www.ref.ac.uk/media/1447/ref-2019_01-guidance-on-submissions.pdf.
18 Pseudonyms were used to preserve anonymity.
19 As denoted by membership of the League of European Research Universities.
20 The impact and the underpinning research must have occurred during prescribed time periods.

References

Bandola, J. and Lyall, C. (2015). 'Interdisciplinarity in the strategic documents of the Russell Group universities'. University of Edinburgh, Edinburgh, Internal Report to Researcher Experience Committee.

Bandola-Gill, J. (2019). 'Between relevance and excellence? Research impact agenda and the production of policy knowledge', *Science and Public Policy*, vol. 46, pp. 895–905.

Bandola-Gill, J. and Smith, K. (2021). 'Governing by narratives: REF impact case studies and restrictive storytelling in performance measurement', *Studies in Higher Education*, published online: 27 Sep 2021 https://doi.org/10.1080/03075079.2021.1978965

Barry, A. (2007). 'The meeting of disciplines. Why interdisciplinarity is a central strategy', *Britain Today*. ESRC, Swindon.

Bruce, A., Lyall, C., Tait, J. and Williams, R. (2004). 'Interdisciplinary integration in the fifth framework programme', *Futures*, vol. 36, pp. 457–470.

Buitendijk, S. (2020). 'Stepping off the hamster wheel: How a limited perspective can obscure the essential', https://simone-buitendijk.medium.com.

de la Mothe, J. (2001). *Science, Technology and Governance*. Continuum, London.

ESRC (n.d.). 'Multidisciplinarity on ESRC grants'. Economic and Social Research Council, Swindon.

Frodeman, R. (2014). *Sustainable Knowledge*. Palgrave, London.

Gombrich, C. and Hogan, M. (2017). 'Interdisciplinarity and the student voice', in R. Frodeman, J. T. Klein and R. C. Dos Santos Pacheco (eds), *The Oxford Handbook of Interdisciplinarity*. 2nd ed. Oxford University Press, Oxford.

Gove, J. (2020). 'Ottoline Leyser: How will new UKRI chief change science?', *Times Higher Education*, 23 July.

Henry, S. (2005). 'Disciplinary hegemony meets interdisciplinary ascendancy: Can interdisciplinary/integrative studies survive, and if so, how?', *Issues in Integrative Studies*, vol. 23, pp. 1–37.

Hulkes, A. (2018). 'The arc of funding', https://blog.esrc.ac.uk/2018/06/26/the-arc-of-funding.

Klein, J. T. (2010). *Creating Interdisciplinary Campus Cultures.* Jossey Bass, San Francisco.

Kooiman, J. (1993). *Modern Governance. New Government-Society Interactions.* Sage, London.

Kuhn, T. S. (1970). *The Structure of Scientific Revolutions.* University of Chicago Press, Chicago.

Laurie, G., Bruce, A. and Lyall, C. (2009) 'The roles of values and interests in the governance of the life sciences: Learning lessons from the 'Ethics+' approach of UK Biobank', in C. Lyall, T. Papaioannou and J. Smith (eds), *The Limits to Governance.* Ashgate, Aldershot.

Lindvig, K., Lyall, C. and Meagher, L. (2017). 'Creating interdisciplinary education within monodisciplinary structures: The art of managing interstitiality', *Studies in Higher Education*, vol. 44, pp. 347–360.

Lowe, P. and Phillipson, J. (2009). 'Barriers to research collaboration across disciplines: Scientific paradigms and institutional practices', *Environment and Planning A*, vol. 41, pp. 1171–1184.

Lyall, C. (1993). 'The 1993 White paper on science and technology. Realising our potential or missed opportunity?', MSc thesis, University of Sussex.

Lyall, C. (2005). 'Concurrent power. The role of policy networks in the multi-level governance of science and innovation in Scotland', PhD thesis, University of Edinburgh.

Lyall, C. (2019). *Being an Interdisciplinary Academic: How Institutions Shape University Careers.* Palgrave, London.

Lyall, C., Bruce, A., Firn, J., Firn, M. and Tait, J. (2004). 'Assessing end-use relevance of public sector research organisation', *Research Policy*, vol. 33, pp. 73–87.

Lyall, C., Bruce, A., Tait, J. and Meagher, L. (2011). *Interdisciplinary Research Journeys. Practical Strategies for Capturing Creativity.* Bloomsbury Academic, London.

Lyall, C. and Fletcher, I. (2013). 'Experiments in interdisciplinary capacity building: The successes and challenges of large-scale interdisciplinary investments', *Science and Public Policy*, vol. 40, pp. 1–7.

Lyall, C., Meagher, L., Bandola, J. and Kettle, A. (2015a). 'Interdisciplinary provision in higher education: Current and future challenges', Report to Higher Education Academy (now Advance HE) Higher Education Academy, York.

Lyall, C., Meagher, L. and Bruce, A. (2015b). 'A rose by any other name? Transdisciplinarity in the context of UK research policy', *Futures*, vol. 65, pp. 150–162.

Lyall, C. and Tait, J. (2005). 'A new mode of governance for science, technology, risk and the environment?', in C. Lyall and J. Tait (eds), *New Modes of Governance.* Ashgate, Aldershot.

Lyall, C. and Tait, J. (2019). 'Beyond the limits to governance: New rules of engagement for the tentative governance of the life sciences', *Research Policy*, vol. 48, pp. 1128–1137.

Matthews, D. (2020). 'Research funders urge caution over demanding 'excellence'', *Times Higher Education*, 23 July.

Meagher, L. and Lyall, C. (2013). 'The invisible made visible: Using impact evaluations to illuminate and inform the role of knowledge intermediaries', *Evidence & Policy*, vol. 9, pp. 409–418.

Meagher, L., Lyall, C. and Nutley, S. (2008). 'Flows of knowledge, expertise and influence: A method for assessing policy and practice impacts from social science research', *Research Evaluation*, vol. 17, pp. 163–173.

Moore, S., Neylon, C., Eve, M. P., O'Donnell, D. P. and Pattinson, D. (2017). '"Excellence R Us": University research and the fetishisation of excellence', *Palgrave Communications*, vol. 3, article 16105.

National Academy of Sciences (2005). *Facilitating Interdisciplinary Research*. National Academies Press, Washington.

OST (1993). *Realising Our Potential: A Strategy for Science, Engineering and Technology*. HMSO, London.

Rayner, S. (2003). 'Democracy in the age of assessment: Reflections on the roles of expertise and democracy in public-sector decision making', *Science and Public Policy*, vol. 30, pp. 163–170.

RELU (2011). 'Innovation in interdisciplinary methods - The RELU experience', Rural Economy and Land Use Data Support Service, UK Data Archive. University of Essex, Colchester.

Science Europe (2020). *Recommendations on Research Assessment*. Position Statement. Science Europe, Brussels.

Sloat, A. (2002). 'Governance: Contested perceptions of civic participation', *Scottish Affairs*, vol. 39, pp. 103–117.

Smith, K., Bandola-Gill, J., Meer, N., Stewart, E. and Watermeyer, R. (2020). *The Impact Agenda: Controversies, Consequences and Challenges*. Policy Press, Bristol.

Spaapen, J. and Van Drooge, L. (2011). 'Productive interactions in the assessment of social impact of research', *Research Evaluation*, vol. 20, pp. 211–218.

Stern, N. (2016). *Building on Success and Learning from Experience. An Independent Review of the Research Excellence Framework*. Department for Business, Energy and Industrial Strategy, London.

Stilgoe, J. (2014). 'Against excellence', *The Guardian*, 19 December.

Tait, J. (1987). 'Research and policy review 14. Environmental issues and the social sciences', *Environment and Planning A*, vol. 19, pp. 437–445.

Tait, J. (1999). 'Help for the academic nomads in search of their own sympathetic tribe', *Times Higher Education*, 5 March 1999.

Thew, N. (2007). 'The impact of the internal economy of higher education institutions on interdisciplinary teaching and learning', The Interdisciplinary Teaching and Learning Group, University of Southampton, Southampton.

Toombs, W. and Tierney, W. (1991). 'Meeting the mandate: Reviewing the college and development curriculum', ASHE-ERIC Higher Education Report No. 6., George Washington University, Washington DC.

Universities UK (2021). 'Cuts to ODA will limit UK universities' role in solving global challenges', 12 March, www.universitiesuk.ac.uk/news/Pages/cuts-oda-limit-uk-universities-role-solving-global-challenges.aspx.

Van der Zwaan, B. (2017). *Higher Education in 2040. A Global Approach*. Amsterdam University Press, Amsterdam.

Watermeyer, R. (2019). *Competitive Accountability in Academic Life. The Struggle for Social Impact and Public Legitimacy*. Edward Elgar, Cheltenham.

Weingart, P. (2000). 'Interdisciplinarity: The paradoxical discourse', in P. Weingart and N. Stehr (eds), *Practising Interdisciplinarity*. University of Toronto Press, Toronto.

3
TAKING INTERDISCIPLINARITY AND TRANSDISCIPLINARITY TO EYE LEVEL WITH SCIENTIFIC DISCIPLINES

Teaching and learning in Complementary Studies at Leuphana College, Lüneburg, Germany

Maik Adomßent

Introducing approach and structure of Complementary Studies at Leuphana College

Leuphana University Lüneburg is a mid-sized public university in Lüneburg, Germany. Founded in 1946 as a college of education, it emerged from a special legal mandate of the Lower Saxony State Parliament to rethink the academy and create a model university for the Bologna Process. It is supported by a foundation under public law and its multi-award-winning study model with three schools (College, Graduate school, and Professional school) is still unique in Germany. Four faculties sponsor transdisciplinary science initiatives, with research in fields of education, culture, sustainability, and management and entrepreneurship. In order to better understand where the uniqueness lies and what steps had to be taken, the following sections describe internal processes and measures then relates them to external conditions. Leuphana College offers an exceptional study model that, in the sense of contemporary liberal education, goes beyond the boundaries of a purely subject-specific course of study, combines specialist knowledge with interdisciplinary skills, and qualifies students for constantly changing demands of the working world. The Leuphana Semester is an introduction to academia for all first-year students at the College. In interdisciplinary and subject-specific modules of their first semester, students gain access to methods, ways of thinking, and understanding processes of science, thereby developing a basis for their bachelor's degrees. From the second semester onwards, all students in Complementary Studies (CS) continue a path begun during the Leuphana Semester, broadening access to alternative solutions for subject-specific, social, and practical professional problems. In addition to their

DOI: 10.4324/9781003129424-4

disciplinary focuses, they also continue becoming familiar with other subjects, their methods and ways of thinking, as well as in-depth reinforcements in their own subject disciplines.

Thus, traditional academic training is combined with an approach to modern humanistic education that creates a crucial foundation for working in inter- and trans-disciplinary contexts. Within subject-specific study components, students deal intensively with two scientific disciplines, consisting of a major and a minor subject. Whereas the major provides a framework for specialization in a field of study that corresponds to particular interests and talents of students, the minor supplements this specialized focus with a second field of knowledge. The general practice at Leuphana University is for bachelor's degree students to select one of 13 majors and combine it with one of 16 minors, completed over a standard period of study at Leuphana College in six semesters with a total of 180 credit points (CP), with one CP corresponding to a workload of 30 hours (Figure 3.1).

Complementary Studies further aim to enable college students to deal with complex (i.e., socio-ecological) scientific problems beyond previous thinking without bias by learning to reflect on their own subjects from the perspective of others. On the one hand, CS is oriented toward classical areas of knowledge by offering courses in social sciences, humanities and arts, and natural sciences. On the other hand, courses move one step further by introducing students to cross-border cooperation between several fields of science and/or actors outside the academy with a transdisciplinary perspective. The focus here is on raising awareness of disciplinary boundaries, gaps between different knowledge domains, and transition zones, and their epistemological and politically legitimizing implications. Toward these ends, each of the four perspectives consists of three different approaches (Figure 3.2):

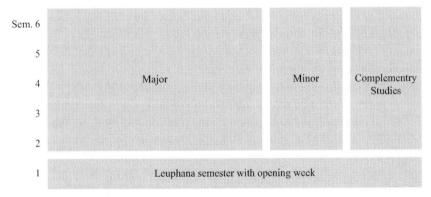

FIGURE 3.1   Study structure of the bachelor's model at Leuphana College. Students acquire 90 CP in their major and 30 CP in their minor. Leuphana Semester and Complementary Studies (30 CP each) together comprise one-third of the entire program.

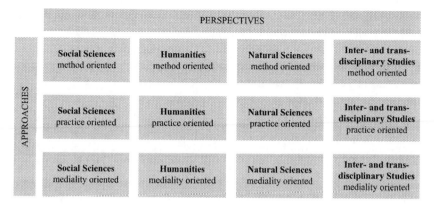

FIGURE 3.2 Structure and modules of Complementary Studies at Leuphana College.

- Seminars in method-oriented modules introduce students to specific approaches from the various subjects or fields that constitute the four perspectives, deepen their principles or methods, and let students explore them to reflect on their relative potentials and limits.
- In practice-oriented seminars, students design, plan, and carry out projects while exploring their links to theories in the perspectives. Critical reflection on project work is a key focus.
- Media(lity)-oriented courses use media (mostly texts) to explore particularly significant or topically relevant theories of and debates on subjects in the perspectives. The definition of "text" is intentionally broad, covering all forms of cultural expression from the written word to visual, audio-visual, and interactive media.

On the whole, these 12 modules (Figure 3.2) exceed subject boundaries in two respects: content and method. In both cases, they aim to (re-)contextualize them and reflect on their plurality in professional perspectives. This goal is advanced by the fact that students get together in subject-heterogeneous learning communities from their very first to their last semesters in the CS part of their studies, thus constantly interchanging disciplinary learning settings in their major and minor. The possibilities are manifold: CS offers up to 150 courses for 3,500–4,000 students each semester.

Situating CS in historical conditions and transformation of the whole institution toward becoming a sustainable university

The university's orientation toward interdisciplinarity and transdisciplinarity in teaching and research goes hand in hand with the broader aspiration of becoming a sustainable institution. Introducing sustainable development at the university level requires learning at all levels, making the entirety of the university a focal point and organizational change necessary. Thus, it is of importance to take a closer look at the whole-institution approach at the center of this strategic change. Adomßent and Michelsen (2006; 2016) described detailed steps of this transformational process elsewhere but some milestones for teaching and learning stand out for this chapter. From a historical standpoint, Leuphana University was one of the first European higher education institutions to follow a systemic view of sustainability-oriented transformation. Its projects "Agenda 21 and University of Lüneburg" (1999–2001) and "Sustainable University–Sustainable Development in the context of university remits" (2004–2008), as well as a UNESCO Chair in "Higher Education for Sustainable Development" (established in 2005), provided a way of envisioning a holistic system. From standpoints of sociology (Serpa and Ferreira, 2019; van Wijk et al., 2019) and organizational theory (Wang and Polillo, 2016; Barbour, 2017; Ferone et al., 2018), this approach combines all three levels of analysis this volume follows, that is, macro (a system analysis of the national and European higher education system and Bologna Process), meso (the university as an organization including basic conditions, structure, management, members, and stakeholders), and micro (inter- and trans-disciplinary collaboration in teaching/learning and research).

Zooming out for a wider picture on the macro level

The prehistory of the institution is situated against the backdrop of larger scientific and political change in Germany, with long-lasting development from the mid-1990s when environmental sciences evolved or were placed alongside existing faculties. This scientific field then evolved to sustainability science, incorporating epistemologically different social, ecological, and economical dimensions of scientific methodology (Heinrichs et al., 2016). Multi-perspectivity and interdisciplinary thinking and working are important principles in the scientific treatment of sustainability-oriented problems. Yet, related research subjects are usually complex, so comprehensive analysis and development of solution concepts cannot be achieved by individual scientific disciplines alone. Rather, joint efforts are required from natural sciences, social sciences, engineering, and humanities. As interdisciplinary research activities, they transcend disciplinary boundaries, and as transdisciplinary research, they span a range from basic research to concrete applications including involvement of stakeholders beyond the academy (Klein, 2010). Each discipline can be located in its own scientific traditions and cultures, characterized by different understandings of science based on different basic assumptions and concepts, procedures, and methods (Becker and Kastenhofer, 2010).

Furthermore, sustainability-oriented research efforts are process-oriented, open-ended search movements that aim, particularly in the case of complex problems that occur in the course of implementing the sustainability principle, to contribute to identifying and expediently overcoming barriers to transformation (Patton, 2011; WBGU, 2011). The focus thereby is on transdisciplinary bridging dualisms of theory and practice, researcher and subject, everyday experiences and academic knowledge (Reason and McArdle, 2006). Thus, with reference to the sustainability concept, dominating knowledge concepts are to be questioned. Understanding knowledge must inevitably include a broader view covering embeddedness in contradictory contexts, social barriers followed by asymmetries from local to global levels, and questioning the need for political and administrative governance (Adomßent, 2008). Because subjects and objects of research necessarily vary considerably depending on their respective contexts, research is increasingly obliged to differentiate by turning its attention to practices and their actors in society who are responsible for this change. The potential range of bodies of knowledge that emerge in contexts of individual cases generally reaches far beyond these and can, in the best case, attain global dimensions by producing

> practical knowledge that is useful to people in the everyday conduct of their lives (...) to contribute through this practical knowledge to the increased well-being – economic, political, psychological, spiritual – of human persons and communities, and to a more equitable and sustainable relationship with the wider ecology of the planet of which we are an intrinsic part.
> *(Reason and Bradbury, 2008, p. 4)*

Rerouting a tanker to ignite and organize the change of a whole institution at the meso level

Generally speaking, the structure of universities is still based on individual pillars. As a result, relations with other educational institutions and organizations of research are not primarily geared to cooperation and trans-institutional collaboration (Adomßent et al., 2007). Similarly, the structure of an organization is generally hierarchical. Change processes that follow the logic of organizational learning, then, will influence a move toward a more horizontal structure and a closer network of cooperation. Thus, universities can be seen as social organizations, loosely coupled systems (Weick, 1976). Cohen and March (1974) coined the term "organized anarchy" for the process of decision-making in universities characterized by vagueness, ambiguity, low degree of self-reflection, and decisions that are often only coincidental. Simple reinforcement at the management level is not the solution to all problems. The anarchical form of decision-making has the positive benefit of showing a high degree of flexibility and players' willingness to change, less than top-down approaches. So, in the end, the culture holds any social organization together, in the sense of a symbolic range of convictions and opinions shared by members of an organization (Keyton, 2017).

A variety of factors influence the development of these cultures including disciplines, values, and norms. Universities have developed specific cultures where convictions, ideas, norms, and symbols are rated highly (Pellert, 1999). Change is easier to achieve, though, when structural and cultural levels are involved in the process. Changes at universities cannot only be achieved through power and force, strong managers, or state intervention (Mintzberg, 1983). Booth (1993) and Pellert (1999) state that approaches that rely on learning processes are more likely to be successful for both individuals and organizations. An approach involves members of an organization in developing new attitudes based on good practice examples that incorporate lessons successfully, supported by communication processes and combined with a learning approach in which the people involved are introduced carefully to the change process (cf. Connaughton et al., 2017).

In the context of Leuphana, during the first aforementioned project, "Agenda 21 and the University of Lüneburg", the idea of organizational change was not yet predominant. The second project, "Sustainable University", followed this pathway precisely. Whereas the first project took initial steps toward spelling out sustainable development in the daily routine of university life, the second project was systematically pursued and extended by a subsequent "Sustainable University" project. In various sectors of the university implementation of specific measures, a change process was initiated that has now passed the point of no return, resulting in a unique sustainability profile including founding a faculty of the same title in 2010 and consolidating a culture of responsibility that characterizes Leuphana's corporate identity and practice. The following paragraphs unravel how this goal was achieved with regard to inter- and trans-disciplinary ways of teaching.

Fine-tuning and adapting the structure by testing and implementing inter- and trans-disciplinary teaching on the micro level

A primary aim of the first project was to develop and test the pilot "Sustainability: A new course of study". It was to involve an interdisciplinary network of various disciplines in developing a program of university study. The program was then tested and finally evaluated by the Interfaculty Coordination Office for General Ecology (IKAÖ) of the University of Bern. The evaluators were generally in favor of continuing the program while giving specific recommendations for its further development. Some content-related and conceptual aspects were considered, but the greatest room for development was the management level: in particular, work- and time-intensive organization of interdisciplinary workflow, continuous support and supervision of students, and the taking up and resolving of comprehension or communication problems that might arise from different approaches of various disciplines.

Recommendations from the evaluation were incorporated into revisions made in the course of the follow-up project. The goal of this follow-up second project, for a sustainable university, was to further develop the study program. It had two main features (Barth and Godemann, 2006): first, an interdisciplinary approach to problem-solving in which both teaching staff and students were to come from various disciplines; and second, a learning process supported by setting up an alternative learning environment with a mixture of in-person and online learning phases. This form of blended learning in the sustainability course took place over two semesters, giving students opportunities to identify social problem areas and global trends in an interdisciplinary dialogue that included political, economic, cultural, and social points of view. The interdisciplinary course was open to students of all disciplines in their third semester and beyond and was conducted as an additional course outside a student's regular study program. This provision allowed students to work collectively on specific concrete solutions to a socially relevant problem. In didactic terms, the objective of the course was to convey broader social and methodological competencies by using a large variety of methods and interchange between group and individual learning phases as well as reflective elements (Barth et al., 2007).

This study program also involved scholars of various disciplines within the university and experts from scientific and practical fields outside the university. Their inclusion enabled transdisciplinary work beyond the limits of science and scholarship. Subject- and actor-specific knowledge of both scientists and actors outside academia, with their different approaches to problems and methods, were all integrated into the program. After two successful runs (Barth and Timm, 2011), the sustainability course became integrated into the new structure of the university, after modification and adaptation to fulfill criteria for a subject within the existing bachelor structure of Lüneburg University. The result was a "Minor Sustainable Development" that spread the establishment of sustainability in higher education through new structures but with a broader, cross-disciplinary focus that showcased an ideal-typical example of what Rusinko (2010) calls the "creation of a new, cross-disciplinary introductory or capstone course" (Figure 3.3).

Even with this approach to change, however, "management by chance" played an important role in this equation. As Chowdhury (2010, p. 388) states, there might always be an unprecedented factor responsible for awesome success or awful failure of any managerial course of action, coined as "the unforeseen or unknown chance cause" (a z factor). At the same time, though, he also states, based on his research, that there is also a "tolerance limit factor" that if properly empowered by knowledge quality can regulate z. In the case of Leuphana University, this phenomenon came into play when a new president had been appointed and could be convinced that following the pathway toward becoming a sustainable university would be a successful strategy for his tenure as president. At least in the beginning, however, it was not his identification with the guiding principles of sustainability that convinced him to steer in this direction. It was rather the fact that the environmental science faculty, by far the smallest in the university, was far ahead in terms of all research performance key indicators (third-party funding, publications, dissertations, etc.).

34 Maik Adomßent

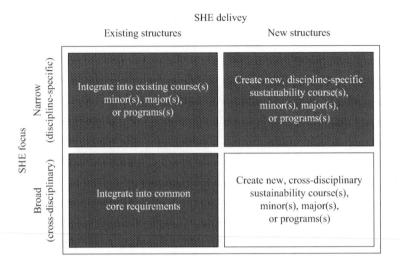

FIGURE 3.3 Localization of Leuphana's holistic approach in implementing inter- and trans-disciplinary teaching in sustainability (the lower-right quadrant) in Rusinko's (2010, p. 253) generic matrix to integrate sustainability in higher education.

Telling the whole CS story about balancing experiential knowledge with strategic goals, or, looking for participative ways of implementation rather than applying explicit theories of institutional change

It is all very well and good to talk about transformative changes and integrations, illustrating possibilities for deep-reaching change. However, an unspoken question remains – how to adapt them to an existing structure. In the case of CS, they existed from the initial implementation of the Leuphana bachelor's degree back in 2009, replacing all former discipline-focused bachelor courses and thereby giving comparably large room to cross-disciplinary teaching and learning. However, many students and lecturers were discontented with the initiative. The university was fortunate to raise external funds for a systematic review of the former concept and, based on thorough evaluation from 2011–2014, came up with a completely new proposal for a structure officially implemented in 2015. Replacement of the outrun CS by the "new" model was carefully conducted. Although not explicitly based on or underpinned by management theories, it can be best described as a participative organizational change and adaptation (Pardo-del-Val et al., 2012; Lamprinakis, 2015). Furthermore, the author's personal experiences with flawed implementation of former study courses in environmental sciences played a significant role, where courses from mainly social and natural sciences were balanced quantitatively but interrelated.

One major motivation of the CS initiators, then, was to replace "side-by-side" coexistence of courses by putting interdisciplinarity and transdisciplinarity more explicitly and genuinely on the map of teaching and learning. However, the whole change process required taking the time, in fact, a whole year, to promote the new model in a collegial atmosphere by inviting all university actors, initiatives, and responsible bodies to discuss, comment, and reflect on the proposed CS renewal in addition to gaining the president's consent. All these efforts made it possible to finally achieve unanimous approval of the new model by the university senate. As a follow-up, constant processes of quality assurance also accompanied these endeavors, depicting a growing identification on the students' side and a growing willingness to teach CS by the teaching staff. For instance, system surveys of current and former students at Leuphana are designed to learn more about the background, needs, satisfaction, and career paths of students to use this information for the quality development of studies and teaching. Toward this end, three levels of surveys are conducted with each student cohort: mid-term, end-of-study, and alumni survey of former students (three years after completing their studies). Other pertinent instruments include regular quality circles with students, teaching staff, and study coordinators, added by accreditation procedures with external experts from different peer groups, leading after the first five years to successful re-accreditation in 2020.

Aligning institutional facilities to foster and safeguard future inter- and trans-disciplinary teaching and research

Coming back to the above-mentioned cross-faculty embeddedness of CS, it is important to mention that Leuphana University follows a methodological pathway of transdisciplinary sustainability research accompanied by transgressive measures and decentralized facilities to scaffold and support both teaching and research across all institutions, illustrated in Figure 3.4.

To elaborate, the inter-departmental Center for Methods focuses on disciplinary, interdisciplinary, and transdisciplinary teaching, research, and methodologies. The objective of the center is to provide support for students at all levels (bachelor's, master's, PhD, and beyond) with respect to education and training in methods, thereby deepening and adding to methods being taught during Leuphana's study programs. Toward this end, the center cooperates closely with the university's faculties and schools, contributing by means of CS within the bachelor program and in subject-specific studies of master's programs.

In addition, the Leuphana Teaching Service supports lecturers, faculties, and schools in the further development of study programs, modules, and courses as well as the expansion of their own teaching competence. The main focus is on teaching-related applications, with possibilities for further qualification and a wide range of support services. In accordance with the university's development plan, five fields of interaction/dialogue-oriented, digital, diversity-oriented,

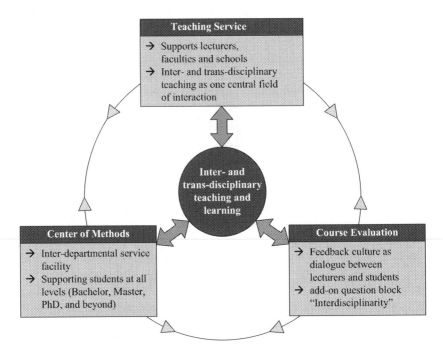

FIGURE 3.4 Aligning institutional facilities at Leuphana University: interplay of the Center for Methods, Teaching Service, and Course evaluations.

experience-oriented, and inter- and trans-disciplinary teaching form focal points of content. By making good teaching visible, the Leuphana Teaching Service is the central hub at which information and experience on teaching, learning, and teaching development are bundled and brought into a lively exchange university-wide, with a constant eye on current developments in the (inter)national educational landscape.

Last, but not least, course evaluations (LVE) provide a systematic, standardized way of collecting written student feedback about teaching, thus promoting dialogue between lecturers and students. The aim is to identify the strengths and weaknesses of a course and ensure teaching quality by developing and implementing opportunities for improvement. Toward this end, student questionnaires and lecturer questionnaires facilitate comparing different perspectives of students and lecturers when evaluating courses. In the 2016 summer semester, in particular, the Leuphana Teaching Evaluation launched a component system for use with course evaluation. This questionnaire is composed of a basic survey and optional question blocks. Members of the teaching staff can currently use the following questionnaires (in German or English) as add-on question blocks: "Practice and application", "Digital in presence", and "Interdisciplinarity" (illustrated in Table 3.1). The latter is recommended to all lecturers in CS. Alternatively, a freely designable

TABLE 3.1 Queries of the optional question block on interdisciplinarity in the component system of Leuphana's teaching evaluation (LVE, 2021)

Additional questions: Interdisciplinarity	Strongly disagree	Rather disagree/ rather agree	Strongly agree	n/r
In this course, I am able to familiarize myself with one or more other scientific disciplines incl. different ways of thinking and methods.	O	O O O O		O
The interaction with other scientific disciplines increases my awareness of similarities and differences between various scientific disciplines.	O	O O O O		O
The course addresses challenges that can arise when various scientific disciplines come together.	O	O O O O		O
This course promotes discussion between students from different disciplines.	O	O O O O		O
In this course, students are able to contribute the varied knowledge they have previously gained in their studies and connect it with the course content.	O	O O O O		O
The course has made it clear to me that various perspectives on the same topic are meaningful.	O	O O O O		O
In the course, I have become familiar with forms of cooperation (various methods, etc.) in order to meaningfully connect various scientific disciplines with each other.	O	O O O O		O

question block can be added optionally, where teachers can design up to six closed and four open questions themselves. As a whole, the component system allows up to two fixed add-on question blocks and the free-design add-on question block to be added optionally in addition to the basic questionnaire. LVE can also be performed on paper or online.

Looking to the future: Learning for transformation

Based on requirements of inter- and trans-disciplinary cooperation in research, the question of the educational claim of a course of study aimed at students before their first academic degree arises. This concern responds to the fact that the expertise and ability to reflect on one's own subject matter is not yet attainable at this point in time, even though it is an indispensable prerequisite for interdisciplinary cooperation (Jacobs, 2013; Di Giulio and Defila, 2017). For this reason, it is appropriate to strive for cross-disciplinary or cross-domain learning as the pedagogical ideal for multi-perspective study programs that can have various facets (DeZure, 2017; Adomßent, 2016). The following quote from the Association of American Colleges and Universities and the Carnegie Foundation for the Advancement of Teaching (2004, p. 1) reflects this pluralistic stance toward integrative learning:

> Integrative learning comes in many varieties: connecting skills and knowledge from multiple sources and experiences; applying theory to practice in various settings; utilizing diverse and even contradictory points of view; and understanding issues and positions contextually. Significant knowledge within individual disciplines serves as the foundation, but integrative learning goes beyond academic boundaries. Indeed, integrative experiences often occur as learners address real-world problems, unscripted and sufficiently broad to require multiple areas of knowledge and multiple modes of inquiry, offering multiple solutions and benefiting from multiple perspectives.

Klein (2010) and DeZure (2017) accordingly emphasize that integrative learning and interdisciplinary learning are by no means equal in content. Rather, they argue that the former should be understood as the broader category and the latter as a subset. Consequently, looking at necessary prerequisites to equip a change of perspective on teaching and learning could be not just helpful but indispensable, not only in but predominantly for higher education contexts. Fischer and Ostwald (2005) propose a relevant change in the understanding of learning communities and settings by recommending a shift from understanding teaching and learning settings and actors more as communities-of-interest than communities-of-practice, as explained in Table 3.2.

Complementary Studies reflect this understanding and its underlying philosophy. If students become aware of the perspectivity of scientific knowledge as well as their own positionality, through reflection on mutual relations to their environments (Plessner, 1975), they lay foundations for accepting other positions and making informed and cautious decisions. The "Agenda 2030 for Sustainable Development" adopted by the United Nations in 2015 is a suitable framework for such a reflection. Industrialized and developing countries alike are aligning their future actions with 17 Sustainable Development Goals (SDGs) in order to promote human rights and a good life for all people through sustainable development. Integration is considered a key principle for implementing sustainability goals. Against this background, research, education, and measures to promote international cooperation are of particular importance for achieving SDGs (Adomßent and Aricò, 2016; Adomßent et al., 2019). In line with the UN's 2030 Agenda and related global SDGs, we encounter contradictions on a daily basis but rarely reflect them in everyday life: for example, when consumer behavior leads to conflicts elsewhere between sustainable food production and nature

TABLE 3.2 Contrasting characteristics of teaching and learning in communities-of-interest with those of communities-of-practice (after Fischer and Ostwald, 2005)

Characteristic	Community-of-practice	Community-of-interest
Nature of problems	Different tasks in the same domain	Common task across multiple domains
Members	From the same domain (novices and experts)	From different domains (stakeholders)
Knowledge development	Exchange of knowledge within the practice; refinement of a domain-specific knowledge system	Exchange of knowledge between domains; integration of multiple knowledge systems
Learning	Growing from novice to expert	Reaching shared understanding
Major objective	Growth in domain-specific knowledge	Resolving a complex problem
Threat	Groupthink	No real communication
Opportunity	Fast progress due to shared background	Creative and robust solutions by making all voices heard

conservation (Obersteiner et al., 2016; International Council for Science, 2017). Here too, practice-oriented educational approaches are helpful, starting with everyday habits and environments and showing sustainable behavioral options (e.g., WESSA and USAID 2016). Exemplary handouts also exist for university environments, which address both institutional and individual actors (SDSN Australia/Pacific, 2017).

To conclude, organizing study programs such as CS across faculties is a promising model with regard to transferability to other universities because it is an appropriate antidote to counter pillarization of the academic system (Fallis, 2009; Adomßent et al., 2007). Put another way, the larger the university, the more often observed. Admittedly though, as in the Leuphana case, it is far easier to implement when a new study model is developed from scratch than to integrate it into existing corset-like curricular structures. In the end, there might be interesting examples at other places to pick and learn from but due to organizational singularity adaptation to distinctive structures, histories, and aspirations of every single institution will be required.

On a broader level, this openness to variety can be shown by a German example of heterogeneous initiatives fostering teaching and learning on institutional dimensions that culminated in nationwide cooperation of a network of dedicated "Sustainability at Higher Education Institutions" (HOCH N), putting emphasis on six different fields of action, teaching and education, as well as research, being the most prominent ("classical") ones. But networks with similar (sustainability-driven) focus on interdisciplinarity and transdisciplinarity do also exist on a continental level, for instance, in Africa (MESA: Mainstreaming Environment and Sustainability in African Universities), Asia and Pacific (ProSPER.Net: Network for the Promotion of Sustainability in Postgraduate Education and Research), North America (AASHE: Association for the Advancement of Sustainability in Higher Education), Latin America (ARIUSA: Alianza de Redes de Universidades por la Sustentabilidad y el Ambiente), and in Europe (COPERNICUS Alliance: European Network on Higher Education for Sustainable Development). Sometimes, these initiatives even work with worthwhile political backing, for example, the range of professionalization at all levels of university staff or the establishment of certification systems of sustainability rating systems for higher education institutions like STARS (Sustainability Tracking, Assessment and Rating System), AISHE 2.0 (Auditing Instrument for Sustainability in Higher Education), or Alternative University Appraisal – all emphasizing inter- and trans-disciplinary teaching and learning.

References

Adomßent, M. (2008) 'Knowledge production and distribution of higher education institutions in the sway of global development trends', in Herwig, R., Uhlig, J. and Küstner, J. (eds), *Wissen als Begleiter!? Das Individuum als Lebenslanger Lerner.* LIT, Münster, pp 153–174.

Adomßent, M. and Aricò, S. (2016) 'Broadening the application of the sustainability science approach', *IAU Horizons*, vol 21, no 4, pp 12–14.

Adomßent, M., Dlouhá, J., Hopkins, C. A., Lotz-Sisitka, H., Razak, D. A. and Vilela, M. (2019) 'Quality education and lifelong learning for all: Trying to get to grips with the iridescent, multifaced, and at the same time universal character of SDG 4', *IAU Horizons*, vol 24, no 1, pp 22–23.

Adomßent, M., Godemann, J. and Michelsen, G. (2007) 'Transferability of approaches to sustainable development at universities as a challenge', *International Journal of Sustainability in Higher Education*, vol 8, no 4, pp 385–402.

Adomßent, M. and Michelsen, G. (2006) 'German academia heading for sustainability? Reflections on policy and practice in teaching, research and institutional innovations', *Environmental Education Research*, vol 12, no 1, pp 85–99.

Adomßent, M. and Michelsen, G. (2016) 'Leuphana University Lüneburg and the sustainability challenge: A review and a preview', in Franz-Balsen, A. and Kruse, L. (eds), *Human Ecology Studies and Higher Education for Sustainable Development: European Experiences and Examples.* Oekom, Munich, pp 57–86.

Association of American Colleges and Universities and the Carnegie Foundation for the Advancement of Teaching (2004) 'A statement on integrative learning', http://wacenter.evergreen.edu/sites/wacenter.evergreen.edu/files/statementintlearning.pdf

Barbour, J. B. (2017) 'Micro/meso/macrolevels of analysis', *The International Encyclopedia of Organizational Communication.* https://doi.org/10.1002/9781118955567.wbieoc140

Barth, M. and Godemann, J. (2006) 'Nachhaltigkeit interdisziplinär studieren: Das Studienprogramm Nachhaltigkeit an der Uni Lüneburg', *Zeitschrift für Hochschulentwicklung*, vol 1, no 1, pp 30–46.

Barth, M., Godemann, J., Rieckmann, M., & Stoltenberg, U. (2007) 'Developing Key Competencies for Sustainable Development in Higher Education', *International Journal of Sustainability in Higher Education, 8*, 416–430.

Barth, M. and Timm, J. (2011) 'Higher education for sustainable development: Students' perspectives on an innovative approach to educational change', *Journal of Social Science*, vol 18, pp 16–26.

Booth, S. A. (1993) *Crisis Management Strategy: Competition and Change in Modern Enterprises*. Routledge, London.

Chowdhury, U. K. (2010) 'Management by chance', *International Journal of Law and Management*, vol 52, no 5, pp 383–403.

Cohen, M. D. and March, J. G. (1974) *Leadership and Ambiguity. The American College President*. Harvard Business School Press, New York.

Connaughton, S. L., Linabary, J. R. and Yakova, L. (2017) 'Discursive construction', The International Encyclopedia of Organizational Communication. https://doi.org/10.1002/9781118955567.wbieoc063

DeZure, D. (2017) 'Interdisciplinary pedagogies in higher education', in Frodeman, R., Klein, J. T., & Pacheco, R. (eds), *The Oxford Handbook of Interdisciplinarity*. Oxford University Press, Oxford, pp 558–572.

Di Giulio, A. and Defila, R. (2017) 'Enabling university educators to equip students with inter- and transdisciplinary competencies', *International Journal of Sustainability in Higher Education*, vol 18, no 5, pp 630–647.

Fallis, G. (2009) 'A liberal education for our age', in Fallis, G. (ed.), *Multiversities, Ideas, and Democracy*. University of Toronto Press, Toronto, pp 381–420.

Ferone, E., Pietroni, D., Petroccia, S. and Antonio Alberto, A. (2018) 'Organizational innovation: A systemic approach', *International Review of Sociology*, vol 28, no 3, pp 419–431.

Fischer, G. and Ostwald, J. (2005) 'Knowledge communication in design communities: And how they may be overcome', in Bromme, R., Hesse, F., and Spada, H. (eds), *Barriers and Biases in Computer-Mediated Knowledge Communication. Computer-Supported Collaborative Learning Series*, vol 5. Springer, Dordrecht, pp 213–242.

Heinrichs, H., Martens, P., Michelsen, G. and Wiek, A. (eds). (2016) *Sustainability Science: An Introduction*. Springer, Dordrecht.

International Council for Science (2017) *A Guide to SDG Interactions: From Science to Implementation*. Paris: International Council for Science. https://doi.org/10.24948/2017.01

Jacobs, J. A. (2013) *In Defense of Disciplines: Interdisciplinarity and Specialization in the Research University*. University of Chicago Press, Chicago and London.

Kastenhofer, K. (2010) 'Zwischen "schwacher" und "starker" Interdisziplinarität: Sicherheitsforschung zu neuen Technologien', in Bogner, A., Kastenhofer, K. and Torgersen, H. (eds), *Inter- und Transdisziplinarität im Wandel? Neue Perspektiven auf problemorientierte Forschung und Politikberatung*. Nomos, Baden-Baden, pp 87–122.

Keyton, J. (2017) 'Culture, organizational', *The International Encyclopedia of Organizational Communication*. https://doi.org/10.1002/9781118955567.wbieoc155

Lamprinakis, L. (2015) 'Participative organizational change and adaptation: insights from a qualitative case study of successful change', *Development and Learning in Organizations*, vol 29, no 2, pp 10–13.

LVE (Leuphana Course Evaluation) (2021) 'Add-on question block interdisciplinarity of student questionnaire', https://www.leuphana.de/fileadmin/user_upload/services/lehrevaluation/01_Dokumente/LEva_2018_basis_interdisciplinarity_students_E_Muster.pdf

Mintzberg, H. (1983) *Structures in Fives: Designing Effective Organizations*. Prentice-Hall, New Jersey.

Obersteiner, M., Walsh, B., Frank, S., Havlik, P., Cantele, M., Liu, J., Palazzo, A., Herrero, M., Lu, Y., Mosnier, A., Valin, H., Riahi, K., Kraxner, F., Fritz, S. and van

Vuuren, D. (2016) 'Assessing the land resource-food price nexus of the sustainable development goals', *Science Advances*. https://doi.org/10.1126/sciadv.1501499

Pardo-del-Val, M., Martínez-Fuentes, C. and Roig-Dobón, S. (2012) 'Participative management and its influence on organizational change', *Management Decision*, vol 50, no 10, pp 1843–1860.

Patton, M. Q. (2011) *Developmental Evaluation: Applying Complexity Concepts to Enhance Innovation and Use*. The Guilford Press, New York.

Pellert, A. (1999) *Die Universität als Organisation. Die Kunst, Experten zu managen*. Böhlau, Wien, Köln, and Graz.

Plessner, H. (1975) *Die Stufen des Organischen und der Mensch*. de Gruyter, Berlin and New York.

Reason, P. and Bradbury, H. (2008) 'Inquiry and participation in search of a world worthy of human aspiration', in Reason, P. and Bradbury, H. (eds), *The Sage Handbook of Action Research: Participative Inquiry and Practice*. 2nd ed. Sage, London, pp 1–14.

Reason, P. and McArdle, K. L. (2006) 'Action research and organization development', in Cummings, T. C. (ed.), *Handbook of Organization Development*. Sage, Los Angeles.

Rusinko, C. A. (2010) 'Integrating sustainability in higher education: A generic matrix', *International Journal of Sustainability in Higher Education*, vol 11, no 3, pp 250–259.

SDSN Australia/Pacific (2017) *Getting Started with the SDGs in Universities: A Guide for Universities, Higher Education Institutions, and the Academic Sector*. Australia, New Zealand and Pacific Edition. Sustainable Development Solutions Network – Australia/Pacific, Melbourne.

Serpa, S. and Ferreira, C. (2019) 'Micro, meso and macro levels of social analysis', *International Journal of Social Science Studies*, vol 7, no 3, pp 120–124.

Thompson Klein, J. (2010) 'A taxonomy of interdisciplinarity', in Frodemann, R. (ed.), *The Oxford Handbook of Interdisciplinarity*. Oxford University Press, Oxford, pp 15–30.

van Wijk, J., Zietsma, C., Dorado, S., de Bakker, F. G. A. and Martí, I. (2019) 'Social innovation: Integrating micro, meso, and macro level insights from institutional theory', *Business & Society*, vol 58, no 5, pp 887–918.

Wang, Y. and Polillo, S. (2016) *Power in Organizational Society: Macro, Meso and Micro*. https://doi.org/10.1007/978-3-319-32250-6_3

WBGU (German Advisory Council on Global Change) (2011) *World in Transition – A Social Contract for Sustainability*. Flagship Report, Berlin.

Weick, K. (1976) 'Educational organizations as loosely coupled systems', *Administrative Journal Quarterly*, vol 21, pp 1–19.

WESSA and USAID (2016) *Stepping Up to the Sustainable Development Goals. A practical guide to integrating the SDGs into our daily lives, including our practical activities, year plan, networking and sustainable centre developments through change-choice-practices*. WESSA, Durban.

4
INTERDISCIPLINARY PROJECTS AND SCIENCE POLICIES IN MEXICO

Divergences and convergences

Juan Carlos Villa-Soto, Mónica Ribeiro Palacios, and Norma Blazquez Graf

Introduction

The process of institutionalizing interdisciplinary education and research is underway in Mexico but faces the challenge of introducing new forms of academic practice in universities currently organized according to markedly disciplinary tenets. Understanding this process is important for arriving at the appropriate assessment and consequent encouragement of interdisciplinary work in traditional academic environments (Padberg, 2014). Among many traits of interdisciplinarity, collaborative work in multidisciplinary and inter-institutional teams is crucial (Klein, 2005; 2013), as well as long timeframes for designing and implementing research projects. Studies examining institutionalizing processes of interdisciplinary education and research have focused on organizational designs that encourage communication, research collaboration (National Academy of Sciences et al., 2005), identity, and legitimacy of new practices (Vienni Baptista et al., 2018), among other issues. The editors of this book, Bianca Vienni Baptista and Julie Thompson Klein, have posed new questions concerning the way(s) in which a comprehensive change can be achieved in institutional cultures in order to boost interdisciplinary work. These include top-down planning strategies and bottom-up methods to overcome obstacles. The primary purpose of this chapter is to understand how these strategies can be combined to examine ways in which public policies in Mexico foster interdisciplinary research, converging with or diverging from initiatives undertaken in university environments in order to develop research projects and undergraduate degree programs.

Jacobs and Frickel (2009) have addressed the issue of evaluation in studies of top-down initiatives that promote interdisciplinary education and research. They report interdisciplinary research evaluations conducted by funding agencies are carried out according to standard indicators of scientific activity, such as

DOI: 10.4324/9781003129424-5

the number of publications, citations, and other criteria that are applied to assess disciplinary work. They also note some areas of interdisciplinary research, such as neuroscience and nanotechnology, do not require special evaluation criteria to compete successfully and get funded, given that they fit conventional criteria such as the number of citations. However, Langfeldt (2006) has pointed out that interdisciplinary research can be less successful in many review settings, including those of grants, as there is greater uncertainty when new approaches are involved. In Mexico, interdisciplinary research projects are directly promoted with top-down planning strategies by using funds from the National Council for Science and Technology (Conacyt, for its Spanish acronym), which are earmarked to finance activities linked to developing scientific and technological research.[1] The impact of these criteria on academic production lies in the National System of Researchers' (SNI, for Spanish initials) view that financial incentives stimulate the work of individuals who are devoted to producing scientific knowledge. Gil-Antón and Contreras (2017) state that the SNI does not only complement salaries, using the logic of merit pay, but that it influences the structure of the scientific profession by defining quality and productivity of the researchers within the system.

In this chapter, we show how the area-specific evaluation criteria applied by the SNI favor superiority of certain modes of collaborative research in interdisciplinary centers at the National Autonomous University of Mexico (UNAM, for Spanish initials). Our findings are relevant to the study of institutionalizing processes of interdisciplinary research because they indicate that a predominant mode of interdisciplinarity exists that is compatible with traditional scientific evaluation criteria established in each separate field of knowledge. These criteria are coupled with cultural factors that each knowledge area has developed in academic environments. Here, the description of cultural characteristics refers to work configuration, the types of products, and the criteria for determining quality in each field of knowledge, drawn from descriptions of the two cultures by Snow (1964) in his well-known distinction between sciences and humanities (Aréchiga, 2014).

The study of how top-down planning strategies are integrated with administrative decisions to overcome obstacles from below is also relevant to reinforcing interdisciplinary approaches in the context of education. This need is particularly pertinent in higher education, as interdisciplinary approaches have expanded in university studies since the turn of the last millennium. In UNAM, for example, one-third of undergraduate degrees are shaped by multi- or interdisciplinary principles. Since 2000, 97% of their curricula were created with this perspective (Villa-Soto and Mendoza, 2020). This chapter also focuses on processes of curricular restructuring in two undergraduate degrees that center on studying environmental issues in order to comply with an interdisciplinary guideline established by central administrations of UNAM and the Autonomous University of Queretaro (UAQ). These are the Bachelor's in Environmental Sciences (LCA, for Spanish initials) and the Bachelor's in Human Development for Sustainability (LDHS, for Spanish initials). We pay particular attention to strategies applied to promoting interdisciplinary work. Finally, we highlight difficulties that have emerged in implementing interdisciplinary guidelines, considering that both degree programs integrate input from the sciences and humanities related to social-environmental studies but they are attached to a single field of knowledge: the LCA is within the jurisdiction of the Academic Council for the Biological, Chemical, and Health Sciences of UNAM, while the LDHS is in the UAQ's Humanities Area.

The chapter is organized as follows. First, evaluation criteria are described for each of SNI's knowledge areas. Next, we present the types of interdisciplinary research developed at UNAM's two interdisciplinary research centers based on the characteristics of SNI researchers' publications in peer-reviewed journals. Then, we describe the curriculum development and restructuring process for the two undergraduate degree programs that address socio-environmental problems from an interdisciplinary perspective, focusing on strategies for establishing the teaching staff and for promoting interdisciplinary work. Finally, the difficulties of complying with interdisciplinary orientation are discussed and some conclusions are drawn.

Methods

For analysis of the Mexican context, we performed two case studies: the Center for Interdisciplinary Research in the Sciences and Humanities (CEIICH, for its Spanish initials), and the Center for the Sciences of Complexity (C3 in Spanish). Both are located at the UNAM. They are the two most important institutions involved in interdisciplinary research at the university, and both aim to build bridges between sciences and humanities (Villa-Soto and Vienni Baptista, 2018a). The CEIICH is part of the UNAM Coordination of Humanities, while the C3 is part of that university's Scientific Research Coordination. We analyzed defining traits of 64 papers published in peer-reviewed journals between 2012 and 2020 by six selected authors from these two centers, which are also members of the SNI. We did so by identifying all the articles by selected authors in journals during the specified time period according to activity reports by the institutions and articles referenced on researchers' personal websites. Analysis of the publications' characteristics entailed identifying the following: (a) in which fields of knowledge authors had their academic degrees; (b) the primary research topic; (c) the thematic coverage or the journal's field of knowledge; and (d) its impact factor. The topic of each article's piece was identified according to a review of its abstracts and keywords. In every case, we consulted the impact factor of journals reported in Scimago Journal and Country Rank (SCImago, n.d.) or the qualification assigned in the Integrated Classification of Scientific Journals (CIRC, for Spanish initials) (CIRC, 2020).

To study the C3 in particular, we selected the work of three researchers who satisfied the criterion of having achieved the SNI's highest level (level 3).[2] These researchers are affiliated with different research institutions within or outside UNAM but are all associated with C3 research programs. For CEIICH, we selected the work of three researchers based on their participation in CEIICH training programs in interdisciplinary research, while considering whether their work explicitly reflected the interdisciplinary approach they conveyed in these programs. For researchers with lower SNI ratings (levels 2 and 1), we consulted the work of those who, apart from meeting the first criterion, had a greater production volume in peer-reviewed journals during the period studied.

In order to understand the context of education, we chose two programs from central and western regions of the country as case studies. The UAQ's Bachelor's in Human Development for Sustainability implemented a curricular change based on its faculty's experience in creating a postgraduate course in interdisciplinary studies. In turn, the National Higher Education School's Bachelor's in Environmental Sciences is affiliated with UNAM in Morelia and was created explicitly to educate young students for an interdisciplinary career. We studied these cases by reviewing activity reports and conducting semi-structured interviews with two teachers who had not only participated in establishing these degree programs and restructuring their curricula but had also been their coordinators (Fuentes, 2020; Ribeiro, 2020). The semi-structured interviews covered the following topics: (a) emergence and restructuring processes of the undergraduate degrees and (b) challenges of integrating faculty and promoting interdisciplinary work among teachers and students. These dimensions enabled us to become familiar with bottom-up measures elaborated by coordinators and collective bodies in order to implement interdisciplinary approaches and thus meet the aims of the UNAM and UAQ central administrations, in the sense of degree programs guided by an interdisciplinary ideal.

The influence of evaluation criteria on modes of interdisciplinary research

Although Conacyt was created in 1970, the National Science and Technology Programs did not promote interdisciplinary projects until 2000, and even then, with limited conceptual precision and few policy instruments to facilitate its implementation (Villa-Soto and Blazquez, 2016). A workgroup from the Scientific and Technological Advisory Forum (FCCT, for its Spanish initials) conducted an in-depth study of the use of government funds to promote interdisciplinary research in Mexico. The report from this workgroup indicated that 64% of the projects approved between 2009 and 2012 that were considered multi-, inter-, or trans-disciplinary were developed by individual researchers. These projects were assessed by an evaluation committee generically named "multidisciplinary" (Bocco et al., 2014). Two of the authors of this chapter, Villa-Soto and Blazquez (2016), reviewed the approved project titles and topics that reported higher financial support in that study and suggested that, in general, the following interdisciplinary research modes are predominant:

- Inter-specialties: convergence of specialties within a single discipline in the fields of natural sciences, e.g., a project entitled "From Genetic Networks to Morphogenesis and Development: Theoretical Models and Experimental Validation" that was restricted to specialties in the biological field.
- Auxiliary interdisciplinarity: enrichment or broadening of one discipline's analytical and interpretational tools by applying knowledge generated in another disciplinary field, e.g., a project entitled "Concentration and Separation of Cells Using Electric Fields in Micro-Devices" in which knowledge from physics is applied in biology.

Our analysis revealed an extreme scarcity of projects that combined natural sciences with social sciences. We also speculated the predominance of individual projects and their concentration in the aforementioned interdisciplinary work modes could be a result of the impact of quality criteria for scientific work that the SNI applies.

Evaluation criteria used by the SNI

A study carried out by Gil-Antón and Contreras (2017) asserted that the SNI's criteria seek to standardize results, practices, and dynamics from different communities and shape scientists without considering the specificities of each knowledge area. They observe that in this system, all the fields of knowledge are assessed with the same criteria, ignoring their diversity (Díaz Barriga, 1996). By comparing SNI's Area 1 (mathematics, physics, and earth sciences) and Area 5 (social sciences), these authors demonstrate there is a tendency to consider characteristics of the former as the model for the latter. However, impact factor is a relevant criterion in several categories: for example, physics, mathematics, and earth sciences (FI > 1 in Journal Citation Reports and in Q1[3] and Q2 quartiles of SCIMAGO), biology and chemistry (FI > 0.5 in Journal Citation Reports), and medical and health sciences (FI > 1). In the case of humanities and behavioral sciences, the impact factor of the journal's indexation and/or prestige is not specified, whereas in social sciences preference is given to indexed international journals, and those in the Conacyt records in the case of national publications (Conacyt, 2020a).

In 2019, the SNI authorized guidelines that governed the functioning of transversal multi-, inter-, and trans-disciplinary committees that are in charge of assessing proposals with coverage of diverse disciplines. These committees evaluated projects that were also linked to a field of knowledge covered by the SNI (Conacyt, 2019a). The fact that these committees were to present their proposal to the one that covers the knowledge area selected by the proposal author indicates that the prevalent criterion is to keep reviews within one knowledge area. The argument wielded to justify this process is that "peer reviewing projects works better when it is carried out within well-defined fields rather than allowing the project to cross boundaries" (Bocco et al., 2014, p. 16). Even though transversal committees were a step ahead in terms of assessment of interdisciplinary work, application of criteria established by each SNI area still persists. Each area determines which products are considered valid to meet requirements for entering or remaining at a given level. The impact factor (FI)[4] of journals in which research articles are published is also part of evaluation criteria. Based on what Jacobs and Frickel (2009) indicated regarding the existence of areas that are better fits for conventional evaluation criteria, and in response to Langfeldt's (2006) comment about less conventional projects having less success in assessment settings, we formed the hypothesis that specific criteria in each of the SNI's areas could favor the development of particular interdisciplinary research modes in this case study's two centers.

The new Regulation for the National System of Researchers issued in 2020 (Conacyt, 2020b) shows further progress in legitimating interdisciplinary research in the National Science and Technology System (SNCyT, for its Spanish acronym),[5] in particular, designing a commission for a new area of expertise called "interdisciplinary" (with specific evaluation criteria that are yet to be defined). The new SNI regulations establish that interdisciplinarity "is produced when two or more disciplines are combined to bring about a new level of integration in which the disciplinary frontiers start to become indistinct" (Conacyt, 2020b). Explicit reference to interdisciplinarity is also present in the general definitions of Conacyt's National Strategic Programs. In this case, interdisciplinarity is defined as "the approach which enables the coproduction of solutions to a common problem by integrating different academic disciplines" (Conacyt, 2019b, p. 3).

These new regulations resulted from the critical review carried out in 2019 by Conacyt of the scientific and technological policy that was applied in Mexico starting in the 1990s, which was based on a development model centered on industrial modernization, trade openness, and economic globalization processes. Following this review, Conacyt's new policy on science and technology has resulted in increasing the prevalence of humanistic, scientific, and technological knowledge in solving the country's priority problems and contributing to development with inclusive and equalitarian well-being (Conacyt, 2020c). This renovation, set forth in Conacyt's 2020–2024 institutional progam, includes a proposal to restructure how the SNI operates to favor social and environmental benefits. This document points out that a large part of SNI members' research products have not responded or contributed to solving the most pressing national problems. This finding is attributed to researchers finding themselves subject to productivist evaluation mechanisms (Conacyt, 2020c).

The influence of SNI evaluation criteria on interdisciplinary research modes at CEIICH and C3

In a previous study, Villa-Soto et al. (2016) described the development of the CEIICH since it was established in 1995. The authors stressed the distinguishing feature that has been its hallmark: building bridges between sciences and humanities when undertaking studies of social problems on a national and a global scale. Based on an academic structure organized according to research programs and with a pluridisciplinary[6] academic staff, the CEIICH comprises diverse interdisciplinary perspectives and modes. Some projects are linked to complex systems theories, either from a constructivist perspective or a mathematical theory of dynamic systems. Within this sphere, the CEIICH has also encouraged the development of hybrid domains, such as historic sociology, political ecology, and philosophy of law, among other interdisciplines (Villa-Soto et al., 2016). In the same journal, Alvarez-Buylla and Frank (2013) discussed the origin of the C3 and its perspectives, highlighting its innovative character in terms of how scientific work can be approached. Since its creation in 2008, this center has set the same objectives as the CEIICH: to build bridges among natural, social, and humanistic sciences. However, the authors note the original goal was to promote research at different organizational levels by integrating many diverse disciplines and using formal and computational tools assumed to emerge from complex systems theory. Although the C3 expresses interest in understanding emerging behaviors that result from associating parts from different levels or hierarchies, the substantial content of complexity is interaction between multiple components, implying the management of large quantities of data. Papers published in journals by researchers from both centers, who have attained higher SNI levels and greater productivity in this area, demonstrate these modes comprise interspecialties in natural sciences, on the one hand, and in social sciences, on the other.

Notwithstanding, both the CEIICH and the C3 stress the importance of bringing together sciences and humanities in interdisciplinary research. However, very few projects actually implement this integration. Those which do at the CEIICH generally do so from hybrid domains, such as political ecology, and only exceptionally from a systemic perspective. With the exception of one article published in a low-impact journal (Q3), publications from the C3 do not report studies of complex systems that coordinate processes from different levels of organization according to a principle of stratified reality. The conception of complexity, which predominates in published journal articles, is grounded in the mathematical theory of dynamic systems and in the physics of nonlinear systems. Applying formal and computational tools to study phenomena from different disciplinary domains does not in any strict sense imply building a complex system in which relationships between different levels of organization are studied. The dynamic and systemic approaches predominant at the C3, for example, study fundamental traits of collective phenomena, such as critical points, attractors, preferential linkups, and other approaches that belong to the same level of organization. These projects tend to be developed in the fields of biology, biomedicine, or economics, and they are undertaken by groups whose education has been restricted to only one knowledge area and led by researchers with interests in physics and mathematics.

Generally speaking, based on this interdisciplinary mode, leaders of these projects still meet the requirement of publishing in journals with a high impact factor (Q1), established by SNI's physics, mathematics, biology, chemistry, and medical and health sciences areas. Moreover, CEIICH researchers generally fulfill requirements established by humanities, behavioral sciences, and social sciences that do not impose specific criteria for impact level and, consequently, have to meet this standard for publication. The CEIICH has set a training program in motion for interdisciplinary research that follows methodological guidelines in multidisciplinary groups and conceptualizes research problems as complex systems from a constructivist viewpoint based on Rolando García's complex systems theory (see García, 2006). Yet, this approach is not dominant in research projects. The predominant focus of individual articles is on a wide range of topics conducted in hybrid spheres by academics with pluridisciplinary training in social sciences and humanities. Collective work only occurred in one case, according to the profile for the C3 project carried out by a level-1 SNI researcher in Area 1 (mathematics, physics, earth sciences). Moreover, these articles are generally published in low-impact journals. The critical observation that quantitative criteria of evaluation systems favor individual work (Castillo et al., 2017) is confirmed in the research this center conducts, which simultaneously conditions the type of interdisciplinary pursuit. However, this criterion also facotrs collective work done in the framework of complexity studies based on the mathematical theory of dynamic systems.

Implementing the interdisciplinary approach in degree programs at UNAM and UAQ

In the context of education, when tasked with creating undergraduate degree programs with an interdisciplinary intent following top-down instructions of central administrations, teachers and degree program coordinators faced the same implementation challenges after an average of five years. They forced early restructuring of curricula based on bottom-up measures to promote interdisciplinary work. Created in 2012, LCA is administered by the National Autonomous University of Mexico's Morelia campus. Founded in 2010, LDHS is run by the Autonomous University of Querétaro. Both Morelia and Querétaro are medium-sized, developing cities whose educational needs are growing. As a result, leaders of these two campuses, established to increase the availability of higher education in the country, seized this opportunity to expand cutting-edge interdisciplinary methods and practices. In both cases, the aim is to approach environmental issues from a social-ecological perspective under the paradigm of sustainability. However, they present differences in approach to environmental problems: LCA has a strong base in ecology, whereas LDHS leans more toward the tradition of environmental humanities. Yet, in both cases, curricula were restructured in a creative, interactive process allowing for adjustments in the study plan and in graduates' profiles. Restructuring curricula implied an intense and prolonged joint effort among members of an academic working group. Professors' training was basically disciplinary, though with clear interests in dialogue with other disciplines. In response, the group implemented strategies for restructuring, including work meetings with the participation of guest researchers from disciplinary areas of other university research centers plus courses and workshops on curriculum development. These activities allowed for building common languages related to basic concepts and common purposes while making it possible to recruit professors for joint projects that ultimately permitted adjustments to the curriculum.

As a result of such changes, collegiate work for restructuring the curricula improved and fostered communication among academic staff, contrary to a previous stage in which academic egos and disciplinary boundaries brought about significant disagreements. In both cases, it is clear that the timeframe from when programs were launched until complete restructuring was vital because the willingness to collaborate and to offer suggestions for work among colleagues required a degree of maturity and trust, and even a certain friendship between teachers. Trust is widely recognized as a core element for tearing down barriers among practitioners of different disciplinary fields of knowledge (Klein, 2005).

We observed five convergence points in institutional restructuring:

1. Graduate profile. Both programs started with a specific graduate profile in view. LCA was meant to last three years and allow graduates to directly join the postgraduate curriculum in order to train young researchers. In the case of LDHS, with a duration of four years, the idea was to train agents who would mediate between government agencies and civil society in human development and sustainability projects. Nonetheless, experiences of graduates in the field indicated adjustments were needed to respond to diverse employment fields. The LCA curricula grew to four years in order to incorporate other dimensions and skills. Yet, most graduates from the LCA enrolled for master's courses, while graduates from the LDHS were more inclined to take jobs in the government sector or in civil associations.
2. New subjects. The restructuration process allowed for incorporating new, integrative, and interdisciplinary subjects that would enable the establishment of a theoretical–methodological basis for developing an interdisciplinary approach. Some subjects were planned on the basis of hybrid theoretical fields, such as nature, culture, and society (in LCA) or complex social-ecological systems (in LDHS), while other subjects were linked to interdisciplinary methodologies, such as social research methods for environmental sciences (in LCA) or epistemology for interdisciplinarity (in LDHS). The institutional challenge has been to find teachers who are capable of handling these subjects and methods from comprehensive viewpoints, without biases dictated by their own disciplines.
3. Integrative subjects. The restructuring process favored promoting interdisciplinarity among students through subjects devoted to integrating

knowledge. Subjects such as integration application and project development, in addition to laboratories for sustainability and sustainability project management, allowed three or four professors and a group of students to generate projects linked to a specific problem. They were to be developed during final semesters, bringing together theoretical and methodological knowledge gained during basic training in order to structure projects responsive to common situations, problems, or interventions. These subjects problematize institutional structures and constitute academic workload for only one teacher while others participate voluntarily, so on occasion resulting in a lack of commitment.

4. Graduation requirements. Although most theses at LCA deal with problems that bridge together several disciplines, the Academic Committee had to intervene when disciplinary projects started becoming more prominent. The restructuring process restricted authorization of theses to only those that conformed to the Academic Committee's request to engage in bridging and integrating, a stipulation that has had a positive influence on encouraging students to research their topics of interest with a multi- or interdisciplinary vision. The regulations for the LDHS focus on requesting that degree work stresses socio-environmental problems in local contexts. This work should promote social well-being and preferably incorporate dialogue with non-academic actors, for example, a project to enhance urban green areas in collaboration with organized civil society or a participative cartography project on water-related conflicts working together with the residents of the affected neighborhood.

5. Evaluation. In both LCA and LDHS, evaluations are a point of vulnerability for professors. It is framed as individual production within the SNI. In both units, formats conform to disciplinary traditions, hindering interdisciplinary work and limiting the type of products that can be created. For example, when the review board of the Academic Council of the Biology, Chemistry and Health Area assessed one professor's research on territorial regulation, ecologists – the primary staff members – did not consider making a map to be a viable result of research. Yet, the geography area would, while distinguishing between creating and copying a map. Facing a negative evaluation, the professor had to request a new appraisal from the Academic Council of the Social Sciences Area's review committee. Such cases tend to be common among professors in these programs. Correcting work basically consists of sending a request for evaluation to another area's review committee because a new interdisciplinary academic council has not been institutionalized.

Conclusions

The examples earlier indicate that the advancement of interdisciplinary approaches is becoming increasingly important in scientific and technological policies in Mexico. This development has been evident in the introduction of different evaluation criteria for interdisciplinary work in funding programs for research projects as well as incentive and commendation programs over the last decade. However, criteria according to specific disciplines and fields still condition the modes of interdisciplinary work that are developed in university environments. Explicit references to interdisciplinarity in these policies are expressed in terms of general conceptions (Conacyt, 2019b; 2020b). Moreover, area-specific evaluation criteria still dominate, similar to the ways they are applied to disciplinary projects. Accordingly, the selection of methods has two priorities: (a) interdisciplinary research projects by multidisciplinary groups with traits of specialization and (b) projects that emerge from hybrid domains but are carried out by a single person. These results coincide with the observation of Jacobs and Frickel (2009) regarding the existence of areas that are better fits for conventional evaluation criteria.

In addition, the top-down strategy does not harmonize with initiatives that originate in a university environment designed to foster bottom-up research projects that tackle complex problems based on the inter-relationship of different levels of organization and the integration of multi/disciplinary groups. The absence of this interdisciplinary mode in centers we studied suggests they face major hurdles when attempting to satisfy productivity requirements and/or impact levels established in each study area's evaluation criteria. This gap confirms Langfeldt's (2006) observation about the lower success rates of non-conventional projects in evaluation settings. To strengthen interdisciplinary research in universities, it is important to consider the potential contributions of undergraduate degrees to training experts in creating, undertaking, and assessing interdisciplinary projects. LDHS and LCA could substantially contribute to training these experts, reinforced by certificate programs in interdisciplinary research similar to those offered by CEIICH. The center relays its interdisciplinary experience to UNAM's academic staff as well as to other institutions given that its academic personnel's teaching methods do not necessarily connect and integrate the interdisciplinary research they conduct with what is taught at UNAM's faculties (Villa-Soto and Vienni Baptista, 2018b). More broadly, teaching programs must also overcome the obstacle of being affiliated with just one knowledge area. When central administrations of universities create interdisciplinary degree programs in a top-down fashion, they must accompany them with a strategy incorporating faculty's bottom-up collegiate work from the beginning.

However, undergraduate programs in this study have, so far, faced disciplinary evaluation, curtailing possibilities of participants' collaborative production. Despite design problems, though, they represent a significant achievement. They have enabled relationships and collective work between teachers and researchers from different disciplines and from diverse departments, centers, or research groups, thus facilitating dialogue over periods longer than those generally available in research settings. In closing, the training of professionals with theoretical and methodological interdisciplinary abilities now underway will enable future possibilities for joint research centers and evaluation committees with new visions and criteria, giving a greater boost to interdisciplinary teaching and research. The model featured in this chapter represents a window of opportunity to couple capacities of the SNCyT with the aim of giving this perspective momentum, including taking on the complexity of problems with a high social impact. To achieve the synergy necessary to create a critical mass of experts in designing, undertaking, and evaluating inter-disciplinary projects, it is important to create spaces that foster an academic culture that readily accepts changes in evaluation criteria to make them more open to interdisciplinary practice. The ways that interdisciplinary research and education have developed at UNAM centers and in undergraduate degree programs at both UNAM and UAQ provide a valuable experience that can guide more structured and comprehensive planning in different areas of the SNCyT, in such a way that these institutions and other similar spaces may create new forms of knowledge. The latter is important, given the fact that, in Mexico, interdisciplinary research is defined by the coexistence of a variety of processes for connecting different types of knowledge that are not governed by a sole approach.

Notes

1 Conacyt is a decentralized public institution charged with designing, planning, executing, and coordinating public policy in all matters related to science, technology, and innovation in Mexico.
2 The SNI levels are established according to specific requisites. For example, among other stipulations, for level 1, the candidate must have conducted original and high-quality scientific or technological research; for level 2, he/she is required to demonstrate leadership in a certain line of research; and for level 3, he/she must have carried out research that represents a relevant scientific or technological contribution to the generation or application of knowledge.
3 The quartile indicates the position of a journal in relation to all those in its area. The journals with the highest impact factor are in the first quartile (Q1).
4 The impact factor measures the frequency at which a journal has been cited in a specific year.
5 The National Science and Technology System (SNCyT, for its Spanish acronym) formally comprises the institutions that promote, coordinate, and undertake these functions, and includes the national science and technology programs.
6 Pluridisciplinary education refers to the achievement of academic degrees in different disciplines; for example, a bachelor's in psychology, a master's in physiology and biophysics, and a doctorate in philosophy. This profile is based on an actual researcher at the CEIICH.

References

Álvarez-Buylla, E. and Frank, A. (2013) "El Centro de Ciencias de la Complejidad de la UNAM: Piedra de Roseta para la ciencia en México", *INTERdisciplina*, vol. I, no. 1, pp. 171–180.
Aréchiga, H. (2014) *La dispersión cultural en la ciencia*. Colección Conceptos. CEIICH-UNAM, Mexico.

Bocco, G., Espejel, I., Hualde, A., Liedo, P. Olivé, L., Reyes, C., Robles, E. and Suárez, R. (2014) *Evaluación de proyectos multi/inter/transdisciplinarios*. Reporte de investigación. Foro Consultivo Científico y Tecnológico, AC, Mexico.

Castillo, E., González, E.O., Félix, D. and Rojas, D. (2017) *Programas de evaluación del trabajo académico en México Políticas, significados y efectos*. Universidad de Sonora/Qartuppi, Sonora.

CIRC (2020) "Clasificación Integrada de Revistas Científicas". https://clasificacioncirc.es/inicio.

Conacyt (2019a) *Lineamientos para el funcionamiento de las comisiones dictaminadoras y comisiones transversales del Sistema Nacional de Investigadores*. Consejo Nacional de Ciencia y Tecnología, Mexico. https://www.conacyt.gob.mx/index.php/el-conacyt/sistema-nacional-de-investigadores/marco-legal/lineamientos-sni/13709-comisiones-dictaminadoras-y-transversales/file

Conacyt (2019b) *Convocatoria 2019 para la elaboración de propuestas de proyectos de investigación e incidencia para la sustentabilidad de los sistemas socioecológicos*. Conacyt, Mexico. https://www.conacyt.gob.mx

Conacyt (2020a) *Criterios SNI*. Conacyt, Mexico. https://www.conacyt.gob.mx/index.php/sni/convocatorias-conacyt/convocatorias-sistema-nacional-de-investigadores-sni/marco-legal-sni/criterios-sni

Conacyt (2020b) "Reglamento del Sistema Nacional de Investigadores", Diario Oficial de la *Federación*. September 21, SEGOB, Mexico. https://www.dof.gob.mx/nota_detalle.php?codigo=5600871&fecha=21/09/2020

Conacyt (2020c) "Programa institucional 2020–2024 del Consejo Nacional de Ciencia y Tecnología", *Diario Oficial de la Federación*, June 23, SEGOB, Mexico. https://www.siicyt.gob.mx/index.php/normatividad/2-conacyt/4-conacyt/programa-institucional/programa-institucional-2020-2024/4925-programa-institucional-2020-2024/file

Díaz Barriga, Á. (1996) "Los programas de evaluación (estímulos al rendimiento académico) en la comunidad de investigadores. Un estudio en la UNAM", *Revista Mexicana de Investigación Educativa*, vol. 1, no. 2, pp. 408–423.

Fuentes, J. (2020) Personal communication, August 21.

García, R. (2006) *Sistemas complejos, conceptos, método y fundamentación epistemológica de la investigación interdisciplinaria*. Gedisa, Barcelona.

Gil Antón, M. and Contreras Gómez, L.E. (2017) "El Sistema Nacional de Investigadores: ¿espejo y modelo?", *Revista de la educación superior*, vol. 46, no. 184, pp. 1–19.

Jacobs, J.A. and Frickel, S. (2009) "Interdisciplinarity: A critical assessment", *Annual Review of Sociology*, vol. 35, pp. 43–65.

Klein, J. (2005) "Interdisciplinary teamwork: The dynamics of collaboration and integration", in Derry, S.J., Schunn, C.D. and Gernsbacher, M.A. (eds), *Interdisciplinary collaboration: An emerging cognitive science*. Lawrence Erlbaum, New Jersey, pp. 23–50.

Klein, J. (2013) "The state of the field: Institutionalization of interdisciplinarity", *Issues in Interdisciplinary Studies*, vol. 3, pp. 66–74.

Langfeldt, L. (2006) "The policy challenges of peer review: Managing bias, conflict of interests and interdisciplinary assessments", *Research Evaluation*, vol. 15, no. 1, pp. 31–41.

National Academy of Sciences, National Academy of Engineering, and Institute of Medicine (2005) *Facilitating Interdisciplinary Research*. The National Academies Press, Washington, DC.

Padberg, B. (2014) "The Center for Interdisciplinary Research (ZiF)—Epistemic and institutional considerations", in Weingart, P. and Padberg, B. (eds), *University*

Experiments in Interdisciplinarity: Obstacles and Opportunities. Transcript Verlag, S, Bielefeld, pp. 95–113.

Ribeiro, M. (2020) Personal communication, August 5.

SCImago (n.d.) *SJR — SCImago Journal & Country Rank* [Portal]. http://www.scimagojr.com

Snow, C.P. (1964) *Two Cultures: And a Second Look. An Expanded Version of the Two Cultures and the Scientific Revolution.* The University Press, Cambridge.

Vienni Baptista, B., Vasen, F. and Villa-Soto, J.C. (2018) "Interdisciplinary centers in Latin American universities: The challenges of institutionalization", *High Educ Policy.* https://doi.org/10.1057/s41307-018-0092-x

Villa-Soto, J.C. and Blazquez, N. (2016) "Interdisciplinary education and research in Mexico", *Issues in Interdisciplinary Studies,* vol. 34, pp. 143–163.

Villa-Soto, J.C., Castañeda, M.P. and Blazquez, N. (2016) "El CEIICH, clave en la institucionalización de la investigación interdisciplinaria en la Universidad Nacional Autónoma de México", *INTERdisciplina,* vol. 4, no. 10, pp. 49–64.

Villa-Soto, J.C. and Mendoza, R.M. (2020) "Criterios para definir el carácter interdisciplinario de diseños curriculares universitarios", *INTERdisciplina,* vol. 8, no. 20, pp. 167–189.

Villa-Soto, J.C. and Vienni Baptista, B. (2018a) "Territorialidad interdisciplinaria: estudio de caso del Centro de Investigaciones Interdisciplinarias en Ciencias y Humanidades (CEIICH, UNAM)", in Castro, A. and Merino, M.I. (eds), *Libro de resúmenes del Segundo Congreso Latinoamericano de Investigación y Educación Superior Interdisciplinaria (IEI 2018)/.* Pontificia Universidad Católica del Perú. Instituto de Ciencias de la Naturaleza, Territorio y Energías Renovables, Lima, pp. 43–44.

Villa-Soto, J.C. and Vienni Baptista, B. (2018b) "Legitimación del quehacer interdisciplinario: el caso de estudio del Centro de Investigaciones Interdisciplinarias en Ciencias y Humanidades", *Ideação. Revista do Centro de Educação, Letras e Saúde,* vol. 20, no. 1, pp. 91–106.

5

A LONG AND WINDING ROAD TOWARD INSTITUTIONALIZING INTERDISCIPLINARITY

Lessons from environmental and sustainability science programs in Brazil

Gabriela Litre, Diego Pereira Lindoso, and Marcel Bursztyn

Introduction

Against the backdrop of a global trend in which complex challenges such as socio-environmental problems demand profound redesign in institutional structures of the academy, this chapter begins by exploring how multi- and interdisciplinary graduate programs (GPs) in Brazil have evolved in recent decades from a few initial tentative programs toward proliferation of courses with different degrees of quality, especially in environmental and sustainability sciences fields. We start by describing the context of historical and geographical conditions over the last half-century, during which Brazil shaped and institutionalized interdisciplinarity through the integration of several disciplinary approaches. Then we identify limits and pitfalls that hinder such initiatives to flourish and after that present concrete examples that illustrate common "pathologies" and misunderstandings that have affected these new interdisciplinary programs since their beginning (Bursztyn and Drummond, 2013; Bursztyn et al., 2016). We also explore how inter- and trans-disciplinary research and teaching are organized in time and space in Brazil, including communities where they emerged. Thus, the chapter concretely shows how some initiatives have contributed to accomplishing national and regional interdisciplinary and transdisciplinary goals.

In addition, the chapter presents "hands-on" insights into how interdisciplinary/transdisciplinary processes operate in Brazil by focusing on the birth and the trajectory of a particular interdisciplinary center founded 25 years ago – the Centre for Sustainable Development (CDS in Portuguese) at the University of Brasília (UnB). The CDS is currently one of the three top-ranked interdisciplinary centers in Brazil devoted to the analysis of socio-environmental challenges and policies (Bursztyn et al., 2016). More broadly, the chapter shows that most interdisciplinary changes in graduate studies in Brazil have been

DOI: 10.4324/9781003129424-6

shaped by theories of institutional change with the defining strategy of the centralizing of governmental regulations regarding the entire national educational system. This government-led strategy has demanded systematic, top-down performance assessments of what constitutes interdisciplinarity and what does not. Finally, and in order to explore what future potentials and advantages interdisciplinary and transdisciplinary research and teaching present in Brazil, including contributions to solving complex societal problems, the chapter scrutinizes the roots and consequences of some of the "pathologies" faced by interdisciplinary programs in the country during the last 30 years. Such an understanding could help interdisciplinary programs and courses overcome institutional barriers in academia both in this country and internationally.

An overview of institutionalization of interdisciplinary programs in the postgraduate system in Brazil

Similar to the rest of the world, universities in Brazil evolved in the 20th century by following the dual trend of fragmentation (e.g., with natural sciences subdivided into biology and geology) and disciplinary aggregation (e.g., with the formation of biochemistry). In the last quarter of the 20th century, the fragmented model of knowledge production and growing demand for integrated knowledge to manage complex problems, such as socio-environmental challenges, prompted epistemological criticisms that led to the global emergence and institutionalization of interdisciplinary approaches in research and teaching. In contrast to disciplinary centers, interdisciplinary programs are a consequence of neither fragmentation nor aggregation of disciplines. As scientific hubs, interdisciplinary programs integrate disciplines and exhibit a problem-oriented and problem-solving identity from their birth. Challenges such as climate change, AIDS, population aging, megacities, and so on are examples of complex problems that demand integrated approaches. Their difficult path toward institutionalization and academic recognition within university structures has a long history that has not reached an end yet. Furthermore, no single trajectory exists: their pathways vary among cases. This plurality is certainly the case for Brazilian interdisciplinary programs, where introduction and implementation took place under particular conditions.

In the 1980s, Brazil underwent a process of re-democratization after 21 years of military dictatorship (1964–1985). Longtime repressed social and intellectual "energies" were channeled in several ways, including the generation of socio-environmental responses that demanded integrated views of long-delayed problems. This liberated energy also resulted in a new wave of mobilization of Brazilian civil society in matters of public interest. As *avant-garde* social spaces, several universities played a key role in advancing such a process, both for their role in resisting the military regime as intellectual cores of re-democratization and, in many cases, for being permeable to new socio-environmental agendas that emerged in Brazil and abroad. This context led to two main factors that triggered the boom of interdisciplinary approaches: international mobilization around an ecological agenda, stemming mainly from the 1972 UN Conference

Interdisciplinary programs in Brazil 59

on the Human Environment, Stockholm, and the growing role of grassroots non-governmental organizations (NGOs). As a result, during the 1990s, political and scientific spaces were consolidated and articulated around the notion of sustainable development and with global environmental agendas, such as climate change and biodiversity conservation. In the technological sphere, the computational and biotechnological revolution also gained traction, fostering innovative interdisciplinary programs in the following decades.

Both top-down and bottom-up forces continued to interact in the process of institutionalizing interdisciplinary programs in Brazil, producing an "interdisciplinary vector" that crossed different fields. In the late 1990s, bottom-up mobilizations led by some cutting-edge academic groups managed to overcome many existing symbolic and institutional barriers to interdisciplinarity, pushing forward interdisciplinary programs into the Brazilian university system (Bursztyn, 2005). Since then, interdisciplinary initiatives have grown exponentially, especially among graduate programs. This development confirms the importance of approaching complex problems through innovative analytical frameworks as well as efforts of institutions to adapt to new scientific arrangements. The "star model" in Figure 5.1 illustrates these efforts to consolidate interdisciplinarity out of existing institutional structures, mainly through the process of "borrowing" scholars on joint appointments to integrate new interdisciplinary centers in the higher education system (Figure 5.1).

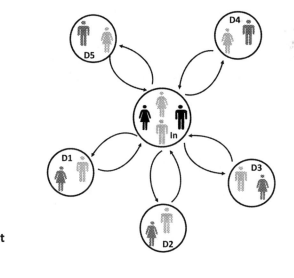

FIGURE 5.1 The "star model". The modes of engagement of faculty members in an interdisciplinary program offered at a major university. **D:** disciplinary faculty; **In:** interdisciplinary program/center (source: adapted by the authors from Bursztyn, 2005).

One unique factor that needs to be taken into account to decipher the Brazilian experience with institutionalizing interdisciplinary courses is the heavily regulated nature of graduate studies in the country. Their regulated nature shows that most interdisciplinary changes in graduate studies in Brazil have been shaped by a theory of institutional change whose defining strategy has been centralizing governmental regulations regarding the entire national educational system. This government-led strategy has demanded systematic, top-down performance assessments. Accordingly, interdisciplinary postgraduate programs have been, and still are, strictly supervised by a national system of accreditation and evaluation managed by the Coordination for the Improvement of Higher Education Personnel (CAPES for its acronym in Portuguese).

Through its centralizing functions, CAPES has a historical and influential role in institutionalizing interdisciplinary programs at a national level. The agency was created in the early 1950s as a branch of the Brazilian Ministry of Education, with a mandate to foster a graduate education system in Brazil. In 1999, prompted by bottom-up mobilization within the academic community, CAPES agreed to create a new area of knowledge named "multidisciplinary". This term was a catchall for a broad variety of cross-disciplinary courses that had started to proliferate and did not "fit" into pre-existing disciplinary slots, for instance, gerontology. In synchrony with an international trend toward creating new graduate programs and courses labeled "interdisciplinary", mobilization from the university's interdisciplinary community continued, and soon, in 2001, the area was renamed "interdisciplinary", followed by exponential growth in the number of courses and graduate programs defined as interdisciplinary (CAPES, 2009). The ensuing "boom" of interdisciplinary GPs was striking. Although Brazilian graduate education as a whole grew at an average rate of 8.4% per year between 2001 and 2011, interdisciplinary GPs showed an average annual growth of 205% (Figure 5.2). This trend continued until 2018, with a record of 590 interdisciplinary graduate courses/programs, most of them with an environmental and agricultural thematic focus. This already impressive figure gains even greater relevance when analyzed in the light of CAPES' strict criteria for authorizing new interdisciplinary graduate courses: annually, only 20 out of 100 proposals for new interdisciplinary courses/programs received the green light from CAPES (CAPES, 2019a). Figure 5.2 depicts the evolution of GPs in interdisciplinary and environmental areas of assessment.

(Re)fragmenting integration

Less than a decade after its creation in 2008, CAPES changed its position and the interdisciplinary area was reformulated. The new architecture included a multidisciplinary committee that operated as a broad knowledge umbrella under which the interdisciplinary area was subordinated along with four other study and research areas: namely, biotechnology, environmental sciences, materials (or engineering sciences), and teaching. The environmental sciences (ES) subarea

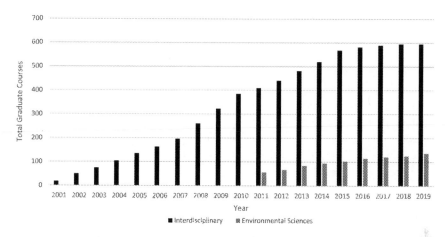

FIGURE 5.2 Evolution of the graduate programs in CAPES' interdisciplinary and environmental assessment areas. The year 2019 had no updated data at the time of publication of this chapter for interdisciplinary courses, so the chart replicates results from the year 2018 (source: prepared by the authors based on CAPES, 2019a, 2019b).

in particular was created as a subdivision of what was until then classified in the interdisciplinary area and received some of its courses and programs. The ES subarea also absorbed some of the new programs that featured interdisciplinary approaches that would be created in the following years[1] (Figure 5.2). CAPES' reformulation of institutionalizing was in part a response to an accelerated expansion of courses/programs, with the result of (re)fragmentation into thematic compartments. This logic, which coincides with the logic of disciplinarization, is an inevitable result of creating the ES subarea as a parceling of the interdisciplinary area. Despite still covering a large number of interdisciplinary epistemologies, the ES "compartment" or subarea was reduced to a more restricted scope, creating barriers around peripheral areas of the research field and eventually limiting collaboration between researchers and disciplines. As a consequence, the initial idea of a "borderless territory", in which any disciplines add to addressing a complex problem could be mobilized in an integrated and collaborative way, was frustrated (as depicted in Figure 5.1).

In addition, several interdisciplinary postgraduate programs with similar interdisciplinary teaching and research profiles were "forced" to choose a new "compartment" or subarea in 2011. Although some programs chose to remain in CAPES' interdisciplinary area, other programs, such as the University of Brasília's Center for Sustainable Development analyzed below, chose to migrate to the ES subarea. Consequently, courses and programs that shared common interdisciplinary profiles started being distant from one another. They began to be evaluated and rated according to different criteria (explained as a "tyranny of metrics"), in addition to being directed by CAPES to follow different quality guidelines. This (re)fragmentation process continues to be a defining feature of the institutional culture of academic recognition of strictly disciplinary fields in Brazil. Despite being the result of consolidating a strong epistemological basis toward more mature interdisciplinary programs, CAPES' interdisciplinary area is still considered a type of incubator or transitional stage that hosts "newcomers" in the form of new interdisciplinary programs before they gain sufficient human resource density and curricular sophistication to form a new area or even a discipline on their own. This process thus took the 21st-century Brazilian academy back to the fragmentation and aggregation path of the 20th century (Bursztyn and Drummond, 2013).

Universalization vs quality?

Exponential increase in interdisciplinary courses and programs also has to be analyzed in the context of a governmental policy aimed at expanding universities in Brazil. The Federal University's Restructuring and Expansion Program (REUNI) is a public initiative that provided funding for territorial expansion and distribution of the Brazilian network of universities in the early 21st century. Between 2003 and 2014, the number of federal (national) universities increased from 45 to 59 while the number of campuses more than doubled, rising from 148 to 327. Between 2007 and 2013, the number of available places for graduate students also grew 80.3% on average per federal university. Furthermore, REUNI supported courses and programs that restructured their curriculum and institutional architecture and that improved faculty quality and capacity (Paula and Almeida, 2000), including interdisciplinary courses/programs. However, the process of institutionalizing interdisciplinarity in Brazil exhibits another unique feature: graduate courses and programs classified in interdisciplinary and ES areas are, for the most part, exclusively at the master's degree level, while centers that offer both master's and PhD degrees or exclusively PhD level courses represent a far smaller proportion depicted in Figure 5.3. A widely held belief – with which the authors agree – is that a relative lack of highly qualified PhD level faculty available to fill newly opened positions limits prospects, since it is a vital condition for CAPES to accredit any new PhD program in any area. This gap, however, is in the process of gradually being filled.

The particular institutional interdisciplinary profile in Brazil sketched above results from two parallel processes. The first consists of the formation of graduation through effort and academic identities of some consolidated interdisciplinary groups. They are concentrated around major scientific centers in the country, have usually been created as master's level courses, and have gradually gained maturity and necessary "density" of qualified faculty to be successfully "upgraded" to PhD programs. The second and less fortunate institutionalization process involves the creation of certain "opportunistic" interdisciplinary programs, a catchall term for disciplinary courses with low faculty density.

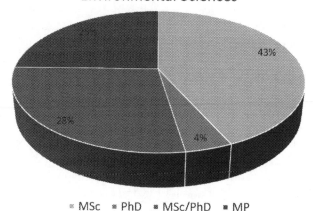

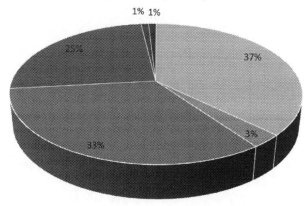

FIGURE 5.3 Proportion of graduate programs classified in CAPES' interdisciplinary (until 2018) and environmental science (until 2019) areas. **MSc:** master's; **PhD:** doctorate; **MSc/PhD:** master's and doctorate; **MP:** professional master's; **DP:** professional doctorate; **MP/DP:** professional master's/professional doctorate (source: prepared by the authors from CAPES, 2019a, 2019b).

Since these programs lack the human resources required to create a "traditional" or "disciplinary" master's level course or program, their proponents frequently request CAPES accreditation as joint interdisciplinary master's programs they consider to be far less defined and strict than disciplinary courses. This type of "opportunistic" process is more frequent, though not exclusive, among private higher education institutions and younger public universities, many of them created in the last 20 years by the REUNI program described earlier. Geographic and historical factors are additional elements for understanding the *sui generis* process of interdisciplinary institutionalization in Brazil.

Brazil is frequently referred to as a country of "continental dimensions", including the existence of several symbolic regions with a rich diversity of livelihoods, identities, and biomes within its wide national borders. Brazil is the fifth-largest nation in the world (8.5 million km^2). Most of its 212 million inhabitants are concentrated along the Atlantic coast, in the south and northeast, with a slow and diffuse expansion toward the north and center of the country, mostly starting in the second half of the 20th century. The result is a unique combination of diverse territories with strong socio-economic asymmetries and cultural and environmental particularities, presenting a varied combination of regional challenges and potential. This heterogeneity is also reflected in the educational system. Most universities and research centers tend to be concentrated in medium to large cities, especially in the central south of Brazil and/or close to the Atlantic coast, which also have the highest concentration of economic and social indicators. The resulting diverse "geography" of national scientific production and academic density necessary for interdisciplinary institutionalization leads to uneven distribution of interdisciplinary and ES courses/programs in the country, as depicted in Figure 5.4.

To elaborate, on the one hand, the relatively wealthy though internally unequal southeast and southern regions house most programs classified in these two areas, even if ES courses/programs show a somewhat more balanced overall distribution at the national level when compared with traditional disciplinary areas (Figure 5.4). On the other hand, the north and center-west regions feature lower percentages of interdisciplinary institutions. These areas have lower population density but are characterized by a more recent flow of population that is expanding rapidly in some areas, especially in the northern Amazon region. At the same time, these geographical regions are home to the most expressive and culturally rich populations of Creole, Maroon, and Amerindian people, among other traditional communities. Additionally, these regions are still covered by vast areas of native vegetation, many of them protected or conservation areas that host biodiversity hotspots. Despite the smaller proportion of interdisciplinary and ES courses/programs in relation to other regions of the country, this diversity has been the object of many socio-environmental case studies with the potential to trigger interdisciplinary approaches, especially in the field of ES.

Interdisciplinary pathologies and syndromes

In order to explore future potentials and advantages inter- or trans-disciplinary research and teaching present in Brazil, including contributions to solving complex societal problems, it is necessary to understand the roots and consequences of some of the "pathologies" faced by interdisciplinary programs in Brazil

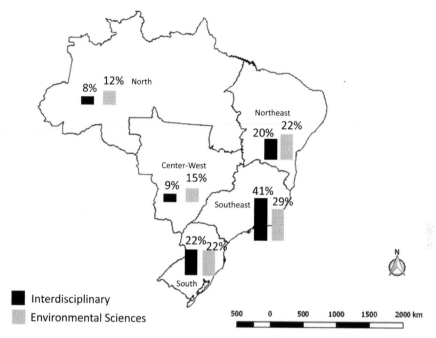

FIGURE 5.4 Distribution of the postgraduate courses/programs evaluated as interdisciplinary and environmental sciences by CAPES according to Brazilian regions (source: prepared by the authors based on CAPES, 2019a, 2019b).

during the last 30 years. Such an understanding could help interdisciplinary programs and courses overcome institutional barriers in academia both in Brazil and in other countries (Bursztyn, 2005). Despite the positive evolution of many interdisciplinary programs, at least four "pathologies" persist. They include: (i) the stigma of generality and shallowness; (ii) the syndrome of refusing otherness (or alternative ways of thinking and/or the marginalization of communities representing those alternative views); (iii) the syndrome of non-peer evaluation; and (iv) the "tyranny" of external metrics. Evaluation of interdisciplinary programs in Brazil, in particular, has generally been performed by "non-peers". That reality is slowly changing, criteria used for measuring interdisciplinary proposals, performance, results, and impacts have been strongly influenced by particularities of fields to which each evaluator belongs.

This approach, which is neither new nor exclusive to Brazil (Jantsch, 1972), directly influences not only the evaluation of curricula and syllabi but also how journals IP researchers publish in are ranked. Most "disciplinary" reviewers naturally tend to favor aspects of a program that have interfaces with their own fields. As a result, important research outputs can be neglected by narrow or biased metrics of academic performance. Inevitably, overvaluation of some aspects and underestimation of others occur. The classical debate between humanities and natural and empirical science scholars about the fairest methods to measure academic productivity and impact in different fields remains relevant in 2020. Most Brazilian interdisciplinary programs are still treated paternalistically by graduate academic authorities as if they are infantile or immature experiences that are not academically self-sufficient. Many interdisciplinary programs when assessed are not compared with one another but to each evaluator's domain of reference. Thus, interdisciplinary programs are frequently considered "incomplete" for not having the full shape of a program that includes a disciplinary background, and/or are judged as "too ambitious", "vague", or even "eccentric" for not fitting into any specific disciplinary approach. Hence, programs end up being evaluated and rated not according to what they offer but what they do not offer or intend to (Bursztyn and Drummond, 2013). On a more positive note, though, the growing presence of "genuine" peers in interdisciplinary assessment committees has started to improve negative aspects of interdisciplinary program evaluation. An increasing number of committee members are being recruited from interdisciplinary fields, and, just as important, some of these "genuine" interdisciplinary peers have obtained advanced degrees in interdisciplinary programs outside Brazil or in already consolidated interdisciplinary programs in the country. They can then capitalize on their day-to-day work in Brazilian interdisciplinary institutions and their experience as doctoral students in interdisciplinary programs.

The CDS: An audacious path toward institutionalizing interdisciplinarity

The authors of this chapter are affiliated with the Center for Sustainable Development (CDS) at the University of Brasília (UnB), both as founder and full professor as well as former graduate students and current associate researchers. Founded in 1995, the CDS illustrates a challenging and audacious path toward interdisciplinary institutionalization in Brazil. Contrary to the trend in most interdisciplinary graduate programs in the country, the CDS' graduate program initially implemented its first PhD course in 1996, and only two years later, in 1998, established the master's program. After consolidating its GP, in 2009, the CDS along with other UnB departments created a joint undergraduate course in ES. Additionally, in 2010, the CDS was strategically located at the geographic center of Brazil in the capital city Brasília, which is host to the Brazilian federal government and most multilateral organizations. It is also surrounded by a socio-biodiverse Cerrado biome (savannas). Within this context, a new degree course was introduced: the master's in Sustainability with Indigenous Peoples and Traditional Territories (MESPT in Portuguese). MESPT is a pioneering transdisciplinary experience in Brazilian higher education based on the paradigm of interculturality. It aims to democratize graduate education by opening doors of academia to historically underrepresented traditional populations in Brazil (Portela et al., 2019).

On the one hand, the MESPT provides formal though still tailored content and methods of graduate training for students who define their identities as traditional Brazilian peoples and communities,[2] with many considered leaders within their communities. On the other hand, the MESPT creates a bridge between formal and traditional knowledge systems built on multiple ontologies and on candidates' personal socio-environmental experiences. The inclusive and innovative profile of the MESPT has generated frequent institutional resistance, even within the Brazilian interdisciplinary community. In its first 25 years of existence, the CDS has also offered seven master's courses and two "inter-institutional" PhD courses, in addition to training several teachers who took interdisciplinary approaches to new universities and campuses created by the REUNI program. Because it hosts one of the pioneering postgraduate courses in the country, the CDS has further played an active role in the institutionalization and experimentation of inter- and trans-disciplinary approaches in Brazil. Moreover, it has reached maximum qualification in terms of academic excellence at the undergraduate level that CAPES verified in 2017 (concept 7/7). This recognition does not necessarily mean its performance was acknowledged as an interdisciplinary center once the CDS chose to be evaluated under the ES area during the aforementioned CAPES reformulation in 2011. It means, indirectly, the interdisciplinary profile of the CDS was somehow "disciplinarized" by CAPES as a prerequisite for academic recognition.

In many ways, the CDS trajectory mirrors larger difficulties and possibilities of interdisciplinary institutionalization in Brazil and abroad (Vienni Baptista and Rojas, 2019). Creation of the CDS provided an opportunity to establish new academic ground within the fragmented institutional framework of the University of Brasília. This common ground allowed faculty and scholars from various backgrounds to collaborate in addressing complex socio-environmental challenges that cannot be solved through single disciplinary approaches. The first step was to define institutional possibilities within Brazilian higher education regulations in order to establish joint faculty appointments that were temporary or permanent. A faculty member from earth sciences, for instance, could allocate part of his or her contractual time to collaborating with colleagues from the social and life sciences. The second step was to offer tenure track positions for full-time members who were meant to interact with holders of joint appointments between the CDS and discipline-based departments. Such interaction ensured that both faculty profiles can enrich one another. The "star model" presented earlier in this chapter is a graphic representation of this conception. From a graduate student perspective, the institutional model adopted by the CDS also created a favorable environment for integrating disciplinary knowledge and for developing transdisciplinary approaches. Candidates of different disciplinary backgrounds who confronted their academic perspectives on science fields such as biology, geology, law, physics, chemistry, agriculture, or engineering attended both master's and PhD courses while debating and collaborating on the transversal curricula provided by the common core of seminars.

The master's and PhD courses also have a high number of candidates who are employees of the federal government or civil society leaders. Some of them even occupy high-level positions at their respective institutions. Many of these candidates with already mature and transdisciplinary profiles (including trans-sector and engaged in participatory work with stakeholders) bring their personal experience and non-academic views and expectations to debates on complex issues to form not only a dialogical space in which interdisciplinary thought is developed but also open spaces for the practice of transdisciplinarity through science-policy-civil society dialogues (Streck, 2021). Interdisciplinary research projects, with a focus on sustainability issues, are also a key aspect of virtually all CDS research proposals. Their implementation involves both students and faculty members from various backgrounds, ages, and life trajectories who collaborate through exchanges of expertise and worldviews, even with related methodological challenges (Litre et al., 2019).

Final considerations

Even if still facing persistent challenges, the rich experience of interdisciplinary graduate programs in Brazil over time yields lessons from both accomplishments and shortcomings. The impressive size of its graduate system compared with other countries and its strict regulation scheme make the Brazilian case a laboratory for analyzing the process of interdisciplinary program design and practice in real time. Abundant data on historical series and modes of implementation of interdisciplinary strategies are available in the country. Therefore, this chapter drew on documented evidence of the tendency in the prevailing institutional culture to transform interdisciplinarity into a new "disciplinarized" discipline in order to achieve legitimacy and academic recognition. This expectation clearly sacrifices the richness of collaboration among researchers and communities from different fields of knowledge. In addition, the pathway toward formal accreditation and criteria for periodical evaluation of interdisciplinary programs has inevitably been rigid and has not left much room for genuine innovation. Openly recognizing and understanding some of the pathologies faced by interdisciplinary programs in Brazil, then, is helping to overcome existing institutional barriers to interdisciplinarity in the Brazilian higher education system, as analyzed in the early 2000s by Bursztyn (2005) and Bammer (2013).

Yet, at the same time, the concrete application of interdisciplinary research results to address complex socio-environmental problems through policymaking is still limited among decision-makers in Brazil (Donadelli, 2016). Moving from interdisciplinarity toward transdisciplinarity while opening dialogue between science and societal actors outside academia is an even more challenging endeavor in the country. Defining the nature of transdisciplinary knowledge is already problematic (Bursztyn et al., 2016), and the inclusion of approaches in courses and programs usually generates mistrust within so-called "normal science". In this search for transdisciplinarity, the idea of knowledge co-production

– connecting social actors with formally trained scientists to jointly generate participatory solutions – is a methodological advance that enables filling the gap between theory and practice (Hirsch Hadorn et al., 2018; Lindoso et al., 2020).

A final overall insight arising from the Brazilian experience in institutionalizing interdisciplinarity and adopting transdisciplinary practices is that this process cannot be reduced to a single, generic model. Each case is unique and has to be approached according to its specific institutional environment and culture. Every experience requires consideration in its context. In addition, familiar complications of pitfalls, clashing interests, perceptions, and goals must be taken into account. Each inter- and trans-disciplinary program, then, needs to find its own concrete pathway toward institutional consolidation and academic legitimization. Hence, the Brazilian roadmap toward institutionalization of interdisciplinarity and transdisciplinarity in academia in general, and the case of CDS in particular, should not be considered as a guideline or model to be followed elsewhere. The study of several cases in Brazil (Bursztyn, 2004) has already shown that each case is a unique experience, shaped by specific situations and communities, with their own challenges and opportunities. Some general features, however, could be mentioned here as references to be considered in other endeavors. First, interdisciplinarity and transdisciplinarity need to be evaluated by peers (people with an interdisciplinary and transdisciplinary profile), and not from a single discipline standpoint. Second, interdisciplinarity and transdisciplinarity are not antagonists to disciplines, but rather complementary. It is not a matter of competition, but rather of collaboration. Third, and as a consequence, scientists from disciplinary backgrounds, interdisciplinary researchers, and their counterparts in the "real world" need to develop skills to understand and communicate with each other.

Acknowledgments

We thank Stéphanie Nasuti for sharing her experience and views on the MESPT program trajectory. This work was supported by the INCT/Odisseia-Observatory of socio-environmental dynamics: sustainability and adaptation to climate, environmental and demographic changes under the National Institutes of Science and Technology Program (Call INCT – MCTI/CNPq/CAPES/FAPs n.16/2014), with financial support from the Coordination for the Improvement of Higher Education Personnel (Capes): Grant 23038.000776/2017-54; National Council for Scientific and Technological Development (CNPq): Grant 465483/2014-3; Research Support Foundation of the Federal District (FAP-DF): Grant 193.001.264/2017).

Notes

1 www.gov.br/capes/pt-br/centrais-de-conteudo/TabelaAreasConhecimento _072012_atualizada_2017_v2.pdf.

2 "Traditional peoples and communities" in Brazil have in practice attributed themselves identities on the basis of at least one out of the following four criteria: (a) ethnic-racial; (b) through the connection to a specific biome or ecosystem; (c) by a predominant work activity that figures as a mark of identity; and (d) by the type of occupation and use of the territory, combined with historical-conjunctural circumstances (Costa-Filho, 2015, pp. 82–83; Costa-Filho, 2020).

References

Bammer, G. (2013). *Disciplining interdisciplinarity. Integration and implementation sciences for researching complex real-world problems*. ANU Press. ISBN (print): 9781922144270. ISBN (online): 9781922144287. http://doi.org/10.22459/DI.01.2013

Bursztyn, M. (2004). 'The environment and interdisciplinarity: Challenges to the academic world', *Desenvolvimento e Meio Ambiente*, vol. 10, pp. 67–76.

Bursztyn, M. (2005). 'A institucionalização da interdisciplinaridade e a universidade brasileira', *Liinc em Revista*, vol. 1, no. 1, pp. 38–53.

Bursztyn, M., Drummond, J. (2013). 'Sustainability science and the university: Pitfalls and bridges to interdisciplinarity', *Environmental Education Research*, vol. 20, pp. 1–20.

Bursztyn, M., Maury, B., Litre, G. (2016). 'Interdisciplinary graduate studies in Brazil: Lessons from sustainability and environmental sciences', in B. Vienni, J. Thompson Klein (eds), *Interdisciplinarity in Latin America*. Issues in Interdisciplinary Studies, no. 34, pp. 122–142.

CAPES. (2009): 'Documento de Área, Área de Avaliação Interdisciplinar'. Brasília. https://www.gov.br/capes/pt-br/centrais-de-conteudo/INTER03ago10.pdf Last accessed on 24th July, 2021

CAPES. (2019a): 'Documento de Área, Área de Avaliação 45: Interdisciplinar'. Brasília. https://www.gov.br/capes/pt-br/centrais-de-conteudo/INTERDISCIPLINAR.pdf Last accessed on 24th July, 2021

CAPES. (2019b): 'Documento de Área 2019, Área de Avaliação 49: Ciências Ambientais'. Brasília. https://www.gov.br/capes/pt-br/centrais-de-conteudo/C_amb.pdf. Last accessed on 24th July, 2021

Costa-Filho, A. (2015). 'Os Povos e Comunidades Tradicionais no Brasil', in E. Cerqueira, et al. (eds), *Os Povos e Comunidades Tradicionais e o Ano Internacional da Agricultura Familiar*. 1ª ed. Brasília-DF: Ministério do Desenvolvimento Agrário, pp. 77–98.

Costa-Filho, A. (2020). 'Traditional peoples and communities in Brazil: The work of the anthropologist, political regression and the threat to rights', *Vibrant – Virtual Brazilian Anthropology*, vol. 17, pp. 1–19.

Donadelli, F. (2016). 'Reaping the seeds of discord: Advocacy coalitions and changes in Brazilian environmental regulation', PhD thesis, The London School of Economics and Political Science (LSE), UK.

Hirsch Hadorn, G., Hoffmann-Riem, H., Biber-Klemm, S., Grossenbacher-Mansuy, W., Joye, D., Pohl, C., Wiesmann, U., Zemp, E. (eds). (2018). *Handbook of transdisciplinary research*. Springer, Bern p. 472.

Jantsch, E. (1972). 'Inter- and transdisciplinary university: A systems approach to education and innovation', *Higher Education*, vol. 1, no. 1, pp. 7–37.

Lindoso, D.P., Sátiro, G., Nogueira, D., Castanho, P.A., Litre, G., Bernal, N., Rodrigues-Filho, S., Bursztyn, M., Saito, C. (2020). 'Uma Odisseia no campo socioambiental da pesquisa transdisciplinar: bases epistemológicas para a co-construção do conhecimento do projeto INCT – Odisseia. Estudo de caso do Baixo Rio São Francisco, Brasil', *INCT Observatory of Socio-Environmental Dynamics*, Working Paper Series, 5.

Litre, G., Bursztyn, M., Rodrigues-Filho, S., Mesquita, P.S. (2019). 'Challenges of performing socio-environmental interdisciplinary research: The experience of the Brazilian Research Network on Climate Change (Rede CLIMA)', *Desenvolvimento & Meio Ambiente (UFPR)*, vol. 51, pp. 141–153.

Paula, C.H., Almeida, F.M. (2000). 'O programa REUNI e o desempenho das Ifes brasileiras', *Ensaio: Avaliação e Políticas Públicas em Educação*, vol. 28, no. 109, pp. 1054–1075.

Portela, C., Nogueira, M., Guimarães, S. (2019). 'Saberes transformativos em prática na academia (Dossiê)', *Revista de Estudos em Relações Interétnicas*, vol. 22, no. 1, pp. 3–10.

Streck, D. (2021). 'Transdisciplinarity as a decolonizing research practice', *Diálogos Latinoamericanos*, vol. 29, pp. 88–100.

Tonneau, J.P., Lemoisson, P., Coudel, E., Maurel, P., Jannoyer, M., Bonnal, V., Bourgoin, J., Cattan, P., Chéry, J.P., Piraux, M., Lestrelin, G. (2011). 'Les observatoires territoriaux. Des outils de la société de la connaissance?', *Revue Internationale de Géomatique*, vol. 27, no. 3, pp. 335–354.

Vienni Baptista, B., Rojas, S. (2019). 'Transdisciplinary institutionalization in higher education: A two-level analysis', *Studies in Higher Education*. doi: 10.1080/03075079.2019.1593347.

6
INTERDISCIPLINARY EDUCATION AND RESEARCH IN NORTH AMERICA

Karri A. Holley and Rick Szostak

Introduction

Interdisciplinary scholars in North America have some advantages relative to scholars in most other regions. The region is replete with colleges and universities. The larger higher education systems in both Canada and the United States have also long possessed an ethos of innovation. Further, research funding has been available to encourage interdisciplinary work and to facilitate new kinds of knowledge production. Higher education in the United States also has a lengthy history with and commitment to General Education (Gen Ed) requirements that provide a breadth of understanding. Those who study interdisciplinarity also benefit from a long tradition of scholarship about other drivers of interdisciplinarity, including the four major drivers today identified in the National Academies of Science, Engineering, and Medicine's state-of-the-art report: the inherent complexity of nature and society, the desire to explore problems and questions not confined to a single discipline, the need to solve societal problems, and the power of new technologies (NASEM, 2005).

Despite these numerous advantages, however, a set of challenges persist. Institutional decisions regarding interdisciplinarity are only rarely informed by familiarity with the scholarly literature. In addition, frequent budget crises and financial shortfalls can threaten novel programs, rendering interdisciplinary programs among the most precarious in terms of economic and cultural capital. For junior faculty and emerging scholars, tenure and promotion standards can penalize interdisciplinary work as well, raising questions about institutional commitment to interdisciplinarity. Across higher education, but especially at larger universities, campuses continue to be characterized by powerful disciplinary structures that severely limit resources for interdisciplinary endeavors. This chapter surveys undergraduate and graduate education, interdisciplinary

DOI: 10.4324/9781003129424-7

research, and interdisciplinary career trajectories, speaking of general trends where possible and noting specific ones in Canada and the United States where relevant. Given the institutional diversity that characterizes the North American landscape of higher education, we give examples of particular programs or research centers. We also explore critiques of interdisciplinarity and why these have emerged.

We write as US American (Holley) and Canadian (Szostak) scholars but approach topics with shared underlying questions about how knowledge production processes across multiple institutional functions, including teaching and research, are structured and prioritized as well as the influence of their structure on practices and outcomes. With respect to the book's five guiding questions, we are most focused on the second, detailing how interdisciplinary research and teaching are organized, and how these structures have evolved historically. We pay special attention to the differences between the United States and Canada. In doing so, we thus embrace the first question posed by the co-editors of this volume about how history and geography have shaped outcomes (see the Introduction). To answer it, we describe processes of gradual change over a period of decades. Our answer to the third question is that change is only rarely transformative, though some significant programs have emerged. We detail how many of the key developments in our theoretical understanding of interdisciplinarity have occurred in North America (question four); nevertheless, interdisciplinary programs are typically little informed by this robust theoretical discourse. In addition, we write throughout with consideration to future prospects (question five).

Undergraduate teaching programs

The Association for Interdisciplinary Studies (AIS) provides a macro lens on underlying questions about how and why to pursue interdisciplinary teaching and research. Originally named as the Association for Integrative Studies, AIS originated in 1979 in the United States with initial attention focused on undergraduate interdisciplinary education. The Association worked over the ensuing decades to identify best practices for curriculum, pedagogy, and program administration. Scholars connected to AIS developed the first textbooks on how to perform interdisciplinary analysis, now in multiple editions (Repko and Szostak, 2020; Repko et al., 2020; Augsburg, 2016). These outcomes followed and built upon publications by AIS pioneers such as Julie Thompson Klein and William H. Newell. More recently, the Association has broadened its scope to address both graduate education and research, mindful that one cannot teach students how to perform interdisciplinary analysis without grappling with how scholars do so. The AIS has also become increasingly international over time, expanding from decades of location in the United States to include presidents and conferences both in Canada and the Netherlands. Machiel Keestra of the University of Amsterdam, for example, has long been associated with AIS and has co-authored a text aimed at graduate students (Menken and Keestra, 2016). The international composition of the Association thus continues to speak to the significance of collaborative efforts in higher education and the global nature of knowledge production.

One of the most important messages from AIS is that students can and should be taught how to integrate insights from different disciplines. This imperative is evident across interdisciplinary education programs in US and Canadian academic institutions. Scholars of interdisciplinarity have identified several key strategies for transcending conflicts in disciplinary insights. At times, seeming differences in disciplinary insights can be resolved by clarifying terminological ambiguity that results from different disciplines defining key terms in different ways. At other times, disciplinarians may disagree simply because each naturally emphasizes phenomena they study. It is often possible to include the phenomena studied by one discipline in a theory grounded in a different discipline. An alternative approach involves mapping arguments made by scholars from different disciplines. This approach is especially useful when phenomena influence each other, including influences neither discipline may pay much attention to. When disciplines are talking about the same concept but still disagree, it is useful to place seeming dichotomies on a continuum. For example, an economist might stress rational decision-making and a sociologist stress peer pressure or cultural influences. An interdisciplinary scholar can ask where on a continuum from rationality to non-rationality a decision-maker might sit, and then draw as appropriate on both analyses. These strategies are useful to students beyond the classroom when engaging differences of viewpoints among fellow citizens. Thus, interdisciplinary education fosters citizenship and constructive work as well as personal interactions. This imperative is the foundational ethos of interdisciplinary education in this case study.

Universities in the United States and Canada have for decades been more open to interdisciplinary teaching programs than universities in Asia, Europe, and other regions of the world (Huber, 1992). Interdisciplinarity was encouraged in the United States within General Education during the first half of the 20th century. Subsequently, interdisciplinary degree programs became common in the 1960s, in part as a response to political tumult (Repko et al., 2020). The growth of programs in ethnic, Black, and women's studies, as well as environmental and urban studies, document the rapid development of interdisciplinary efforts during this era. Programs are sometimes broadly general in scope such as majors in Interdisciplinary Studies or Liberal Studies, but they are more often thematic programs with titles such as Gender Studies or Area Studies or Environmental Studies. The latter type of programs, though, tends to be more multidisciplinary than interdisciplinary. Students are exposed to different disciplines but left to integrate insights of different disciplines on their own due to a lack of institutional commitment for a program or an inability of faculty to devote time and resources needed to ensure integrative aspects of interdisciplinary work as a formal part of the curriculum. In addition, some programs (notably gender studies and biochemistry, but also others) have formalized as hybrid "interdisciplines", benchmarking the development of a core set of theories and methods and fostering discipline-like status to the exclusion of other possible approaches.

The scope of and commitment to interdisciplinary education varies according to institutional factors, including the mission and the culture of a particular campus. The large number of smaller liberal arts colleges in the United States (about 15% of the total institutional population) is a unique facet of North American higher education. These enclaves focus on education in human and natural sciences, with generally no or limited professional or graduate programming. They also have small numbers of scholars in any one discipline, finding it congenial to structure degree programs that require coursework from multiple disciplines. These colleges usually prioritize teaching over research as well. Thus, faculty members are willing to devote considerable energies to team teaching and the development of interdisciplinary curricula that actually guide students through an integrative process. Although these institutions face an uncertain financial future and even more uncertainty related to student enrollment and post-pandemic realities, they will likely continue to be the most innovative and interdisciplinary areas moving forward (see Brint et al., 2009). Brint et al. (2009) hypothesize that such colleges have at times seen interdisciplinary programs as a strategy for attracting students interested in particularly complex areas such as cultural studies, race and ethnic studies, environmental studies, international studies, gender studies, and brain and biomedical studies.

In contrast, interdisciplinarity has faced greater challenges at larger research-oriented universities. Augsburg and Henry (2009) spoke of the "disciplinary hegemony" that characterizes such universities: interdisciplinary teaching programs exist, but the dominant power in such institutions is wielded by disciplines. In worst cases, interdisciplinary programs that had been successful were nevertheless closed as a result of competition over resources during times of financial stringency in North America. In other cases, interdisciplinary programs failed to achieve necessary resources. Team teaching, in particular, is not cheap and provides a tempting target when budgets are cut. Interdisciplinary programs also faced skepticism and even outright opposition in their status due in no small part to their experimental missions. Similar to liberal arts colleges, interdisciplinary education at larger research-oriented universities also faces uncertainties in the post-pandemic reality. It is too early to predict whether these uncertainties will change the ways programs are designed and delivered in addition to what students are attracted to such programs and what faculty teach in them.

In addition, experience of interdisciplinarity varies by field. In applied natural sciences, increasing funding from granting agencies and governments from the 1960s forward, guided by demands for practical outcomes, led to the expansion of interdisciplinary research with spillover into increased interest in interdisciplinary teaching, especially in brain and biomedical science. Social sciences and humanities, in particular, had less funding but a growing intellectual and cultural interest in social concerns that transcended disciplinary boundaries.

This trend in part reflected increased numbers of women, immigrants, and visible minorities among both the professoriate and student bodies. These developments encouraged the creation of interdisciplinary programs addressing gender, race, area and international studies, and the environment (Brint et al., 2009). Given challenges for stability and long-term development, the best administrative structure for teaching programs is not a universal model. Autonomous departments of Interdisciplinary Studies give these programs equivalent administrative structure and appearance to disciplinary departments. However, while departments may provide stability, they do not necessarily ensure truly interdisciplinary approaches or their sustainability.

Case studies in Augsburg and Henry (2009) show that interdisciplinary departments may still be disbanded and their faculty and staff distributed across disciplinary departments. One common alternative is to house interdisciplinary scholars in disciplinary departments with cross-appointments, so part of their teaching and service time is dedicated to interdisciplinary programs. The advantage is increasing the number of potential advocates for interdisciplinarity in disciplinary departments. Yet, the danger is that scholars come to identify with their departments over time, and interdisciplinary teaching programs become defenseless. This outcome happened at co-author Szostak's campus: the administrative structure he lauded in Szostak (2009) has been disbanded due to a combination of administrative whim and professorial apathy.

One of the conclusions that emerges is the fact that faculty evaluations – including decisions about salary, tenure, and promotion – need to explicitly account for interdisciplinarity. This impediment is the most common complaint of interdisciplinary scholars in North America: that they are evaluated by disciplinary scholars in accordance with disciplinary standards (NASEM, 2005). On the teaching side, it can take longer to prepare interdisciplinary courses. On the research side, interdisciplinary research is typically slower, often involves many co-authors, and appears in outlets unfamiliar to disciplinary scholars. Toward remedying these challenges, the Association for Interdisciplinary Studies has developed a set of guidelines that universities should follow in evaluating interdisciplinary scholarship, although getting such guidelines heeded in an environment of disciplinary hegemony is challenging (Klein et al., 2016). Universities are predominantly disciplinary organizations, reflected in core functions such as hiring, evaluation, and faculty promotion.

General Education

All colleges and universities in the United States are regularly evaluated by one of several regional accrediting agencies, all of which require General Education requirements for undergraduate students. To maintain accreditation, all colleges and universities must require students to take several courses outside of their majors. The purpose of Gen Ed is to ensure that students have some broader knowledge beyond their majors, though models range from multidisciplinary menus of discipline-based courses to integrative cores. The imperative for Gen Ed can be traced to the emergence of disciplinary majors in the late 19th and early 20th centuries at a time of widespread concern that universities would churn out narrow experts lacking broad perspectives to be well-informed and constructive citizens. Scholars in the United States also hoped initially that Gen Ed might encourage cultural unity at a time of mass immigration (Boyer & Levine, 1981). The most common approach is a "cafeteria" style in which students are required to select courses in sciences, social sciences, and humanities and arts. A few institutions pursue a "great books" approach, but these lack a coherent approach to interdisciplinary components of Gen Ed. Students may have little understanding or appreciation of why they are forced to take these courses. Furthermore, they are rarely given advice on how they might integrate material in different courses into a coherent understanding of the world.

In Canada, there is no pressure from outside the university toward General Education, and the phrase is little used, but some faculties in English-speaking universities still have what are often termed "core" requirements (unknown outside vocational programs in French-speaking universities). These approaches are also often cafeteria in style and idiosyncratic by institution, though reflecting similar motives as Gen Ed programs in the United States. However, interdisciplinarity could infuse Gen Ed or core requirements by giving students a sense of how scholarship is organized and equipping them with tools for integrating insights from different specialties. Interdisciplinarity can also prepare students for citizenship and lifelong learning by helping students place their majors in larger contexts and preparing them to be more broad-minded and open to new knowledge and information in their careers. Students would learn about the nature of disciplines, and how they have divided studies of the human and natural worlds. Students would also come to appreciate the value and limitations of specialized research, along with advantages that flow from a symbiotic relationship between specialized and integrative research. They would ideally learn how to grapple with differences originating in values. An interdisciplinary education should facilitate creativity, since it encourages students to search broadly, appreciate diverse perspectives, and draw novel connections (Szostak, 2017).

Graduate interdisciplinary teaching and degree programs

As noted earlier, undergraduate interdisciplinary teaching programs have been disbanded, and their teachers reassigned to disciplinary departments, or cross-appointed faculty choose to prioritize their disciplinary identities within such programs. This process occurs in part because many instructors in interdisciplinary programs have disciplinary PhDs and their tenure homes are typically discipline-based departments. As a result, these faculty have had to learn how to teach in an interdisciplinary manner after becoming professors in a specialty. Steady expansion in the number of undergraduate interdisciplinary teaching programs during recent decades or the development of interdisciplinary Gen Ed might have expanded the number of job openings for scholars with interdisciplinary PhDs, but little data exist to document this connection. However, widespread budgetary challenges in recent decades have lowered horizons. Furthermore, graduate education has long prioritized disciplinary specialties. Where interdisciplinary graduate programs do exist, these have tended to expand more in natural sciences than in human sciences, while most undergraduate interdisciplinary teaching has been focused on other areas. This trendline means that interdisciplinary undergraduate teaching programs at research universities can lack synergies with graduate programming and expectations for graduate teaching assistants (see Brint et al., 2009).

Even with these drawbacks, examples of interdisciplinary programming at the master's and doctoral levels are evident. For example, surveying the report of AIS doctoral programs, Holley (2018) noted that almost 300 doctoral programs at US research universities in interdisciplinary STEM fields alone (neuroscience, bioinformatics, materials science, etc.) existed in 2014. Contemporary graduate programs tend to link not only across disciplinary campus units but also with themes, topics, and issues that resonate locally and globally. These emphases enable academic institutions, faculty, and students to capitalize on residential expertise while also providing community impact. Arizona State University is a recent exemplar, including the introduction of interdisciplinary, cross-campus laboratory structures called "Interdisciplinary Solutions for Social Impact". With support from the ASU Graduate School as well as individual academic colleges, these structures emphasize team-based and project-oriented learning on rotating topics of importance across various fields. The Spring 2021 theme of *Impacting Inequality*, for example, is designed in part with input from interested graduate students and faculty; this crowd-sourced approach extends to outcomes that prioritize solution-based models. In upcoming semesters, administrators and faculty will solicit new input for different themes. These curriculum initiatives are reflected in structural changes on the graduate level that prioritize interdisciplinary efforts, including reorganization around theme-based and interdisciplinary federated schools.

In the same way that undergraduate interdisciplinary programs connect to campus traditions, graduate programs do as well – serving as signature areas or ways in which an institution can showcase its strengths (Holley, 2017). Accordingly, and as emphasized elsewhere in this chapter, interdisciplinary efforts also address the need for organizational change, as seen at ASU. Other examples are worthy of note. The Fletcher School at Tufts University in Massachusetts, with a long history of emphasizing graduate studies in law and diplomacy, recently re-organized along 11 areas of specialization to reflect the need for interdisciplinary practice and engagement in global affairs. Similarly, at Virginia Tech, a new Infectious Disease Interdisciplinary Graduate Education Program is located within a newly formed research center, and the program is funded by six participating colleges in addition to the VT Graduate School. This approach has been commonplace for interdisciplinary graduate programming in the last three decades: the design of a research center provides a hub for activity that brings together scholars from individual colleges. Ultimately, the effective design of graduate interdisciplinary curricula requires (re)design of organizational structures that allow for delivery of such curricula.

External partners also continue to drive interdisciplinary graduate initiatives across higher education. The US National Science Foundation's Research Traineeship Program (NRT) is a primary example, preceded by the groundbreaking Integrative Graduate Education and Research Traineeship Program (IGERT). The impact of these efforts is not just funding new research topics and curriculum models. It also institutionalizes those efforts to make good on the oft-extolled promise of a "next generation" of scholars. As part of funding, institutions are required to consider how to make these interdisciplinary approaches self-sustaining when external funding concludes. Tumultuous events of 2020 have also brought change to self-sustaining efforts including addressing social needs. In Fall 2020, graduate student researchers at the University of Texas at San Antonio (UTSA) competed in the COVID-19 Transdisciplinary Team Grand Challenge to strengthen collaborations not only across academic departments and colleges on campus but also with community partners. The Challenge involved funding from the UTSA Graduate School and the Office of the Vice President for Research, Economic Development, and Knowledge Enterprise. Winning graduate student teams included one focused on wastewater surveillance and another on countering the spread of health misinformation, with both teams representing academic colleges across the institution.

Efforts to date have largely focused on ways to foster an interdisciplinary culture on campus or to create structures conducive to interdisciplinary engagement. A growing consensus asserts that transformative interdisciplinary learning requires attention to both culture and structure. The growth of interdisciplinary work at Duke University can be traced to a self-study report in 1988 and the creation of an Office of the Vice Provost for Interdisciplinary Activities in 1993. Subsequent strategic plans reinforced cultural and structural foundations including signature interdisciplinary areas, interdisciplinary faculty hiring initiatives, and a university-wide collaborative learning model that includes undergraduate and graduate students that focuses on compelling social issues. This degree of attention is expensive, though, not only in terms of financial commitments from internal and external stakeholders but also cognitive, physical, human, and organizational resources. Moreover, institutional structures and policies still serve as barriers to cross-disciplinary engagement by students and faculty (O'Meara and Culpepper, 2020). A commitment to interdisciplinary graduate efforts of necessity means that the university is committing time and energy toward one endeavor, usually at the expense of another. Linking interdisciplinary efforts across a campus or across an institution's strategic plan reduces this either/or dichotomy and instead allows for theme-based coherence across units. These same principles apply to the undergraduate curriculum and

Gen Ed requirements discussed earlier in the chapter. In short, they represent institutional commitment beyond a course catalog listing directed at legitimacy, personnel, and financial resources.

Interdisciplinary research

Interdisciplinarity has become a buzzword among university administrators, national granting agencies, science-policy bodies, and educational commissions in both Canada and the United States. However, it is often shorn of reflection on what interdisciplinarity means or how interdisciplinary research is best pursued. The ideal institutional structure for supporting interdisciplinary research is not obvious, either. Interdisciplinary research centers are common at universities, generally based on external grant funding, although occasionally set up to pursue such funding. Leahy et al. (2019) documented the prevalence of such centers at high prestige, top-tier universities, usually members of the Association of American Universities (AAU), those with medical schools, and those with high revenues and/or research and development spending. More general centers across the range of college and university types with a remit to encourage interdisciplinary research, and sometimes teaching, are rarer. The Center for Interdisciplinarity at Michigan State University is noteworthy: it sponsors regular seminars and mixers where scholars with shared interests can meet, has been successful in accessing external research grants, and offers a transdisciplinary graduate fellowship. Other universities have attempted to compile databases that allow scholars to identify others for collaboration on shared interests. Still other campuses have developed centrally operated research offices with support from the highest level of administration. The professional association National Organization of Research Development Professionals (NORDP) was formed in 2010 as a response to this trend; its global membership seeks to foster competitive interdisciplinary research activities in higher education. These are admirable attempts to stimulate bottom-up interdisciplinarity and provide institutional legitimacy but the results of such efforts have not been carefully evaluated.

In Canada, the Social Sciences and Humanities Research Council (SSHRC) had for many years operated an interdisciplinary grant competition in tandem with competitions in a variety of disciplines. In practice, any grant proposal that was judged not to fit any particular discipline was channeled to the interdisciplinary adjudication committee. Interdisciplinary applicants were then asked to explain the interdisciplinary nature of their projects but few did so well. One of the co-authors of this chapter – Szostak – came to this conclusion after serving on such a committee a couple of times. More recently, SSHRC has moved to a system of larger adjudication committees that each span multiple disciplines. This initiative has had ambiguous effects on interdisciplinarity. A dedicated interdisciplinary committee no longer exists, but all proposals are now judged by scholars from multiple disciplines. These may or not be open to interdisciplinary approaches. In addition, SSHRC has occasionally collaborated with granting agencies from natural and health sciences, both of which have called for greater valuing of interdisciplinarity in sponsoring joint granting programs that span the three areas.

In the United States, the National Cancer Institute was the initial catalyst for the International Network for the Science of Team Science (SciTS) (www.inscits.org/). Recognizing an increase in the number and size of research teams involving scholars from different disciplines, the Network aligned health science research and transdisciplinarity while addressing common challenges and strategies for collaborative research. The 2015 NASEM state-of-the-art report on *Enhancing the Effectiveness of Team Science* cited data showing that team research tends to be more productive and important while acknowledging many teams fail to achieve their potential. The annual SciTS conference is a professional home for related interests, and numerous works present overviews of the emerging field with strategies for choosing team members and leaders, understanding cognitive and social dimensions of collaboration, and identifying impediments in the reward system including protocols of authorship (Hall et al., 2019). The Network's strategy is analogous to that of scholars associated with AIS in identifying common challenges and strategies for overcoming them with guidance for theory and practice. Moreover, scholars from both organizations have interacted.

In addition to other challenges, lack of education and training for requisite expertise is a prominent factor in not only conducting interdisciplinary research but also assessing it. As a result of their doctoral training, faculty are traditionally immersed deeply in their entrenched disciplinary norms and related criteria of quality. Furthermore, no uniform approach exists for interdisciplinary research in Canada or the United States; even institutions of similar type and mission exhibit different approaches and degrees of willingness to support it. Leahy et al. (2019) found the greatest distinctions exist between universities with a medical school and those without one, in part due to differences of research infrastructure in different institutional types. The ability of faculty to foster bottom-up change related to interdisciplinary dynamics can combine with top-down administrative commitments shaping interdisciplinary prospects and outcomes. Even when faculty have a commitment to interdisciplinarity supported by external funding agencies such as Canada's SSHRC and the US-based National Science Foundation (NSF) and National Institutes of Health, or perhaps to NSF's emphasis on transdisciplinarity and creative, innovative collaboration through convergence research, interdisciplinary engagement is influenced by administrative support and willingness to undertake and support change efforts.

Interdisciplinary careers

Choice of a doctoral program has long-term effects on the trajectory and the nature of an academic career, including both academic field and host institution. With the growth of interdisciplinary doctoral programs, an increasing number of emerging scholars are starting their post-PhD careers with a depth of interdisciplinary expertise. The CGS/GRE Survey of Graduate Enrollment and Degrees, published jointly by the US Council of Graduate Schools and the Graduate Record Examinations (GRE) Board, monitors doctoral recipients in interdisciplinary studies (broadly grouped in "other fields" along with multi-disciplinary studies and "fields not previously classified", among other options). Degree recipients in this classification have shown steady growth in the last decade, and now represent 8% of all doctoral degrees awarded in the United States (Okahana et al., 2020). Given the nature of interdisciplinary work, and the fact that interdisciplinary degrees are likely awarded under disciplinary classifications such as social/behavioral sciences and math/computer sciences, this figure is probably an undercount.

However, the challenging academic job market in North America is a concern, with fewer long-term positions compared with previous decades. These challenges have almost surely been exacerbated by the current pandemic and contributed even more uncertainty to the careers of emerging researchers. For example, an early response to the COVID-19 pandemic in North America was a hiring freeze on faculty and staff. While this freeze may have been lifted at most institutions in the months hence, the academic job market has not yet rebounded to its pre-pandemic levels, which already reflected a precipitous decline, especially in the number of permanent or tenure-earning positions (Berdahl et al., 2020). The (perceived and/or real) disconnect between interdisciplinary skills and job positions is an added concern as well as declining federal support for research. Given the scarcity of permanent positions, those with interdisciplinary PhDs can find themselves in competition with those who hold disciplinary-based PhDs (Holley, 2018). Calls from a range of stakeholders have consistently emphasized the need to prepare doctoral graduates for alternative careers. Yet interdisciplinary PhDs graduates face similar challenges as their disciplinary PhD peers in terms of competing for jobs in industry, government, or other employers outside the academic sector.

The piecemeal approach toward implementing interdisciplinarity in higher education is evident when considering careers of interdisciplinary PhD graduates. Two issues are important to address. First, we need a greater understanding of the skills interdisciplinary degree recipients gain in their doctoral program. This knowledge would allow not only for more effective curriculum design and delivery but also permit graduates to embark more effectively and efficiently on their career paths. Little research exists on this gap. Future research, census, and institutional assessment efforts should consider this question related to doctoral degree recipients. Second, we need to understand the environment in which graduates practice and deepen these skills – for graduates who pursue careers in academia as well as those in other sectors. The variant and ad hoc nature of Gen Ed and undergraduate interdisciplinary programs as well as uncertain commitments to interdisciplinary research suggest that answers to these questions reveal a potential mismatch of interdisciplinary efforts. Evaluation to understand not only how institutions develop interdisciplinary programming, but also staff, support, and evaluation of these programs would be beneficial.

Critiques of interdisciplinarity

Criticism has been inevitable. Disciplinary scholars worry that interdisciplinarity is taking resources away from disciplines. They wonder if interdisciplinary research can maintain the same academic standards as disciplinary research. And they question how disciplinary expertise and advancement can be maintained or broadened alongside interdisciplinary efforts. Some critiques are reasonable. Universities and granting agencies have not always pursued viable strategies for fostering interdisciplinarity. However, universities also exhibit an "either/or" mindset, especially in times of financial constraints and social turmoil that demand a results-driven approach to higher education coupled with degrees prioritizing employability in the job market. They might pursue interdisciplinarity as an experiment but seek a range of outcomes related to socio-economic impact, high graduation rates, or high levels of community engagement – outcomes that may have never been given resources and support to be realized.

Many critiques also attack an interdisciplinarity that bears no resemblance to conception and practice by scholars of interdisciplinarity. Jacobs (2013) conflated interdisciplinarity with anti-disciplinarity, whereas most interdisciplinary scholars are well aware of both the strengths and weaknesses of disciplines. Frickel et al. (2016) also argued incorrectly that interdisciplinarians think they are better than disciplinarians and worry that scholars of interdisciplinarity ignore the status hierarchies within universities. In fact, scholars of interdisciplinarity worry a great deal about disciplinary hegemony. Graff (2015) further accused scholars of interdisciplinarity of being ahistorical when the literature indicates an awareness of the history of disciplines and interdisciplinarity. Since there is an audience for such critiques, interdisciplinarity continues to be misunderstood and thus unduly feared in the academy. It is crucial, then, that interdisciplinary researchers disseminate pertinent academic standards, make important intellectual contributions, and build upon disciplinary research. Disciplinary scholars can, in turn, learn from interdisciplinary scholarship by placing their own research in a broader context while learning the value of alternative theories, methods, or variables. They can then work collaboratively toward addressing urgent societal challenges.

The greatest lesson, though, is that the main threat to quality interdisciplinary research and teaching is superficial interdisciplinarity performed by scholars who do not seriously engage disciplines they draw upon or the large body of expertise on the nature of interdisciplinarity, providing an easy target for those who wish to criticize the concept (see Szostak, 2019). Temporal and resource demands constitute another threat to interdisciplinary research and teaching. This threat is aggravated by the uncertain present and future of higher education brought upon by years of tenuous financial contributions, declining public support, and now a global pandemic and public health crisis. The promises long associated with interdisciplinarity – including innovation or thinking "outside of the box" – are now embedded in a context of greater uncertainty. In this financial environment, it is particularly critical that advocates of interdisciplinarity address both legitimate and misguided critiques outlined earlier, for otherwise, university administrators will find it too convenient to cut back on support for interdisciplinary initiatives.

Concluding remarks

Administrators often extol the virtues of interdisciplinarity without reflecting deeply on what this rhetorical endorsement requires in the way of both institutional structure and culture. Scholars in North America have developed an extensive literature regarding the nature of interdisciplinarity and how this is best pursued. (The *About Interdisciplinarity* section of the website of the Association for Interdisciplinary Studies provides an overview of this literature; see also the textbooks by Augsburg, and Repko and Szostak and Buchberger). Administrators are often only dimly aware at best of this literature. The pressing need to address a range of complex societal concerns ensures a future for interdisciplinary research and teaching. However, failure to learn lessons from the past ensures that these enterprises are not so successful as they could be.

We can return here to the book's five guiding questions. With respect to the first question about how history and geography have shaped developments, the importance of General Education requirements in the United States but their absence in Canada and much of the world highlight their role in shaping possibilities and limits. General Education creates an opportunity for interdisciplinary education that has not been broadly capitalized upon. As for the second question, we stressed the institutional diversity that characterizes the North American scene (especially in the United States): initiatives have been pursued at a local level, often little informed by developments elsewhere, but nevertheless reflecting broader social movements that have shaped programs of research and education. With respect to the third question, we have described a process of gradual change over a period of decades rather than dramatic transformation. The fourth question regarding the theorization of interdisciplinarity is perhaps the most intriguing. On the one hand, North America has been the home of a robust academic conversation regarding best practices for interdisciplinary research and teaching. On the other hand, university and granting agency administrators often neglect this literature as they make decisions regarding teaching programs and research centers. Our conclusions about the prospects for the future (question five) are thus nuanced. It is clear that interdisciplinary research and teaching have a vital role to play in addressing pressing social problems and promoting a breadth of knowledge. Moreover, there is a robust literature that explains how interdisciplinarity is best pursued. However, it is less clear how quickly university administrators will move to better and more fully institutionalize interdisciplinarity.

References

Augsburg, T. (2016). *Becoming Interdisciplinary: An Introduction to Interdisciplinary Studies*, 3rd ed. Dubuque, IA: Kendall Hunt.

Augsburg, T., and Henry, S. (Eds). (2009). *The Politics of Interdisciplinary Studies: Essays on Transformations in American Undergraduate Programs*. Jefferson, NC: McFarland & Company.

Berdahl, L., Malloy, J., and Young, L. (2020). Faculty perceptions of political science PhD career training. *PS: Political Science & Politics*, 53(4), 751–756. https://doi.org/10.1017/S1049096520000839

Boyer, E.L., & Levine, A. (1981). *The Quest for Common Learning: The Aims of General Education*. Washington, DC: Carnegie Foundation.

Brint, S.G., Turk-Bicakci, L., Proctor, K., and Murphy, S. (2009). Expanding the social frame of knowledge: Interdisciplinary, degree-granting fields in American colleges and universities, 1975–2000. *The Review of Higher Education*, 32(2), 155–183.

Frickel, S., Albert, M., & Prainsack, B. (Eds). (2016). *Investigating Interdisciplinary Collaboration: Theory and Practice across Disciplines*. New Brunswick, NJ: Rutgers University Press.

Graff, H. (2015). *Undisciplining Knowledge: Interdisciplinarity in the Twenty-First Century*. Baltimore, MD: Johns Hopkins University Press.

Hall, K.L., Vogel, A., and Croyle, R. (Eds). (2019). *Strategies for Team Science Success: Handbook of Evidence-Based Principles for Cross-Disciplinary Science and Practical Lessons Learned from Health Researchers*. Berlin: Springer. https://link.springer.com/chapter/10.1007/978-3-030-20992-6_45

Holley, K. (2017). The administration of interdisciplinary programs. In J. Klein, R. Frodeman, and R. Pacheco (Eds), *The Oxford Handbook of Interdisciplinarity*, 2nd ed. (pp. 530–543). New York: Oxford University Press.

Holley, K. (2018). The longitudinal career experiences of interdisciplinary neuroscience PhD recipients. *The Journal of Higher Education*, 89(1), 106–127.

Huber, L. (1992). Towards a new studium generale: Some conclusions. *European Journal of Education*, 27(3), 285–301.

Jacobs, J.A. (2013). *In Defense of Disciplines*. Chicago, IL: University of Chicago Press.

Klein, J.T., Moranski, K., and Schindler, R. (2016). Association for interdisciplinary studies (AIS) guidelines for tenure and promotion for interdisciplinary faculty. https://interdisciplinarystudies.org/wp-content/uploads/2019/06/AIS_Tenure_Promotion_Guidelines.pdf.

Leahey, E., Barringer, S., and Ring-Ramirez, M. (2019). Universities' structural commitment to interdisciplinary research. *Scientometrics*, 118, 891–919.

Menken, S., and Keestra, M. (Eds). (2016). *An Introduction to Interdisciplinary Research: Theory and Practice*. Amsterdam, The Netherlands: University of Amsterdam Press.

National Academy of Sciences. (2005). *Facilitating Interdisciplinary Research*. Washington, DC: National Academies Press.

O'Meara, K., and Culpepper, D. (2020). Fostering collisions in interdisciplinary graduate education. *Studies in Graduate and Postdoctoral Education*, 11(2), 163–180. https://doi.org/10.1108/SGPE-08-2019-0068

Okahana, H., Zhou, E., and Gao, J. (2020). *Graduate Enrollment and Degrees: 2009 to 2019*. Washington, DC: Council of Graduate Schools.

Repko, A., and Szostak, R. (2020). *Interdisciplinary Research: Process and Theory*, 4th ed. Thousand Oaks, CA: Sage.

Repko, A., Szostak, R., and Buchberger, M. (2020). *Introduction to Interdisciplinary Studies*, 3rd ed. Thousand Oaks, CA: Sage.

Szostak, R. (2009). A Canadian and collaborative perspective: The office of interdisciplinary studies at the University of Alberta. In T. Augsburg and S. Henry (Eds), *The Politics of Interdisciplinary Studies* (pp. 212–226). Jefferson, NC: McFarland Press.

Szostak, R. (2017). Interdisciplinary research as a creative design process. In F. Darbellay, Z. Moody, and T. Lubart (Eds), *Creative Design Thinking from an Interdisciplinary Perspective*. (pp. 17–33) Berlin: Springer.

Szostak, R. (2019). Manifesto of interdisciplinarity. https://sites.google.com/a/ualberta.ca/manifesto-of-interdisciplinarity/manifesto-of-interdisciplinarity.

PART II
Transdisciplinary institutional spaces and timeframes

7
THE RISE OF TRANSDISCIPLINARY "BOUNDARY ORGANISATIONS" WITHIN THE AUSTRALIAN TERTIARY EDUCATION SECTOR

Beyond the disciplined university

Isabel Sebastian, Dena Fam, and Jason Prior

Introduction

Since the 1980s, the number of university-based boundary organisations has risen, including industry-linked institutes and funding programmes that have enabled a parallel rise of inter- and trans-disciplinary research and learning within Australian universities. At the same time, Australian universities have to a large extent retained traditional disciplinary-based structures. This chapter explores what constitutes university-based boundary organisations (BO) and an overview of their emergence in the Australian tertiary education sector with a focus on one particular model, the Institute for Sustainable Futures (ISF). The focus then shifts to ISF's history as a transdisciplinary, university-based boundary organisation (TD-BO) within the University of Technology Sydney (UTS). By adopting theories on boundary organisations (Guston, 2001; Miller, 2001; Gustafsson and Lidskog, 2018; Cvitanovic et al., 2018), we developed a tripartite model to explore dimensions enabling ISF to operate and evolve as a TD-BO: (1) structure and organisation; (2) practices and function; and (3) strategy. We conclude by considering three key questions explored in this chapter, including:

1. How have historical conditions shaped the institutional possibilities and limits of TD-BOs in Australia?
2. How were transdisciplinary initiatives enabled within UTS to facilitate ISF's evolution as a TD-BO?
3. How might we theorise and analyse institutional dynamics in TD-BOs, drawing on an analysis of ISFs evolution and endurance over the last 25 years?

DOI: 10.4324/9781003129424-9

University-based boundary organisation: Beyond the disciplined university

The disciplined university, with its departments spanning mathematics, architecture, and planning remains firmly grounded within Australian tertiary education. The recent global COVID-19 pandemic (2019–present) significantly impacted Australian universities due to two key factors: (1) strict travel restrictions prevented international students from entering Australia and (2) the government's "Job Keeper" programme, a subsidy for businesses and not-for-profit organisations affected by the pandemic, was not extended to public universities. As a result, the academic workforce reduced by approximately 15–20% (some 17,000 academics) in 2020 (Visentin, 2021). Yet, Australian universities with their disciplinary siloes appear to remain intact for now, though with reduced staffing numbers both across and within disciplinary faculties. Potential longer-term impacts include maintaining reduced staff–student ratios triggered by a reduced academic workforce, limiting academic appointments and international doctoral scholarships for the foreseeable future, and the increasing norm of online teaching.

A current battle is raging about the relevance of disciplinary education within Australian universities. For example, present fees for STEM disciplines – science, technology, engineering, and mathematics – are being reduced by more than 60%, while the cost of AHSS disciplines – arts, humanities and social sciences – is doubling, based on the belief that STEM graduates are more "employable" and "job relevant" (Carmody and Hunter, 2020). These recent developments ignore the rise of inter- and trans-disciplinary initiatives in the Australian university sector, commencing in the 1980s with over 600 new research centres developed in one decade alone (Turpin, 1997). Current government policy and differential pricing of higher education subjects ignore that "interdisciplinary training will become ever more important" (Evans et al., 2020, p. 1) and that growing inter- and trans-disciplinary research and learning can only exist at the intersection of STEM and AHSS disciplines. The answer to this question is found in the way in which inter- and trans-disciplinary research and learning has been integrated into Australian universities since the 1980s through university-based BOs. These BOs allow the university to retain the illusion of disciplinary focus, while at the same time moving beyond the disciplined university.

In discussing the rise of BOs within the Australian tertiary sector, we draw on a well-established body of BO theory (Guston, 2001; Miller, 2001; Tribbia and Moser 2008; O'Mahony and Bechky, 2008; Frame and Brown, 2008; Parker and Crona, 2012; Wehrens et al., 2014; Franks, 2016; Gustafsson and Lidskog, 2018; Cvitanovic et al., 2018). BO theory provides insight into appropriate structures, organisations, and practices for entities aiming to create change that addresses complex multi-stakeholder socio-ecological challenges (Franks 2016). Guston (2001) initially framed BOs as specific entities to bridge science-policy interests, achieving both scientific and policy goals. Parker and Crona (2012) subsequently expanded BO theory to accommodate contemporary university-based boundary organisations by opening up the science-policy dichotomy to a multi-stakeholder space, recognising continuous role-tensions that come with demands and accountability relationships of university-based BOs (Wehrens et al., 2014). Parker and Crona (2012, p. 282) suggested university-based BOs operate in hybrid spaces, requiring specific hybrid management strategies that allow them to navigate "landscapes of tension". Miller (2001) contributed further to BO theory by distinguishing four hybrid management strategies that characterise the processes within BOs, including activities of convening, translating, collaborating, and mediating.

How have historical conditions shaped the institutional possibilities and limits of TD-BOs in Australia?

Since the 1980s, the number of BOs associated with Australian universities has increased significantly to address the need for inter- and trans-disciplinary research and learning. However, at the same time, disciplinary siloes have remained intact. The rise of BOs was driven in part by extensive structural reforms of the Australian tertiary education sector during the "Dawkins Reforms" of 1988, resulting in the "enterprise" universities model (Howes, 2018) prevailing today. The reforms coincided with government-led initiatives steering academic research towards centre-based structures and concerns of national socio-economic importance (Turpin, 1997). These BOs have taken many forms triggered by significant research programmes, such as the national Cooperative Research Centre (CRC) programme, to the discrete BOs such as the Institute for Sustainable Futures within UTS.

Introduced in 1990, the CRC programme has been the flagship programme of Australia's National Innovation System for the past 30 years (Noble et al., 2019). Funding CRC BOs as interdisciplinary centres consisting of industry-society-science partnerships avoids disruption of universities' disciplinary structures and aims at commercial solutions to complex societal challenges. The CRC Association (2021) estimates the CRC programme involved more than 1,200 industry partners and generated over 12,600 patents by 2015 and generated a net economic impact of AU$14.5 billion by 2017 to the community, exceeding costs of the programme by a factor of three to one. More recently (2012 onwards), the Australian Research Council (ARC, 2016) has also offered funding for Industrial Transformation Research Hubs, a type of BO that supports collaborative research between science, industry, and the university. However, as Bammer et al. (2020) have noted, attempts by the ARC to fund interdisciplinary research have been thwarted by the ARC's use of traditional disciplinary panels, which disadvantage applicants aiming to transverse disciplinary fields in their research proposals. As a result, "interdisciplinary grant applicants have lower success rates than discipline-based proposals" (2020, p. 2). Yet, BOs remain an essential feature of Australian universities to protect inter- and trans-disciplinary research and learning from the hegemony of disciplinarity. Like many other university-based BOs, the ISF was created to facilitate solutions-driven, transdisciplinary collaborations, with many focused on sustainability research that fosters boundary crossing (Cvitanovic et al. 2018; Hirsch Hadorn et al., 2006; Jahn et al., 2012; Pohl et al., 2019). We now turn to analyse ISF as an example of an evolving TD-BO.

How were transdisciplinary initiatives enabled within UTS to facilitate ISF's evolution as a transdisciplinary boundary-organisation?

The ISF was established in 1997 as a flagship research institute with seed funding for an initial three-year period. It is a transdisciplinary university-based boundary organisation with UTS that was itself formed in 1989 as a result of the Dawkins Reforms. As a TD-BO, the ISF has had three distinct phases of development between 1997 to 2021, which are presented in Figure 7.1.

Phase 1: 1997–2000

ISF began with a staff consisting of a director, one administrator/institute manager, and eight higher-degree-by-research (HDR) students. During its early years, it carried out several major projects tackling boundary-crossing research questions in partnership with industry and government partners. From its inception, as a TD-BO, the ISF was established as a research-only entity and deliberately positioned outside traditional faculty structures. This separation was

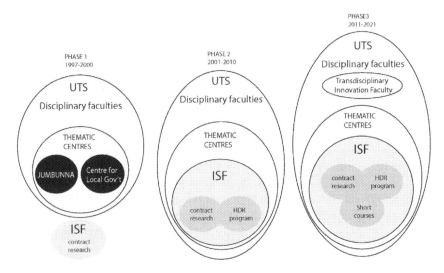

FIGURE 7.1 The evolution of ISF within the University of Technology Sydney 1997–2021.

geographically reinforced by the fact that the ISF was located off-campus, at the Australian Technology Park (ATP), several kilometres from the UTS city campus. The location within the ATP, which is an incubator for start-up enterprises, reinforced the purpose of ISF as an outward-facing BO for research engagement with the community and industry. ISF's outward-facing role was reinforced by the expectation that after an initial period it would become a largely self-funding institute dependent on external funding. ISF's founding director, Professor Mark Diesendorf, aligned its transdisciplinary mission with theoretical frameworks, such as participatory action research and soft systems methodology, thereby further distancing ISF from the disciplinary structure of the university.

By 2000, the "Developmental Review Report for Institute for Sustainable Futures" defined ISFs role as a TD-BO associated with UTS, "as a focus and public symbol of the University's commitment to the quest for sustainable futures" its purpose was "to work with industry and community to develop solutions leading to sustainable futures through programs of research, teaching and consultancy" (UTS, 2000, p.1). ISF was to initiate joint projects across relevant faculties within and external to UTS. The review set out further expectations for ISF, including acting as a "window" to sustainability activities at UTS; coordinator of sustainability activities across faculties; and a focus on postgraduate research training (UTS, 2000).

Phase 2: 2001–2010

The ISF review (UTS, 2000) ushered in leadership change and ISF's second phase. Professor Stuart White's role as director cemented ISF's focus on contract research. When Dr Cynthia Mitchell joined in 2001 as Postgraduate Program Director, she began building a community of scholars. The concept of transdisciplinary research came into focus in the HDR student programme in 2003 and was followed in 2006 by a national teaching and learning fellowship in postgraduate education to explore the supervision of TD-HDR students (Mitchell, 2009). The pragmatic focus of creating change in the world led students and staff to develop a practice-oriented approach to transdisciplinarity informed by the transdisciplinary scholarship of the day. For example, an "outcome spaces framework" emerged from ISF's practice in the mid-2000s and was steadily revised. While ISF's unique role as a TD-BO associated with UTS continued, it was physically relocated to UTS's city campus in 2004, making in White's words "a material difference" in the ISF's "interaction and engagement with the rest of the University" (Mitchell, pers comm, 12 November 2020). During this phase, ISF grew rapidly in scale, including 60 contract research staff and 30 HDR students with ten distinct research areas by 2010.

Phase 3: 2011–2021

ISF's most recent phase is marked by stature as a well-recognised sustainability-oriented TD-BO within the Australian tertiary education sector. During this period, ISF has increased its engagement across disciplinary faculties and industry, including the Australian CRC programme and partnerships on industry-funded contract research. In 2020, ISF successfully led a bid for Australia's largest-ever CRC, securing AU$350 million of industry and government contributions for research into reliable affordable clean energy (RACE, 2030). ISF has a long history of membership within CRC programmes, such as the CRC for Contamination Assessment and Remediation of the Environment (CRC CARE). During this phase, the ISF began to promote its accumulated knowledge as an outwardly facing TD-BO within UTS with the publication of the transdisciplinary outcomes spaces framework and lessons learned during ISF's two-decade history of boundary crossing and praxis (Mitchell et al., 2015). In recent years, teaching and learning initiatives have included online short courses (e.g., systems thinking and deliberative democracy) based on ISF's practice-based knowledge and experience. Over its 25-year history, ISF grew considerably as a TD-BO. In 2019 alone, it conducted over 200 contract research projects and was raising AU$7.9 million in external transdisciplinary research funding. In the same year, ISF employed 78 research and professional staff, supervised 56 HDR students, hosted 24 adjunct professors and visiting scholars, and produced 142 publications (ISF, 2020).

An analytical model for transdisciplinary boundary organisations

The evolution of ISF as a TD-BO external to UTS's existing faculty structure was analysed by drawing on advancements in BO literature and discourse. Figure 7.2 lists the literature referenced and proposes an analytical model to investigate ISF's evolution as a TD-BO, with the recognition and need for further case studies to test the robustness of this model.

We propose three dimensions (Table 7.1) as a way of characterising university-based BOs engaged in TD: (1) structure and organisation; (2) practice and function; and (3) strategy. The three dimensions do not function in isolation but rather enable and reinforce each other. Thus, we depict ISF's development as a TD-BO using the three dimensions and associated characteristics mentioned earlier. Together, they offer insight into how ISF endured as a TD-BO and supported the institutionalisation of transdisciplinarity within UTS while allowing the university to retain its disciplinary structure.

Structure and organisation

In this section, we discuss how ISF addresses each of the seven characteristics of structure and organisation for a TD-BO (per Table 7.1).

Legitimate hybrid space

Creation of a *legitimate hybrid space* to facilitate collaboration between scientific and non-scientific stakeholders at ISF preceded the first phase of ISF's

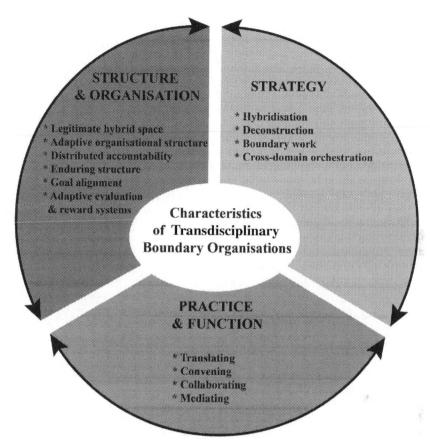

FIGURE 7.2 Characteristics of a transdisciplinary boundary organisation (TD-BO) (created by the authors, adapted from Guston, 1999; Miller, 2001; O'Mahony and Bechky, 2008; Frame and Brown, 2008; Tribbia and Moser, 2008; Parker and Crona, 2012; Wehrens et al., 2014; Mitchell et al., 2015; Franks, 2016; Gustaffson et al., 2018).

development (1997–2000). Senior UTS management in 1997 conceived the hybrid space of sustainability research to coexist alongside, yet importantly outside, the traditional model of the UTS disciplinary-based faculties, structures, and processes. ISF was structured around an evolving set of research areas that related to client and funding agency sectors – for example, water, energy, resources, transport, and international development – rather than disciplinary-focused areas. Within this theme-based structure, ISF operated as a hybrid space in both its contract research projects and the HDR programme where students from a range of disciplines worked on sustainability themes across research areas.

TABLE 7.1 Characteristics of a transdisciplinary boundary organisation (TD-BO)

1. **Structure and organisation**
   a) **Legitimate hybrid space**: BOs create dedicated hybrid spaces for scientific and non-scientific stakeholders; hybrid spaces are constructed to support a mix of social worlds, norms, facts, and values and help navigate landscapes of tension due to often incommensurable stakeholder demands.
   b) **Adaptive organisational structure**: BOs implement adaptive governance and operational systems and practice agile and responsive management.
   c) **Distributed accountability**: BOs have distinct lines of accountability to different social worlds of science, politics, and other stakeholders.
   d) **Durable structure**: BOs are characterised as a continuing organisational entity facilitating the transformation of social relationships through knowledge co-production and mutual adapted learning.
   e) **Aligning to university goals**: BOs are characterised by a high degree of goal alignment with the host university and aligned values and expectations.
   f) **Adaptive evaluation and reward systems**: BOs are characterised by ongoing external evaluation to foster reflection, adaptive learning, and adaptation.

   Franks, 2016; O'Mahony and Bechky 2008, p. 453; Frame and Brown, 2008, p. 237; Parker and Crona, 2012; Miller, 2001; Gustaffson et al., 2018; Guston, 2001.

2. **Practice and function**
   a) **Convening**: BOs bring stakeholders together for face-to-face contact and discussion, and exchange information and perspectives to foster trust-building.
   b) **Translating**: BOs ensure information and resources are accessible and relevant to the stakeholders involved.
   c) **Collaborating**: BOs facilitate transparent dialogue, fostering mutual understanding, and knowledge co-production (scientific and applied knowledge), leading to agreed practical measures.
   d) **Mediating**: BOs mediate between multiple stakeholders and ensure fair representation of divergent interests; professionals can play the mediation role.

   Adapted from Franks, 2016, p. 32; O'Mahony and Bechky, 2008, p. 452; Guston, 1999, pp. 105–106; Tribbia and Moser, 2008, p. 317.

(Continued)

TABLE 7.1 Continued

3. Strategy a) **Hybridisation**: BOs aim to integrate normative and scientific elements to meet epistemological and normative criteria of multiple stakeholders. Defined by Miller (2001) as hybridisation. b) **Deconstruction**: BOs aim to deconstruct scientific facts, evidence, and theories to reveal value-laden assumptions and tensions. c) **Boundary work**: BOs establish and maintain dynamic boundaries between scientific and other domains (e.g., societal, political) in a continuous process of identifying and negotiating stakeholder tensions. d) **Cross-domain orchestration**: BOs engage in activities across multiple domains, formal and informal, to identify and overcome cultural boundaries to ensure mutual benefit for those involved.	Adapted from Miller, 2001; Wehrens et al., 2014; Parker and Crona 2012.

Adaptive organisational structures

With the increasing growth of ISF, its internal governance structures were reinvented three times through institute-wide reviews: (1) with an initial director in a position of top-down management; (2) with a director and deputy director; and (3) with director, deputy director, business manager, team leaders, and postgraduate directors configured in a horizontal rather than a hierarchical model of leadership. The focus shifted to *adapting organisational structures*, processes to improve effectiveness and productivity in working with clients, partner organisations, and UTS faculties. This change included project management and tracking systems, institute-wide portfolios on research outcomes, business development, sustainable workplace issues, management of planning and quality, and internationalisation of research.

Distributed accountability

One of the challenges BO's face is the accountability mechanism for both the scientific community and stakeholders while depending on review mechanisms outside established structures (Guston et al., 2000). This challenge remains one of the continuing areas of tension for ISF as it is accountable to its clients for delivering project outcomes and stakeholders involved within the projects for fair representation, while scientific outputs are needed to meet academic standards. Due to the ISF's client focus, co-created knowledge from transdisciplinary projects may be perceived by others as biased and therefore not meeting objective scientific accountability. Recognition of expertise in knowledge co-production steadily increased alongside UTS' expanding institutional commitment to transdisciplinarity with investment in a Faculty of Transdisciplinary Innovation (in 2016) initially focused on undergraduate skills development. However, transdisciplinary literacy of knowledge co-production methods and practices among scholars, university administration, and client communities is required for university-based BOs such as ISF to be recognised and evaluated as managing *distributed accountability*.

Durable structure

ISF faced major challenges during its first phase due to competing goals and expectations that threatened its existence, relevance, and remit. Challenges emerged due to expectations that ISF has "a legitimate function to coordinate, initiate and bring together trans-disciplinary research projects" (UTS, 2000, p. 7), but without necessary funding mechanisms and resources. To achieve this goal of becoming self-funding, ISF's focus was on viable management and financial systems to support industry-funded contract research projects, embedded and refined as ISF's operating model during the second phase and thereby stabilising its structure as an enduring entity within UTS.

Subsequently, early in the third phase, ISF successfully made the case for a greater level of financial support for activities associated with the growing HDR programme, and engagement with industry and the community. This phase also resulted in a greater level of inclusion in central university administrative fora, which until then had been focused on teaching faculties. ISF's inclusion in UTS' Senior Management Planning committees and creation of the UTS Faculty of TD Innovation (currently the School of Transdisciplinary Innovation) attests to its durability and contribution to UTS planning and development, despite being outside the faculty structure. UTS-wide contributions include the creation of a university-wide "Transdisciplinary Soiree" to bring colleagues together across the university quarterly to identify areas for collaboration, leading the first analysis of projects for mapping to the UN Sustainable Development Goals, publications, and UTS-wide sustainable development policy and strategy.

Aligning to university goals

The early focus of ISF's industry-funded contract research model was stakeholder engagement, research, and practice to improve sustainability-oriented problems in partnership with government and industry. Meanwhile, UTS-wide strategic goals evolved to facilitate *community partnerships, connected research,* and *social change* (UTS, 2021), closely aligning with ISFs remit of engaged transdisciplinary research and practice to "create change towards sustainable futures" (ISF, 2020). TD-BOs while outside the faculty structure have an expectation of meeting the aligned university goals and expectations.

Adaptive evaluation and reward systems

ISF's evolution required developing organisational structures to include appropriate evaluation and reward systems, such as external client evaluation of projects and feedback to ensure client satisfaction. As a university-based institute, ISF was also accountable to the Deputy Vice Chancellor – Research, including evaluation of the business model and income from research outputs, HDR completions, and publications. Multiple and often contrasting evaluation and reward systems must therefore be negotiated. Criteria of academic publications and descriptive research projects by the traditional disciplinary-based academy can contrast to the more normative approach required for research objectives of a TD-BO. Balancing contrasting evaluation and reward systems, therefore, requires investing more time, resources, and importantly, capacity to adapt to client needs when required. Connecting evaluation mechanisms with distributed accountability will aid TD-BO's success and longevity.

Practice and function

In this section, we discuss how ISF addresses each of the four characteristics of practice and function for a TD-BO (per Table 7.1).

Convening

ISF's position as a university-based BO outside faculty structures provides a unique opportunity to facilitate exchange between disciplinary fields. Over the last two decades, *convening* both informal and formal collaborative initiatives have included thought leadership and dialogue to seed future partnerships between industry, government, and community. Examples include (1) ISF convening/co-convening community engagement dialogue initiatives, for example, World Wide Views on Global Warming dialogue (WWVD, 2009); (2) international symposia, for example, World Resources Forum Asia-Pacific (2015); and (3) conferences in collaboration with industry and government.

Translating

Throughout ISF's three phases, research outcomes were translated from over 2,000 contract research projects and 48 HDR completions to date (almost all doctoral thesis) into academic publications and non-academic outputs (e.g., industry-specific reports, stakeholder reports, websites, guidebooks, media articles, social media, blogs). HDR students had translated scholarly work for practitioners into teaching materials in online short courses such as "systems thinking" and "deliberative democracy", the latter providing a tangible translation of theory into practice for political leaders, civil servants, and facilitators.

Experimentation, theoretical development, and transdisciplinary initiatives have also led to insight on how to achieve transdisciplinary outcomes (Mitchell et al., 2015; Fam et al., 2017a; Duncan et al., 2020; Fam and O'Rourke, 2020), support collaboration and collective thinking (Fam et al., 2018a; Prior et al., 2018; Ross and Mitchell, 2018), supervise (Mitchell, 2009), assess quality within transdisciplinary postgraduate programmes (Mitchell and Willetts, 2009), manage tensions within transdisciplinary doctorates (Willetts et al., 2012), and build capacity and skills for postgraduate students (Fam et al., 2017b; Riedy et al., 2018), in addition to meta-considerations for planning integrative postgraduate degree programmes (Fam et al., 2018b).

Collaborating

Australian government funding programmes (as discussed earlier) have created a research culture focused on industry engagement and *collaboration* between multiple partner organisations since the 1990s. Within this research culture, ISFs convening capacity to initiate, build, and formalise transdisciplinary collaborations has culminated in successful CRCs and ARC transformation research hubs.

Mediating

BOs involve multiple stakeholders from across multiple sectoral boundaries, as well as professionals who serve a mediating role (Guston, 2001). In its role as a university-based BO that undertakes industry-funded contract research, ISF often mediates between its clients and stakeholders to facilitate innovative solutions to complex sustainability problems. For example, the deliberative democratic processes facilitated in the World Wide Views project (WWVD, 2009) carried out by ISF compiled recommendations derived from a deliberative process learning from voices of ordinary Australians on climate change. Such processes require mediation in representing stakeholder views fairly and have the potential to influence policy, providing evidence of community support on contested issues such as climate change responses.

Strategy

We turn now to how ISF addresses each of the four characteristics of strategy for a TD-BO (see Table 7.1).

Hybridisation

According to Miller (2001), *hybridisation* in BOs integrates normative and technical choices or judgements to meet epistemological and normative criteria of multiple audiences. ISF's mission "to create change towards sustainable futures" has a normative intent to create change by co-producing knowledge, drawing on and integrating disparate disciplinary knowledge, networks, and expertise. Fulfilling this mission requires an "open-ended learning process without pre-determined outcomes" and continually establishing new relations "between elements not previously related" (Pohl et al., 2021, p. 18). Defining *hybridisation* as a form of integration – which we propose in this chapter – will require further studies to test the robustness of the TD-BO model. Institutionally, UTS-wide strategies and funding mechanisms with a focus on "industry and community engaged research", "practice-based learning", "connected research", "social change" and "precinct and community partnerships" (UTS, 2021) continue to enable *hybridisation* by integrating disparate disciplinary knowledge, networks, and expertise.

Deconstruction

Miller (2001) described *deconstruction* in hybrid management of BOs as making value choices and assumptions explicit and transparent. Deconstruction is closely aligned to the concept of reflexivity in transdisciplinary literature, which Miller (2006) contends is necessary to attend to uncertainties and assumptions. Recent scholarship further highlights the importance of reflexive processes for transformational learning in BOs (Borie et al., 2020). Throughout ISF's second and third phases, reflection has been central to the evolution of ISF, along with increasing recognition of diverse practices, assumptions, and perspectives. Within the HDR programme, several activities fostered reflexivity: including annual planning retreats, peer support groups (e.g., Groups for Accountability and Support [GAS] in Fisher et al., 2003), Knowledge and Accountability for the Progression of Women (KAPOW), and space and time for reflection on the HDR programme (Riedy et al., 2018). Within ISF more broadly, reflection occurs in annual ISF planning days, staff meetings at different levels of management including weekly operations meetings, monthly research area meetings, and quarterly management meetings. In addition, self-reflection in staff supervision and review processes prompts staff to reflect on enablers and disablers of contributing to the institute. However, due to the pressure of an industry-funded contract research model, which rarely funds evaluation and impact analysis of individual projects, reflection is challenging to implement at a project level. Although voluntary stakeholder and client feedback is collected as a standard procedure in all projects, it is mostly limited to quality assurance rather than enabling deep reflection, a tension associated with the industry-funded research model for ISF as a university-based BO.

Boundary work

As Miller put it, *boundary work* involves "translation, negotiation and communication among multiple parties" (2006, p. 9). ISF's *boundary work* is expressed in practices and functions elaborated earlier involving convening, translating, collaborating, and mediating. ISF is involved in a continual process of navigating "landscapes of tension" (Parker and Crona, 2012) within UTS as it is positioned external to faculty structures. ISF's institutional structure and funding model enable it to work across and between disciplines and sectors. This flexibility in conducting research beyond disciplinary boundaries has resulted in ISF's implementation of research projects aligned to core TD principles of co-producing knowledge, high participation, and transcending disciplinary boundaries.

Cross-boundary orchestration

During the second and third phases, ISF invested in *cross-boundary orchestration* through formal and informal initiatives. Early examples in the second phase include the instigation of weekly "operations" meetings within ISF, where all new proposals and projects were shared, teams formed, and social events planned. These meetings facilitated boundary crossing at an internal level. For example, informal externally focused events include quarterly industry targeted presentations and discussions inviting faculties to exchange knowledge and explore potential opportunities for collaboration in a relaxed social setting. A formal UTS-wide initiative includes #UTS4Climate emerging from UTS signing a climate emergency declaration in 2019. This initiative is hosted by ISF as a cross-boundary platform, pooling initiatives from across UTS faculties and offering discussion events hosted by the former Premier of New South Wales, Industry Professor of Climate and Business, Bob Carr. More recently with the advent and uptake of online collaborative and data storage platforms at ISF, such as Microsoft Teams, Trello, Google docs, and Jamboard, novel forms of collaboration are emerging to support cross-boundary orchestration.

How might we theorise and analyse institutional dynamics in TD-BOs?

The model presented above is one way of potentially analysing institutional dynamics in TD-BOs, drawing on boundary organisation theories as a starting point for theorising and developing greater insight into how university-based TD-BOs such as ISF operate and evolve within the wider historical context of tertiary education in Australia. The model was valuable in identifying enablers and barriers to institutionalising transdisciplinary initiatives through BOs in universities. Some of the characteristics of the TD-BO model such as "hybridisation" and "deconstruction" would benefit from further conceptual development from a transdisciplinary context. In addition, other characteristics could be a beneficial contribution. For example, under the "strategy" dimension, exploring the possibility of conceptually linking "hybridisation" with the concept of "integration" as it is formulated in current transdisciplinary scholarship. Similarly, the characteristic "deconstruction" could be explored for its conceptual relationship and relevance to "reflexivity". Other characteristics of TD-BOs currently excluded from the model but emerge as relevant in the analysis as ISF as a TD-BO include leadership, transformation, and social impact. We offer the TD-BO model as a work in progress that will benefit from further investigation to fill conceptual gaps and refine its robustness.

Conclusion

This chapter explored three areas of inquiry: (1) the historical conditions shaping institutional dynamics of university-based TD-BOs in the Australian tertiary education sector; (2) enablers of transdisciplinary initiatives with UTS facilitating ISF's evolution as a TD-BO; and (3) a conceptual model of TD-BOs to theorise and analyse institutional dynamics and ISFs evolution as a TD-BO. We summarise our key findings under each area of inquiry.

1. Historical conditions shaping institutional dynamics of university-based TD-BOs in the Australian tertiary education included:
    - Structural reforms within the Australian tertiary education sector in 1988 created the "enterprise" university model driving universities to secure research funding from diverse sources such as industry and community organisations.
    - Australian Research Council programmes have evolved historically to embed a collaboration and transdisciplinary research culture, resulting in industry-society-science partnerships guiding the establishment of TD-BOs.
    - TD-BOs established external to the traditional faculty structure enable transdisciplinary initiatives while maintaining these structures.
2. Enablers of transdisciplinary initiatives with UTS, facilitating ISFs evolution as a TD-BO included:
    - Establishing ISF as an outward-facing research-focused BO, creating a legitimate hybrid space for transdisciplinary research with the expectation for it to become self-funding while improving complex sustainability-oriented problems.
    - Establishing adaptive structures, collaborative practices, and boundary-crossing strategies to enable distributed accountability mechanisms for both industry and academia.
    - Aligning to university-wide strategies with a focus on community partnerships, connected research, and social change provided greater legitimacy for ISF's transdisciplinary agenda.
3. Insights from the development of a conceptual model to theorise and analyse institutional dynamics in TD-BOs included:
    - Insights from the current discourse on boundary organisations that offer conceptual guidance on institutional development and enabling factors in ISF's evolution as a TD-BO.
    - The TD-BO model offers key insight into institutional characteristics (and dimensions) in ISF's evolution including: (1) structure and organisation; (2) practices and function; and (3) strategy.
    - The TD-BO model allowed identification of enablers and barriers to institutionalising transdisciplinary initiatives within ISF and is offered as a work in progress that will benefit from further investigation to fine-tune its conceptual robustness.

Acknowledgements

We thank Professor Stuart White and Emerita Professor Cynthia Mitchell for sharing their insights on ISF's history.

References

Australian Research Council (2016) 'ARC statement of support for interdisciplinary research', www.arc.gov.au/policies-strategies/policy/arc-statement-support-interdisciplinary-research, accessed 10 February 2020.

Bammer, G., O'Rourke, M., O'Connell, D., Neuhauser, L., Midgley, G., Klein, J.T., Grigg, N.J., Gadlin, H., Elsum, I.R., Bursztyn, M. and Fulton, E.A. (2020) 'Expertise in research integration and implementation for tackling complex problems: When is it needed, where can it be found and how can it be strengthened?', *Palgrave Communications*, vol 6, no 1, pp 1–16.

Borie, M., Gustafsson, K.M., Obermeister, N., Turnhout, E. and Bridgewater, P. (2020) 'Institutionalising reflexivity? Transformative learning and the intergovernmental science-policy platform on biodiversity and ecosystem services (IPBES)', *Environmental Science & Policy*, vol 110, pp 71–76.

Carmody, B. and Hunter F. (2020) 'Gobsmacking: Writers savage humanities fee hike', *The Sydney Morning Herald*, 19 June.

Cooperative Research Centres Association (CRCA) (2021) 'Innovation-led prosperity for a post-COVID Australia 2021–22 pre-budget submission', crca.asn.au/wp-content/uploads/2021/03/2021-2022-Pre-Budget-Submission.pdf, accessed 12 April 2021.

Cvitanovic, C., Löf, M.F., Norström, A.V. and Reed, M.S. (2018) 'Building university-based boundary organisations that facilitate impacts on environmental policy and practice', *PloS one*, vol 13, no 9, pp 1–19.

Duncan, R., Robson-Williams, M. and Fam D. (2020) 'Assessing research impact potential: Using the transdisciplinary outcome spaces framework with New Zealand's national science challenges', *Kotuitui: New Zealand Journal of Social Sciences Online*, vol 15, no 1, pp 217–235.

Evans, N., Beveridge, C., Turney, C., Quiggin, J. and Damousi, J. (2020) 'An open letter to Australia's Education Minister Dan Tehan—signed by 73 senior professors', *The Conversation*, 21 July, theconversation.com/an-open-letter-to-australias-education-minister-dan-tehan-signed-by-73-senior-professors-142989, accessed 12 April 2021.

Fam, D., Neuhauser, L. and Gibbs, P. (2018a) *Transdisciplinary theory, practice and education: The art of collaborative research and collective learning*. Springer, Cham,.

Fam, D. and O'Rourke, M. (2020) *Interdisciplinary and transdisciplinary failures as lessons learned – A cautionary tale*. Routledge, Oxon.

Fam, D., Palmer, J., Riedy, C. and Mitchell, C. (eds) (2017a) *Transdisciplinary research and practice for sustainability outcomes*. Routledge, Oxon.

Fam, D.M., Leimbach, T., Kelly, S., Hitchens, L. and Callen, M. (2018b) 'Meta-considerations for planning, introducing and standardising interdisciplinary learning in higher degree institutions', in D.M. Fam, N. Neuhauser and P. Gibbs (eds), *Transdisciplinary theory, practice and education: The art of collaborative research and collective learning*. Springer, Cham.

Fam, D.M., Smith, T. and Cordell, D. (2017b) 'Being a transdisciplinary researcher: Skills and dispositions fostering competence in transdisciplinary research and practice', in D.

Fam, J. Palmer, C. Riedy and C. Mitchell (eds), *Transdisciplinary research and practice for sustainability outcomes*. Routledge, Oxon.

Frame, B. and Brown, J. (2008) 'Developing post-normal technologies for sustainability', *Ecological Economics*, vol 65, no 2, pp 225–241.

Franks, J.R. (2016) 'An application of boundary organisation theory to develop landscape-scale conservation in formal agri-environment schemes', *Sociologia Ruralis*, vol 56, no 1, pp 48–73.

Fisher, K., Bennett-Levy, J. and Irwin, R. (2003) 'What a GAS! Action research as a peer support process for postgraduate students', *ultiBASE Articles*, November edition, pp 1–20.

Gustafsson, K.M. and Lidskog, R. (2018) 'Boundary organizations and environmental governance: Performance, institutional design, and conceptual development', *Climate Risk Management*, vol 19, pp 1–11.

Guston, D. H. (1999). Stabilizing the boundary between US politics and science: The role of the Office of Technology Transfer as a boundary organization. *Social studies of science*, vol 29, no 1, pp 87–111

Guston, D.H. (2001) 'Boundary organizations in environmental policy and science: An introduction', *Science, Technology and Human Values*, vol 26, no 4, pp 399–408.

Guston, D.H., Clark, W., Keating, T., Cash, D., Moser, S., Miller, C. and Powers, C. (2000) 'Report of the workshop on boundary organisations in environmental policy and science', 9–10 December 1999, Kennedy School of Government, Harvard University, Cambridge, MA.

Hirsch Hadorn, G., Bradley, D., Pohl, C., Rist, S. and Wiesmann, U. (2006) 'Implications of transdisciplinarity for sustainable research', *Ecological Economics*, vol 60, no 1, pp 119–128.

Howes, T. (2018) 'Effective strategic planning in Australian universities: How good are we and how do we know?', *Journal of Higher Education Policy and Management*, vol 40, no 5, pp 442–457.

Institute for Sustainable Futures (ISF) (2020) 'ISF annual report 2019', University of Technology Sydney (UTS), Sydney.

Jahn, T., Bergmann, M. and Keil, F. (2012) 'Transdisciplinarity: Between mainstreaming and marginalization', *Ecological Economics*, vol 79, pp 1–10.

Miller, C. (2001) 'Hybrid management: Boundary organizations, science policy, and environmental governance in the climate regime', *Science, Technology, & Human Values*, vol 26, no 4, pp 478–500.

Miller, C. (2006) 'Boundary organizations: Strategies for linking knowledge to action', in *Draft based on the December 9 workshop on boundary organizations in environmental policy and science*, Global Environmental Assessment Project, John F. Kennedy School of Government, Harvard University, Cambridge, MA.

Mitchell, C., Cordell D. and Fam, D. (2015) 'Beginning at the end: The outcome spaces framework to guide purposive transdisciplinary research', *Futures*, vol 65, pp 86–96.

Mitchell, C.A. and Willetts, J.R. (2009) 'Quality criteria for inter and trans-disciplinary doctoral research outcomes', prepared for *ALTC Fellowship: Zen and the Art of Transdisciplinary Postgraduate Studies*. Institute for Sustainable Futures, Sydney, UTS.

Mitchell, C.A. (ed.) (2009) 'Quality in inter- and trans-disciplinary postgraduate research and its supervision: Ideas for good practice', prepared for *ALTC Fellowship: Zen and the Art of Transdisciplinary Postgraduate Studies*. Institute for Sustainable Futures, UTS.

Noble, D., Charles, M.B., Keast, R. and Kivits, R. (2019) 'Desperately seeking innovation nirvana: Australia's cooperative research centres', *Policy Design and Practice*, vol 2, no 1, pp 15–34.

O'Mahony, S. and Bechky, B.A. (2008) 'Boundary organizations: Enabling collaboration among unexpected allies', *Administrative Science Quarterly*, vol 53, no 3, pp 422–459.

Parker, J. and Crona, B. (2012) 'On being all things to all people: Boundary organizations and the contemporary research university', *Social Studies of Science*, vol 42, no 2, pp 262–289.

Pohl, C., Fam, D., Hoffmann, S. and Mitchell, C. (2019) 'Exploring Julie Thompson Klein's framework for analysis of boundary work', *Issues in Interdisciplinary Studies*, vol 37, no 2, pp 62–89.

Pohl, C., Klein, J.T., Hoffmann, S., Mitchell, C. and Fam, D. (2021) 'Conceptualising transdisciplinary integration as a multidimensional interactive process', *Environmental Science & Policy*, vol 118, pp 18–26.

Prior, J., Cusack, C.M. and Capon, A. (2018) 'The role of pliability and transversality within trans/disciplinarity: Opening university research and learning to planetary health', in D. Fam, L. Neuhauser and P. Gibbs (eds), *Transdisciplinary theory, practice and education: The art of collaborative research and collective learning*. Springer, Cham.

Riedy, C., Fam, D.M., Ross, K. and Mitchell, C. (2018) 'Transdisciplinarity at the crossroads: Nurturing individual and collective learning', *Technology Innovation Management Review*, vol 8, no 8, pp 41–49.

Ross, K. and Mitchell, C. (2018) 'Transforming transdisciplinarity: An expansion of strong transdisciplinarity and its centrality in enabling effective collaboration', in D. Fam, L. Neuhauser and P. Gibbs (eds), *Transdisciplinary theory, practice and education: The art of collaborative research and collective learning*. Springer, Cham.

Tribbia, J. and Moser, S.C. (2008) 'More than information: What coastal managers need to plan for climate change', *Environmental Science & Policy*, vol 11, no 4, pp 315–328.

Turpin, T. (1997) 'CRCs and transdisciplinary research: What are the implications for science?', *Prometheus*, vol 15, no 2, pp 253–265.

University of Technology Sydney (2000) *Developmental review report for Institute for Sustainable Futures*. University of Technology Sydney, Sydney.

University of Technology Sydney (2021) 'UTS 2027 strategy, vision and goals', www.uts.edu.au/about/uts-2027-strategy/vision, accessed 31 March 2021.

Visentin, L. (2021) 'Universities facing $2 billion loss as job cuts total more than 17,000', *The Sydney Morning Herald*, 3 February.

Wehrens, R., Bekker, M. and Bal, R. (2014) 'Hybrid management configurations in joint research', *Science, Technology, and Human Values*, vol 39, no 1, pp 6–41.

Willetts, J., Mitchell, C., Abeysuriya, K. and Fam, D. (2012) 'Creative tensions: Negotiating the multiple dimensions of a transdisciplinary doctorate', in Alison Lee and Susan Danby (eds), *Reshaping doctoral education: Changing programs and pedagogies*. Taylor & Francis, London, pp 128–143.

World Resources Forum (2015) 'Knowing, wanting and being able, keywords for change at WRF Asia-Pacific', www.wrforum.org/tag/wrf-asia-pacific/, accessed 31 March 2021.

World Wide Views Dialogue (WWVD) (2009) 'Giving the voice of ordinary Australians on climate change', wwviews.org.au, accessed 31 March 2021.

8
A CONTEXTUAL APPROACH TO INSTITUTIONAL CHANGE

Transdisciplinarity in Ghanaian higher education

Beatrice Akua-Sakyiwah

Introduction

After decades of independence, Ghana continues to face development problems. Infrastructural deficit, lack of skilled labour, inefficient management of natural resources, a high rate of illiteracy, and other problems hinder societal development. This composite of challenges has kept the nation dependent on colonial masters for assistance in order to accelerate its post-colonial needs. As a result, creating transformative knowledge that shifts Ghanaian society towards more sustainable futures has become crucial in the 21st century. Integrative features of transdisciplinarity (TD) that cross academic borders into community and other professional domains have the potential to solve Ghana's specific national problems. Policy outcomes, for instance, depend on a multisectoral approach to collaborating with various stakeholder groups to achieve a common goal. This need underscores the urgency of the country's universities to prioritise an approach that meets complex socio-economic, political, and cultural dimensions of pressing problems. Unfortunately, in most Ghanaian universities, transdisciplinarity is used sparingly, as it is unfamiliar to most. Only a few have been introduced to it through academic involvement in South Africa or a Western conference (Akua-Sakyiwah, 2020), and most literature is based on Western research (Bernstein, 2015; van Breda and Swirling, 2018). A few scholars also know TD is a requirement for funding aimed at solving problems. However, the need for more higher education to address sustainable context-specific solutions is a necessary condition for dealing with complex problems the nation faces.

This chapter investigates narratives of university faculties and students about the use of TD in research projects from three higher education institutions, gleaned from 30 semi-structured interviews and documentary evidence. The aim is to examine how incorporating transdisciplinarity in the curriculum

DOI: 10.4324/9781003129424-10

can contribute to national initiatives in order to solve complex problems while advancing Ghana's sustainable development agenda. In keeping with the purpose of this volume, it uses a time–space binary relationship to unearth complexities associated with "creating structures and spaces to generate epistemological, methodological, and organisational innovations that pave the way to new forms of knowledge" (Vienni Baptista and Klein, 2020, p. 2). The aim is to understand how a policy framework interacts with practice and to facilitate translating transdisciplinary activities into teaching and learning through a transformative curriculum. This guiding question for the book leads to exploring challenges and strategies for solutions.

The first section examines relevant discussions of TD as the context for approaching transformation. It elaborates on the collaborative nature of TD in creating and integrating knowledge, a feature that also allows permeating systems and crossing boundaries of fields. Discussion is linked to specific developmental case studies in Ghana, highlighting the usefulness of TD to promoting success while raising concerns about the slowness of academia to embrace the concept in the higher education curriculum. The second section presents the methodological approach, highlighting theoretical underpinnings, sampling and procedures, research instruments, and data analysis. The third section diagnoses the time–space concept to illuminate structural challenges facing higher education institutions in Ghana. Participants' views further reveal empirical understandings in the institutionalisation of transdisciplinary research (TDR) for a transformative curriculum and as a course in higher education institutions. The chapter concludes by focusing on current global demands for a new workforce requiring knowledge that crosses disciplinary boundaries while transferring skills and thinking into real-life scenarios for societal advancement.

Institutionalising transdisciplinarity in Ghanaian higher education

Many authors have discussed TD's contribution to an expanding literature. The purpose here is not to dwell on definitions but to focus on TD's transformative nature and role. The concept itself has existed for decades but became more visible in the 1980s. Echoing van Breda and Swilling (2018), TD is not a new science, rather a new way of doing science. The authors infer that TD cannot be replicated by other approaches and that context matters in design, implementation, and outcomes. This assertion is crucial for this chapter, given its purpose is to see TD's viability in solving environmental problems facing Ghana today. Research studies that have suggested a transformation to a higher education research approach argue universities' capacity to solve societal problems is yet to be fully realised (Jantsch, 1972; Klein, 2004; Schneidewind, 2001; Weingart, 2014). TD research forms the key focus for its integrative realisation and adoptability for addressing complex social challenges (Spoun, 2017 in Vienni Baptista and Rojas-Castro, 2019). Traditionally, knowledge generation within academia has mostly been achieved through a monodisciplinary paradigm, requiring students to specialise in different kinds of knowledge (Habermas, 1987). But this system limits their knowledge-creating prowess in complex areas (Winberg, 2006). Solely discipline-based academic knowledge dissociates students from real-world problems, constraining their ability to relate the content and context of their study to societal relevance (Jansen, 2002). The need to address emerging environmental changes in our current socio-cultural, political, and economic world has, thus, prompted a widespread transitional move towards interdisciplinarity (Winberg, 2006).

In South Africa, policy adjustments in higher education documents brought (Kraak, 2001) tremendous improvement in the knowledge gap. Gibbons et al.'s (1994) thesis about emergent new forms of Mode 2 knowledge production, in particular, purported higher education is producing students with needed skills and knowledge to contribute to national reconstruction and competition in the global economy. Though researchers (Muller and Subotsky, 2001; Ensor, 2001) have questioned Gibbons and co-authors' claim, the move away from purely disciplinary academic context to sites where knowledge is applied is a significant innovation that echoes South Africa's socio-political and economic agendas (Gibbons et al., 1994; Klein et al., 2001). Thus, the past decade has witnessed increased institutionalisation of TD in South African higher education, fostering an innovative academic setting where integrative knowledge production could thrive. As part of institutionalising TD, disciplinary-based knowledge is being infused with other knowledge forms. This process has resulted in a hybridised form of undergraduate study pathways where employable skills are pivotal (Winberg, 2006). Academic collaborative works are stored in different disciplinary hubs, but they are linked with institutional representatives outside academia, workplaces, state, and academics. The result is a connection between departments of education and labour. The institutionalisation of TD in South Africa started with policy design resulting in the Qualifications Authority Act (SAQA) (1995), bringing about a National Qualifications Framework. In 1998, the Skills Development Act was introduced to provide systemic work-based educational interventions. Skills Levy and the National Skills Fund were additionally introduced to obtain resources that sustain the implementation of new programmes (Winberg, 2006).

Similarly, in 2019, Vienni Baptista and Rojas-Castro explored the process of institutionalising TD at Leuphana University in Germany and using qualitative research methodology, highlighted two procedural approaches to institutionalising TD. These include policy and practice. Like South Africa, Germany has implemented several initiatives, beginning with enacting policies that facilitated decisions, and explained the process of implementation (Palonen, 2003; Hugue and Harrop, 2004). Following policy directives, transdisciplinary research and activities became part of the university's academic culture. Vienni Baptista and Rojas-Castro (2019) cautioned, however, that policy alone does not guarantee the implementation of proposed objectives, rather, a determination to develop activities that ensure the realisation of TD in practice. In raising this caveat, they followed Klein's (2014) taxonomy on the development of transdisciplinary research to contextualise discourses that shape trends, narratives, and social formations in the institutionalisation of transdisciplinarity. In contrast to the German example, though, in most third-world countries, transdisciplinarity institutionalisation is yet to be evidenced, and research findings (Akua-Sakyiwah, 2020, research notes) suggest the academic community assume the time is due for Ghana to embrace an institutionalising transdisciplinary research culture and narratives from participants affirm this. Though participants agree that implementation requires a policy agenda, they also bemoan constraints on time, space, and resources. These obstacles are discussed further below.

Institutionalisation of transdisciplinarity in Ghana

Ghana is a former British colony and the first African country to acquire independence from European rule (BBC News, 2020; The Commonwealth, n.d.). Its population is approximately 30 million people (BBC News, 2020; Worldometer, 2020), growing at a rate of 3% per year. About two-thirds of the people live in rural regions and are involved in agriculture. Ghana is located midway between Senegal and Cameroon, bordered by Côte d'Ivoire and Burkina Faso, Togo, and the Atlantic Ocean (The Commonwealth, n.d.). The land is rich in mineral resources, such as gold and diamonds. Yet, in 2011, the International Finance Corporation (IFC) accorded the county a lower middle-level income (World Bank, 2011). Currently, Ghana faces numerous social, economic, environmental, and health challenges, including coastal erosion and flooding, waste management and recycling, environmental management, and improper land reclamation in the mining industry (Nartey 2020; Srivastava and Pawlowska, 2020). A report by the Ministry of Environment Science and Technology (MEST, 2012) suggests that Ghana's environmental pillar faces depletion, degradation, and pollution challenges with only a small share of the revenue from natural resource exploitation due to a weak value of primary products. Adding to weak growth in the manufacturing sector, challenges in job creation, education, water and sanitation, urbanisation, and health, structural transformation of the economy remain a major challenge.

According to Srivastava and Pawlowska (2020), environmental degradation costs $6.3 billion annually or nearly 11% of Ghana's 2017 GDP. Non-renewable resources such as gold and oil cannot sustain growth as resources deplete while renewable resources such as cocoa, timber, and other tree and food crops depend on good environmental stewardship. There are clear signs and scientific evidence that erosion of the natural capital may put at risk growth, livelihoods, and human health (Nartey, 2020). Coupled with the government's proposed project on *Ghana Beyond AIDS* (The Presidency, 2018), requiring robust engagement of all stakeholders, the kind of knowledge systems needed, that is, built-up integrated approaches, are lacking. Undeniably, research is crucial for all universities, and individual faculty promotion is appraised on the basis of research, not excellence in teaching. The central role of research and education is thus being recognised as crucial to achieving a sustainable environment, particularly for grappling with modern ecological complexities (Blessinger et al., 2018). Nonetheless, ongoing discussions suggest that our current global socio-economic system cannot be dealt with using traditional, mono- and inter-disciplinary approaches. Higher education is the sight of knowledge creation, but without policy directives, and institutional willingness to embrace TD, institutionalising TD is unlikely.

Insights from three higher institutions in Ghana

Higher education is well established in Ghana. NAB (2020) indicates that it has ten technical universities, 12 traditional universities, and 101 private universities. Together, these offer degrees in a Higher National Diploma (HNC). This section presents the background of the universities in the study.

Thirty participants were chosen from three institutions: Comnasda University, Nanoas University, and the Institute of Ancolas. They are situated in two different regions in Ghana, chosen for their active research participation and reputation for research with local, national, and global impacts. Comnasda University, for instance, is one of the traditional universities, with the largest population of students taking research-based courses. It is well known for numerous research institutes, including medical, population, environmental, social, and economics (CU, 2014–2024). As of July 2020, Comnasda University recorded approximately 53,643 in population count (Enrolment and Graduation Statistics, 2020). It has a high-ranking score in the country and is one of the best within the subregion (Times Higher Education, 2020). With a fairly good infrastructure, it prides its research-intensive reputation, with one of four priority areas being TDR into climate change adaptation (CU, 2014–2024).

Like Comnasda, Nanoas University is one of the oldest traditional universities in the country with a population of about 74,000 students (NU, n.d.). In response to the changing needs of Ghanaian society and the world, the university has increasingly added to its traditional functions, which consists of training educational planners, administrators, agriculturalists, actuarial scientists, optometrists, information technologists, and other professionals. It also has a reputation for admitting students from less privileged schools/areas through its remedial science programme, mature students' entrance examinations, and consensus selection from deprived schools identified by the Joint Admissions Board (NU, n.d.). Currently, it is seeking redress in the law to amend the original mandate of training skilled and qualified human power to fill educational institutions in Ghana, expanding to other industrial capabilities across Africa and elsewhere. The Institute, in turn, has provided education and training since its inception to the Ghanaian community and elsewhere in Africa, retaining its original mandate. It has a small population of about 10,600. With a concentration of students from the public/private sectors, the Institute prides itself on its emerging culture of intensive research. Over the past decade, it has strengthened its facilities to expand its programme to undergraduate/postgraduate programmes with the focus of attracting students globally (IoA, Staff Durbar, 2017, p. 8).

Both universities and the Institute engage with the state on topical issues and have good reputations for conducting external collaboration in research and securing funding. They are also representative of similar institutions in Ghana and have collaborative links with similar universities in Africa, North America, and Europe. The conceptual framework undergirding this study is a composite of general systems theory (von Bertalanffy, 1975), complex adaptive system (Holland, 1992), and systems knowledge (Bliss, 1935; Levy and Williams, 1998). All three concepts consider how social context allows the integration of knowledge, reconfiguring it into new and useful knowledge to solve complex environmental problems. Von Bertalanffy's general system theory focuses on interactions and reactions, as well as their integration in our world. Relationships and interactions between sub-systems (Broderick, 1993) are further embedded in supra-systems, combined to function in a unified way rather than "standing alone" (von Bertalanffy, 1975). Thus, they are related to Pereira et al.'s (2020) concept of transformative spaces. As humans interact with the environment and each other, systemic transformation occurs through a process of generating new forms of meaning. Holland's (1992) concept of an adaptive system explores complexities involved in reorganising and integrating natural sciences and social sciences to adapt to environmental problems. The process crosses boundaries of scientific disciplines and local knowledge, co-producing hybridised knowledge systems to solve societal problems.

Complex socio-economic and ecological challenges our planet faces are propelling an increasing focus on co-creating and co-producing knowledge aligned with transdisciplinarity, which is aimed at solving complex problems in a rapidly changing environmental system (Pohl et al., 2010; Lemos et al., 2018). Cash et al. (2003) further observed that institutional mechanisms for human interactions help in understanding how systems are mediated through human actions across a variety of boundaries. This process results in lessons for harnessing sustainable environmental growth dependent on effective management of boundaries between knowledge and action. Recognising this composite conceptual framework, this chapter draws on DeRose's (1992) perspective on systems knowledge, which offers an understanding of how context matters in knowledge production. DeRose's approach explains how willingness to attribute knowledge to a given subject is sensitive to contextual variation due to differing experiential realities. "Meaning making", "knowing", "having a reason to", and "being true" or "being right" only make sense within a specified context (DeRose, 1992). Therefore, the context in which an action, utterance, or expression occurs is crucial to meaning. Yet, while knowledge is dependent on context and practical experience, variability of data is also important.

The significance to TD's integrative knowledge production is that interacting with context helps to transform existing knowledge into viable co-produced knowledge (Tengö et al., 2014; Díaz et al., 2015) and helps to solve complex ecological challenges that the Anthropocene presents (Brondizio et al., 2016). Zgambo (2018) assumes that spaces and context allow participants to narrate their own experiences in their voices. However, Ndlovu (2018) has questioned the authenticity of context in the face of colonial domination. Emerging writers in Africa and socio-political movements in Latin America are also sceptical about the neoliberal ideal of colonial discourses that endorse knowledge systems of the colonised (Mapara, 2009; Hanson et al., 2011; Chilisa, 2012; Ndlovu, 2018). In their discussions of coloniality, Hanson et al. (2011) prompted rethinking concepts of development, the global economy, and modernity, including re-examining the role of scholarship and knowledge production that sustain or break down power relations that propagate colonial epistemologies. These scholars have raised concerns about ways colonial discourses have exploited practices of the colonised, disempowered them, muted their voices to a third party, and created a loss of identity. Such a historical stance creates conceptual and theoretical difficulties in understanding intersectionality of "race, knowledge and capital and how these result in forms of unequal development and social inequality" (Mapara, 2009; Hanson et al., 2011; Chilisia, 2012; Ndlovu, 2018).

Scholarly research from third-world countries has suffered as a result of deferring to and over-relying on Western knowledge. It is not surprising, then, that post-colonial African states continue to rely on aid and expertise from colonial masters. African scholars such as Chillisa (2012) have long raised concerns about the relationship between research subjects and the academic community while arguing that Indigenous research, when made participatory, empowers a "colonised other". Researchers learn to understand and analyse their contexts, helping to effect changes to subjects' conditions. She also questions ways that colonial discourses have perpetuated narratives of Africans while calling for social sciences to create spaces that allow the colonised to find their voices. Though in his coloniality of knowledge, Ndlovu (2018), raised concerns about how colonial domination of Africa has influenced ways of "knowing, seeing and imagining". Understanding multifaceted complexities in TD, then, is crucial to enhancing structural adjustments to policy, curriculum, and human attitudes towards desired societal change. For higher educational institutions, adoption of TD becomes a starting point to understanding how bringing together Indigenous knowledge systems and scientific knowledge will enhance new insights into reclaiming the lost and marginalised identity of African scholarly works. Widening understanding of the potential of TD will help Africans assert and affirm their voices in their own narratives, in addition to deconstructing colonial discourses that subjugated African scholarship. Analysis of data from an empirical, qualitative study of three institutions illustrates related challenges and potentials.

A review of a number of Ghanaian research articles and journals yielded no traces of transdisciplinary practice. Further insights emerged from purposive sampling (Nakkeeran, 2016) using a snowball approach to identify and involve faculty members as well as both male and female PhD students. The goal was to understand the views of students who have started research and hence may have been introduced to various forms of approaches. Involving faculty aimed to solicit views on how funding and other related activities are linked to TD and the concept's use in teaching. The research instruments were mainly interviews and documentary analysis, conducted in a focus group in face-to-face dialogue. About a quarter of participants were interviewed through telephone conversations when the COVID-19 pandemic interrupted direct communications. In addition, a review of reports on research funding and samples of research approaches by faculty from universities' websites revealed visions and mission statements about research focus, curriculum, and other aspects of academic culture. Interviews also followed a thematic pattern, framed by a preprepared topic list that yielded data on the main research themes. Categorising and coding the data helped identify emerging themes. Their categorisation shed sharper light on common themes while enhancing understanding of how individual perceptions shaped their willingness to embrace new ideas. Theoretical analyses of data, in turn, were mainly based on complex systems theory and contextualism.

In addition, ethical considerations were crucial because individuals needed to preserve confidentialities despite difficulties in soliciting ethical clearance for institutional research that often goes through vigorous processes (Akua-Sakyiwah, 2012). As a result, the focus shifted to individuals, rather than institutions, with schedules for interviews relocated from universities to sites participants chose. This change has implications for the primary objective of a book focused on institutionalisation, as participants channelled discussions more towards their individual experiences instead of higher education generally. Probing questions solicited information reflecting how TD is practised within their universities. The location change, though, made the snowballing approach very useful, as participants suggested other people to be interviewed. These additional informants were faculty who have been involved in research funding and attended conferences on TD, students involved in transdisciplinary projects, and faculty who have informally incorporated TD into their research methodology class. Following protocol, participants were also informed about the dynamics of the interview process, its discretion and voluntary nature, as well as the objectives of the research and options to either opt-out or participate.

The time–space concept and establishment of transdisciplinary research in higher education institutions of Ghana

To reiterate, in the course of research for this chapter, faculty and students discussed their perceptions of TD and the role of higher education institutions in utilising the benefits of TDR, particularly in the face of Ghana's environmental crisis and the government's initiation of the project *Ghana Beyond AIDS*. This section channels these views through the conceptual lens of the time–space dichotomy. Universities are crucial spaces for generating epistemological, methodological, and organisational innovations that pave the way for new forms of knowledge. At the same time, they struggle for legitimation as environments for boundary work (Vienni Baptista and Klein, 2020). According to Marshall et al. (2018), the environmental space of TDR goes beyond a restrictive location in time and space separated from context. Rather, it is a transformative space within cognitive, normative, social, and material arenas of a knowledge system. Vilsmaier et al. (2017) suggest that transdisciplinary activities create "in-between" spaces in the environment. Nowotny et al. (2001) call these "transaction spaces", as they allow the "macro, meso and micro" issues to be communicated to, including processes through which educators can "talk back" to other contexts. Transaction spaces are significant to allowing effective cooperation between knowledge producers and contexts of application, ensuring that the process of producing knowledge is "socially robust". This enables the "co-evolution" of knowledge producers and society (Winberg, 2006).

Using transformative space as a metaphor, Marshall and Dolley (2019) suggest TDR signifies the extent to which its connectivity extends beyond multiple dimensions and permeates its surroundings. Its key feature is linked to diverse local experiential knowledge and actions. However, universities are hampered by restrictive spaces of curriculum, governing policies, and financial challenges, thereby impeding adjustments to innovations. In addition, Scholz et al. (2006) observed that whereas TDR focuses on problems, academics are often concerned with the kind of epistemology needed. The involvement of diverse disciplinary experts, practitioners, and social groups complicates the kind of epistemic system to adopt. During interviews, 99% of participants contested the existing educational curriculum already has time constraints, making it inappropriate for TD's complexities. This links well with the second guiding question for this book on institutionalising TD. Ghana has yet to embrace TD, and yet has to go through complexities involved in the institutionalisation process through policy formulation and curriculum transformation. During the interview, at least 99% of participants proposed the need for institutionalising TD. As discussed further, a few faculty who have had experience in the approach are informally incorporating it in their teaching, but mostly to impart knowledge about the concept.

In the paragraphs that follow, respondents shed further light on TD, mostly centred on benefits but also factoring in challenges and reasons why higher education institutions may be reluctant to adopt the approach despite its value and strength. Some believe that TD will offer appropriate skills to tackle the economic and developmental needs of Ghana. Alofusu, for example, embraced this need:

> I have not had [a] direct encounter with TDR, but I read about it when I became part of a group applying for funding. I was amazed about the elaborated collaboration and engagements … This is what Africa needs, but it starts with higher institution[s] embracing it [TD].
>
> *(Alofusu, Faculty, 2020)*

Along with Alofusu, many other interviewees have not had direct encounters with TD and, like him, only read about it so they can get through their funding proposals. Some have also heard of it from others, while a few have heard about it from conferences they attended. Another handful have been involved directly through securing project funding. Views, therefore, varied according to perspectives and experiences. However, 90% of participants agreed that higher institutions should embrace the concept. Maxino, for example, commented that designing measures to institutionalise the approach could be capital intensive and time constraining, but the benefit is worth the effort:

> I have learnt that for anything to be good, it must go through refinery. Nothing comes easy and on a silver platter. Ghana cannot go "Beyond AIDS" if we are still dependent, knowledge wise, resources wise, and financial wise. What our medical team did during the Covid-19; to raise statistics about where we are and where we can go, shows that we can do it if we start from somewhere. At least Ghana too made a voice, and we did not have to wait for the "Whiteman" to do it and tell us. We also told the world what we did in our own words. Yes, it is expensive, and our "contact tracing approach" during the Covid-19 was elaborated like this transdisciplinary approach, but we were able to do it.
>
> *(Maxino, a final year PhD student, 2020)*

Both Alofusu and Maxino further agreed it may take some time to see results, but the starting point is for higher education institutions to embrace and attempt to utilise it in their teaching activities. Both Adomkwaa and Ankoma addressed how that goal might be accomplished:

> It starts with curriculum adjustments, and even if students are not going to be able to use it on their research projects because of the cost and time involved, they must be taught the concept and get the understanding so they can apply it in practical terms, in their future projects.
>
> *(Adomkwaa, Master student, 2020)*

> Institutions can involve research students on their funding projects so they will have hands-on experience about the concept. Too much emphasis on a lack of money and a lack of resources are jeopardising our economy, and it's about time this stops, because we have everything here in Ghana. What we don't have is [an] independent knowledge bank and managerial skills. I see TD restoring this lost identity.
>
> *(Ankoma, Faculty, 2020)*

In addition, about 95% of all participants believed without the proactive engagement of higher education institutions, students who will be future leaders of our country will continue to depend on foreign knowledge and aid. Interviewees also believe that institutional engagement is crucial for utilising TD, lest it is sidelined due to lack of understanding and overemphasis on the time–space dichotomy. As Ampong's comments below suggest, without institutional adjustments in the curriculum, any effective efforts individual lecturers make by trying to integrate them in their teaching will be hampered:

> I have had direct experience through some funding project[s] we had with a South African institution. We had to undergo transdisciplinary training as part of the requirement, but for me this is very useful. I have in my own ways tried to incorporate this in my teaching to allow my undergrad students [to] understand the concept and my master research students are on board [with] my project.
>
> *(Ampong, Faculty, 2020)*

Several informants with transdisciplinary encounters admitted they have not been proactive in talking about their experience of TD with colleagues and the university community to help advance the need for institutionalising TD proactively, and that they need to do more to awaken that spirit. Akin sums this view up in his narration:

> Those of us with the transdisciplinary experience can help to make institutionalisation a reality. We all know the huge benefit, so our first move is joining ourselves together, even if we have to do that with those from other universities. A transdisciplinary club could be our starting point and we can rotate the meetings within universities involved. Inviting non-transdisciplinary encounters including management to join our meetings, done through seminars, workshops, symposi[a], etc., will foster understanding.
>
> *(Akin, Faculty, 2020)*

Hansa, though, interrupted:

> It is a lack of confidence and a commitment towards the approach which is stopping such [a] move. Because institutionalising TD in higher education in Ghana is possible.
>
> *(Faculty, 2020)*

In addition, there was a clear indication that knowledge about TD among members of the university community was scanty, and the few who have had a positive encounter also lacked confidence to initiate conversations that may open access to collective discussions, thereby leading to institutional acceptance. There was also a concern that without institutional involvement even those students who have been introduced to the concept will not take it seriously:

> Some colleagues say they have introduced their students to the concept and transdisciplinary projects. The problem I have is the limited study period.

These students have no way of continuing utilising the knowledge gained. Institutionalising TD may prompt others who are interested to take it up as a course of study.

(Regio, Faculty, 2020)

Beyond these insights, about 80% of participants agreed that a decisive approach to institutionalising is a way forward, framed by policy design that reflects transformed curricula. This step will prepare students to contribute to the socio-economic, political, and cultural reconstruction of Ghana. Almost 75% of them also agreed the time has come for academic institutions to move away from stand-alone disciplinary-based curricula that lack the capacity to solve the world's complex challenges. About 1% of faculty who mentioned encountering the approach from South African, including those who chanced upon it through involvement in research funding, akin to Ampong above, incorporate the concept into their teaching. They testified that students are very enthusiastic about the concept and its approach while being optimistic that institutions adopting it will see a positive dividend. Roughly 70% of participants, though, echoed concerns that benefits outweigh costs, including inadequate space, time, and resources as well as the difficulty of adjusting programmes to incorporate a pragmatic connotation of TD. Watkins (1972) notes in the immediate post-independent period that Ghana has already gone through curricula changes and revisions. Yet, university education needs to be further in line with the realities of current environmental complexities to institutionalise measures allowing students to be innovative.

Conclusions

Both literature and interview data affirmed that transdisciplinarity has the potential to equip students with skills that can make them innovators of change. Research is still needed, though, to ascertain how funding can become a tool for curriculum change that will institutionalise transdisciplinarity in Ghanaian higher institutions. Discussions throughout this chapter have demonstrated sustainable solutions to challenges many African societies face today that cannot only be achieved from a mono-/inter-disciplinary analysis, which offers partial solutions to complex socio-ecological challenges. Emerging concerns in literature (Molz and Edwards, 2013; van Breda and Swilling, 2018) suggest interdisciplinarity enables pulling ideas from separate domains together. Yet, integrating existing approaches is not enough. The past five decades have prompted the need for transdisciplinary responses that embrace the co-production of knowledge for the participatory transformation of science, humanities, and society. Within the context of Africa, Chilisa's (2011) calls for the integration of "Indigenous knowledge" systems into a wider conception of "post-colonial research". To recall, she suggests the history of colonialism has problematised African narratives and their lived experiences, requiring an innovative approach that allows African people to reclaim their lost identity.

To conclude, given that higher education is central to solving Ghana's complex environmental problems and future economic development, broad social and cultural advantages to curriculum reforms are required for upcoming generations to face our social, economic, cultural, and political environmental challenges. Objectives in the agenda for *Ghana Beyond AIDS* as well as the need for academic knowledge to respond to socio-cultural, political, and economic needs played a key role in this chapter. They were framed by a wide range of contexts that underscore the critical role research and innovation can play in realising a transformation and developmental agenda in Ghanaian society. A robust transdisciplinary approach is key to achieving this goal, affirmed by respondents' broad consensus on the need for universities to participate in curriculum reforms in order to allow education and research to tackle socio-economic, cultural, political, and environmental needs of Ghana. They are responsible for training students who can engage in innovative efforts. Research is also needed to ascertain how funding can become a tool for adjusting curriculum towards institutionalising TD in higher institutions in Ghana. In closing, four major recommendations emerge for transformative change:

- Universities receiving research funding and experiencing the utility of TD can set good examples by reviewing and consolidating their curriculum. This effort should be supported by financial resources from the government of Ghana to engage all stakeholders.
- Higher education management can approach the government to set money aside for useful projects. This step will entail opening-up dialogue with the government and policymakers to solicit ways that TD can become a nationwide agenda.
- With COVID-19 and accompanying economic downturns, everything is open for change, including the prospect of another global pandemic in the future. Therefore, planning and preparation are important for institutionalising TD.
- Higher institutions can provide spaces for faculty members to encounter TD and discuss its benefits with the university community as a way of educating members on its potential for sustainable development. Transdisciplinary clubs, seminars, workshops, symposia, and mini-conferences can be useful tools for attracting wider university engagement with TD and facilitating a cultural approach to using TD and its activities in teaching/learning and research in higher institutions of Ghana.

References

Akua-Sakyiwah, B. (2012). *Somali Refugee Women's Perception of Social Services in the UK.* Thesis, Centre for Women Studies, White Rose E-theses Online (WREO), The City of York, UK.

Akua-Sakyiwah, B. (2020). *Transdisciplinarity for Transformative Curriculum*. Unpublished Research Notes. Ghana Institute of Management and Public Administration (GIMPA), Accra Ghana.

BBC. (2020). Ghana country profile. https://www.bbc.com/news/world-africa-13433790.

Bernstein, J.H. (2015). Transdisciplinarity: A review of its origins, development, and current issues. *Journal of Research Practice*, 11(1), Article R1. http://jrp.icaap.org/index.php/jrp/article/view/510/412.

Blessinger, P., Sengupta, E., and Makhanva, M. (2018). Higher education's key role in sustainable development. *University World News*. https://www.universityworldnews.com/post.php?story=20180905082834986, accessed 6/3/2021.

Bliss, H.E. (1935). The systems of science and organisation of knowledge. *Philosophy of Science*, 2(1), 86–103.

Broderick, C. B. (1993). Understanding family process. Newbury Park, CA: Sage.

Brondizio, E.S., O'Brien, K., Bai, X., Biermannd, F., Steffence, W., Frans Berkhoutf, F., Cudennecg, C., Lemosh, M.C., Wolfei, A., Palma-Oliveiraj, J., and Chen-Tung, A.C. (2016). Re-conceptualizing the Anthropocene: A call for collaboration. *Global Environmental Change*, 39, 318–327. https://doi.org/10.1016/j.gloenvcha.2016.02.006, accessed 12/12/2020.

Cash, D.W., Clark, W.C., Frank Alcock, F., Dickson, N.M., Eckley, N., et al. (2003). Knowledge systems for sustainable development. *Proceedings of the National Academy of Sciences*, 100(14), 8086–8091.

Chilisa, B. (2011). *Indigenous Research Methodologies*. Los Angeles, CA: SAGE Publications.

Chilisa, B. (2012). Indigenous Research Methodologies. University of Botswana, London: Sage Publication.

CU. (2014). Institutional strategic plan report, 2014–2024. http://www.uc.edu.gh/publicaffairs/uc-strategic-plan-2014-2024, accessed 26/3/2021.

CU. (2020). Enrolment and graduation statistics Camnasda University. https://www.camnasda.edu.gh/about/enrolment-and-graduation-statistics, accessed 1/3/2021.

De Rose, K. (1992). Contextualism and knowledge attributions. *Philosophy and Phenomenological Research*, 52(4), 913–929.

Díaz, S., Demissew, S., Carabias, J., Joly, C., Lonsdale, M., Ash, N., Larigauderie, A., Ram Adhikari, J., Arico, S., Baldi, A., Bartuska, A., Andreas, I.B., Bilgin, A., Brondizio, E., MAChan, K., Figueroa, E.V., Duraiappah, A., Fischer, M., and Zlatanova, D. (2015). The IPBES Conceptual Framework connecting nature and people. *Current Opinion in Environmental Sustainability*, 14, 1–16. https://doi.org/10.1016/j.cosust.2014.11.002.

Ensor, P. (2001). *Academic Programme Planning in South African Higher Education: Three Institutional Case Studies*. Bellville: University of the Western Cape, Education Policy Unit Publication.

Gibbons, M., Limoges, C., Nowotny, H., Schwartzman, S., Scott, P., and Trow, M. (1994). *The New Production of Knowledge*. London: Sage Publishers.

Jansen, J.D. (2002). Mode 2 knowledge and institutional life: Taking Gibbons on a walk through a South African university. *Higher Education*, 43(4), 507–521.

Jantsch, E. (1972). Inter- and transdisciplinary University: A systems approach to education and innovation. *Higher Education*, 1(1), 7–37. https://doi.org/10.1007/BF01956879.

Habermas, J. (1987). *Theory of Communicative Action. 2, System and Lifeworld: The Critique of Functionalist Reason*. Boston, MA: Beacon Publishers.

Hague, R., and Harrop, M. (2004) *Comparative Government and Politics: An Introduction*. 6th (ed.). Basingstoke, New York: Palgrave Macmillan.

Hanson, A., Jacob, M., and Rafael Routson, R. (2011). Coloniality at large: Latin America and the postcolonial debate: A book review. *A Radical Journal of Geography*. https://doi.org/10.1111/j.1467-8330.2011.00933_1.x.

Holland, J.H. (1992). *Complex Adaptive System*, Daedalus, 121(1), 17-30, http://www.jstor.org/stable/20025416.

IoA. (2017). *Staff Durbar, Annual Report*. Institute of Ancolas, Unpublished.

Klein, J.T. (2004). Prospects for transdisciplinarity. *Future*, 26, 515–526.

Klein, J.T. (2014). Discourses of transdisciplinarity: Looking back to the future. *Futures*, 63, 68–74. https://doi.org/10.1016/j.futures.2014.08.008.

Kraak, A. (ed.). (2001). *Changing Modes: New Knowledge Production and Its Implications for Higher Education in South Africa*. Pretoria: HSRC Publication.

Lemos, M.C., Arnolt, J.C., Ardoin, N.M., Baja, K., Bednarek, A.T., et al. (2018). To co-produce or not to co-produce. *Nature Sustainability*, 1, 722–724. https://doi.org/10.1038/s41893-018-0191-0.

Levy, P., and Williams, J.R. (1998). The role of perceived system knowledge in predicting appraisal reactions. *Journal of Organizational Behavior*, 19(1), 53–65.

Mapara, J. (2009). Indigenous knowledge systems in Zimbabwe: Juxtaposing postcolonial. https://www.researchgate.net/publication/228427362_Indigenous_Knowledge_Systems_in_Zimbabwe_Juxtaposing_Postcolonial_Theory, accessed 23/6/20.

Marshall, F., and Dolley, J. (2019). Transformative innovation in peri-urban Asia. *Res Policy*, 48, 983–992. https://doi.org/10.1016/j.respol.2018.10.007.

Marshall, F., Dolley, J., and Priya, R. (2018). Transdisciplinary research as transformative space making for sustainability: enhancing propoor transformative agency in periurban contexts. *Ecology and Society*, 23(3):8. https://doi.org/10.5751/ES-10249-230308

MEST. (2012). *National Assessment Report on Achievement of Sustainable Development Goals and Targets for Rio+20 Conference*. Ministry of Environment Science and Technology. https://sustainabledevelopment.un.org/content/documents/1016ghanationalreport.pdf, accessed, 23/3/2021

Molz, M., and Edwards, M. (2013). Research across boundaries: Introduction to the first part of the special issue. *Integral Review, A transdisciplinary and transcultural Journal for New Thought, Research and Praxis*, 9(2), 1–11.

Muller, J., and Subotzky, G. (2001). What knowledge is needed in the new millennium? *Organization*, 8(2), 163–182. https://doi.org/10.1177/1350508401082004.

NAB (2020) Accredited Institutions. http://nab.gov.gh/accredited_institution, accessed, 16/12/2021.

Nakkeeran, N. (2016). Is sampling a misnomer in qualitative. *Sociological Bulletin*, 65(1) 40–49.

Nartey, S. (2020). Back to environment, health and safety law committee publications. https://www.ibanet.org/Article/NewDetail.aspx?ArticleUid=6EFEC52C-1177-4F99-98A7-1A5638BC826F, accessed 23/3/2021.

Ndlovu, M. (2018). Coloniality of knowledge and the challenge of creating African futures. *Mufahamu, A Journal of African Studies*. https://escholarship.org/uc/item/7xf4w6v7, accessed 23/3/2021.

Nowotny, H., Scott, P., and Gibbons, M. (2001). *Re-Thinking Science, Knowledge and the Public in an Age of Uncertainty*. Cambridge: Polity Press.

NU. (n.d.) History. Nanoas University. https://www.nu.edu.gh/main/about/history#:~:text=From%20an%20initial%20student%20enrolment,sandwich%20postgraduate%20students%2048989%20distance, accessed 19/3/2021.

Palonen, K. (2003). Four times of politics: Policy, polity, politicking, and politicization. *Alternatives: Global, Local, Political*, 28(2), 171–186. https://doi.org/10.1177/030437540302800202.

Pereira, E., Mascarenhas, M., Flores, A., Chalip, L., and Pires, G. (2020). Strategic leveraging: Evidences of small-scale sport events. *International Journal of Event and Festival Management*, 11(1), 69–88.

Pohl, C., Rist, S., Zimmermann, A., Fry, P., et al. (2010). 'Researchers' roles in knowledge co-production…' Science and *Public Policy*, 37, 267–281.

Schneidewind, U. (2001). Mobilizing the intellectual capital of universities. In J. T. Klein, R. Häberli, R. W. Scholz, W. Grossenbacher-Mansuy, A. Bill, and M. Welti (eds), *Transdisciplinarity: Joint Problem Solving among Science, Technology, and Society* (pp. 94–100). Basel: Birkhäuser. https://doi.org/10.1007/978-3-0348-8419-8_9.

Scholz, R.W., Lang, D.J., Wiek, A., Walter, A.I., and Stauffacher, M. (2006). Transdisciplinary case studies as a means of sustainability learning: historical framework and theory. *International Journal of Sustainability in Higher Education*, 7, 226–251.

Srivastava, S., and Pawlowska, A.E. (2020). Ghana: Balancing economic growth and depletion of resources. https://blogs.worldbank.org/africacan/ghana-balancing-economic-growth-and-depletion-resources, accessed 23/3/2021.

Tengö, M., Brondizio, E.S., Elmqvist, T., Malmer, P., and Spierenburg, M. (2014). Connecting diverse knowledge systems for enhanced ecosystem governance: the multiple evidence base approach. *Ambio*, 43, 579–591.

The Commonwealth. (n.d.). Ghana, history. https://thecommonwealth.org/our-member-countries/ghana/history.

The Presidency, Republic of Ghana. (2018). President Akufo-Addo Attends Africa CEO Forum in Geneva, Switzerland. http://presidency.gov.gh/index.php/briefing-room/news-style-2/179-president-akufo-addo-attends-africa-ceo-forum-in-geneva-switzerland, accessed, 3/12/2019.

Times Higher Education. (2020). Best universities in Africa. https://www.timeshighereducation.com/student/best-universities/best-universities-africa.

van Breda, J., and Swilling, M. (2018). *The Guiding Logics and Principles for Designing Emergent Transdisciplinary Research Processes. Sustainability Science*, 14(3). DOI:10.1007/s11625-018-0606-x

Vienni Baptista, B., and Rojas-Castro, S. (2019). Transdisciplinary institutionalization in higher education: A two-level analysis. *Studies in Higher Education*, 45(6), 1075–1092. https://doi.org/10.1080/03075079.2019.1593347.

Vienni Baptista, B., and Klein, J.T. (2020). Dynamics of inter- and trans-disciplinarity within institutions: Cultures and communities, spaces and timeframes. In *Conference Proceedings*, Gothenburg University.

Vilsmaier, U., Brandner, V., and Engbers, M. (2017). Research in-between: The constitutive role of cultural differences in transdisciplinarity. *Journal of Engineering and Science*, 8. https://doi.org/10.22545/2017/00093.

von Bertalanffy, L. (1975). *Perspectives on General Systems Theory: Scientific-Philosophical Studies*. New York: Braziller.

Watkins, M.O. (1972). *The University's Role in a Developing Country: An Open Lecture Delivered at the University of Ghana*. Accra: Ghana University Press.

Weingart, P. (2014). Interdisciplinarity and the new governance of universities. In *University Experiments in Interdisciplinarity - Obstacles and Opportunities*. https://pub.uni-bielefeld.de/publication/2673487, accessed 26/3/2021.

Winberg, C. (2006). Undisciplining knowledge production: Development driven higher education in South Africa. *Higher Education*, 51, 159–172. https://doi.org/10.1007/s10734-004-6378-5, accessed 23/3/2021.

World Bank. (2011). Ghana looks to retool its economy as it reaches middle-income status. https://www.worldbank.org/en/news/feature/2011/07/18/ghana-looks-to-retool-its-economy-as-it-reaches-middle-income-status, accessed, 26/3/21.

Worldometre. (n.d.). Ghana demographics. https://www.worldometers.info/demographics/ghana-demographics.

Zgambo, O. (2018). *Exploring Food System Transformation in the Greater Cape Town Area*. Thesis, Stellenbosch University. https://scholar.sun.ac.za/handle/10019.1/103445?show=full, accessed 13/02/2021.

9
DEVELOPMENT OF INTERDISCIPLINARITY AND TRANSDISCIPLINARITY IN MODERN RUSSIAN SCIENCE AND HIGHER EDUCATION

Vladimir Mokiy and Tatyana Lukyanova

Introduction

This chapter considers nuances that influence the limitations and prospects of the institutional development of interdisciplinarity (ID) and transdisciplinarity (TD) in academic research institutions and universities in Russia. They were shaped by specific historical conditions that contributed to the formation of features of Russian society, as well as institutional structures and interactions between academic institutions and universities. In this chapter, we briefly describe their features. Discussion begins, first, with how science and education in modern Russia are represented by different structures: including federal state budgetary institutions of science (The Russian Academy of Sciences, 2013) and federal and regional state budgetary institutions of higher education (The Government of the Russian Federation, 2018). The structure of the Russian Academy of Sciences (RAS) has different scientific units, including centers, institutes, and laboratories. Therefore, its scientific units are associated in Russia with academic science and are called "academic" institutes. To solve fundamental practical problems in breakthrough areas (such as weaponry, space, energy), academic science is located in a separate division of sectoral science. Development of an "industry-oriented" science is determined by significant target factors that stimulate disciplinary scientists to conduct interdisciplinary research (Russian Academy of Sciences, 2013). Broadly speaking, higher education in Russia is also represented by the structure of its institutions. In addition to teaching students, leading universities are engaged in innovative research activities (Erokhin et al., 2018, p. 242). Academic institutions and higher education institutions also interact with each other, as discussed further below.

Second, from that base, maintaining the internal stability of the post-Soviet state implies perpetuating an authoritarian style of governance of science and education, with a gradual transition to a state-public style of governance (Kozyrin, 2014). Third, the authoritarian style of science and education management perpetuates a cautious attitude in relation to scientists and teachers' involvement in ID and TD. Yet, integration and generalization of disciplinary knowledge can lead to a different, non-authoritarian explanation of the essence of laws of social development. In this regard, it is important to note that many scientists and teachers of modern Russia formed their scientific worldviews at universities of the Soviet Union. This demographic fact is evident in the average age of researchers in modern Russia, which exceeds 50 years, and the share of scientists over 60 years is 36%. In Russian universities, the average age of researchers and teachers is also over 47, and the composite share of researchers and teachers over 60 is 24% (Voynilov et al., 2017, p. 42). Fourth, higher education in the country is in a state of transformation. Russia only signed the Bologna Declaration in 2003 (Krainov, 2008). In 2009, the transfer of educational programs in Russian universities from specialist degrees for bachelor's and master's degrees also began, and in 2012, state regulation of higher education started. The latter development was accompanied by numerous reductions, associations, and reorganizations of higher education institutions (Odegov and Garnov, 2019, p. 44).

The established structure of the higher education network, then, has largely determined institutional limitations and opportunities for the development of interdisciplinarity and transdisciplinarity. Kuzminov et al. (2013, pp. 51–52) argue that by 2013 four types of higher education institutions had been formed in Russia: (i) research universities; (ii) infrastructural universities; (iii) sectoral universities; and (iv) universities of factual higher education. Research universities have the status of federal universities and national research universities, with the necessary infrastructure and specialists to conduct large-scale research activities. Infrastructural universities admit regional applicants and do not conduct large-scale research activities. Sectoral universities are linked to one or more large companies, including state companies, thus providing a sustainable labor market for their graduates. Universities of factual higher education, in turn, provide total access for the wider population. The fourth type offers students higher and better socialization than secondary schools but does not guarantee a qualitative basis of professional competence. Today, three-quarters of Russian students are studying in higher education institutions of factual higher education, meeting the population's demand for diplomas but not in institutions conducting innovative research activities.

Thus, and fifth, Russia has historically developed a hierarchical structure that supports a centralized authoritarian leadership of science and education. Given this structure, academic institutions specialized in scientific disciplines provide theoretical and methodological support to universities, as well as controlling the process of the formation of a scientific worldview and the development of university science (Ablazhej, 2015, pp. 29–37). Under the influence of the above features, scientists and teachers of different age groups experience interdisciplinarity and transdisciplinarity in science and higher education differently in modern Russia.

Therefore, we have singled out from these various assessments a description of personal and professional, academic-epistemological, institutional, and socio-political factors that, according to Vienni Baptista and Klein (in this volume), can objectively influence the intensity of limitations and prospects for the development of interdisciplinarity and transdisciplinarity. Further, we summarize and describe these factors in the sections on interdisciplinarity and transdisciplinarity in academic institutions and in higher education institutions. To conclude, following these sections, we describe a unique experience of developing transdisciplinarity within the framework of autonomous non-profit organizations in Russia.

To turn first to prospects for developing interdisciplinarity and transdisciplinarity in the Russian higher education system, we conducted a bibliometric content analysis of the literature using the keywords "interdisciplinarity" and "transdisciplinarity". As a result, we managed to study the perceptions of Russian scientists and teachers about the prospects for the development of interdisciplinarity and transdisciplinarity, as well as providing links to the most informative literature on this topic.

Definitions of interdisciplinary and transdisciplinary interactions

Our choice of bibliographic content analysis was aimed at gaining insights into the reform of science and education in Russia conducted by the Higher School of Economics (Voynilov et al., 2017), gleaned from 150 articles and reports written by scientists of academic institutions and university professors on interdisciplinary and transdisciplinary topics (2017–2020), as well as 30 years of experience in the Russian School of Transdisciplinarity (1990–2020). This chapter reflects our systematization of the perspectives of Russian scientists and teachers about the prospects for developing interdisciplinarity and transdisciplinarity and incorporating insights from the publications with links to the most informative literature on this topic. In the process of systematizing and reflecting on this data, we found that the lack of accepted definitions – including explicit signs of interdisciplinarity, a particular interdisciplinary approach, transdisciplinarity, and a particular transdisciplinary approach – complicates the analysis of the content of articles and conference abstracts, while reducing their scientific value (Mokiy and Lukyanova, 2016, p. 5). However, our analysis revealed that in modern Russia, interdisciplinarity is associated with the integrative nature of the modern stage of scientific knowledge (Mokiy and Mokiy, 2016, p. 6). In most cases, transdisciplinarity is associated with a special kind of multidisciplinary research that goes beyond specific disciplines, a connotation that follows from the meaning of the prefix "trans-" itself (Knyazeva, 2011, pp. 193–194). This finding of collaborative interactions allowed us to propose the following definitions of interdisciplinary approaches, used in this chapter to assess prospects for interdisciplinarity and transdisciplinarity in modern Russia (Mokiy and Lukyanova, 2017, pp. 10–11).

Mokiy and Lukyanova's (2017) definitions follow:

(i) The interdisciplinary approach is a way of expanding the horizon of the scientific worldview in the direction of mutual enrichment of knowledge, methodology, and languages of two complementary scientific disciplines.
(ii) The transdisciplinary approach is a way to expand the horizon of a scientific worldview through the implementation of integrative trends in disciplinary, interdisciplinary, and multidisciplinary knowledge and models of the object.

In Russia, though, scientists tend to believe "disciplinarity is order, and interdisciplinarity is freedom", hence a search for a "no man's land" between two disciplines. Thus, both in Russia and in the West, definitions of interdisciplinarity and transdisciplinarity often have an associative character. Therefore, we were forced to give generalized definitions of approaches that differ in degrees of integrating trends, knowledge, and disciplines. The general association in this case is an image of the horizon of a scientific worldview.

Our classification of academic and corresponding systems approaches, then, also allowed us to assess negative and positive impacts of factors limiting the development of interdisciplinarity and transdisciplinarity in modern Russia. Toward that end, we further include the following definitions of these systems approaches (Mokiy, 2019a, pp .251–252):

(i) A systems interdisciplinary approach is a way to identify and model an object in the image of a local interdisciplinary system, allowing the application of complementary systemic disciplinary methods to study the system.
(ii) A systems transdisciplinary approach is a method of identifying and modeling a complex object in the image of a transdisciplinary system, which allows applying a universal systems transdisciplinary methodology to its study. In the context of such a definition, the system transdisciplinary approach is associated with the meta-discipline "systems transdisciplinarity".

Limitations for the development of interdisciplinarity at academic institutes and universities

Mindful of limitations for developing interdisciplinarity in Russian academic institutions and universities, in the absence of significant practical factors that stimulate scientists of sectoral science to pursue interdisciplinary interaction, academic scientists prefer to ask rhetorical questions. For example, Kirdina (2017, pp. 144–145) interrogates whether all participants in interdisciplinary projects are able to present subjects of their research in mathematical form or whether they should hope for a universal language for groups of disciplines. Division of academic institutions into disciplinary groups does not facilitate an active search for answers to such questions. However, as in other countries, it contributes to the formation of concrete limitations for developing interdisciplinarity. Kirdina and Kleyner (2016, p. 50) highlight two such limitations. The first is directly related to the organization of interdisciplinary cooperation within a particular project. Each new project requires developing or revising a disciplinary apparatus. The second restriction is related to the loss of a single understanding of interdisciplinary interaction that requires taking into account all results of various disciplinary approaches in the project. Considering all disciplinary results can lead to a high level of abstraction, in which individual disciplinary results are dissolved and the outcome is trivial. Lysak (2016) adds a third restriction, connected with the evaluation of interdisciplinary research by mono-disciplinary specialists. However, such practice leads to misunderstandings and inaccurate interpretations of results, understating their practical value. Furthermore, in Russian universities, interdisciplinarity is perceived in two ways, traditional interdisciplinary links and complex interdisciplinary links.

Illustrating one perception, Mamatov et al. (2010, pp. 308–309) clarified that traditional interdisciplinary links are perceived as relations between individual elements of academic disciplines in order to coordinate their content in training programs. In turn, complex interdisciplinary relationships facilitate integrating disciplinary knowledge. Thus, two interrelated trends of interdisciplinarity are typical for modern university education: integration and coordination. Interdisciplinary integration is the highest form of unity of aims, principles, educational content, and expanded didactic units that interrelate academic disciplines. Interdisciplinary coordination is also reflected in the interdisciplinary teaching of students. Mirsky (2010) reports that universities actively using interdisciplinarity in research and teaching are trying to solve four types of problems:

(i) Methodological problems concerning the formation of the subject of study in an interdisciplinary research project in which different disciplines participate.
(ii) Organizational problems related to the creation of communication networks and interaction between researchers from different scientific disciplines, in which they could participate professionally to achieve and discuss results of an interdisciplinary research project.
(iii) Information problems concerning the transfer of results from an interdisciplinary research setting to the field of practical decision-making.
(iv) Vakhshtayn (2016, pp. 242–243) contends language problems are the most difficult to solve because interdisciplinary research models can only be built when there is a language of description beyond the boundaries of only one discipline. This process requires immersion in the axiomatics of other disciplines and using its ways of encoding the world.

In the context of these problems, we follow Shevchuk's (2014) assessment of prospects for the development of interdisciplinarity. In 2014, she was one of the organizers of a set of interdisciplinary research seminars on human resources held at the Higher School of Economics from the National Research University (HSE, Moscow). In evaluating the success of these seminars, she admitted uncertainty about whether the interdisciplinary approach had taken root in the professional minds of HSE scientists and professors. At present, the university administration endorses this approach, but it is not an independent choice of researchers, affirming our findings of the reluctance of professors to go beyond the boundaries of their disciplines on their own initiative. This gap makes it difficult to predict prospects for interdisciplinarity.

Reflecting on factors that hinder or help interdisciplinary development, we argue they result from a tension between goals and objectives of second- and third-generation universities. Second-generation universities are mainly aimed at solving disciplinary problems. In this case, it is enough for students to form a disciplinary worldview, the expansion of which is mainly due to general cultural competencies. Third-generation universities are aimed at solving complex multifactorial interdisciplinary problems. To solve them, a disciplinary worldview is not enough. Therefore, the university should teach students to expand the horizons of the disciplinary worldview through the use of all types of academic and systems scientific approaches then appropriate them to the context of a particular problem. General cultural competencies encompass a wide range of issues, including knowledge and experience in national and international arenas, as well as spiritual and moral foundations, traditions of families and social groups, and the role of science and religion. In Russia, in particular, a student acquires general cultural competence in classes on philosophy and cultural studies, typically in the first year of study.

Prospects for the development of interdisciplinarity in universities

The combination of personal and professional interests of teachers with the management of a particular university in developing quality educational processes aimed at solving multifactorial regional problems will contribute to the expansion of institutional opportunities for the development of interdisciplinarity in modern Russia. Implementation of such opportunities in Russian universities has been going in two directions since 2015. To start with, the first direction was prompted by the need to solve problems of regions where universities are located. To address them, universities have begun to actively form specialized interdisciplinary laboratories and centers, focusing on particular environmental, economic, and social concerns. These subdivisions brought together scientists and professors who have an interdisciplinary worldview. Results from these organizational units contribute to accumulating experience in interdisciplinary research, while also having a positive impact on the ranking of universities. For example, the rector of the Tyumen Industrial University, V. V. Efremova, reported that after analyzing problems and development plans of the region and industrial partners by 2020, the university managed to create 12 laboratories and modernize 20 laboratories. These laboratories are aimed at solving problems in five areas: (i) digitalization of the economy and education; (ii) improved efficiency of production and deep processing of hydrocarbon raw materials; (iii) development of environmentally friendly and resource-saving energy; (iv) integrated development of the Arctic zone of Western Siberia; and (v) creation of new materials and import substitution (Efremova, 2020).

The second direction of new opportunities for interdisciplinary implementation arose as a result of strengthening intellectual activity of scientists and university teachers. This activity is aimed at identification features of interdisciplinarity, as well as finding solutions to problems of interdisciplinary interactions in universities. The Southern Federal University (SFU) illustrates this second direction. It was established in 2006 as the first Federal University in Russia. In 2015, by the decision of the rector of the university, a working group was formed on "Interdisciplinary socio-economic research of SFU".[1] It was headed by the corresponding member of the Russian Academy of Sciences, the Deputy Director of the Central Economic, and the Mathematical Institute of the Russian Academy of Sciences, G. Kleiner. From 2015 to 2020, the working group has labored extensively. It organized a quarterly scientific and interdisciplinary seminar for young scientists. The university also implemented many interdisciplinary research projects supported by internal grants. Between 2016 and 2020, the working group also held five national and international conferences on "Interdisciplinarity in Modern Social and Humanities Knowledge". Representatives of other Russian universities in these conferences helped to disseminate the experience of Southern Federal University in implementing institutional opportunities for developing interdisciplinarity.

Limitations for developing transdisciplinarity in academic institutions

To reiterate, the authoritarian style of science and education management does not welcome their development through "bottom-up initiatives" generated by scientists. This style, which does not welcome the development of interdisciplinary and transdisciplinary approaches in humanities and social sciences, might change the content of the worldview on which the state ideology stands. Mindful of this threat, in 2008, E. Kruglyakov, Chairman of the Commission on Combating Pseudoscience and Falsification of Scientific Research of the RAS, officially declared transdisciplinarity to be a pseudoscience (Kruglyakov, 2008, pp. 8–9). Until his death (in 2012), Kruglyakov continued to struggle with the "spirit" of transdisciplinarity. This "struggle" had a negative impact on the assessment of the practical importance of transdisciplinarity. A monograph published in 2015 under the auspices of the Russian Academy of Sciences and the Institute of Philosophy of the RAS – "Transdisciplinarity in philosophy and science: Approaches, problems and prospects" – illustrates the negative consequences (Institute of Philosophy RAS, 2015). In their annotation to this collective monograph, the editors called it the first publication dedicated to understanding the phenomenon of transdisciplinarity in Russia, new for the development of modern science and culture. It was published in the Russian Academy of Sciences only two years after Krugliakov's death. For this reason, the authors of articles giving direction to discussions of transdisciplinarity are not Russian, rather foreign scholars who have been dealing with theoretical and practical issues of developing transdisciplinarity for many years in international contexts (Klein, 2015, pp. 80–93; Nicolescu, 2015, pp. 62–79; Scholz et al., 2015, pp. 31–61).

When Porus (2015) summarized the opinions of Russian participants in the monograph, he considered transdisciplinarity just one of the vectors of a multidimensional transgression of modern science beyond its classical self-identification, in the mode of a philosophical discussion. However, this characterization is a rather modest understanding of transdisciplinarity by Russian academic scientists that does not factor in 50 years of developing the concept in world science and higher education.

A second example comes from the XII International Scientific and Practical Interdisciplinary Symposium 2020 "Reflexive Processes and Management". This meeting was a rehearsal for the international conference WOSC 2020 (the World Organization of Systems and Cybernetics). Organizers of the symposium (Lepsky, 2019, p. 7) declared that transdisciplinarity is the basic approach to integrating knowledge areas and subjects in the management of cybernetics of the third order. However, the term "transdisciplinarity" can be found in only five of 82 articles and reports published in this collection. In three of them, the term "transdisciplinarity" is mentioned only in the introduction or in the conclusion. Of the remaining two, one briefly describes the philosophical issues of transdisciplinarity. Thus, authors do not always specify definitions of ID and TD. And only one report is fully devoted to the theoretical and practical application of a systems transdisciplinary approach in solving problems of the global management of society development. As we reported earlier, the authoritarian style of science management does not allow initiation of this movement up "from the bottom", favoring "from above". Therefore, taking into account the negative attitude of the Academy of Sciences of Russia to transdisciplinarity, prospects of institutional development of transdisciplinarity will depend directly on its institutional development in science on a world scale.

A transdisciplinary approach implies the implementation of integrative trends in disciplinary, multidisciplinary, and interdisciplinary modes. However, unsolved problems of interdisciplinarity and interdisciplinary interactions discussed earlier have largely contributed to the topic of transdisciplinarity not being seriously considered in most modern Russian universities. To illustrate, in 2013, staff of the National Research University Higher School of Economics met in Moscow with authors of the ARISE II report, K. Canizares and R. Morgan, who are vice-presidents of the Massachusetts Institute of Technology. They focused on related goals of higher education in the United States, including the transition from interdisciplinarity to transdisciplinarity capable of creating new disciplines

(ARISE II, 2013, p.14). In the United States, colleagues have attempted to learn what successful transdisciplinarity may look like in Russian higher education. HSE first vice-rector, L. Gokhberg (Seregin, 2013) commented that a complex system of government decisions and initiatives lies behind recommendations in the ARISE II strategy. However, the mechanism for preparing such a strategy differs from Russian traditions. "ARISE II" is an attempt to define directions of scientific development "from below" by the scientific community itself. In Russia, it is still difficult to imagine organizing public discussions on similar topics affecting society as a whole. The process of transforming higher education, though, is seeking new institutional forms of transdisciplinarity "from above". For example, the national project "Science" provides for creating a federal network of completely new structures for Russia – scientific and educational centers (SECs). In 2019, five such centers were already opened. The SECs could become a fundamentally new form of interaction between education, science, business, and government, breaking down disciplinary barriers and achieving transdisciplinary solutions. In the meantime, according to L. Kiryanova, vice-rector of Tomsk Polytechnic University (Kiryanova, 2019), transdisciplinarity remains an aspirational goal of the near future for most of the centers being created.

Prospects for developing transdisciplinarity in autonomous non-profit organizations

In 1996, a new element was added to the structure of Russian science and higher education – autonomous non-profit organizations (Federal Law, 1996). With this step, Russia began to advance the scientific potential for innovation in civil society. Significantly, per area of activity from SECs to universities of higher education and openness to interaction with civil society is increasing. In this regard, Nowotny et al. (2001) explained, the recognition of stakeholders' perspectives and alternative knowledge lead to dismantling the dichotomy of experts versus non-professionals, promoting new partnership relations between academia and society. The Institute of Transdisciplinary Technologies develops these relations within the framework of an autonomous non-profit organization that celebrated its 13th anniversary in 2020. The Institute uses theoretical and practical experience in transdisciplinary approaches, accumulated by the Russian School of Transdisciplinarity over 30 years. The Russian school was founded in 1990 (Brief History, 2020). Its launch coincided with the creation of a public research laboratory at Kabardino-Balkarian State University (Nalchik, Russia) – created on the initiative of ordinary citizens interested in the challenge of presenting results of interdisciplinary scientific research. All laboratory staff are trained in the fields of science but do not have degrees. However, this fact did not prevent them from creating a universal method of unification and generalization of disciplinary knowledge. Unification is a process for bringing disciplinary knowledge and/or its classifications to uniform transdisciplinary systems of classification. In other words, existing classifications are specified within limits of isomorphic transdisciplinary systems models for space, time, and information units. This context conditions a unity of the world and of each object and process. Generalization is a method to fill transdisciplinary systems models of order units with disciplinary knowledge, which describes the objective essence of the object or problem. Transdisciplinary systems unification and generalization do not break disciplinary classifications and do not cancel their criteria, indices, and parameters. But they allow interpreting these criteria, indices, and parameters in terms of the order conditioning a unity of the environment, as well as objects and processes that are its elements (**Mokiy** and Lukyanova, 2021a, p. 13).

In retrospect, the enthusiasm and personal interests of the staff of the research laboratory at Kabardino-Balkarian State University allowed achieving serious results in a short period of time and in the absence of external funding. Successful scientific contacts with personally interested scientists of academic institutions, university professors, specialists of industry-specific science, and government officials allowed filling the gap of lacking knowledge in philosophy and methodology, as well as developing and testing in practice the first models of unification and generalization of disciplinary knowledge. As a result, as early as 1996, the methodology for summarizing disciplinary information was approved by specialists from medicine, economics, education, ecology, and energy at the state level and officially recommended for solving complex multifactorial state problems (**Mokiy** and Lukyanova, 2021b, p. 87). This step contributed to the opening in 1997 of the first Russian research laboratory for transdisciplinary planning and forecasting, on the initiative of the rector of the Kabardino-Balkarian State University. Further development of the theory and methodology of a systems transdisciplinary approach contributed to the creation in 2007 of an autonomous non-profit organization called the "Institute of Transdisciplinary Technologies". By 2020, this Institute remained the only organization in Russia that continues to develop the theory and methodology of the systems transdisciplinary approach while also providing information and consulting services to interested organizations in many areas of science and technology. The success of the Russian School of Transdisciplinarity is due to the following circumstances. To delineate them:

(i) Targeting. The systems transdisciplinary approach was originally created to solve complex multifactorial problems. Therefore, the main goal of the approach is to find and improve the method of generalizing disciplinary knowledge within a special meta-discipline – systems transdisciplinarity.
(ii) Strict philosophical and conceptual substantiation. The establishment and development of the systems transdisciplinary approach was initially based on a special philosophical (following Plotinus) and conceptual (following E. Jantsch) rationale of transdisciplinarity. This rationale did not contradict general philosophical decisions and the natural science picture of the world.
(iii) Availability of language and methodological tools. Basic concepts of a systems transdisciplinary approach (information, time, space, system, etc.) were

initially given increased semantic potential, expanding descriptive possibilities of disciplinary languages. The main methodological tools (models of information, time, space units of order) do not declare but demonstrate practical possibilities.

(iv) High adaptability. Ability to adapt (retell and interpret) the concept and methodology of a systems transdisciplinary approach to different disciplines has eliminated conflict in personal and professional communications. Teachers, scientists, and specialists became convinced the new approach does not destroy their disciplinary worldviews, rather it expands their horizons by participating constructively in discussing the concept and practical testing of models of systems of transdisciplinary approaches within their disciplines.

Conclusions

Summarizing the factors that have had an impact on the development of interdisciplinarity and transdisciplinarity in science and higher education in modern Russia, we drew the following conclusions:

(i) The development of interdisciplinary interactions in modern Russia is regulated by socio-political factors (in line with the transformation of higher education "from above" from the Ministry of Science and Higher Education of the Russian Federation and Russian Academy of Sciences).

(ii) The common factor of interdisciplinary interactions is the hierarchical structure of the scientific worldview (on inter-, multi-, and trans-disciplinary levels) in most Russian universities. Consistent expansion of its horizon contributes to replacing factors that initiate interdisciplinary interactions, in this case, tending to a gradual transition to academic and institutional factors.

(iii) In research universities, a transition is occurring from interdisciplinary approaches to a multidisciplinary perspective of the scientific worldview and organization of students' education. But for most Russian universities, transdisciplinarity remains a promising future.

Viewed against the background of such conclusions, it is necessary to distinguish transdisciplinarity in a theoretical sense as a way of expanding the scientific worldview by implementing integrative tendencies of disciplinary, multidisciplinary, and interdisciplinary approaches, and in a practically useful sense, as a meta-discipline (systems transdisciplinarity). In such a sense, systems transdisciplinarity aims to bring results of higher education in line with the level required for solving urgent problems of the state and society as a whole. In turn, it is expedient to develop systems transdisciplinarity in two directions:

(i) In the direction that can strengthen the practical capabilities of disciplinary specialists in solving their professional problems.

(ii) In the direction of training students, if necessary, to solve problems of interdisciplinary interactions as well as multifactor problems of modern society.

It is important to add that while for Russian universities transdisciplinarity is a promising future, the introduction of systems transdisciplinarity in universities in Western Europe and America is a timely and urgent need. To substantiate this statement, we used the methodology of the systems transdisciplinary approach. The starting point for the development of systems transdisciplinarity was the groundbreaking international seminar on interdisciplinarity in universities in Paris from 7–12 September (Apostel et al., 1972). According to our forecasted results, the development and recognition of systems transdisciplinarity as a meta-discipline may be completed by September 2026. Since September 2019, awareness of the need to train students to address the pressing problems of modern society has entered its final phase (Mokiy, 2019b, pp. 85–86). This fact is confirmed by the purpose of the editors of this book: to establish a comparative framework for thinking about institutional and cultural conditions for inter- and trans-disciplinary research and teaching in higher education. All findings in this and other chapters, as well as the larger literature, reinforce appeals to the organizers of higher education, rectors of universities, government officials, and grantees in different countries with a call to organize and support international cooperation in a timely fashion and in the formation of a meta-discipline (called systems transdisciplinarity). This goal can be achieved through a specialized regional innovation center, which will develop and implement a strategic "bottom-up" plan to adapt such meta-discipline (systems transdisciplinarity) to the disciplinary structure of universities.

Note

1 Details are available from the working group's website (http://msgi.sfedu.ru/).

References

Ablazhej, A.M. (2015). 'Тенденции взаимодействия академической науки и высшего образования в современных условиях' ['The trends of interaction between academic science and higher education in modern conditions'], *Sociology of Science and Technology*, vol 6, no 3, pp 29–37.
Apostel, L., Berger, A. and Michaud, G. (1972). *Towards interdisciplinarity and transdisciplinarity in education and innovation. Interdisciplinarity: problems of teaching and research in universities*, OECD Publishing, Paris.
ARISE II (2013). *Unleashing America's research and innovation enterprise*, American Academy of Arts and Sciences, Cambridge, p 14.
Brief History (2020). 'Brief history of the Russian school of transdisciplinarity', *Informational Portal "Transdisciplinarity"*. http://td-science.ru/index.php/history, accessed 25 September 2020.

Efremova, V.V. (2020). 'Консорциумы вузов – это драйверы регионального развития' ['University consortia are drivers of regional development']. Tyumen Industrial University. https://www.tyuiu.ru/rektor-tyumenskogo-industrialnogo-universiteta-konsortsiumy-vuzov-eto-drajvery-regionalnogo-razvitiya/, accessed 15 September 2020.

Erokhin, A.K., Vlasenko, A.A. and Tsareva, N.A. (2018). 'Организационная структура современной российской системы высшего образования: проблемы и тенденции развития' ['Organizational structure of Russia's modern system of higher education: Issues and trends in development'], *Baltic Humanitarian Journal*, vol 7, no 1(22), pp 241–245.

Federal Law (2020). 'Федеральный закон о некоммерческих организациях' ['Federal law "about non-profit organizations"'] 12.01.1996, no 7, chapter 1, article 2(2). https://legalacts.ru/doc/FZ-o-nekommercheskih-organizacijah/, accessed 10 September 2020.

Institute of Philosophy RAS (2015). 'Трансдисциплинарность в философии и науке: подходы, проблемы и перспективы' ['Transdisciplinarity in philosophy and science: approaches, problems and prospects'], in V. Bazhanov and R.W. Scholz (eds) Navigator, Moscow.

Kirdina, S.G. (2017). 'Особенности внутридисциплинарного и междисциплинарного дискурсов: сравнительный анализ' ['Features of intradisciplinary and interdisciplinary discourses: Comparative analysis'], *Proceedings of the Second Annual All-Russian Scientific Conference (Rostov-on-Don, 22–24 June 2017, Southern Federal University)*, Southern Federal University Publ., Rostov-on-Don, pp 134–149.

Kirdina, S.G. and Kleyner, G.B. (2016). 'Социальное прогнозирование как междисциплинарный проект' ['Social forecasting as an interdisciplinary project'], *Sociological Research*, vol 12, pp 44–51.

Kiryanova, L.G. (2019). 'Томский научно - образовательный центр должен стать локомотивом научно-технического развития России' ['Tomsk scientific and educational center should become a driver of scientific and technical development of Russia'], *News of the Siberian Science*. http://www.sib-science.info/ru/heis/drayverom-06082019, accessed 20 September 2020.

Klein, J.T. (2015). 'Discourses of transdisciplinarity: Looking back to the future', in V. Bazhanov and R.W. Scholz (eds), *Transdisciplinarity in philosophy and science: Approaches, problems and prospects*, Navigator, Moscow, pp 80–93.

Knyazeva, E.N. (2011). 'Трансдисциплинарные стратегии исследования' ['Transdisciplinary research strategies'], *Bulletin of the Tomsk State Pedagogical University*, vol 10, pp 193–194.

Kozyrin, A.N. (2014). 'Государственная политика Российской Федерации в области образования: понятие и законодательные принципы' ['State policy of the Russian Federation in the field of education: The concept and legislative principles'], *Federal Centre for Educational Legislation*. http://fcoz.ru/obrazovatelnoe-pravo/analitika/detail.php?ELEMENT_ID=646, accessed 11 September 2020.

Krainov, G.N. (2008). 'Болонский процесс и проблемы модернизации высшего образования в России' ['The Bologna process and the problems of modernization of higher education in Russia'], *Fundamental Research*, vol 9, pp 76–78.

Kruglyakov, E.P. (2008). 'Подковерная наука' ['Undercover science'], *Science in Siberia*, vol 10, no 2645, pp 8–9.

Kuzminov, Y.I., Semenov, D.S. and Frumin, I.D. (2013). 'Структура университетской сети: От советского к российскому генеральному плану' ['Structure of the university network: From the soviet to the russian master plan'], *Education Issues*, vol 4, pp 8–63.

Lepsky, V.E. (2019). 'Предисловие редактора' ['Editor's preface'], *Reflexive processes and management. Collection of materials of the XII International scientific and practical interdisciplinary symposium "Reflexive processes and management", October 17–18, 2019*, Kogito-Center, Moscow, p 7.

Lysak, I.V. (2016). 'Междисциплинарность: преимущества и проблемы применения' ['Interdisciplinarity: Advantages and problems of application'], *Modern Problems of Science and Education*, vol 5.

Mamatov, A.V., Sitnikova, M.I., Tarasova, S.I. and Konovalov, D.V. (2010). 'Междисциплинарная подготовка в университете по направлению нанобиотехнологии' ['Interdisciplinary training at the university in the direction of nanobiotechnology'], *Scientific reports*, vol 2, no 97, pp 305–310.

Mirsky, E.M. (2010). 'Междисциплинарные исследования' ['Interdisciplinary research'], in *New philosophical encyclopedia*, Thought, Moscow.

Mokiy, V.S. (2019a). 'Systems transdisciplinary approach in the general classification of scientific approaches', *European Scientific Journal*, vol 15, no 19, ESJ July Edition, pp 247–258. https://doi.org/10.19044/esj.2019.v15n19p247

Mokiy, V.S. (2019b). 'International standard of transdisciplinary education and transdisciplinary competence', *Informing Science*, vol 22, pp 73–90. https://doi.org/10.28945/4480

Mokiy, V.S. and Lukyanova, T.A. (2016). 'От дисциплинарности к трансдисциплинарности в понятиях и определениях' ['From disciplinarity to transdisciplinarity in concepts and definitions'], *Universum: Social Sciences*, vol 7, no 25, pp 1–11.

Mokiy, V.S. and Lukyanova, T.A. (2017). 'Междисциплинарные взаимодействия в современной науке: подходы и перспективы' ['Interdisciplinary interactions in modern science: Approaches and perspectives'], *Economics of contemporary Russia*, vol 3, no 78, pp 7–21.

Mokiy, V.S. and Lukyanova, T.A. (2021a). 'Transdisciplinarity: Marginal direction or global approach of contemporary science?', *Informing Science*, vol 24, pp 1–18. https://doi.org/10.28945/4752

Mokiy, V.S. and Lukyanova, T.A. (2021b). Методология научных исследований. Трансдисциплинарные подходы и методы [*Methodology of scientific research. Transdisciplinary approaches and methods*], Urait, Moscow.

Mokiy, V.S. and Mokiy, M.S. (2016). 'От дисциплинарности к трансдисциплинарности в федеральных государственных стандартах высшего образования' ['From disciplinarity to transdisciplinarity in the federal state standards of higher education], *Universum: Social Sciences*, vol 9, no 27, pp 1–7.

Nicolescu, B. (2015). 'The hidden third and the multiple splendor of being', in V. Bazhanov and R.W. Scholz (eds), *Transdisciplinarity in philosophy and science: Approaches, problems and prospects*, Navigator, Moscow, pp 62–79.

Nowotny, H., Scott, P. and Gibbons, M. (2001). *Re-thinking science: Knowledge and the public in an age of uncertainty*. Polity Press, Cambridge.

Odegov, Y.G. and Garnov, A.P. (2019). 'Реформа российского образования: проблемы, результаты, перспективы' ['The reform of Russian education: Problems. Results. Prospects'], *Standard of Living of Russian Regions*, vol 3, no 213, pp 36–51. https://doi.org/10.24411/1999-9836-2019-10071

Porus, V.N. (2015). 'От междисциплинарности к трансдисциплинарности: мосты между философией науки и философией культуры' ['From interdisciplinarity to transdisciplinarity: Bridges between philosophy of science and philosophy of culture'], in V. Bazhanov and R.W. Scholz (eds), Navigator, Moscow, pp 416–432.

Scholz, R., Lang, D., Wiek, A., Walter, A. and Stauffacher, M. (2015). 'Transdisciplinary case studies as a means of sustainability learning: Historical framework and theory', in V. Bazhanov and R.W. Scholz (eds), *Transdisciplinarity in philosophy and science: Approaches, problems and prospects*, Navigator, Moscow, pp 31–61.

Seregin, O. (2013). 'Развитие науки и техники: опыт США' ['Development of science and technology: the US experience'], *News of HSE*. https://www.hse.ru/news/ev/83641955.html, accessed 11 September 2020.

Shevchuk, P. (2014). 'Междисциплинарность: Pro et contra. География НИУ ВШЭ' ['Interdisciplinarity: Pro et contra. Geography of HSE'], *Appendix to the Newsletter "Windows of Academic Growth"*, vol 1, no 10, pp 1–4.

The Government of the Russian Federation (2018). 'Распоряжение правительства Российской Федерации от 27 июня 2018 года N 1293-р. Об утверждении перечня организаций, подведомственных Министерству науки и высшего образования Российской Федерации, Министерству просвещения Российской Федерации и Рособрнадзору' ['Order of the Government of the Russian Federation No. 1293-r of June 27, 2018. On approval of the list of organizations under the jurisdiction of the Ministry of science and higher education of the Russian Federation, the Ministry of education of the Russian Federation and Rosobrnadzor']. *Electronic fund of legal and regulatory and technical documentation*. http://docs.cntd.ru/document/550510169, accessed 10 September 2020.

The Russian Academy of Sciences (2013). 'Структура Российской Академии Наук' ['Structure of the Russian Academy of Sciences'], *Information portal of the Russian Academy of Sciences*. http://www.ras.ru/sciencestructure.aspx, accessed 10 September 2020.

Vakhshtayn, V.S. (2016). 'Салоны и клубы. Междисциплинарность как идеология академического мира' ['Salons and clubs. Interdisciplinarity as an ideology of the academic world'], in *Proceedings of the all-Russian scientific conference (Rostov-on-Don, 22–23 June 2016, Southern Federal University)*, Southern Federal University Publ., Rostov-on-Don, pp 235–246.

Voynilov, Y., Gorodnikova, N., Gokhberg, L., Ditkovskiy, K., Kotsemir, M., Kuznetsova, I., Lukinova, E., Martynova, S., Ratay, T., Rosovetskaya, L., Sagieva, G., Streltsova, E., Suslov, A., Fridlyanova, S. and Fursovet, K. (2017). 'Researchers by gender and age', in *Science and technology indicators: 2017: Data book*, in L.M. Gokhberg, Ya.I. Kuzminov, K.E. Laikam and S.Yu. Matveev (eds), National Research University Higher School of Economics. HSE Publ., Moscow, pp 39–42.

10
"LEAPING OVER" DISCIPLINES

Historical context and future potential for interdisciplinarity and transdisciplinarity in Chinese higher education

BinBin J. Pearce

Introduction

Increasing emphasis on inter- and trans-disciplinary research and education has been fueled by a recognition of the inadequacy of a purely disciplinary point of view for addressing the complexity of social, economic, political, and intellectual problems in society (Gibbons et al., 1994). Boundaries between disciplines were drawn in a time and place distant from questions being raised today, rendering their applicability now questionable. In order for academic endeavors to maintain relevance for society at large, collaboration between disciplines and the inclusion of knowledge from outside of academia are required. This premise is evident, for example, by the increased number of publications using interdisciplinarity and transdisciplinarity as keywords, rising by 50% between 1978 and 2005 within natural sciences alone in the last decades (Porter and Rafols, 2009). In the United States, this expansion has been further fueled by a US$40 million, 15-year *National Academies Keck Futures Initiative* to bolster interdisciplinary research focused on understanding ecosystem services, complex systems, aging, and the control of infectious diseases (NRC, 2018). At the same time, however, the documented popularity of interdisciplinary approaches camouflages a path dependency for disciplinary organization, linked to academic paths for recognition and success (Chen, 2014). Further limiting prospects, institutes of higher education in China are inheritors of a wholly different cultural, political, and institutional tradition. What, then, is the prospect and potential for inter- and trans-disciplinarity research to be further developed in a different cultural and historical context other than in North America and Europe?

Etymology provides a starting point. In Chinese, interdisciplinarity is literally translated as the "crossing" between disciplines (交叉学科) and transdisciplinarity is "leaping over" disciplines (跨领域学科). "Crossing" between disciplines

DOI: 10.4324/9781003129424-12

points to an understanding of interdisciplinarity as "interacting", "integrating", or "linking" between disciplines (Klein, 2018, pp. 18–23). "Leaping over" disciplines capture a particular aspect of transdisciplinarity – the connotation of "transcending" or "transgressing" but not necessarily "transforming" disciplines (Klein, 2018, pp. 24–26). The term "interdisciplinarity" is now emerging in the context of research grant calls by the National Natural Science Foundation of China and emerging bachelor's level liberal arts education in some elite Chinese universities (Poo and Wang, 2014). However, transdisciplinarity is not yet visible in official policy documents. The future influence of both concepts in Chinese academia is still to be seen, then, though there are promising institutional signals.

This chapter asks three related questions. First, do these concepts have ties to historical notions of higher education within Chinese culture or are they imports of recent internationalization of a globalized educational system? Second, how are inter- and trans-disciplinary approaches to research and teaching visible in institutes and programs that have been or are being created in China? Third, are concepts of interdisciplinarity and transdisciplinarity as developed in Western literature relevant in higher education in China? To answer these questions, this chapter starts with a description of past traditions in higher education in China, then continues with developments that influenced the contemporary higher education system under the regime of the Chinese Communist Party (CCP). Finally, it concludes by linking components of past developments with manifestations of interdisciplinarity and transdisciplinarity within the contemporary and future system of Chinese higher education.

Historical development

Two separate but interlinked types of higher institutes of education persisted throughout Chinese history, neither one of them similar to the European medieval model of the university. The *taixue* (太学, "supreme learning") emerged – starting in CE 400 then reached its full stage of development by CE 907. It was a civil service examination system supported by accompanying preparatory organizations that provided a path to governmental positions (Hayhoe, 1994). According to their exam performance, scholars received a position within a local, prefectural, or national government hierarchy. This system was refined during the Song dynasty (CE 960–1279) by Neo-Confucianist scholar Zhu Xi and persisted until 1911. The subject of these examinations was based on the Four Books and Five Classics (四书五经). They were canonical texts embodying core values and beliefs in Confucianism, collections of poetry, speeches, and documents from the Zhou dynasty, descriptions of ancient rituals and a divination system, and history (Hayhoe, 1994; 1989).

This system created a community of scholar-officials who held a monopoly over the official body of knowledge that led to worldly success. Intellectual power was predicated on the loyalty of these scholars to the state, the classical texts, and the emperor himself. Critical questioning or debates about the validity of fundamental principles were not part of that tradition. In addition, communities of learning centered on a single great scholar or libraries constituted another type of institution. These were the independent *shuyuans* (书院, "book institute"), exhibiting parallels to Plato's Academy where learning took place through an informal society of scholarly discussion (Yoshihiko and Chien, 2020). These *shuyuans* integrated Confucian, Buddhism, and Daoist traditions while providing renewed interpretations of classical texts from these traditions, largely independent and funded by private endowments of land. Members did not focus on developing specialist knowledge or theories. They were preoccupied with interpretation of classical texts and developing the application of these interpretations for government affairs. The autonomy enjoyed by *shuyuans* was tenuous, though, since the knowledge produced in these organizations was seen as potentially subversive to the state. Hence, its members lacked collective rights and were at times subject to imperial suppression (Hayhoe, 1994).

These two traditional institutional types were linked by a Confucian approach to scholarship emphasizing connectedness and integration "between theory and practice, fact and value, individual and community, institution and political-social-natural context" (Hayhoe, 2001, p. 347). Boundaries between academic knowledge and practical knowledge were not made distinct within the Chinese epistemological tradition, which maintained a "holism in knowing". This holistic vision of learning combined an expectation that knowledge is demonstrated to be true through practice and application, rather than through theoretical argumentation or experimentation, and that all knowledge should have an ethical basis. Knowledge is not only a mirror through which to reflect empirical reality but rather a demonstration of values and their deepening inextricable from the development of one's morals (Tu, 2001). Refinement of this moral character is the goal toward which knowledge strives because it is seen as the basis for a peaceful family life that then becomes the basis for the peaceful governance of state. Thus, understood, knowledge in the Confucian tradition did not merely create categories of understanding of the world, in the form of disciplines, but rather served as the basis for political ideology, social ethics, and family values (Chan, 1969).

From a historical perspective, precedents for inter- and trans-disciplinary approaches to education in China include, primarily, (1) knowledge as an integrated corpus, rather as belonging to discrete categories and (2) acquisition of knowledge for the common good, rather than its own sake. In the *shuyuan*, for example, knowledge was not divided into disciplines. Rather, the focus was on cultivating holistic knowledge and education for its impact on character development and the ability to think critically and clearly. However, the extent of interdisciplinarity was limited, since science, math, and engineering did not belong to an academic body of knowledge. Rather, they belonged to a trade and developed in apprenticeships outside of the *shuyuan* and *taixue* (Altbach, 1989). Knowledge in both types of institutions was oriented toward the common good applied to the practice of governance. The importance of application, rather than acquisition of knowledge alone, was implicit in the *shuyuans* through the production of alternative and subversive commentaries of classical texts with the aim of improving approaches to governance. For this reason, the imperial government simultaneously used new developments found in *shuyuans* and suspected them as a potential source of revolt. In the *taixue*, knowledge application was explicit where education became part of societal meritocracy for attaining governmental positions. The "common good" was indirectly achieved by directing knowledge toward one's own cultivation, exhibited in improving one's social position by attaining a position. Knowledge was valued as a means to maintain peace in society through the cultivation of wise individuals (Chan, 1969). Thus, precedents for interdisciplinarity and transdisciplinarity characteristics of academic scholarship in China were historically evident and serve as a touchstone for future development and acceptance of inter- and trans-disciplinary learning in China.

These traditions of learning were disrupted when the CCP came to power on 1 October 1949. Prior to adopting the Soviet model from the late 19th century to the early 20th century, models of university education from America, England, Germany, and France operated in parallel in China. Their values were preserved through the 18th and 19th centuries, especially in colonial powers such as France, Germany, and Great Britain as well as the United States and the Soviet Union, though each context emphasized different elements of this Western tradition. In France, specialist knowledge, for example, was linked to a scholarly ideal. In Germany, theory was emphasized over practice in universities, with philosophy as the integrator of all other fields of knowledge. Practical studies were relegated to "Technische Hochschulen" (technical universities or institutes of technology) thus occupying a lower status than universities and less autonomy (Ringer, 1969). The "college" model of British universities was carried to the United States. It fostered close connections between students and their tutors, guided by the vision of creating a community of scholars. American universities married this British collegiate model with the German university model with an emphasis on research and focus on the unity of knowledge (Altbach, 1989; Veysey, 1965). Between 1911 and 1949, this diversity of academic models coexisted in China. Tsinghua University pioneered the adapted American research university model, becoming a premier institute by the 1920s led by Chinese scholars who had returned from the United States. They were recipients of a scholarship that was a part of the Boxer Indemnity, a result of China's defeat in 1901 by the Eight-Nation Alliance of Western countries (Hayhoe, 1994). The German Humboldtian university, in turn, served as a model for Peking University, starting in 1917 (Duiker, 1977), placing emphasis on autonomy and academic freedom that made it a center of major student-led political movements (4 May, Tiananmen Square protests).

Between 1949 and 1966, the Soviet model of higher education dominated the educational landscape. The People's University became the central institute influencing all teaching and research in social sciences, while also responsible for educating all experts in national planning, finance, and trade, and political instructors to ensure "absolute intellectual orthodoxy" (Hayhoe, 1989) throughout the intellectual life of a university. The higher education system was thus remolded to meet the demands of a socialist agenda for economic development. The system of institutes, curriculum, textbooks, specialization, and even disciplinary names followed the Soviet model. Thus, the CCP created a period of complete Soviet dominance in restructuring higher education in the period from 1940–1966. As a result, many decades passed before diverse influences from other traditions would reemerge. All teaching material and instruction were unified throughout the country through lesson scripts (Hayhoe, 1989). As a consequence of this restructuring, the boundary between basic and applied disciplines and specializations became ossified in institutional organizations. The Soviet system also emphasized delineation of disciplines to increase the efficiency of higher education in responding to the needs of a centrally planned economy. Most Chinese institutes of higher education became associated with a single discipline (Liu, 2016), in a system where the "Academy" played a major role in defining higher education. It was an elite association of scholars with nationally recognized intellectual authority. Separation between research and teaching was emphasized, with the Academy primarily taking charge of research activities and universities responsible for teaching.

By 1953, only 14 of the 182 colleges and universities were "comprehensive universities" in the sense of institutes with expertise in more than one field, but even they only had programs in arts and sciences (Yang, 2000). Colleges and universities were highly specialized and organized into single disciplinary areas such as teacher education, engineering, and agriculture (Li, 2012). Division made integration and collaboration between fields nearly impossible. Moreover, this model elevated the polytechnical university to a leading role, designating engineering expertise in clearly marked professional and geographical sectors that served central planning (Hayhoe and Zha, 2010). By 1960, then, polytechnics and specialist engineering universities were considered the elite institutes within academia. Most communist leaders were graduates of these institutes, not "comprehensive" universities covering a broader range of subjects. In contrast, polytechnic universities focused on applied fields, not basic science, with highly specialized disciplinary programs. Between 1966 and 1976, though, the country was thrown again into chaos during the Cultural Revolution. A generation of students was lost as all institutes of higher education were shut down, except those affiliated with the military. Primary and secondary schools were also closed. Not until 1977 was the first cohort of university students admitted into universities after an entire decade of paralysis (Yang, 2000). Starting in the 1980s, reforms were proposed, spearheaded by Deng Xiaoping in response to a changing socialist market economy and in recognition of the inadequacy of the Soviet model for socio-economic changes (Kwong, 2016). The goal was to raise the level of technology, national output, and a market economy in the country. Reforms resulted in mergers between specialized institutes, a first move toward breaking down institutionalized borders between disciplines. Yet, the entire educational system of China was devastated by the previous ten years of neglect.

Even though higher education was dissembled by the Cultural Revolution, however, during this period, a particular type of transdisciplinarity emerged among a generation of students forced to experience personal and social development outside of any academic institution, aligning the concept with personal learning outside strictures of academic disciplines. They learned through working in factories and fields and a small number of lucky ones had the opportunity to incorporate these experiences back into an academic institution. These complexities show the potential of interdisciplinarity and transdisciplinarity in China for enriching higher education in the future and may have more touchstones than at first glance. The period left an indelible mark on the role of education and universities in the political, social, and cultural landscape of China, though it is not openly discussed today. Li (2012) and Hayhoe (1989) described differences between Western and Chinese modes of higher education in terms of limits to scholars' academic freedom and the degree of control the state has over institutes of higher education. Traditionally, academic freedom in the West is associated with freedom in the search for understanding natural and social worlds but discouraged for application to political or social activism or including a political or activist agenda in the search for knowledge. Hayhoe (1996) has proposed "self-mastery" and "intellectual freedom" and similar concepts in China, though with some differences. Self-mastery in Chinese institutes of education is caught between the need to serve governmental interests and their own survival and internal administration, opening the possibility of bottom-up initiatives within top-down plans (Li, 2016). While academic freedom in a Western connotation is not apparent in the Chinese tradition, intellectual freedom is a familiar concept. It is the intellectual authority to criticize the government in the case of scholar-officials who qualified in imperial exams (Li, 2016). For independent scholars, this freedom manifested in a sense of moral responsibility to put knowledge to use for the highest common good (Li, 2016). Yan (2020) described the relationship between Chinese and Western knowledge paradigms for higher education as a hybrid paradigm, incorporating elements of different systems in response to the changing demands of social circumstances.

Contemporary evolution

Traditional openness to practice-oriented and holistic knowledge stands in contradiction to the focus on strategy in government projects for building up Chinese universities to compete on the world stage. Elite universities received the bulk of government funds in an effort to rebuild the higher education system. From 1995 to 2013, for a cumulative US$5 billion, two national-level plans invested in "Project 211" and "Project 285". These funding schemes identified and supported the elite 100 universities with the best chances of competing on the global academic stage, in terms of research output. Subsequently, this program was expanded to support 39 additional universities by 2004 (Zha et al., 2019). Six of the nine original universities were polytechnics and that trend has continued since. Funding is concentrated in China's technology-focused polytechnic universities that have a limited curricular focus outside of natural sciences and engineering (Hayhoe and Zha, 2010). While some have merged with medical universities (Tsinghua University, Zhejiang University, Shanghai Jiaotong University, and Huazong University of Science and Technology), few have been able to recover teaching and research in social sciences, humanities, and arts, subjects many of these institutes were famous for prior to the adoption of the Soviet model. As a consequence, some of China's most elite educational institutes, the polytechnic universities, are unable to contribute to advancing a program of cross-cultural dialogues and cultural diplomacy that may be important for China in the coming years, in addition to economic growth. This strategy of concentrating resources in elite institutes has contributed to both increasing the quantity and quality of research outputs, evident in the growing number of published articles and journals, as well as top-cited researchers.

To reiterate, official institutes of higher education in China have always been an apparatus of the state and did not exist independently. However, at the same time, these institutes have a certain degree of operational autonomy ("self-mastery" per Hayhoe, 1996) and are expected to develop ideas and initiatives that would allow them to be competitive with world-class universities. Much of the funding, for example, is raised through consulting for some of China's major multinational companies. This channel steers focus toward applied areas of research rather than basic research (Hayhoe and Zha, 2010). A "strong state" notion supports the role that Chinese universities play as the educational and research arm of the government for social and economic development (Zha et al., 2016). While the strength of this approach is undeniable in terms of funneling resources for specific, quantifiable objectives in higher education, China's top-down planning of higher education has also inhibited innovation and creativity. The technocratic approach of top-down plans assumed that cultural change needed for innovation could be state-engineered, without a holistic consideration of complex societal and cultural factors that can lead to transformational change. Incorporation of a liberal arts education, again within elite universities, has been one response to this lag in innovation, broadening the curriculum while aligning with the native humanistic tradition of the *shuyuan*. Expansion of university autonomy and the power of professors in institutional management is another response to lagging strides in innovation. China's latest blueprint for education reform and development, the *National Outline for Medium and Long Term Educational Reform and Development* (2010–2020), includes provisions for democratic internal governance, autonomy over program development, faculty hiring, and pedagogical reform. An initial group of 17 institutes is serving as the test field for these policy reforms (Zha and Yang, 2014). Yet, although expansion of the Chinese higher education systems has been impressive, there is still a significant gap compared with Western systems. For example, in 2012, the total budget of the National Science Foundation of China was about 13% (US$2.8 billion) of equivalent funding for the National Science Foundation and the research funding for the National Institutes of Health in the United States (US$22 billion). Basic research received 4.7% of R&D funding compared with over 10% in the United States, UK, and Korea, indicating that applied research remained the main focus of resources (Poo and Wang, 2014). Discrepancy of research funding would indicate a potential gap in research breadth and depth, Chinese institutes' ability to compete on a global stage with relatively less funding, and the need for leveraging international collaboration. The Sino-German Science Center, for example, is an example of this interdisciplinary collaboration in life sciences, natural sciences, management, and engineering sciences, where each country funds 50% of the costs (Poo and Wang, 2014).

Future potential for inter- and trans-disciplinary research

Concrete changes have been underway. In 2000, Zhejiang University established the first interdisciplinary research center in China, the Micro System Research (Chen, 2014). Peking University also has a group of 12 research centers labeled interdisciplinary, including the Academy for Advanced Interdisciplinary Studies focused on life sciences, Institute of Humanities and Social Sciences, and the Institute of Molecular Medicine.[1] However, the span of disciplines within each institute is still narrow. Tsinghua University, though, has established 13 "university-affiliated" or university-wide interdisciplinary research centers oriented around topics of societal relevance, including the Institute of 21st Century Development, Institute of Sustainable Development Goals, Center for Science, Technology and Education Policy, and Center for Crisis Management Research.[2] Based on a study about NSFC-sponsored interdisciplinary research (Shao et al., 2018), top-tier universities[3] carry out research projects with greater researcher disciplinary diversity than second- or third-tier institutions. In elite universities, a growing trend for supporting interdisciplinary education within both bachelor and graduate programs is also apparent. For example, Shanghai Tongji University established a transdisciplinary minor program on Sustainable Development in 2012, expecting students to take courses across departments and carry out a transdisciplinary group project (Jia et al., 2019). The Jinling College[4] at Nanjing University was founded in 1998 to provide an interdisciplinary environment for top students studying humanities and social sciences, while the Xinya College at Tsinghua University, established in 2014,[5] emulates a residential liberal arts college in a pilot project to reform undergraduate education and is developing an affiliated honors degree.[6]

Responses also appear at the policy level. In 2000, the National Natural Science Foundation of China (NSFC) laid out a plan for interdisciplinary research (Ledford, 2015). Then, in 2006, the State Council issued a development plan for science and development that identified the need to cultivate the growth of interdisciplinary subjects, research, and education (National Science and Technology Development Plan in Medium and Long-Term (2006–2020)). Today, the NSFC Funding Guide continues support for interdisciplinary research by naming it one of the five basic selection criteria for funding new projects (NSFC, 2018). The *11th Five-Year Development Strategy* of the National Science Foundation of China (NSFC) also mentioned the importance of interdisciplinary research and education (Cao et al., 2006). On closer inspection, however, "interdisciplinary research" is defined specifically by the categories of projects belonging to divisions of "Biophysics/Biochemistry/Molecular Biology" and "Biomaterials/Imaging/Tissue Engineering" in these documents. This categorization indicates interdisciplinarity is thought of as a concept that belongs to certain orders of problems to be solved, rather than a general concept to be applied broadly. Also in the *National Science and Technology Development Plan*, interdisciplinary research is mentioned in connection with strengthening the link between basic research and technology, rather than a means to build bridges between disciplines. While China has identified the importance of the concept and term of "interdisciplinarity" in policy, the meaning and practice of the concept are motivated by the power of new technologies, rather than, for example, exploring the inherent complexity of nature and society or solving societal problems (NAS et al., 2005).

Further, the term "transdisciplinary" research is not found in any official documents of Chinese higher educational policy. If an aspect of transdisciplinary research is defined by an exchange with practitioners (Gibbons et al., 1994) and joint problem framing (Pearce and Ejderyan, 2019), however, then there is evidence of this type of activity. A number of organizations co-founded by universities and industry are working with non-academic actors. These collaborations have been manifested in a variety of models, including the "university national science park", university spin-off companies, joint project development with small and medium-sized companies focused on solving specific technical problems, technology transfer with local governments, and joint R&D institutes (where companies and universities co-fund a laboratory that serves effectively as the R&D department of a company) (Wang, 2007). These collaborations have been characterized as "learning alliances" where companies are seeking, and as an essential element, technological innovation (Wang, 2007). As of 2014, Tsinghua University hosted 102 research institutes in collaboration with domestic industry (Chen, 2014). As of 2016, more than 1,100 joint R&D institutes have also been created in universities across the country with enterprises from more than 100 countries (Ma, 2019). These collaborations address Chinese enterprises' need for research capacity and provide a source of funding for universities. However, in comparison with the United States, Chinese universities are still less active in terms of industry–university collaborations and publication productivity (Zhou et al., 2016).

The potential for the proliferation of interdisciplinarity and transdisciplinarity concepts then, if adopted in a meaningful way by Chinese higher education, is vast. As of 2019, China matriculated eight million graduates, more than the number of graduates matriculating in the United States and India combined (Gu and Zheng, 2019). China is home to 514,000 higher educational institutes and 270 million students are enrolled (MOE, 2018). Furthermore, enrollment in universities grew by 17% per year starting in 1998. Reaching 22.3 million in 2010, this increase amounted to a 26.5% participation rate for the 18–22 age group. In parallel with the growth in enrollment, the number of institutes grew from 1,022 to 2,358 during this same period (Zha et al., 2016). By 2007, the Chinese higher education system overtook the United States to become the world's largest in terms of enrollment. A study of 24 top universities in China found that the number of publications in foreign journals increased by an average of 14.6% every year between 1993 and 2010 (Zhang et al., 2013). Yet, the landscape of higher education presents both challenges and opportunities for future developments of inter- and transdisciplinary research and teaching. Striving for innovation and being competitive on the world stage is a dynamic force moving Chinese higher education forward.

Final remarks

In summary, traditional openness to practice-oriented and holistic knowledge stands in contradiction to the focus on strategy in government projects for building up Chinese universities to compete on the world stage. However, increasing attention is being paid to the need for inter- and trans-disciplinary research and education, backed up by concrete programs and funding. And the potential for the proliferation of such concepts is still vast and unmet. The perspective I took in writing this chapter is affected by a personal connection to the evolution of higher education in China. My parents, both born in 1954, were forced to leave school in the sixth grade during the Cultural Revolution. Later, my father was a part of the first cohort of university students to be admitted into an institute of higher education in 1977 after the end of the Cultural Revolution in China. As a result of this educational opportunity, my parents were able to immigrate to the United States to continue in a graduate program. Yet, the consequences of the political upheaval and trauma that China experienced in the 20th century are still being unraveled. Therefore, the evolution and vagaries of Chinese higher education are part of this legacy. The past has to be considered in congruence with the impressive growth and development of Chinese higher education, mirroring its economic development over four decades. The concepts and institutional arrangements needed for supporting inter- and trans-disciplinary research and teaching within Chinese higher education could serve as a means to link historical context and future goals while bridging the native goal of establishing and promoting a greater number of world-class universities. It could be a means of building on historical foundations while moving forward to develop an innovative institutional organization for higher education.

Notes

1 http://english.pku.edu.cn/academics.shtml.
2 www.sppm.tsinghua.edu.cn/english/ResearchCenters/UniversityAffiliated/.
3 Top-tier universities were identified by the national government in 1998 as a part of the "985 Project". Second- and third-tier universities were funded by the "211 Project" throughout the 1990s (Zhang et al., 2013).
4 www.jlxy.nju.edu.cn/xygk/xxjj.htm.
5 www.xyc.tsinghua.edu.cn/#.
6 www.xyc.tsinghua.edu.cn/publish/xinya/10624/index.html.

References

Altbach, P. G. (1989). Twisted roots: The Western impact on Asian higher education. In P.G. Altbach & Viswanathan Selvaratnam (Eds.), *From Dependence to Autonomy* (pp. 1–24). Dordrecht: Kluwer Academic Publishers.

Cao, C., Suttmeier, R. P., & Simon, D. F. (2006). China's 15-year science and technology plan. *Physics Today*, *59*(12), 38–43. https://doi.org/10.1063/1.2435680

Chan, W.-T. (1969). *A Source Book in Chines Philosophy* (Paperback, pp. 1–883). Princeton, NJ: Princeton University Press.

Chen, B. (2018). China's education: 40 years of epic achievements. Ministry of Education China. The People's Republic of China. Retrieved 25 January 2021, from http://en.moe.gov.cn/news/press_releases/201812/t20181224_364525.html

Chen, S. (2014). *Interdisciplinary Research & Education in China: Achievements & Challenges* (pp. 19–22). Presented at the 8th Annual Strategic Leaders Global Summit, Newfoundland, Canada. https://cgsnet.org/ckfinder/userfiles/files/Chen_P1_2014_Global_Summit_web_proceedings.pdf

Duiker, W. J. (1977). *Tsʻai Yüan-pʻei, Educator of Modern China* (pp. 1–124). University Park, PA, and London: Pennsylvania State University Press.

Gibbons, M., Limoges, C., Helga, N., Schwartzman, S., Scott, P., & Trow, M. (1994). *The New Production of Knowledge*. London: Sage.

Gu, M., & Zheng, C. (2019). Education in China. Retrieved 25 January 2021, from https://wenr.wes.org/2019/12/education-in-china-3

Hayhoe, R. (1989). China's universities and Western academic models. In P. Altbach & V. Selvaratnam (Eds.), *From Dependence to Autonomy* (pp. 25–62). Dordrecht: Kluwer Academic Publishers.

Hayhoe, R. (1994). Ideas of higher learning, east and west: Conflicting values in the development of the Chinese University. *Minerva*, *32*, 361–382.

Hayhoe, R. (1996). *China's Universities 1895–1995: A Century of Cultural Conflict*. New York: Garland Press.

Hayhoe, R. (2001). Lessons from the Chinese academy. In R. Hayhoe & J. Pan (Eds.), *Knowledge across Cultures A Contribution to the Dialogue among Civilizations* (pp. 334–370). Hong Kong: Comparative Education Research Centre.

Hayhoe, R., & Zha, Q. (2010). China's polytechnic transformation. *International Higher Education*, *60*. https://doi.org/10.6017/ihe.2010.60.8501

Jia, Q., Wang, Y., & Fengting, L. (2019). Establishing transdisciplinary minor programme as a way to embed sustainable development into higher education system. *International*

Journal of Sustainability in Higher Education, 20(1), 157–169. https://doi.org/10.1108/IJSHE-05-2018-0095

Klein, J. T. (2018). Learning in transdisciplinary collaborations: A conceptual vocabulary. In D. Fam, L. Neuhauser, P. Gibbs (Eds.), *Transdisciplinary Theory, Practice and Education: The Art of Collaborative Research and Collective Learning* (pp. 11–24). Cham: Springer International Publishing.

Kwong, J. (2016). Embedded models of development: Educational changes in the People's Republic of China. In C. P. Chou & J. Spangler (Eds.), *Chinese Education Models in a Global Age* (Vol. 31, pp. 3–14). Singapore: Springer.

Ledford, H. (2015). Team science. *Nature, 525*, 308–311.

Li, J. (2012). World-class higher education and the emerging Chinese model of the university. *Prospects, 42*(3), 319–339. https://doi.org/10.1007/s11125-012-9241-y

Li, J. (2016). The Chinese University 3.0 in a global age: History, modernity and future. In C. P. Chou & J. Spangler (Eds.), *Chinese Education Models in a Global Age* (Vol. 31, pp. 15–36). Singapore: Springer Singapore. https://doi.org/10.1007/978-981-10-0330-1

Liu, S. (2016). *Quality Assurance and Institutional Transformation*. Singapore: Springer.

Liu, Y. (2016). *Higher Education, Meritocracy and Inequality in China* (pp. 11–34). Singapore: Springer.

National Academy of Sciences, National Academy of Engineering, and Institute of Medicine. (2005). *Facilitating Interdisciplinary Research*. Washington, DC: The National Academies Press. https://doi.org/10.17226/11153

National Natural Science Foundation of China. (2018). *National Natural Science Fund Guide to Programs 2019* (pp. 1–330). Beijing: NSFC.

National Research Council. (2018). *Collaborations of Consequence: NAKFI's 15 Years Igniting Innovation at the Intersections of Disciplines*. Washington, DC: The National Academies Press. https://doi.org/10.17226/25239

Pearce, B. J., & Ejderyan, O. (2019). Joint problem framing as reflexive practice: Honing a transdisciplinary skill. *Sustainability Science, 15*(3), 683–698. https://doi.org/10.1007/s11625-019-00744-2

Poo, M. M., & Wang, L. (2014). A new face at Natural Science Foundation of China—An interview with NSFC President Wei Yang. *National Science Review, 1*(1), 157–160. https://doi.org/10.1093/nsr/nwt031

Porter, A. L., & Rafols, I. (2009). Is science becoming more interdisciplinary? Measuring and mapping six research fields over time. *Scientometrics, 81*(3), 719–745. https://doi.org/10.1007/s11192-008-2197-2

Ringer, F. (1969). *The Decline of the German Mandarins*. Cambridge, MA: Harvard University Press.

Shao, Z.-Y., Li, Y.-M., Hui, F., Zheng, Y., & Guo, Y.-J. (2018). Interdisciplinarity research based on NSFC-sponsored projects: A case study of mathematics in Chinese universities. *PloS ONE, 13*(7). https://doi.org/10.1371/journal.pone.0201577

Tu, W. (2001). The ecological turn in new Confucian humanism: Implications for China and the world. *Daedalus, 130*, 243–264. https://doi.org/10.2307/20027726

Veysey, L. (1965). *The Emergence of the American University*. Chicago, IL: University of Chicago Press.

Wang, N. (2007). *The Way Chinese Companies Collaborate with Chinese Universities*. Thesis dissertation, University of Kalmar (pp. 1–71). http://www.diva-portal.se/smash/get/diva2:224970/FULLTEXT03.pdf

Yan, F. (2020). Identity of China's modern academic system: A Chinese–Western interaction perspective. *Journal of Educational Change*. https://doi.org/10.1007/s10833-020-09389-w

Yang, R. (2000). Tensions between the global and the local: A comparative illustration of the reorganisation of China's higher education in the 1950s and 1990s. *Higher Education, 39*(3), 319–337. https://doi.org/10.1023/A:1003905902434

Yoshihiko, M., & Chien, I. (2020). An enquiry into the origins of Confucian academies and the Mingtang in the Tang period. In V. Glomb, E.-J. Lee, & M. Gehlmann (Eds.), *Confucian Academies in East Asia* (pp. 45–67). Beaverton, US: Ringgold Inc.

Zha, Q., Shi, J., & Wang, X. (2016). Is there an alternative university model? The debate around the Chinese model of the university. In J. E. Côté & A. Furlong (Eds.), *Routledge Handbook of the Sociology of Higher Education* (pp. 273–286). London and New York: Routledge.

Zha, Q., Wu, H., & Hayhoe, R. (2019). Why Chinese universities embrace internationalization: an exploration with two case studies. *Higher Education, 78*(4), 669–686. https://doi.org/10.1007/s10734-019-00364-w

Zha, Q., & Yang, Q. (2014). A quiet revolution in Chinese universities: Experimental colleges. *International Higher Education, 77*, 25–27. https://doi.org/10.6017/ihe.2014.77.5685

Zhang, H., Patton, D., & Kenney, M. (2013). Building global-class universities: Assessing the impact of the 985 Project. *Research Policy, 42*(3), 765–775. https://doi.org/10.1016/j.respol.2012.10.003

Zhou, P., Tijssen, R., & Leydesdorff, L. (2016). University-industry collaboration in China and the USA: A bibliometric comparison. *PloS ONE, 11*(11), e0165277. https://doi.org/10.1371/journal.pone.0165277

11
CHALLENGES AND OPPORTUNITIES FOR IMPLEMENTING TRANSDISCIPLINARY CASE STUDY APPROACHES IN POST-SOVIET ACADEMIC SYSTEMS

Experiences from Armenia and Georgia

Tigran Keryan, Andreas Muhar, Tamara Mitrofanenko, Kristine Tanajyan, and Lela Khartishvili

Introduction

Countries of the Caucasus region, like many other post-Soviet countries, still face challenges of decentralizing governance and ensuring participatory processes to support sustainable development. Universities can make an important contribution to sustainable development processes in the Caucasus, thus fostering a balance between ecological and social systems (Clark and Dickson, 2003). Implementation of transdisciplinary approaches is a major way of facilitating collaboration between universities and communities while contributing to the sustainability of a region (Keryan et al., 2020a). Extensive experience exists in universities of Western countries in facilitating co-creation of knowledge and jointly addressing societal problems with actors in other social sectors via transdisciplinary teaching and research (Klein et al., 2001; Balsiger et al., 2017). Yet, few documented attempts exist to implement these approaches in academic systems of post-Soviet countries (Huisman et al., 2018). Integration of transdisciplinary approaches into university practices requires structural adaptations, such as curriculum development, as well as behavioral changes in the teaching and research culture of academic institutions (Fam et al., 2018; Nicolescu, 2018). Continuous and collaborative work among all academic actor groups, including students, teachers, and leadership, is also crucial to establishing transdisciplinarity (TD) at the institutional level (Vienni Baptista and Rojas-Castro, 2019). This chapter focuses on the Republics of Armenia and Georgia, both situated in the South Caucasus region.

In the past, innovations in the academic systems of these countries have usually been implemented via a top-down approach (Karakhanyan, 2011; Charekishvili,

DOI: 10.4324/9781003129424-13

2015). As a result, many efforts to address challenges proved to be less productive because the local mentality and specific geographic and cultural contexts were not considered sufficiently (Karakhanyan et al., 2012; Chakhaia and Bregvadze, 2018). Vilsmaier et al. (2017) highlight the strong influence of power relationships, decision-making traditions, and research ethics on outcomes of transdisciplinary processes. In this regard, cultural features of the region are essential to consider when introducing innovations. Yet, TD is a new concept for academic systems in the South Caucasus region (Keryan et al., 2020a), and collaboration with actors from local communities has not been sufficiently considered in research and teaching strategies. Moreover, vice versa, local communities do not consider universities as potential partners in development processes (Keryan et al., 2020b).

We begin by proposing the integration of transdisciplinary approaches into the academic systems of Armenia and Georgia that could increase universities' involvement in addressing issues relevant to society and contribute to the transformation of problem-oriented institutions. The following research questions, related to those guiding this book, frame our discussion: (1) What are the challenges and opportunities for transdisciplinary approaches implementation in the academic institutions of Armenia and Georgia? (2) How can transdisciplinary teaching and research address societal challenges in Armenia and Georgia? The next section discusses post-Soviet academic systems and the implementation of TD in higher education institutions. Then we describe the methods and materials used in this study, followed by the results and discussion section. The last section presents conclusions and provides recommendations for the successful integration of transdisciplinary approaches in Armenian and Georgian academic institutions.

Academic systems in transition

Armenia and Georgia shared all aspects of the Soviet academic system, including university structure and curricula, as well as an absence of tuition fees and guaranteed employment for all graduates (Smolentseva et al., 2018). However, centrally imposed curricula and teaching methods resulted in a lack of capacity for innovation and development in the educational system, while university education primarily aimed at disseminating socialist political propaganda and providing qualified employees for Soviet industries (Heyneman, 2010). Because industrialization was also a priority of the Soviet Union, the focus was on the development of natural and technical sciences, while social sciences, humanities, and arts received less attention. Universities' main task was teaching, while research was assigned to the National Academies of Sciences (Karakhanyan, 2018). After the collapse of the Soviet Union, universities in Armenia and Georgia became important actors in the development of democratic societies, undergoing processes of internationalization and integration into a globalizing world. With the support of international organizations such as the World Bank, major educational reforms were initiated, including universities' legacy and management (Balasanyan, 2018).

However, the deep-seated Soviet bureaucracy as well as insufficient consideration of culture, beliefs, and values of Armenian and Georgian societies resulted in resistance to reforms (Karakhanyan et al., 2012; Charekishvili, 2015). Lack of experience in planning and management of higher education and sometimes overly hasty implementation of Western academic practices also caused disorientation and loss of capacity (Dobbins and Khachatryan, 2015). As a result, many well-qualified researchers and university professors left the South Caucasus countries for better jobs or prospects of better livelihoods. Chakhaia and Bregvadze (2018) reported that in Georgia during that period, higher education institutions were passive receivers of innovation and few cases of participatory innovation existed. This situation is similar for Armenia. Keryan et al. (2020b) showed that even today universities are not actively involved in educational innovation and policy development processes. After 2000, Armenia and Georgia joined the European Higher Education Area (EHEA), and therefore its core element, structuring curricula according to the "Bologna Process", became obligatory. Because it promotes intergovernmental cooperation between European countries in higher education, the Bologna Process aims at ensuring comparability of curricula and qualifications based on European standards. Using the European Credit Transfer and Accumulation System (ECTS), three cycles of higher education qualifications were adopted in both countries: bachelor's, master's, and doctoral degrees (Huisman, 2019). However, a Soviet mentality persists among academic staff as well as socio-political instability of the region, thwarting the implementation and integration of innovations in both countries.

Studying implementation of transdisciplinarity in academic systems

The role of universities in society has long been a topic of discussion among scientists and practitioners, although the concept of TD has contributed a new dimension (Russell et al., 2008; Scholz, 2020) in the connotation of tackling complex societal issues in a non-reductionist way while reinforcing demands for academia to fulfill its social mission (Hirsch Hadorn et al., 2008). It is defined in multiple ways, although we adopt Klein et al.'s (2001) emphasis on mutual learning between science and society and on the co-production of societally robust knowledge by integrating relevant stakeholders from inside and outside of academia. Fam et al. (2018) also emphasize that TD prompts universities to address real-world problems, integrates abstract and case-specific knowledge, and provides solutions for complex issues. In addition, transdisciplinary teaching provides a new model of social learning for students, teachers, and practitioners (Balsiger et al., 2017). Practical implementation of TD is often initiated via case-based research and teaching (Steiner and Posch, 2006), advancing understanding of real-life problems, and the co-production of societally robust solutions among different actors (Scholz and Tietje, 2002). Augsburg (2014) further emphasizes that the success of transdisciplinary implementation depends on individual researcher's personal characteristics such as attitude, creativity, intellectual capacities, ethics, and ability to accept different realities. Integrating transdisciplinary approaches sustainably into an academic system requires considering the internal structure, the culture of research and teaching, and the mentality of teachers and students. Klein et al. (2001) also emphasize the academic culture of collaboration between different disciplines when institutionalizing interdisciplinarity and TD, while Vienni Baptista and Rojas-Castro (2019) state successful institutionalization requires integrating transdisciplinary approaches into both university activities and the policy level.

Clearly, the literature cited earlier addresses multiple and varied aspects relevant for the implementation of TD in an academic system, from the role of the individual researcher to the university system as a whole. Given their historic development and the current transition process, we use a dimension analysis proposed by Keryan et al. (2020b), in order to examine current challenges and future potentials of integrating TD into post-Soviet academic systems. The scheme comprises four fundamental aspects depicted in Figure 11.1:

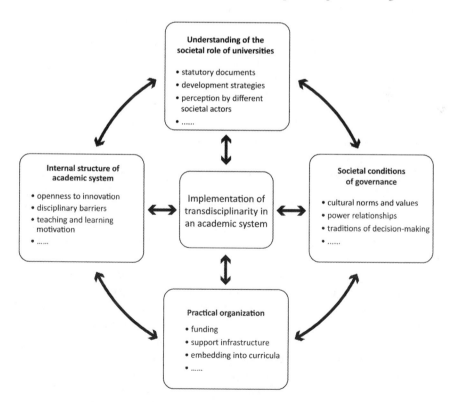

FIGURE 11.1 Dimensions for investigating the implementation of transdisciplinarity into academic systems. Source: Keryan et al. (2020b).

(1) understanding the societal role of universities including perceptions of different actors from academia and society; (2) the internal structure of the academic system encompassing innovation capacities and openness to crossing disciplinary barriers; (3) practical organization of TD considering funding opportunities, supporting infrastructure, and integrating transdisciplinary approaches into curricula; and (4) societal conditions of governance including all kinds of actions and processes influencing the governance of the academic system in view of case-specific cultural norms and values.

Materials and methods

The context of this study was a project named "Transdisciplinarity for Sustainable Tourism Development in the Caucasus Region (CaucaSusT)", funded by the Austrian Partnership Programme in Higher Education and Research for Development (APPEAR). Between 2015 and 2020, project partners from Austria (BOKU University Vienna, IMC Krems), Armenia (Armenian State Pedagogical University, ASPU), and Georgia (Tbilisi State University, TSU) jointly planned and integrated transdisciplinary approaches into university curricula of ASPU and TSU, as well as developed and implemented transdisciplinary case study courses. A CaucaSusT team introduced a case study format based on Scholz and Tietje (2002) in four different regions of the South Caucasus: two in Armenia and two in Georgia. In addition, preparatory activities including seminars and workshops in ASPU and TSU also aimed at training teachers and involving students in transdisciplinary activities. The preparatory phase included: selecting case areas, establishing cooperation with local stakeholders, conducting needs analysis, and arranging a working space in the case study regions.

To elaborate, during each case study course, 24–25 students were placed in groups of four to five based on different disciplinary backgrounds and facilitated by one to two university teachers. Working together, project partners, teachers, and students co-designed the research steps and timeline, based on the availability and interest of local stakeholders. During field studies, university teachers and students from different disciplines (e.g., geography, landscape planning, cultural studies, economics, and sociology) also worked with local community members to address local sustainability-related challenges.

The findings presented in this chapter are based on data from multiple research methods including the analysis of scientific and legal documents, discussions with project partners, and participant observations during project events on the experience of co-developing, integrating, and implementing transdisciplinary case study courses with colleagues in Armenia and Georgia. At the end of each case study, we conducted semi-structured individual interviews and focus groups on implementation with students, teachers, and stakeholders in order to evaluate results and adapt courses accordingly. In addition, we distributed anonymous questionnaires (Flick, 2014). In total, 81 students, 22 teachers, and 40 local stakeholders participated, as well as 41 experts from the field of education and sustainable development. Interviews were conducted in three languages: English, Armenian, and Georgian, recorded and literally transcribed then qualitative content analysis was based on breaking text into different segments based on similarities/contiguity (Maxwell and Chmiel, 2014). Theoretical categories, in turn, were derived through inductively generated open coding of the data. And, finally, codes were explicitly placed into the four dimensions of Figure 11.1 (societal role of universities, internal structure of academic system, practical organization of TD, and societal conditions of governance).

Results

Our findings encompass the four interrelated dimensions, including within each one, obstacles to transdisciplinary approach implementation in Armenia and Georgia as well as recommendations for how transdisciplinary teaching and research can address societal challenges in both countries.

Understanding the societal role of universities

One of the main factors influencing understanding the societal role of universities is the perceived responsibility of academia toward society (Keryan et al., 2020b). Our research participants from and outside academia in both countries perceived this responsibility as an ability of universities to solve local, regional, and national problems. However, they saw a lack of social responsibility at both institutional and individual levels reflected in missing competencies of graduates, lack of motivation among university staff, and detachment of research conducted at universities from real-life problems. Although some lecturers cooperate with stakeholders outside universities, academics are generally not perceived as useful contributors to solving societal issues. As a result, universities are not considered centers of innovation and knowledge creation. Hence, they are not sufficiently involved in the design and implementation of national development policies and strategies, such as educational law in the case of Armenia, leading to diminished trust and hindering the establishment of collaboration between universities and actors in society (Keryan et al., 2020a). Interviewees from university leadership also mentioned that during the Soviet period, top-down orders from the government determined cooperation between universities and practitioners. Even today, universities are still not accustomed to initiating cooperation, especially when financial incentives are unclear. Even though local communities are willing to cooperate with universities, they also do not have the resources and budget to cover associated costs.

Our findings about CaucaSusT experience in implementing transdisciplinary approaches indicate that the involvement of lecturers and students in case study activities positively contributes to the societal role of universities. Specifically, university staff and students recognize they could help address challenges of a particular case faced by a community, and they feel motivated to contribute their knowledge and time in order to provide useful inputs. Local stakeholders, in turn, are beginning to view universities as potential collaborators and experts when research questions of case studies are created in close cooperation with local stakeholders based on their needs. These factors contribute to understanding local real-world problems among participating teachers and students while increasing their inclination to be engaged in societally relevant research. Participatory discussion formats and positioning of local stakeholders as knowledgeable case experts, as well as careful consideration of local power relations and customs, also contribute to building trust across boundaries of the academy and communities. As mentioned by most residents during the interviews, previous interactions with academics were based on a top-down approach such as academics as experts and local practical knowledge was not sufficiently considered. Yet even though a course format may be helpful for motivating the participation of some stakeholders, who are glad to support students' learning, it may also cause initial skepticism about the potential benefits of collaboration with university students for the community, confirmed in our interviews with local stakeholders.

Internal structure of academic system

Despite innovative efforts, top-down approaches to decision-making still prevail in the academic systems of Armenia and Georgia. Strict hierarchical relationships among university leadership and teachers as well as among teachers and students are still common. Students, in particular, are accustomed to following predefined tasks and not arguing with professors or questioning their teaching. Our interviews with early-career university teachers and educational experts also showed that superiors who often occupy decision-making positions, such as department heads, sometimes prevent lecturers from introducing innovative teaching and research approaches, thereby constraining their career growth and prospects for TD. Almost all interviewed teachers and educational experts mentioned that changes in study curricula are often artificially implemented without considering the special needs of the two countries. Moreover, changes often do not take into account professional competencies of teachers or provide resources for training. At the same time, inflexible bureaucracy impedes establishing formal cooperation among departments and with stakeholders outside of academia, necessary for official implementation and recognition of a transdisciplinary course.

In contrast to the Soviet regime, when the higher education system was fully state-funded, university budgets are also dependent on students' tuition fees. Thus, institutions are encouraged to accept more students regardless of their competencies and interests, negatively influencing academic progress at the institutional level. Low salaries of lecturers and researchers are also discouraging highly qualified professionals from academic careers. The average monthly salary of a full-time teacher in public universities of Armenia and Georgia is only between 300 and 500 euros so academics have to take on additional work, reducing time for preparing lectures and conducting research. Some staff try to be involved in grant projects, providing additional income as well as funds for travel and equipment. During the Soviet period, field studies within a country or abroad were embedded as a compulsory part of the curricula. As a result, universities were equipped with supporting infrastructure, including summer base camps in different regions of the country. After the collapse of the Soviet Union, field research was limited to the boundaries of each state, and in recent years has been discontinued in order to decrease expenses even in geography, where fieldwork is necessary.

Even so, our experience and findings demonstrate transdisciplinary case study courses increase students' and lecturers' motivation for both teaching and learning. Department heads also play a crucial role. Receiving additional funds and collaboration with international academics help convince the academic leadership to adopt new approaches and provide opportunities for innovative research. Adaptation of curricula can also be done in stages, based on local policies, in order to bypass bureaucratic delays. Our partners, for example, modified existing courses.

For their part, students appreciate working with real-life cases instead of attending passive lectures. One Georgian student's feedback in an anonymous evaluation form from 2019 is consistent with opinions expressed by other students: "During these two weeks, I learned more than during a semester". Working in multidisciplinary groups with teachers from different disciplines expands students' knowledge and broadens their outlooks through collaborative learning. Transdisciplinary case-based research in particular provides students with freedom and opportunity to formulate their own research questions as well while identifying possible solutions for specific problems. Yet, the limited experience of both lecturers and students with participatory and interdisciplinary approaches remains challenging for conducting successful transdisciplinary case study courses. Nonetheless, even when newly introduced, this format supports establishing inter- and trans-disciplinary cooperation that leads to mutual learning, joint research and teaching, joint student supervision, and cooperation on study material development among the lecturers. Collaborative activities during transdisciplinary case study research, such as working in small groups, field trips, and joint lunches, contribute to overcoming power relationships between teachers and students. Yet, a number of practical considerations arise.

Practical organization

Lack of funds constitutes a key challenge for implementing a transdisciplinary field course. Cumbersome bureaucracy in both Armenian and Georgian public universities, as successors of the Soviet education system where the majority of students are concentrated, can impede practical organization of fieldwork, even when funds are available. Time and effort required from students and lecturers for preparing and conducting transdisciplinary research and teaching constitute yet another challenge. Ensuring the availability of all students and lecturers for the entire duration of a two-week field course can be a demanding task. It requires considering university and individual schedules and obligations, as well as societal norms and conditions such as availability of appropriate accommodation for female and male students, and possibilities for lecturers to bring their children in case they cannot arrange care. And, to reiterate, practical implementation is exacerbated by a lack of teachers' and students' overall experience in conducting field research, along with addressing organizational tasks, coordinating students' group work, planning meetings, and conducting interviews with stakeholders.

Our experience showed that some obstacles of practical organization, especially those related to lack of experience, can be addressed via cooperation with more experienced partners or lecturers, building on their accumulated wisdom of practice. Applying for and receiving external funds also proved useful for increasing teachers' motivation and covering associated costs of extended fieldwork. Teachers who participated in the interviews further mentioned that facing real-world challenges during the implementation of transdisciplinary case study courses fostered critical reflection on the relevance of materials and methods they used. As a result of these reflections, they adjusted curricula, degree work, and master theses strongly linked with real-life problems. In addition, social media platforms such as Facebook, which publicized course progress, further increased students' motivation in Armenia and Georgia. Moreover, mass media coverage of transdisciplinary courses, which can be arranged by alerting local or national media as well as local community partners, led to a greater appreciation by the general public, while increasing support by the university leadership and encouraging the integration of transdisciplinary approaches at the institutional level. Arranging for students to spend a longer time, such as part of or an entire day with local stakeholders and helping them with daily duties, proved to be useful as well, fostering a better understanding of local traditions, customs, and challenges that are key to establishing mutual trust and co-creating relevant solutions.

Societal conditions of governance

Interview results reveal that political instability in Armenia and Georgia has often led to governmental change. Rapid shifts of political leaders and decision-makers on national and subnational levels bring new agendas and strategies, but without sufficient discussions with all relevant stakeholders including academia, practice, and the general public. This process is a formidable challenge to participatory governance, as well as long-term sustainable cooperation between universities and decision-making bodies. Moreover, lack of transparency and awareness about decision-making processes causes misunderstanding and prevents stakeholders, including universities, from participating in governance processes. Engaging in transdisciplinary research, focused on understanding and solving certain societal challenges, while also using systems thinking and producing transformation knowledge, inevitably leads to questions of governance, whether on the local level or beyond. In the CaucaSusT case, close collaboration with relevant stakeholders and the university's neutral position as an "external" actor reveal power relations and gaps in decision-making while enabling a university team to offer advice to stakeholders. However, many teachers found it challenging to shift their roles from experts transferring academic knowledge to partners and collaborators while engaging in the co-production of knowledge with the local population.

Our analysis of the data from interviews and participant observations revealed that cultural barriers prevented case study community members from speaking out about local problems. These barriers could be overcome through collaboration with participating students and teachers, evident in findings from interviews and focus groups that were organized mindful of power relations among participants. In this regard, ASPU and TSU universities play a bridging role between decision-makers and the general public, as members of a case study community, by helping to clear misunderstandings and close communication gaps. Here too, a transdisciplinary case study course provides opportunities for more informal discussions and stakeholder meetings, helping to overcome certain barriers to decision-making. Consistent with findings in the larger literature on TD, in the long-term, more intense involvement of universities in addressing societal problems, including establishing communication and collaboration with decision-makers as relevant stakeholders, further enhances universities' role in contributing useful knowledge for informed decision-making. Finally, a better understanding of power relations and participatory governance is crucial to rendering university graduates more active members of civil society.

Discussion

While interdisciplinarity and transdisciplinarity have relatively long traditions in Western academic institutions, they are still rather new in Armenia and Georgia. Thus, while integrating TD into academic culture, international experience should be adapted to local specificities to avoid resistance to change and negative perceptions about a new concept (Karakhanyan et al., 2012; Charekishvili, 2015; Balasanyan, 2018; Huisman et al., 2018). Furthermore, local needs and interests need to be acknowledged. TD discourse can shape university departments or even entire development strategies of some European institutions (Vienni Baptista et al., 2020). However, in Armenia and Georgia, our findings indicate it should first be implemented at a project or a course level. Only later can it be expanded to a wider discourse. Many authors suggest that the most common way to sustainably integrate TD in an academic system is to establish strong cooperation across disciplines at an initial stage of introducing it, gradually intensifying the collaboration with stakeholders outside academia (Klein et al., 2001; Hirsch Hadorn et al., 2008). However, in our experience, external interventions such as transdisciplinary project implementation initiated interdisciplinary cooperation for both universities. Although the departments of the Armenian State Pedagogical University and Tbilisi State University share an interdisciplinary nature, little cooperation across disciplines has been undertaken in practice before the CaucaSusT project. Teachers found common benefits from cooperating on jointly producing teaching materials and addressing sustainability challenges of local communities.

However, the existing research and teaching culture coupled with skepticism among the general public about the role of academia have made progress challenging. Consistent with Balsiger et al. (2017) and Barth et al. (2019), our results affirmed that transdisciplinary case study courses increase students' and teachers' motivations for learning and teaching while inclining research activities more toward societal interests and needs. TD-related knowledge and skills, such as systems analysis, scenario development, and local knowledge integration, students gain during case study activities are also vital for providing solutions to real-life problems (Wiek et al., 2011; Pohl et al., 2017). Yet, overcoming traditional hierarchical relationships among teachers and students in Armenia and Georgia requires a longer time, in addition to the systematic application of student-centered approaches and explicit reflection on interactions between students and lecturers. Echoing Vilsmaier et al. (2017), a strong focus on discipline-oriented research and teaching traditions is an added obstacle. Lack of research on real-life challenges in Armenian and Georgian universities limits capacity for innovation and responses to complex sustainability problems (impediments echoed in Klein et al., 2001; Steiner and Posch, 2006; Hirsch Hadorn et al., 2008; Lang et al., 2012; Radinger-Peer and Pflitsch, 2017). Taken together, challenges render university involvement in transdisciplinary research activities difficult (Klein, 2004; Scholz, 2020). Bammer et al. (2020) state that long-term institutional support is crucial to accumulating sufficient knowledge and expertise for addressing complex sustainability problems. Our results also show transdisciplinary case study research increases responsibility at both individual level and institutional levels, supporting the perception of universities as contributors to sustainable development (Augsburg, 2014; Mochizuki and Yarime, 2016; Balsiger et al., 2017).

In further keeping with the authors of previous studies (Lang et al., 2012; Nicolescu, 2018; Scholz, 2020), our results show that lack of trust toward academia is a barrier to initiating transdisciplinary collaborations. At the same time, however, integration of transdisciplinary approaches into teaching and research activities contributes to overcoming deficits of trust while fostering mutual learning and joint problem-solving among scientists and the general public (Klein, 2004; Muhar et al., 2006; Hirsch Hadorn et al., 2008). ASPU and TSU established new transdisciplinary courses and adapted existing curricula by making them more society oriented. Even so, Barnett et al. (2001) argued this strategy is insufficient for transformative curricula development, which requires interrelated patterns including knowledge, action, and self (p. 438). The authors also emphasized that the curriculum development process should receive greater attention and discussion at the institutional level. In academic systems of post-Soviet countries, it is common to have discussions at the departmental level (Huisman et al., 2018). Deeper transformation in partner universities, with respect to both curriculum development and university governance, will take more time and effort. Like Bergmann et al. (2021), we also find that long-term involvement in a particular region is important. However, sufficient integration of transdisciplinary approaches at all levels usually cannot be achieved within the context of a sole project (Nicolescu, 2018; Barth et al., 2019; Vienni Baptista et al., 2020). Continuous work, enthusiasm, and long-term collaboration with all relevant stakeholders within and outside universities, as well as additional resources, are required to sufficiently integrate transdisciplinary approaches into the academic culture of the Caucasus countries.

Conclusions and recommendations

While noting correspondences between our findings and other case studies and analyses in literature, we acknowledge several limitations to our study. We based our results on collaborations with two Caucasus universities, one in Armenia and one in Georgia. Four of the implemented transdisciplinary case studies also focused on sustainable tourism development in rural communities. Changing the case study format, or focusing on urban areas, might have revealed additional challenges or recommendations. However, comparability of results between Armenia and Georgia and among individual case studies, combined with discussions with experts, affirmed the results are applicable to the Armenian and Georgian academic systems. Moreover, many post-Soviet countries today face similar challenges (Huisman et al., 2018; Smolentseva et al., 2018; Chankseliani et al., 2021).

To conclude, the integration of inter- and trans-disciplinary approaches into the academic systems of Armenia and Georgia can contribute to the sustainable development of the Caucasus region. Figure 11.1 provides a suitable structure for identifying the potentials of transdisciplinary research and teaching integration in post-Soviet countries as a way of contributing to the complex societal problem-solving process. TD brings a new culture of collaboration between academia and society for Armenia and Georgia, and case-based research provided a useful way to integrate it into both universities. The top-down approach, common in the Soviet Union, influenced many academics and university administrations as they expect innovations to come from the government and do not feel comfortable taking the initiative. On the other hand, lack of educational management experience causes problems at the policy level, leaving universities without support for initiating and adapting innovations.

A bottom-up approach can help overcome these challenges, but it requires longer-term, collaborative projects with sufficient funding and support from government and university leadership as well as cooperation with Western peers. Teachers' encouragement to conduct transdisciplinary research and link studies with social problems drive them to become local actors in the field of sustainability, initiating integration of TD in local contexts. Based on results and lessons learned, several features are particularly vital for the successful implementation of transdisciplinary approaches. In closing, we present general recommendations for achieving better outcomes for transdisciplinary case study research in Caucasus countries:

- Organizing non-formal meetings and gatherings before and during case studies can help overcome hierarchical relationships common to many post-Soviet countries, not only between students and lecturers but also representatives of the university and local community members.
- Personal contacts and networks with active stakeholders, including practitioners as well as community members and local non-governmental organizations (NGOs), need to be established and can help build trust with case study community members.
- Engaging local youth in research activities can help gain an in-depth understanding of societal issues, capitalizing on the openness of youth to cooperate and the free sharing of existing problems that confront both students and teachers.
- At the initial stage, stakeholders need to know whether financial resources are available since some might expect them based on previous experience with NGOs or international organizations. Explaining how they could benefit from cooperation with the university is also important.
- In Caucasus countries, gathering and sharing food is an important part of the culture, which contributes to the trust-building process between universities and stakeholders. In most communities, hospitality and offerings of food and drinks should be accepted without suggesting money.
- Results of transdisciplinary research should be presented to participating stakeholders, and problems that were identified should be brought to the attention of responsible institutions and authorities.

We encourage the scientific community to engage with more cases in Armenia and Georgia, as well as in other countries in the Caucasus region, to deepen our understanding of challenges and opportunities for implementing transdisciplinary in post-Soviet academic systems.

References

Augsburg, T. (2014) 'Becoming transdisciplinary: The emergence of the transdisciplinary individual', *World Futures*, 70(3–4), pp.233–247.

Balasanyan, S. (2018) 'From pedagogy to quality: The Europeanised experience of higher education in post-Soviet Armenia', *European Educational Research Journal*, 17(4), pp.584–601.

Balsiger, J., Förster, R., Mader, C., Nagel, U., Sironi, H., Wilhelm, S. and Zimmermann, A.B. (2017) 'Transformative learning and education for sustainable development', *GAIA-Ecological Perspectives for Science and Society*, 26(4), pp.357–359.

Bammer, G., O'Rourke, M., O'Connell, D., Neuhauser, L., Midgley, G., Klein, J.T., … Richardson, G.P. (2020) 'Expertise in research integration and implementation for tackling complex problems: When is it needed, where can it be found and how can it be strengthened?', *Palgrave Communications*, 6(1), pp.1–16.

Barnett, R., Parry, G. and Coate, K. (2001) 'Conceptualising curriculum change', *Teaching in Higher Education*, 6(4), pp.435–449.

Barth, M., Lang, D.J. and Michelsen, G. (2019) 'Transdisciplinary learning to foster sustainable development: Institutionalizing co-engaged South-North collaboration', *GAIA-Ecological Perspectives for Science and Society*, 28(4), pp.382–385.

Bergmann, M., Schäpke, N., Marg, O., Stelzer, F., Lang, D.J., Bossert, M., … Sußmann, N. (2021) 'Transdisciplinary sustainability research in real-world labs: Success factors and methods for change', *Sustainability Science*, 16(2), pp.541–564.

Chakhaia, L. and Bregvadze, T. (2018) 'Georgia: Higher education system dynamics and institutional diversity', in *25 Years of Transformations of Higher Education Systems in Post-Soviet Countries*, J. Huisman, A. Smolentseva, and I. Froumin, (eds.) pp.175–197. Cham: Palgrave Macmillan.

Chankseliani, M., Qoraboyev, I. and Gimranova, D. (2021) 'Higher education contributing to local, national, and global development: New empirical and conceptual insights', *Higher Education*, 81(1), pp.109–127.

Charekishvili, L. (2015) 'Higher education system in Georgia: Reforms and modern challenges', in *Proceedings of Teaching and Education Conferences* (No. 2403787). Prague: International Institute of Social and Economic Sciences.

Clark, W.C. and Dickson, N.M. (2003) 'Sustainability science: The emerging research program', *Proceedings of the National Academy of Sciences*, 100(14), pp.8059–8061.

Dobbins, M. and Khachatryan, S. (2015) 'Europeanization in the "Wild East"? Analyzing higher education governance reform in Georgia and Armenia', *Higher Education*, 69(2), pp.189–207.

Fam, D.M., Neuhauser, L. and Gibbs, P., eds. (2018) *The Art of Collaborative Research and Collective Learning: Transdisciplinary Theory, Practice and Education*. Dorschet: Springer.

Flick, U., ed. (2014) *The SAGE Handbook of Qualitative Data Analysis*. London: Sage Publications.

Heyneman, S.P. (2010) 'A comment on the changes in higher education in the former Soviet Union', *European Education*, 42(1), pp.76–87.

Hirsch Hadorn, G., Hoffmann-Riem, H., Biber-Klemm, S., Grossenbacher-Mansuy, W., Joye, D., Pohl, C., Wiesmann, U. and Zemp, E., eds. (2008) *Handbook of Transdisciplinary Research*, Vol. 10, Dordrecht: Springer.

Huisman, J. (2019) 'The Bologna process in European and post-Soviet higher education: Institutional legacies and policy adoption', *Innovation: The European Journal of Social Science Research*, 32(4), pp.465–480.

Huisman, J., Smolentseva, A. and Froumin, I., eds. (2018) *25 Years of Transformations of Higher Education Systems in Post-Soviet Countries*. Cham: Palgrave Macmillan.

Karakhanyan, S. (2011) *Reforming Higher Education in a Post-Soviet Context: The Case of Armenia*, Ph.D. Thesis. Radboud Universiteit, Nijmegen, The Netherlands, 13 July 2011.

Karakhanyan, S. (2018) 'Armenia: Transformational peculiarities of the Soviet and post-Soviet higher education system', in *25 Years of Transformations of Higher Education Systems in Post-Soviet Countries*, J. Huisman, A. Smolentseva, and I. Froumin pp.73–96. Cham: Palgrave Macmillan.

Karakhanyan, S.Y., van Veen, K. and Bergen, T.C. (2012) 'What do leaders think? Reflections on the implementation of higher education reforms in Armenia', *Educational Management Administration & Leadership*, 40(6), pp.752–771.

Keryan, T., Mitrofanenko, T., Muhar, A. and Khartishvili, L. (2020a) 'UNESCO's education for sustainable development framework and the reality of university-community cooperation in the Caucasus mountain region', *Mountain Research and Development*, 40(4), pp.D1–D9.

Keryan, T., Muhar, A., Mitrofanenko, T., Khoetsyan, A. and Radinger-Peer, V. (2020b) 'Towards implementing transdisciplinarity in post-Soviet academic systems: An investigation of the societal role of universities in Armenia', *Sustainability*, 12(20), p.8721.

Klein, J.T. (2004) 'Prospects for transdisciplinarity', *Futures*, 36(4), pp.515–526.

Klein, J.T., Grossenbacher-Mansuy, W., Häberli, R., Bill, A., Scholz, R.W. and Welti, M., eds. (2001) *Transdisciplinarity: Joint Problem Solving among Science, Technology, and Society: An Effective Way for Managing Complexity*. Basel: Birkhäuser Verlag.

Lang, D.J., Wiek, A., Bergmann, M., Stauffacher, M., Martens, P., Moll, P., Swilling, M. and Thomas, C.J. (2012) 'Transdisciplinary research in sustainability science: Practice, principles, and challenges', *Sustainability Science*, 7(1), pp.25–43.

Maxwell, J.A., and Chmiel, M. (2014) 'Notes toward a theory of qualitative data analysis', in Flick, U., ed., *The SAGE Handbook of Qualitative Data Analysis*, pp.21–34. London: SAGE Publications.

Mochizuki, Y., and Yarime, M. (2016) 'Education for sustainable development and sustainability science: re-purposing higher education and research', in *Routledge handbook of higher education for sustainable development*, M. Barth, G. Michelsen, M. Rieckmann, and I. Thomas (eds) pp.11–24. London, New York: Routledge.

Muhar, A., Vilsmaier, U., Glanzer, M. and Freyer, B. (2006) 'Initiating transdisciplinarity in academic case study teaching: Experiences from a regional development project in Salzburg, Austria', *International Journal of Sustainability in Higher Education*, 7(3), pp.293–308.

Nicolescu, B. (2018) 'The transdisciplinary evolution of the university condition for sustainable development', in *Transdisciplinary Theory, Practice and Education*, D. Fam, L. Neuhauser, and P. Gibbs, pp.73–81. Cham: Springer.

Pohl, C., Krütli, P. and Stauffacher, M. (2017) 'Ten reflective steps for rendering research societally relevant', *GAIA-Ecological Perspectives for Science and Society*, 26(1), pp.43–51.

Radinger-Peer, V. and Pflitsch, G. (2017) 'The role of higher education institutions in regional transition paths towards sustainability', *Review of Regional Research*, 37(2), pp.161–187.

Russell, A.W., Wickson, F. and Carew, A.L. (2008) 'Transdisciplinarity: Context, contradictions and capacity', *Futures*, 40(5), pp.460–472.

Scholz, R.W. (2020) 'Transdisciplinarity: Science for and with society in light of the university's roles and functions', *Sustainability Science*, 15, pp.1033–1049.

Scholz, R.W. and Tietje, O. (2002) *Embedded Case Study Methods: Integrating Quantitative and Qualitative Knowledge*. Thousand Oaks: Sage Publications.

Smolentseva, A., Huisman, J. and Froumin, I. (2018) 'Transformation of higher education institutional landscape in ost-Soviet countries: From Soviet model to where?', in *25 Years of Transformations of Higher Education Systems in Post-Soviet Countries*, J. Huisman, A. Smolentseva, and I. Froumin, pp.1–43. Cham: Palgrave Macmillan.

Steiner, G. and Posch, A. (2006) 'Higher education for sustainability by means of transdisciplinary case studies: An innovative approach for solving complex, real-world problems', *Journal of Cleaner Production*, 14(9–11), pp.877–890.
Vienni Baptista, B., Maryl, M., Wciślik, P., Fletcher, I., Buchner, A., and Pohl, C. (2020). "Final report on Understandings of Interdisciplinary and Transdisciplinary Research and Factors of Success or Failure". Shaping Interdisciplinary practices in Europe. https://doi.org/10.5281/zenodo.3760417
Vienni Baptista, B. and Rojas-Castro, S. (2019) 'Transdisciplinary institutionalization in higher education: A two-level analysis', *Studies in Higher Education*, 45(6), pp.1075–1092.
Vilsmaier, U., Brandner, V. and Engbers, M. (2017) 'Research in-between: The constitutive role of cultural differences in transdisciplinarity', *Transdisciplinary Journal of Engineering & Science*, 8(1), pp.169–179.
Wiek, A., Withycombe, L. and Redman, C.L. (2011) 'Key competencies in sustainability: A reference framework for academic program development', *Sustainability Science*, 6(2), pp.203–218.

12
RESEARCH INSTITUTE FOR HUMANITY AND NATURE

A Japanese center for inter- and trans-disciplinary consilience of socio-cultural dimensions of environmental sustainability

Yasuhisa Kondo, Terukazu Kumazawa, Naoki Kikuchi, Kaoru Kamatani, Satoe Nakahara, Natsuko Yasutomi, Yuta Uchiyama, Kengo Hayashi, Satoko Hashimoto, Akihiro Miyata, and Shin Muramatsu

Introduction

Research Institute for Humanity and Nature (RIHN) is a Japanese national inter-university research institute that conducts advanced collaborative research for socio-cultural dimensions of environmental sustainability. The current mission and structure of RIHN appear in the Institute's formal description:

> RIHN research starts from the premise that environmental problems are rooted in human society, culture, and values. The goal of RIHN is to seek concepts, theories, and mechanisms capable of describing and enabling transformation of human-environment interactions. This implies that RIHN research involves a normative dimension, driven by questions such as what the relationship between humanity and nature ought to be like. To this end, RIHN solicits, funds, and hosts integrative research projects investigating environmental change problems in specific settings. Research projects are undertaken by interdisciplinary teams at RIHN, partner institutions, and societal stakeholders in Japan and abroad.
>
> *(RIHN, 2020, p. 4)*

The authors have participated in RIHN's interdisciplinary projects, situated in a unique research environment that has been changing over time. To identify how intellectual developments occurred at individual and project levels with respect to institutional characteristics and their changes, we conducted meta-research investigations at RIHN. This chapter presents the framework and findings of

DOI: 10.4324/9781003129424-14

our meta-research, which are relevant to the guiding questions of this book in several ways. The next section presents our methodological framework for meta-research on projects and their rationales. It sorts discourses extracted from semi-structured interviews with project leaders (PLs, equal to principal investigators) and active members by key factors in terms of intellectual developments. Then, in light of the findings, we discuss how institutional changes are shaped at RIHN and how individual projects and researchers respond to those changes. The chapter concludes with some remarks on institutional possibilities and limitations in promoting inter- and trans-disciplinary research and education in Japan, particularly for socio-ecological synthesis toward environmental sustainability in historical and geographical contexts.

The stage-gate project development system

Collaborative research at RIHN is characterized by the stage-gate project development system depicted in Figure 12.1. It comprises sequentially an incubation study (IS), feasibility study (FS), pre-research (PR), and full research (FR). IS proposals are open for university faculty members or other relevant researchers. A Project Review Taskforce (PRT) composed of in-house executives then screened both IS and FS proposals, followed by an External Research Evaluation Committee (EREC). Formerly called the Project Evaluation Committee, or PEC, the EREC consists of distinguished experts from Japan and abroad. Currently, one or two projects are elected for FR per year. The FR-elect PL moves to RIHN during the PR stage.

A typical FR project lasts five years and involves 30 to 150 project members (RIHN IR Unit, unpublished source) with a balance of social and natural scientists, including several in-house members (a project leader, postdoctoral researchers, research associates, and assistants). The current annual budget for an FR project is 50 million Japanese yen, approximately 440,000 US dollars or 388,000 euros. FR projects undergo both mid-term and final evaluations by EREC. Thus far, 35 have been completed, and seven others are ongoing. These projects mainly focused on, but were not limited to, socio-cultural dimensions of local environmental problems, mainly in Asia, including Japan, and in Africa.

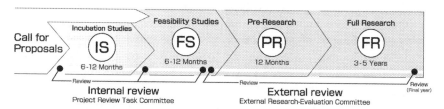

FIGURE 12.1   Ideal timeline of a research project of the Research Institute for Humanity and Nature. Source: RIHN (2020, p. 8).

The ongoing projects report and share their updates with Institute colleagues at annual general meetings. In 2020, approximately 65 in-house research staff members were working at the Institute, in collaboration with more than 700 external affiliates indicated by fields and institutions in Figure 12.2.

Institutional changes over time

RIHN is one of the oldest socio-ecological synthesis centers worldwide, although this aspect is often overlooked (e.g., Specht, 2017). It was established in April 2001 under the auspices of the Ministry of Education, Culture, Sports, Science and Technology (MEXT or *Monkashō*) that was also established in January 2001 by merging the Ministry of Education, Science, Sports and Culture, in charge of higher education and pure sciences, and the Science and Technology Agency. In parallel with this administrative reform, RIHN responded to the need for a new national center to conduct a synthetic approach to complex socio-ecological problems that cannot be solved by single disciplines or laboratories and joined the National Institutes for the Humanities (NIHU) in 2004. Since that time, the medium-term plan has been revised every six years, moving from Phase I from 2004 to 2010, then Phase II from 2010 to 2016, and recently Phase III from 2016 to 2022. In 2003, research projects were classified under five "research axes": (1) environmental change impact assessment; (2) human activity impact assessment; (3) spatial scale; (4) history and time scale; and (5) conceptual framework for global environmental issues (RIHN, 2006). In 2007, the axes were then reorganized into five "research domains": (1) circulation; (2) diversity; (3) resources; (4) ecohistory; and (5) ecosophy. At the beginning of Medium Term Phase II in 2010, the Core Research Hub was established to develop cross-cutting projects based on the concept of "design science" (RIHN, 2012). This system was reorganized at the beginning of Phase III in 2016 to promote transdisciplinarity in the declining of the budget for FR projects (Figure 12.3), and ongoing projects were reclassified to three research programs covering (1) environmental changes and society, (2) fair use of resources, and (3) well-being and lifestyles (RIHN, 2016, p. 7).

Framework for meta-research

In order to address complex socio-ecological problems, RIHN promotes solution-oriented intellectual syntheses and collaborations with research experts. It also collaborates with practitioners such as governments, funders, industries, non-profit organizations, and civil members for transdisciplinary research (TDR), particularly in Medium Term Phase III and later (Mauser et al., 2013; Klein, 2014; OECD, 2020). Table 12.1 depicts differences in interdisciplinary research (IDR) and TDR processes, outcomes, and perceptions (European Commission, 2015). IDR is primarily situated in academia, where experts from different areas collaborate to identify problems and work toward consensus on

Research Institute for Humanity and Nature **171**

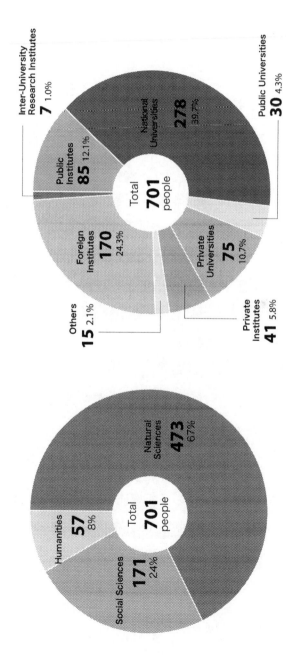

FIGURE 12.2 External affiliates of Research Institute for Humanity and Nature in March 2020. Source: RIHN (2020, p. 49).

172 Yasuhisa Kondo et al.

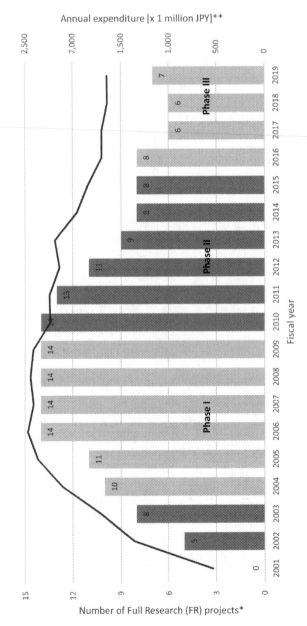

FIGURE 12.3 Number of full research (FR) projects per year (bars) and the gross annual expenditure of Research Institute for Humanity and Nature (broken curves). Source: *RIHN prospectus booklets (www.chikyu.ac.jp/publicity/publications/brochure/); **NIHU financial statements (www.nihu.jp/ja/opendoor/h-zaimu).

TABLE 12.1 Major characteristics of inter- and trans-disciplinary research

Viewpoint		Interdisciplinary research (IDR) (Repko and Szostak, 2020)	Transdisciplinary research (TDR) (Mauser et al., 2013; OECD, 2020)
Process	Problems are identified by …	experts from different research areas	multi-actors: research experts, practitioners, and stakeholders (co-design of research agenda)
	Knowledge is produced by …	experts from different research areas	multi-actors (co-production of knowledge)
	Outcome reaches	experts from different research areas	multi-actors (co-dissemination of results)
	Methods are …	often cutting edge	**socially restricted**
Out-come	**Solution is …**	**to obtain a consent**	to obtain multidimensional consents, and then **dissolve the problem**
Perception	Boundaries	remain?	spanned and dissolved?
	Mindsets are …	hardly transformed?	expected to be transformed

a solution. Outcomes are then disseminated to peer academic researchers. Since IDR explores in-between spaces between established research areas (Vilsmaier et al., 2017), applied research methods are often cutting edge. In contrast, the TDR process is open to society, so characterized by co-design of a research agenda, co-production of knowledge, and co-dissemination (or co-delivery) of results with diverse societal actors, including research experts and practitioners (Mauser et al., 2013). Therefore, problems and solutions may be multidimensional, and methods may be socially limited (Kondo et al., 2021).

Changes in perceptions of socio-psychological boundaries and mindsets, including values and thoughts through participating in IDR and TDR projects, remain a matter of scientific inquiry while being an essential factor of intellectual development. TDR theories assume that socio-psychological boundaries between actors will be spanned and even dissolved through co-creative research; furthermore, values and thoughts must be transformed through mutual learning (e.g., Burger and Kamber, 2003; Gray 2008; Lang et al., 2012). However, our experience indicates that boundaries between research areas remain, and individual research mindsets are not readily transformed. The firmness of socio-psychological boundaries and mindsets leads to individual mental resistance to external or institutional changes as well as disciplinary worldviews.

The consilience hypothesis

In order to define perceptual changes in intellectual developments, we employed the concept of "consilience" as a working hypothesis. Edward O. Wilson (1998) based the concept on William Whewell's premise that unity of knowledge is aimed at integrating branches of scientific inquiries. Charles P. Snow referred to the practical division of natural sciences and humanities as "the two cultures" gap (Wilson, 1998; Snow, 2013), a connotation that became a benchmark for working toward unified knowledge. In IDR projects, though, consilience is often aligned with producing integrative knowledge and wisdom that overarch both scientific and social realms (e.g., Slingerland and Collard, 2011). Thus, research experts can learn something by and beneficial to exploring new intellectual dimensions. The theory of consilience has been criticized as biological reductionism (Klein, 2009), and for not doing justice to "problem solving" and "transgression" in TDR (Klein, 2014). Recent studies of TDR have also stressed cultural differences rather than unity of knowledge (Scholz and Steiner, 2015; Vilsmaier and Lang, 2015).

In our experience, IDR and TDR do not consist only of bridging together different epistemic cultures but also heeding the etymological meaning of "consilience", of "jumping together" phenomena hitherto dealt with in separate fields. A "consilient perspective" does not necessarily imply a reductionist view, and could provide a basis for the co-production of knowledge and wisdom revised jointly by researchers and social actors. For IDR and TDR, then, consilience is a process of intellectual innovation through iterative cycles of differentiation and unification. Consilience might occur when perceiving intellectual development or changes during collaborative projects. Abe and Hiyama (2014) pointed out that, at RIHN, a good project proposal is distinguished by means of (1) research questions, (2) organizational design, particularly in the intersection of research areas, (3) well-planned approaches toward consilience, and (4) participants' deep engagement in collaborative works.

Following these criteria, we classified pre- and in-project conditions for consilience during a research project, depicted in Table 12.2. Pre-project conditions include the academic background and career trajectory of the PL. In-project conditions comprise checkpoints in project management, including: (1) leadership; (2) working hypothesis and goals; (3) selection and capacity building of project members (particularly for in-house postdocs); (4) organization and governance; (5) tools developed and applied; and (6) issues that emerged during the project. We also sought information on outcomes (how problems were dissolved or perceptually transformed) and perceptual changes (how perceptions, values, and thoughts of participants have changed through the project).

Semi-structured interviews

In order to provide a fuller view, we conducted semi-structured interviews with a total of 20 informants, including leaders and active members of nine

TABLE 12.2 Checkpoints for management and intellectual development of collaborative research projects

Process	1. Pre-project conditions for intellectual developments • Academic backgrounds and careers before the project 2. In-project conditions for intellectual developments • Leadership • Working hypothesis and goals • Selection and capacity building of project members • Organization and governance • Tools • Cares for project members
Outcome	Have the problems been solved?
Perception	How have perceptions, values, and thoughts changed through participation in the project?

completed projects identified in Table 12.3. For five projects (1, 2, 3, 4, and 7), we conducted two two-hour interviews with the PL and two-hour interviews with two active members the PL suggested during 2014 and 2015 (plus one additional for Project 7). For other projects (5, 6, 8, and 9), we conducted two two-hour interviews with the PL between 2016 and 2020 (plus two additional interviews for Project 6 on request). Two to four RIHN colleagues conducted every interview with one informant. This many-to-one-style interview is unusual in conventional social surveys, but motivated informants to tell their life histories in a relaxed mood.

In accordance with checkpoints for project management and intellectual development in Table 12.2, each interview was divided into four parts chronologically: prologue, pre-project, in-project, and epilogue. Guidelines for the full sequence and details appear in Table 12.4. Interviews always began with a question, such as "Where are you from?", to encourage informants to tell their personal histories of becoming research experts, with episodes in some cases associated with interests in scientific research. The interviews gradually shifted to professional careers and how informants were engaged in the RIHN project. For PLs, we asked why and how to develop a collaborative research project at RIHN, in response to comments and suggestions from PRT, EREC, and other advisory members. In the later part, based on the consilience hypothesis, we also asked if informants perceived any intellectual developments during the project. Finally, we recorded all interviews and transcribed voice data for discourse analysis.

Key factors of intellectual development from discourse analysis

The discourses extracted from interviews included the following five key factors for productive project management and intellectual development: (1) boundary

TABLE 12.3 List of the interviewed projects (anonymized)

Project number mentioned in the text	Medium-term plan phases at FR	Core research areas	Main study areas	Maximum number of registered project members*	Informants (PL is highlighted in bold with an asterisk)	Year of interviews
1	I to II	Ecology, history	Japan	132	A*, B, C	2014
2	I to II	Hydrology, history	Central Asia	109	D*, E, F	2014
3	I to II	Archaeology, Palaeoenvironment	South Asia	60	G*, H, I	2015
4	I to II	Area studies, local ecosystems	The Middle East and North Africa	91	J*, K, L, M	2015
5	II	Architectural history, urban studies	Jakarta and megacities in Global South	70	N*	2016
6	II to III	Marine ecology, development studies	Japan and Southeast Asia	155	O*, P, Q	2014
7	II to III	Agroecology, area studies	Africa and Asia	32	R*	2016
8	II to III	Paleoclimatology, history	Japan	79	S*	2018
9	II to III	Ecology, environmental sociology	Japan and The Philippines	115	T*	2020

Source: RIHN IR Unit.

*Source: RIHN IR Unit.

TABLE 12.4 Guidelines for semi-structured interviews

Prologue: Personal history before becoming a research expert
- What was your experience associated with your interests in scientific research in your childhood?
- How did you develop your research interests?

Part 1: Pre-project research experience
- How did you develop your professional career before joining RIHN?
- Who inspired you and how?

Part 2: In-project research experience
- What was the first contact with RIHN?
- *Why did you want to coordinate a research project at RIHN?
- *How did you develop working hypotheses and goals in IS, FS, and FR proposals?
- *How did you select project members and build their capacities?
- *How did you respond to the comments from PRT and EREC (formerly PEC)?
- How did you lead, manage, or take care of the project?
- Who influenced the project development and how?
- What tools did you use for collaboration?
- Did you perceive any intellectual developments during the project?

Epilogue: Intellectual experience after completion of the project
- How do you perceive your research experience at RIHN now?
- How are the study area and people there now?
- What are your new directions of research?

The questions with an asterisk are for PLs only.

TABLE 12.5 Key factors of intellectual development extracted from the interviews

Key factors	Project number (Table 12.3)								
	1	2	3	4	5	6	7	8	9
Setting boundary objects (3.1)	+			+	+	+		+	
Multifaceted viewpoints (3.2)	+						+		
Empowerment of early-career researchers (3.3)		+			+				
Scalable organization (3.4)			+		+				
Transition from IDR to TDR (3.5)								+	+

objects; (2) multifaceted viewpoints; (3) empowerment of early-career researchers; (4) scalable organization; and (5) transition from IDR to TDR, as summarized in Table 12.5 and subsequent discussion. These factors explicitly appeared in discourses of two or more projects and were largely consistent with research on real-world labs for TDR in Germany (Bergmann et al., 2021).

Boundary objects

Boundary objects are both adaptable to different viewpoints and robust enough to maintain identity across them (Star and Griesemer, 1989, p. 387). Five of the nine projects set boundary objects in the form of research questions, fields, models, or tools shared with and commonly referred to by project members without explicitly using this technical term. For instance, Project 1 (in Table 12.3) developed central research questions for exploring socio-ecological interactions in Japan through the lens of cultural and historical dimensions. The PL in this case (Informant A) intentionally set questions researchers from different domains were willing to tackle with their own interests and motivations. Project 4 also shared key concepts and research targets to foster consilience, using a scientific framework focused on strengthening subsistence productivity and rehabilitation in the Middle East and North Africa: in particular, keystone species such as camels, date palms, dugongs (a sea mammal in the Red Sea and the Indian Ocean), mangrove trees, and coral reefs, and local environmental knowledge to sustain communities. The PL in this project (Informant J) used key concepts with multiple meanings for individual case studies, along with designated research targets. Joint fieldwork by anthropologists and ecologists also yielded a new research question inquiring how to improve the lifeways of local people.

Models and tools can be boundary objects as well. Project 6 reviewed good practices of community-based ecosystem management in Japan and Southeast Asian countries, resulting in a proposed conceptual model for both local economy and environmental sustainability. Interviews with the PL (O) and two active members (P and Q) revealed three points of consilience. First, the development of the conceptual model resulted in significant intellectual innovation for the participants. Second, feedback from the EREC fostered developing business models from the original conceptual model. Third, the introduction of new devices such as underwater robots and drones attracted local youths to work together for environmental monitoring and care. These transformations contributed to fostering community-based ecosystem management.

Multifaceted viewpoints

Multifaceted viewpoints may provide new insights to project members. The interviews revealed that viewpoints of humanities inspired natural scientists to widen their research scope. For example, in Project 1, the PL (A) encouraged project members to discuss their studies of local ecosystem histories from differing outlooks and approaches of other research experts. Repeated discussions fostered consilience among project members, particularly individual early-career researchers. Project 7 explicitly applied a concept of environmental philosophy for agricultural science and development. It aimed to identify social, cultural, and ecological characteristics of livelihood and adaptation strategies to desertification in semi-arid regions of Asia and Africa. The PL (R) is an agricultural scientist with teaching experience at a university in Kenya, as a Japanese overseas cooperation volunteer. When he developed an FR project, he added wind and humans and earth to the project title (風と人と土; *kaze to hito to tsuchi*). This change inserted humans (人; *hito*) into Watsuji Tetsurō's *fūdo* (風土 human milieu; Berque, 1996).

Empowerment of early-career researchers

Collaborative research projects at RIHN are based at the powerful headquarters for administration, management, and promotion of research, providing good opportunities for early-career researchers to learn these aspects of large-scale projects on the job. PLs also encourage them to develop their research capabilities with some interventions. For instance, in Project 2, which aimed to describe the history of adaptations by human beings to both environmental and societal changes in arid to semi-arid regions of Central Asia, the PL (D) encouraged two early-career researchers specialized in remote sensing (E) and political history (F), respectively, in order to conduct fieldwork with an experienced cultural anthropologist. This "top-down" team building let early-career researchers broaden their research scopes. Consequently, the remote sensing specialist (E) worked for community-based disaster risk reduction in a rural area of Japan after completion of the project. In this case, consilience occurred at an individual level driven by group dynamics.

Scalable organization

Projects are allowed to add or remove project members at any time. In the Japanese business practice of long-term employment, the removal of members during projects rarely occurs. Thus, the number of members tends to increase over time. This aspect of collaboration was corroborated by the words of a PL (D), "[W]hen I found a good potential research partner, I added this person to the team". Project 3 provided another episode. It aimed at conducting an interdisciplinary study of environmental changes and the decline of the ancient civilizations in South Asia. The interviews revealed that the PL (G) and active members (H and I) worked in a genuinely collaborative fashion, respecting colleagues with different skills and thoughts and trying to update a shared scenario as the project progressed. Nonetheless, they had to terminate a membership when someone did not follow the PL's coordination.

Transition from IDR to TDR

Interviews also revealed the PL's notion of the scientific merits of TDR and the motivations to foster it. Project 9 developed a transdisciplinary framework for adaptive watershed governance by linking nutrient cycling more broadly to human well-being and facilitating social engagement in biodiversity conservation and environmental restoration. Interviews with the PL (T) revealed perceptual changes over the course of the project. The PL developed his academic career as a field ecologist lacking former experience collaborating with local actors. Yet, when he visited potential sites to study phosphorus cycling in a river catchment during the FS, his conversations with local community members revealed that they interpreted the same topic with indigenous knowledge. The PL eventually recognized that scientists could empower local communities by sharing experiences and implications of fieldwork, which were evaluated by local actors, and how experiences enhance regional ecological conservation activities with a consilience of scientific and socio-cultural knowledge specific to TDR.

Purely scientific projects can also lead to transformations by the concept of TDR. Project 8 investigated how Japanese societies have reacted to large abrupt climate changes since the prehistoric era. This project reconstructed past climate variability in annual or even monthly time resolutions using tree-ring cellulose oxygen isotopic ratios. High-resolution paleoclimatic information was expected to aid the reinterpretation of historical and archaeological records. However, interviews with the PL (S) revealed perceptual gaps between natural scientists (i.e., climatologists) and social scientists (historians and archaeologists) when interpreting paleoclimatic information. For instance, climatologists tended to consider socio-ecological changes at global or superregional scales, while historians and archaeologists focused on changes at a local scale. The PL also noticed a gap in authorship preference. Social scientists prefer single authorship while natural scientists are accustomed to multi-authored publications. Upon completion of the project, the PL recognized it could be developed as TDR if historians were regarded as representative of past people or societies and conducted dialogues with the present people as a future generation (Saijo, 2020).

Consilience in response to top-down pressures

Summing up, interviews revealed several patterns in perceiving consilience through IDR or TDR projects at RIHN. Most notably, it always happened in a tacit manner, often driven by individual intellectual curiosity in solo interdisciplinary research. PLs perceived a curiosity-driven consilience, particularly at planning phases (i.e., IS and FS), but seldom perceived it on a project-wide scale because they were busy coordinating their own projects, pressured by external evaluations. Most PLs, particularly those who faced declining budgets during the Medium Term Phases II and III (Figure 12.3), felt responding to comments from the PRT at planning phases, and from the EREC (or formerly PEC) after transferring to FR, was a burden. In general, though, feedback and suggestions from evaluation bodies contributed to transforming institutional culture.

In the end, institutional changes did not largely affect the intellectual developments of project employees who were loyal to a particular project rather than the Institute. Thus, they experienced consilience *ad hoc* when individual intellectual curiosity matched the direction of research a PL facilitated, exemplified by early-career researchers in Project 2. However, it was difficult to grasp large-scale consilience at the project level because PLs tended to achieve the original goals approved by external reviewers at the beginning. Moreover, projects are regularly reviewed and evaluated by an external committee. Most PLs reported their projects went as planned, though they tried to modify directions to an extent based on reviewers' suggestions. Top-down interventions associated with institutional changes, then, cannot always foster intellectual developments. For example, Project 5, aiming at investigating how megacities, particularly in the Global South, became earth-friendly by improving the welfare of their inhabitants. As trends of TDR gradually prevailed during this project, the PEC suggested quantifying an outcome to share with stakeholders and decision-makers. In response, the project team developed a city sustainability index. The PL (N) perceived consilience in the development of the index, but the project timetable was too short to disseminate it internationally.

Conclusions and prospects for IDR and TDR institutionalization in Japan

Our interviews with participants in RIHN projects demonstrated that curiosity-driven intellectual developments, which happened mainly at an individual level rather than a project-wide level, were not always impacted by top-down pressures for institutional changes in the mode of TDR at a time of shrinking budgets at RIHN. In other words, projects improved through self-motivated intellectual innovations rather than external interventions. This finding indicates that changes are shaped *ad hoc*. However, a combination of internal and external stimulations transformed the local institutional culture of collaborative research to address socio-cultural dimensions of environmental problems over time. Interviews also revealed the importance of sharing lessons learned from research implementation with other projects in order to recognize, transmit, and transform tacit knowledge about institutional cultures regarding IDR and TDR. This requirement is the first step for satisfactory and productive collaboration. It is essential to create an institutional culture to champion IDR and TDR (Kelly et al., 2019) through sharing "bewilderments" (Kondo et al., 2021, p. 179) rather than success stories. These findings should also be cross-checked with complementary approaches such as questionnaire surveys and bibliometric analyses in the near future.

From a broader perspective, Japan has been experiencing emerging socio-ecological problems for decades, such as an aging population with a declining birthrate (Muramatsu and Akiyama, 2011) as well as devastating disasters (Claremont, 2014). These challenges are often perceived as wicked problems with no clear-cut solutions (Norris et al., 2016; Rittel and Webber, 1973), so cannot be simply solved by research experts from a single and homogeneous research field. The most important outcome of IDR and TDR projects that RIHN has coordinated for 20 years is the emergence of a social network of research experts and practitioners dedicated to addressing wicked socio-ecological problems, particularly in Japan and neighboring Asian countries. External collaborators repeatedly contribute to collaborative projects because they are attracted to and motivated by the kind of consilience that can only be made possible through working with experts and practitioners from different domains at RIHN. In this regard, RIHN is a "transaction space" (Gibbons, 2000, p. 162) making it possible to achieve inter- and trans-disciplinary consilience for socio-cultural dimensions of environmental sustainability in Japan and worldwide.

References

Abe, K. and Hiyama, T. (2014) 'Introduction', in RIHN (ed.), *Global Environmental Studies Manual: An Introduction to Collaborative Research*. Asakura Shoten, Tokyo, pp i–vii (in Japanese) [阿部健一, 檜山哲哉「序に代えて」総合地球環境学研究所（編）『地球環境学マニュアル』朝倉書店, 東京]

Bergmann, M., Schäpke, N., Marg, O., Stelzer, F., Lang, D. J., Bossert, M., Gantert, M., Häußler, E., Marquardt, E., Piontek, F. M., Potthast, T., Rhodius, R., Rudolph, M., Ruddat, M., Seebacher, A. and Sußmann, N. (2021) 'Transdisciplinary sustainability research in real-world labs: Success factors and methods for change', *Sustainability Science*, vol 16, pp 541–564. https://doi.org/10.1007/s11625-020-00886-8

Berque, A. (1996) 'The question of space: From Heidegger to Watsuji', *Ecumene*, vol 3, no 4, pp 373–383. https://doi.org/10.1177/147447409600300401

Burger, P. and Kamber, R. (2003) 'Cognitive integration in transdisciplinary science', *Issues in Integrative Studies*, vol 21, pp 43–73. http://hdl.handle.net/10323/4400

Claremont, Y. (2014) 'Disaster in Japan: A case study', in Butt, S., Nasu, H. and Nottage, L. (eds), *Asia-Pacific Disaster Management*. Springer, Berlin, Heidelberg, pp 79–99. https://doi.org/10.1007/978-3-642-39768-4_3

European Commission. (2015) *Indicators for Promoting and Monitoring Responsible Research and Innovation: Report from the Expert Group on Policy Indicators for Responsible Research and Innovation*. https://doi.org/10.2777/9742

Gibbons, M. (2000) 'Mode 2 society and the emergence of context-sensitive science', *Science and Public Policy*, vol 27, no 3, pp 159–163. https://doi.org/10.3152/147154300781782011

Gray, B. (2008) 'Enhancing transdisciplinary research through collaborative leadership', *American Journal of Preventive Medicine*, vol 35 Supplement, pp S124–S132. https://doi.org/10.1016/j.amepre.2008.03.037

Kelly, R., Mackay, M., Nash, K., Cvitanovic, C., Allison, E. H., Armitage, D., Bonn, A., Cooke, S. J., Frusher, S., Fulton, E. A., Halpern, B. S., Lopes, P. S. M., Milner-Gulland, E. J., Peck, M. A., Pecl, G. T., Stephenson, R. L. and Werner, F. (2019) 'Ten tips for developing interdisciplinary socio-ecological researchers', *Socio-Ecological Practice Research*, vol 1, pp 149–161. https://doi.org/10.1007/s42532-019-00018-2

Klein, J. T. (2009) 'Unity of knowledge and transdisciplinarity: Contexts of definition, theory and the new discourse of problem solving', in Hirsch Hadorn, G. (ed.), *Unity of Knowledge (in Transdisciplinary Research for Sustainability)*. UNESCO-EOLSS, Paris, pp 35–69.

Klein, J. T. (2014) 'Discourses of transdisciplinarity: Looking back to the future', *Futures*, vol 63, pp 68–74. https://doi.org/10.1016/j.futures.2014.08.008

Kondo, Y., Fujisawa, E., Ishikawa, K., Nakahara, S., Matsushita, K., Asano, S., Kamatani, K., Suetsugu, S., Kano, K., Kumazawa, T., Sato, K. and Okuda, N. (2021) 'Community capability building for environmental conservation in Lake Biwa (Japan) through an adaptive and abductive approach', *Socio-Ecological Practice Research*, vol 3, no 2, pp 167–183. https://doi.org/10.1007/s42532-021-00078-3

Lang, D. J., Wiek, A., Bergmann, M., Stauffacher, M., Martens, P., Moll, P., Swilling, M. and Thomas, C. J. (2012) 'Transdisciplinary research in sustainability science: Practice, principles, and challenges', *Sustainability Science*, vol 7, pp 25–43. https://doi.org/10.1007/s11625-011-0149-x

Mauser, W., Klepper G., Rice, M., Schmalzbauer, B. S., Hackmann, H., Leemans, R. and Moore, H. (2013) 'Transdisciplinary global change research: The co-creation of knowledge for sustainability', *Current Opinion in Environmental Sustainability*, vol 5, no 3–4, pp 420–431. https://doi.org/10.1016/j.cosust.2013.07.001

Muramatsu, N. and Akiyama, H. (2011) 'Japan: Super-aging society preparing for the future', *The Gerontologist*, vol 51, no 4, pp 425–432. https://doi.org/10.1093/geront/gnr067

Norris, P. E., O'Rourke, M., Mayer, A. S. and Halvorson, K. E. (2016) 'Managing the wicked problem of transdisciplinary team formation in socio-ecological systems', *Landscape and Urban Planning*, vol 154, pp 115–122. https://doi.org/10.1016/j.landurbplan.2016.01.008

OECD. (2020) 'Addressing societal challenges using transdisciplinary research', *OECD Science, Technology, and Industry Policy Papers*, no 88. https://doi.org/10.1787/0ca0ca45-en

Repko, A. F. and Szostak, R. (2020) *Interdisciplinary Research: Process and Theory*. 4th ed. SAGE Pub, Thousand Oaks, CA.

RIHN (2006) *Research Institute for Humanity and Nature 2006–2007*. https://www.chikyu.ac.jp/rihn_13/archive/brochure/2006/brochure2006e.pdf, accessed 18 March 2021.

RIHN (2012) *Research Institute for Humanity and Nature Prospectus 2012–2013*. https://www.chikyu.ac.jp/rihn_13/archive/brochure/2012/yoran-e_2012.pdf, accessed 18 March 2021.

RIHN (2016) *Research Institute for Humanity and Nature Prospectus 2016–2017*. https://www.chikyu.ac.jp/publicity/publications/brochure/2016E.html, accessed 21 February 2021.

RIHN (2020) *Research Institute for Humanity and Nature Prospectus 2020–2021*. https://www.chikyu.ac.jp/publicity/publications/brochure/2020E.html, accessed 21 February 2021.

Rittel, H. W. and Webber, M. M. (1973) 'Dilemmas in a general theory of planning', *Policy Science*, vol 4, pp 155–169. https://doi.org/10.1007/BF01405730

Saijo, T. (2020) 'Future design: Bequeathing sustainable natural environments and sustainable societies to future generations', *Sustainability*, vol 12, no 16, p 6467. https://doi.org/10.3390/su12166467

Scholz, R. W. and Steiner, G. (2015) 'The real type and ideal type of transdisciplinary processes: Part I—theoretical foundations', *Sustainability Science*, vol 10, no 4, pp 527–544. https://doi.org/10.1007/s11625-015-0326-4

Slingerland, E. and Collard, M. (eds) (2011) *Creating Consilience: Integrating the Sciences and the Humanities*. Oxford University Press, Oxford.

Snow, C. P. (2013) *The Two Cultures and the Scientific Revolution*. Reissue ed. Martino Fine Books, Eastford (originally published by Cambridge University Press in 1959).

Specht, A. (2017) 'Synthesis centres: Their relevance to and importance in the Anthropocene', in Chabbi, A. and Loescher, H. W. (eds), *Terrestrial Ecosystem Research Infrastructure*. Routledge, London.

Star, S. L. and Griesemer, J. R. (1989) 'Institutional ecology, 'translations' and boundary objects: Amateurs and professionals in Berkeley's Museum of Vertebrate Zoology, 1907–39', *Social Studies of Science*, vol 19, no 3, pp 387–420. https://doi.org/10.1177/030631289019003001

Vilsmaier, U. and Lang, D. J. (2015) 'Making a difference by marking the difference: Constituting in-between spaces for sustainability learning', *Current Opinion in Environmental Sustainability*, vol 16, pp 51–55. https://doi.org/10.1016/j.cosust.2015.07.019

Vilsmaier, U., Brandner, V. and Engbers, M. (2017) 'Research in-between: The constitutive role of cultural differences in transdisciplinarity', *Transdisciplinary Journal of Engineering & Science*, vol 8, pp 169–179. https://doi.org/10.22545/2017/00093

Wilson, E. O. (1998) *Consilience: The Unity of Knowledge*. Knopf, New York.

PART III
Intersections between cultures and communities

13
EPISTEMIC CULTURES IN EUROPEAN INTERSECTIONS OF ART–SCIENCE

Paulo Nuno Vicente and Margarida Lucas

Introduction

This chapter focuses on art–science as an interstitial dialogue zone among arts, sciences, and technologies. More precisely, it is about identifying emerging patterns from an examination of individual practitioners' perspectives on heterogeneous collaborations. The foundational questions that give rise to this work emanate from the recurring "two cultures" problem in modern knowledge construction. More than 60 years after an influential lecture by C. P. Snow (1959) on relations between arts/humanities and sciences, including what those relations meant for an industrial economy, we update this debate in the European context with new empirical data, including contemporary perspectives on the role of educational specialization and academic department structure and Snow's subsequent conception of a "third culture" bridging arts and science (Snow, 1963). In the course of updating, we articulate two complementary concepts. The first is *epistemic living spaces* in the form of actual material settings, or landscapes in Felt's (2009) formulation, that shape and are shaped by specific and tangible renderings of knowledge organization. The second concept outlines material instances within *epistemic cultures* (Knorr Cetina, 1995), acknowledging their own diversity and flux. This acknowledgment includes contemporary diverse integrations and intersections between arts and techno-scientific research (Wilson, 2002), understood in terms of Born and Barry's three logics of interdisciplinarity and transdisciplinarity and motivated toward "altering existing ways of thinking about the nature of art and science, as well as transforming relations between artists and scientists and their objects and publics" (2010, p. 105). For operational purposes, we sampled living spaces of art–science from current European institutional and programmatic contexts that bring artists, scientists, and technologists physically and cognitively together to foster collaborative research based on

DOI: 10.4324/9781003129424-16

mutual realms of investigation. Individual practitioners' perspectives are at the core of our investigation of interactions in art–science as the main constituents of an epistemic culture.

Over the past 20 years, discourses on collaboration among art, science, and technology have often been specifically aligned with building instrumental and/or organizational strategies conducive to innovation: whether by designating the site of art–science and its pre-history hybrid activities such as the studio–laboratory (Century, 1999; Schnugg, 2019a), by profiling the individual role of catalysts (Edwards, 2008), by advancing global frameworks based on artist residencies for innovation (Henchoz et al., 2019), or by examining organizational contexts in which they are and/or can be embedded (King, 2020; Paterson et al., 2020; Reinsborough, 2020; Schnugg, 2019b). At the same time, art–science has been expected to cultivate and/or generate new audiences for science (Barry et al., 2008). Exemplary of its adoption in research and development (R&D), policymaking stands out in the recent call for "a new European Bauhaus movement – a collaborative design and creative space, where architects, artists, students, scientists, engineers, and designers work together to make this vision a reality" (von der Leyen, 2020).

We align these three approaches with three imperatives: (a) innovation; (b) public understanding of science; and (c) political administration. Each of these perspectives makes use of a portion of the art–science proposal for their own benefit and/or legitimization. However, each on its own fails to fully incorporate an art–science holistic project for knowledge production while recognizing, even if implicitly, that mutual marginalization "has come about because of three levels: a lack of respect [between the two domains], a specialized focus embedded in disciplinary institutions, and differences in commercial structure and funding" (Scott, 2010, p. 8).

There is objective ground for questioning this assumption, asking what premises inform the expectation that by putting individual artists and scientists together in high-tech environments they will achieve collaborative, innovative results. From a chronological perspective, we approach a historic reaffirmation of Renaissance values and practices and of the artist-engineer as a border-crossing figure, with Leonardo da Vinci as the ultimate archetype. Only after the Enlightenment (17th and 18th centuries) and Romanticism (19th century) did ontological contrast and even opposition between models of the emotional artist and the rational scientist become crystalized, continuing to the present in both public understandings and reciprocal attitudes between artists and scientists. Institutionalization of this separation would eventually result in organizing knowledge into disciplines and corresponding departmentalization of academic life. In the context of this dualism, art–science emerged as "an integrated way to produce new creative insights, which could not be achieved through either art or science alone, or as a new philosophy of research that combines artistic and scientific modes of investigation" (Heylighen and Petrović, 2020, p. 2). In 1959, C.P. Snow shared his regrets about "how very little of twentieth-century science has been assimilated into twentieth-century art" (p. 17). Today, the art–science movement encourages hybridity as an ontology that seeks to formalize an integrative culture by assimilating previously non-dialoguing silos and to normalize boundary crossing in research (Rock and Howard, 2018).

While theoretical works about art–science – notwithstanding the different and even opposing lineages that constitute them (Barry and Born, 2013) – have sought to legitimize an epistemic culture in its own right while establishing suitable epistemic living spaces, and while applied projects have been developed to improve methods and tools of work across distinct contexts of co-creation, less attention has been paid to individual protagonists' perspectives and how different institutional frameworks sustain or constrain them. One way of formulating the problem is to inquire into how epistemic living spaces (institutional landscapes) influence and are influenced by epistemic cultures, here inspected at the micro level (individual values). This chapter is an exploratory attempt to fill this knowledge gap, aimed at answering the general guiding question of this book, asking, How are inter- and trans-disciplinary research and teaching organized in time and space including immediate communities where they emerged?

In order for our study to be connected to the wider European context and history, we will begin by briefly reviewing some of the key ideas of art–science in relation to the premise of the "two cultures" problem. From there, we advance toward the conceptual framework of epistemic cultures to present and operationalize our data collection instrument. We finish this chapter with the presentation and analysis of the results, sharing some reserve notes and recommendations for future research.

Context of the study: Art–science in Europe

One of the most influential ideas in modern knowledge, at least since the Industrial Revolution, is a polarization of the intellectual life of Western societies into two groups according to C.P. Snow's original distinction between (1959) literary intellectuals and scientists (in particular, physical scientists). In the scope of this chapter, it is reasonable to interpret Snow's dualism around artists and scientists. Between the two, he wrote, there is "a gulf of mutual incomprehension – sometimes (…) hostility and dislike, but most of all lack of understanding. They have a curious distorted image of each other" (p. 4). At the core of this mid-century diagnosis, we find early recognition that "scientific culture really is a culture, not only in an intellectual but also in an anthropological sense", as it is structured by "common attitudes, common standards and patterns of behaviour, [and] common approaches and assumptions" (p. 10). Thus, deduction of two cultures followed: one scientific and the other artistic. Approximately 20 years later, Pierre Boulez, composer and founding director of the avant-garde Institut de Recherche et Coordination Acoustique/Music (IRCAM) in Paris, echoed Snow's ideas when acknowledging that "collaboration between scientists and musicians (…) seen from outside, does not appear to be inevitable", considering that "many representatives of the scientific world (...) doubt whether this utopian marriage of fire and water would be likely to produce anything valid" (Boulez, 1977, pp. 5–6).

Since then, a vast array of work has further conceptualized and embodied the validity of synergies between artists and scientists (e.g., Candy et al., 2002; Candy and Edmonds, 2018; Edmonds and Candy, 2010; Edwards, 2011). Indeed, the relationship between the two is inseparable from the very foundation of modern Europe (Eldred, 2016; Gamwell, 2020; Smith, 2006). Following suit, several initiatives, institutions, and academic study programs that exist today were founded to counterbalance disciplinary-centered research practices and institutional forms, recognizing they are "associated in a broader sense with questions of new methods of knowledge production, knowledge and innovation policies and their implications for social differentiation" (Glauser, 2010, p. 12). Nevertheless, "there is a ferment of activity but as yet little codification; practice runs ahead of theory", so following Barry et al. "we might consider Art–Science, then, as an emergent field" (2008, p. 38).

In the scope of our study, we aimed to engage with scientists, artists, technologists, and science and technology managers working in European research institutions and/or on European projects founded on the explicit mission of intersecting/integrating art, science, and technology and of stimulating dialogue across knowledge disciplines. By doing so, we affirmed the assumption that by

> shifting the focus from the outcome to the process of art–science collaboration, it is possible to discover in more depth value-added contributions of art–science experiences on an individual level (e.g., new ways of knowing and thinking, understanding of materials and processes, and learning).
>
> *(Schnugg and Song, 2020, p. 1)*

Theoretical framework: Epistemic cultures

Seminal works in sociology and the philosophy of science, in particular, epistemology, have revealed how the scientific method is not a contextless procedure. It is culturally structured impelling science and technology researchers, as Knorr Cetina put it, to "move inside the epistemic space within which scientists work and identify the tools and devices which they use in their 'truth-finding' navigation" (1991, p. 7). Science, or more precisely research following Latour (1998), constructs plural forms of reason that feed (and are fed by) particular epistemic cultures. Knorr Cetina called them "machines deployed in fact construction". Scientists construct "ontologies of organisms and machines that result from the reconfiguration of self-other-things implemented in different fields". They do so by using "'liminal' and referent epistemologies" and "strategies to put sociality to work" (1995, p. 158). By acknowledging "epistemic cultures constitute specific ways of producing knowledge as well as relating to that which is not known and uncertain" (Kastenhofer, 2007, p. 360), the possibility of convergent, divergent, and emergent processes within and across scientific fields arises. These epistemic anchors ground knowledge construction in a dynamic and diverse process of characterizing scientific disciplines and, correspondingly, their boundary work. The manner in which epistemic cultures construct scientific knowledge is evident in distinct ways in which disciplines organize themselves around relations between privatization of endeavors (i.e., the individual researcher as an epistemic unit) and systematic strategies of validation (i.e., the experiment as an epistemic unit). In this sense, embodied experimental knowledge often remains implicit, "partly encapsulated within the person and partly encapsulated within the narrative culture of the laboratory" (Knorr Cetina, 1991, p. 115).

While useful in the administrative organization of scientific units and subunits, Knorr Cetina contended the culturological notion of discipline proves to be "less felicitous in capturing the strategies and policies of knowing that are not codified in textbooks but do inform expert practice" (1999, p. 2). Accordingly, we reiterate her hypothesis that "epistemic issues are inextricably intertwined with the organization of epistemic groups" (1991, p. 12). While recognizing "a wide gulf still separates the worlds of art and of science, in terms of culture, education, public perception, funding, and societal impact" (Heylighen and Petrović, 2020, p. 3), this starting point allows theoretically consolidating art–science as an epistemic culture and considering scientists, technologists, artists, and science and technology managers in European research institutions and/or on European projects as an epistemic group, while operationalizing empirical examination of the premise. We are not implicating a crystalized characterization of art–science as a uniform culture or this group of participants as monolithic. Rather, we recognize their epistemic knowledge-building activities in European research institutions and/or on European projects, and personal experience in interdisciplinarity and/or transdisciplinarity, renders them an epistemic group hypothetically sharing common values and practices. This acknowledgment allows studying contexts of epistemic organization, including institutions and projects, from the view knowledge "practiced within structures, processes, and environments that make up specific epistemic settings" (Knorr Cetina, 1999, p. 8).

Following suit, we attribute equal importance to the complementary concept of epistemic living spaces in material settings, or landscapes, and investigate how knowledge construction agents frame contemporary knowledge production. More precisely, we seek to examine how they grapple with, as Felt put it, "messiness, embattledness and practical significance of what seems to delimit researchers' capacity to act in, to think and imagine research" as they "inhabit the different cognitive and material landscapes and participate in giving shape to them, how they organise their social, spatial or temporal environments and are organised by them" (2009, p. 18). In pursuing this goal, to sum up, we treat explicit research as a cultural practice and practice as a collective action of "socially recognized forms of activity, done on the basis of what members learn from others, and capable of being done well or badly, correctly or incorrectly" (Barnes, 2001, p. 27). By mapping individual researchers' epistemic (cognitive) values in the context of material knowledge production, we were able to identify, albeit on an exploratory basis, entanglements between personal perspectives and structures of research at the micro level of meaning-making. In other words, we surveyed "specific assumptions about which kinds of research questions are central, how knowledge should be produced, and which properties and procedures constitute good knowledge" (Felt and Fochler, 2012, p. 5). Examining the epistemic structure of interdisciplinarity and transdisciplinarity in the scope of art–science puts us closer to the "nexus of lifeworlds (contexts of existence that include material objects) and lifeworld processes" (Knorr Cetina, 2007, p. 364), and closer to advancing a basis for further examination of the machineries in contemporary knowledge construction.

Method

The present study aimed to characterize epistemic foundations of art–science in Europe, particularly based on individual practitioners' values. Toward this end, we analyzed perceptions of artists, scientists, technologists, and science and technology managers working in European research institutions and/or on European projects explicitly stating inter- and trans-disciplinary objectives to answer the following research questions (RQs):

RQ1. Do scientists, technologists, artists, and science and technology managers working in European research institutions and/or on European projects consider that scientists and artists belong to two different cultures?

RQ2. Do scientists, technologists, artists, and science and technology managers working in European research institutions and/or projects consider that scientists and artists lack mutual understanding?

RQ3. Do scientists, technologists, artists, and science and technology managers working in European research institutions and/or projects consider that educational specializations reinforce a cultural divide among the arts, science, and technology?

RQ4. Do scientists, technologists, artists, and science and technology managers working in European research institutions and/or projects consider that the academic department structure reinforces a cultural divide among the arts, science, and technology?

RQ5: Do scientists, technologists, artists, and science and technology managers working in European research institutions and/or projects consider that solutions to contemporary societal challenges (e.g., climate change, migration-related issues) require an integrated approach by artistic, scientific, and technological disciplines?

The following tools furnished insights for testing the hypotheses.

Online questionnaire

In order to collect data, we organized an online questionnaire using the Qualtrics Survey web-based platform, categorizing items into four topical sections: (a) direct experience in interdisciplinarity and/or transdisciplinarity (ID/TD); (b) drivers of and barriers to ID and/or TD; (c) perceptions of the "two cultures" problem; and (d) socio-demographics. Items (a) and (c) applied to the research question, aimed at inspecting how epistemic living spaces (institutional landscapes) influence and are influenced by epistemic cultures, addressed in this study at the micro level of individual values. Section (a) was based on a contingency/skip-logic question (Sue and Ritter, 2012): respondents who indicated they did not have direct experience in interdisciplinarity and/or transdisciplinarity were directed to the end of the questionnaire since the online instrument was exclusively aimed at artists, scientists, technologists, and science and technology managers in European research institutions and/or projects with related experience. In section (c), we asked participants to respond to items using a Likert scale ranging from "Strongly Disagree" to "Strongly Agree". Section (d) then provided background information about participants. We pretested the online questionnaire with a group of ten faculty members, administering a pilot questionnaire to identify and add revisions or improvements for the survey, mainly wording, technical jargon, conceptual clarity, spelling, and navigation structure. Based on the pilot group's feedback, we then implemented minor adjustments to optimize readability and participants' comprehension of instructions (e.g., normalization of expressions), as well as digital user experience (e.g., introduction of a backspace button). These adjustments facilitated definitive data collection. The SPSS V23 statistics software package, in particular, enabled assessing the internal consistency of the questionnaire and data analysis (with a Cronbach's alpha score of .766).

Sample, data collection, and data analysis

To contribute to the literature with substantial and updated groundwork for a more nuanced discussion of inter- and trans-disciplinary collaboration, we adopted an exploratory research framework aimed at generating empirical data that could lead to a clearer problem formulation, as well as research design improvements. Since a list of all researchers working in inter- or trans-disciplinary settings in Europe was not available, we began by composing a purposive/judgmental and theoretical nonprobability sample (Neuman, 2014) based on public identification as a scientist, technologist, artist, and/or science and technology manager on the official web page of a European institution (e.g., academic department, laboratory, institute, research project) aimed at the intersection of arts, science, and technology. In addition to sampling research institutions and projects identified through a non-systematic literature review (articles and monographs), we surveyed research projects and associated institutions funded by the European Union Horizon 2020 framework (in the European Commission's Community

Research and Development Information Service—CORDIS online database). Furthermore, we conducted snowball sampling: asking questionnaire participants to name one inter- and/or trans-disciplinary project and/or institution of reference in the European context.

Although useful in an exploratory study, nonprobability sampling methods present limitations to external sample validity concerning the relationship with the target population it is meant to represent, as well as possible selection bias inherent in volunteer sampling (Neuman, 2014). The population is not fully known and individuals could choose whether to self-affiliate with proposed characteristics of scientist, technologist, artist, and/or science and technology manager in a European research institution and/or on a European project with direct experience in interdisciplinarity and/or transdisciplinarity: while the first way integrates and establishes links, the second seeks to transcend and, in an epistemological sense, transgress disciplinary boundaries (Klein, 2010). Participants were individually contacted via institutional email publicly available on their institutional and/or project websites. To secure informed consent, we explicitly explained the survey's research objectives, the study authors and their institutions, and applicable privacy and anonymity regulations both in the email body and the questionnaire header. In total, 81 responses were collected. Of these, eight respondents (9.87%) indicated that they did not have direct individual experience in inter- and/or trans-disciplinary research, while 12 respondents (13.58%) did not answer all survey questions. These 20 respondents (24.69%) were, therefore, excluded from data analysis. As such, our final sample consisted of 61 scientists, technologists, artists, and science and technology managers (Table 13.1) in European research institutions and/or projects with personal experience with interdisciplinarity and/or transdisciplinarity across 17 different European countries (Table 13.2).

TABLE 13.1 Demographic characteristics of survey respondents

Characteristics	Categories	Frequency (n)	Percentage (%)
Gender	Male	22	36.1%
	Female	39	63.9%
Age	20–24	–	–
	25–29	1	1.4%
	30–34	5	7.1%
	35–39	16	22.9%
	40–44	11	15.7%
	45–49	10	14.3%
	50–54	9	12.9%
	55–59	4	5.7%
	60–64	3	4.3%
	> 65	2	2.9%
	M	44.64	
	SD	9.06	

TABLE 13.2 Countries represented by survey respondents

Country	n (%)
Austria	1 (2%)
Belgium	1 (2%)
Bulgaria	1 (2%)
Estonia	1 (2%)
France	1 (2%)
Germany	18 (30%)
Italy	1 (2%)
Lithuania	1 (2%)
Netherlands	3 (5%)
Poland	1 (2%)
Portugal	3 (5%)
Russia	1 (2%)
Slovenia	1 (2%)
Spain	1 (2%)
Sweden	3 (5%)
Switzerland	13 (21%)
UK	10 (16%)
Total	61 (100%)

Results

We then analyzed the sample using descriptive statistics (Holcomb, 2017), including frequency distribution, central tendency (mean), and dispersion (standard deviation), as well as calculating interquartile range (IQR) to detect outliers. Additionally, Pearson coefficients enabled measuring the extent to which several variables fluctuated together. We organized our results in five subsections, each corresponding to the research question that guided the survey.

Perceptions regarding the "two cultures" problem

The findings revealed that participants moderately agreed that scientists and artists belong to two different cultures (M = 3.57, SD = 0.158). An aggregate of 63.9% of participants agreed with this view: 39.3% somewhat agreed and 24.6% totally agreed. Analysis further showed that male participants reported higher levels of agreement (M = 3.95, SD = 1.046) than female participants (M = 3.36, SD = 1.287). The 30- to 34-year old (M = 4.20, SD = 0.447) and 45- to 49-year-old (M = 4.10, SD = 0.994) age groups contained the highest majorities of participants who agreed with perceptions of a cultural divide. Figure 13.1 depicts a small number (*n* = 4) of mild outliers on the bottom end (case numbers 33, 54, 22, 43). These participants strongly disagreed with the existence of two separate cultures. The Pearson product correlation of the "two cultures" perspective and the perception of a lack of mutual understanding between scientists and

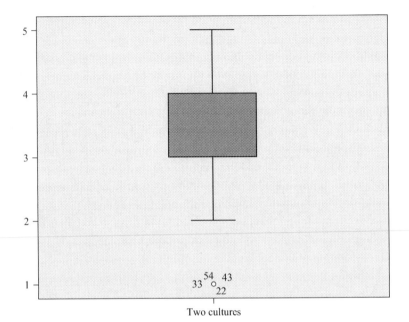

FIGURE 13.1 Boxplot of the perceptions of "two cultures" problem.

artists were moderately positive and statistically significant ($r = 0.387$, $p \leq 0.001$). A moderately positive and statistically significant correlation also appeared in Figure 13.1 between the "two cultures" perspective and the perceived impact of educational specialization on reinforcement of a cultural divide among arts, science, and technology ($r = 0.305$, $p \leq 0.005$).

Perceptions regarding lack of mutual understanding between scientists and artists

Participants tended to moderately agree that scientists and artists lack mutual understanding ($M = 3.25$, $SD = 0.132$). While 41% of participants somewhat agreed with this perspective, 19.7% neither agreed nor disagreed, and 29.5% somewhat disagreed. Our analysis revealed that male participants reported higher levels of agreement ($M = 3.50$, $SD = 1.102$) than female participants ($M = 3.10$, $SD = 0.968$). The 55- to 64-year-old age group ($M = 3.75$, $SD = 1.258$) included the highest majority of participants who agreed with this view. In this instance, no outliers appeared. As previously mentioned, the Pearson product correlation of the "two cultures" perspective and perception of a lack of mutual understanding between scientists and artists was found to be moderately positive and statistically significant. Our analysis also revealed a moderately positive and statistically significant correlation between the mutual understanding variable and the viewpoint that academic department structures reinforce a cultural divide among arts, science, and technology ($r = 0.340$, $p \leq 0.001$).

Perceptions of the impact of educational specialization

An aggregate of 85.2% of participants in our study believed that educational specialization reinforces a cultural divide among arts, science, and technology (M = 4.20, SD = 0.125): 45.9% of respondents strongly agreed and 39.3% somewhat agreed with this view. Female participants reported higher levels of agreement (M = 4.31, SD = 0.950) than male participants (M = 4, SD = 1.024). Our analysis also revealed that the 60- to 64-year-old (M = 4.67, SD = 5.77) and 40- to 44-year-old (M = 4.36, SD = 0.924) age groups of scientists, technologists, artists, and science and technology managers working in European research institutions and/or projects were those with the highest majority who reported this perception. As depicted in Figure 13.2, a small number ($n = 5$) of outliers appeared on the bottom end (case numbers 33, 41, 28, 51, 45), disagreeing with the notion that educational specialization reinforces a cultural divide of arts, science, and technology. Additionally, the Pearson product correlation of the impact of educational specialization and the impact of academic department structure on the epistemic dichotomy was moderately positive and statistically significant ($r = 0.626$, $p \leq 0.001$).

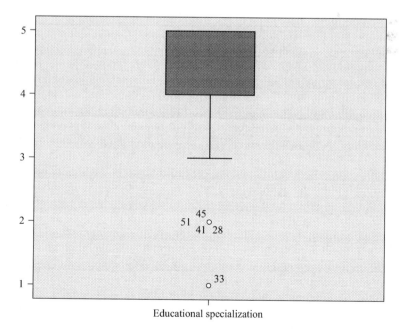

FIGURE 13.2 Boxplot on the impact of educational specialization.

Perceptions of the impact of the academic department structure

Participants also indicated a high level of agreement with the statement that academic department structure reinforces a cultural divide separating arts, science, and technology (M = 4.11, SD = 0.124). An aggregate of 82% of respondents agreed, with 41% strongly agreeing and 41% somewhat agreeing with that claim. Female participants reported higher levels of agreement (M = 4.18, SD = 0.970) than male participants (M = 4.00, SD = 0.976). The 60- to 64-year-old (M = 4.67, SD = 0.577) and 30- to 34-year-old (M = 4.40, SD = 0.894) age groups included the highest majorities of participants who agreed with this perspective. As shown in Figure 13.3, a few (n = 5) outliers appeared at the bottom end (case numbers 33, 30, 28, 36, 31).

Perceptions of the integrated approach to addressing contemporary societal challenges

Finally, data analysis demonstrated that scientists, technologists, artists, and science and technology managers working in European research institutions and/or projects consider that solutions to contemporary societal challenges (e.g., climate change, migration-related issues) require an integrated approach offered by artistic, scientific, and technological disciplines (M = 4.57, SD = 0.129). Indeed, an aggregate of 88.5% supported this position, which included 80.3% who strongly

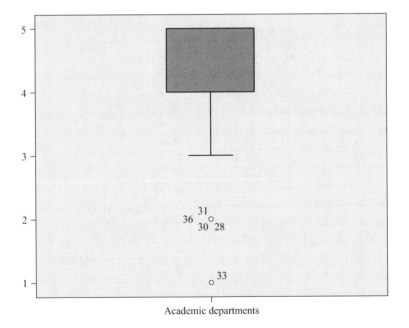

FIGURE 13.3 Boxplot on the impact of academic department structure.

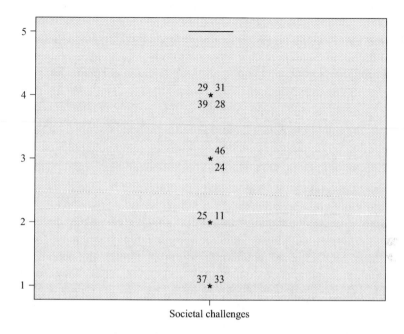

FIGURE 13.4 Boxplot on the integrated approach to addressing contemporary societal challenges.

agreed and 8.2% who somewhat agreed with the premise. The level of agreement between male respondents (M = 4.59, SD = 0.959) and female respondents (M = 4.56, SD = 1.046) was statistically identical. Participants aged 55 to 59 years old were in absolute agreement (M = 5.00, SD = 0.000), and participants aged 45 to 49 years old indicated a very high level of agreement (M = 4.90, SD = 0.316). Despite these very high mean values, some extreme outliers (case numbers 37, 33, 25, 11), as well mild outliers (case numbers 24, 46, 39, 28, 29, 31) appeared at the bottom end as Figure 13.4 shows. In this case, the Pearson product coefficient did not reveal any statistically significant correlation.

Discussion

Our exploratory results concerning epistemic cultures in European intersections of art–science opened two main lines of interpellation:

(a) **Institutional design and management**. Participants externalized ontological opposition between the "two cultures" to the modern social organization of education and academic institutions, namely through specialization and departmentalization. They cited both are contributing factors to a cultural divide of arts, science, and technology while considering a more integrated approach is needed to address contemporary societal challenges. This observation gains particular relevance in view of the design and release of STEAM programs (science, technology, engineering, arts, and mathematics) – and indeed of a New Bauhaus – often taken as a solution to attenuate a culture of silos (e.g., de la Garza and Travis, 2019). A cultural divide is perpetuated by the way in which activities are institutionalized, and interdisciplinarity and transdisciplinarity are constrained by conventional antinomies perpetuated by administrative procedures of higher education and R&D institutions. Given this scope, our study reiterates the importance of institutionalizing at both material and epistemic levels formal mechanisms to encourage and nurture inter- and trans-disciplinary collaboration (e.g., Bruce et al., 2004; Van Heur, 2010).

(b) **(Re)emergence of a frontier intellectual**. If the realization of the holistic vision of art–science requires the physical and administrative assembly of proper epistemic living spaces' mechanisms, that step is inseparable from the institutional legitimization of "frontier" intellectuals, or, as previously designated, of a transdisciplinary attitude (Nicolescu, 2014) of researchers who fully recognize themselves and their endeavors in the hybridity, interspace, and interlanguage of phenomena and methods. Although their individual traits have been previously advanced (Augsburg, 2014), we argue that a key tension exists in modern knowledge organization: (i) between already legitimate modes of research and (ii) emergent modes in search of legitimation. We consider essential an intervention in and by institutions in order to explicitly recognize the inter- and/or trans-place of these individuals becoming transdisciplinary, defending them from being held disciplinary hostages to academic institutions' non-places, left unoccupied or under disciplinary dispute in the day-to-day running functionality of organizations.

Final remarks

A final word on the limitations of this study. We are aware that a quantitative study such as ours risks excluding or minimizing contextual practices that can only be qualitatively examined. For this reason, our results remind all of us of the need of ethnographic studies on interdisciplinarity and transdisciplinarity in art–science contexts. In particular, we are mindful that it is not possible to determine probabilities when using nonprobability sampling methods. As such, inferences using such samples have unknown reliability. For this reason, the current study needs to be replicated through the consolidation of a random sampling process in the European context and elsewhere. Similarly, volunteer sampling can also result in sampling bias, as individuals may choose whether to participate in the online questionnaire and/or whether to self-affiliate with proposed conceptual categories. Guaranteed a random sampling process, it will be particularly fruitful to develop a predictive analysis based on hypothetical correlations of an inter- and trans-disciplinary culture with variables such as age, gender, number of years of experience in research, and scientific and artistic subdomains, among others.

References

Augsburg, T. (2014). Becoming transdisciplinary: The emergence of the transdisciplinary individual. *World Futures*, 70(3–4), 233–247. https://doi.org/10.1080/02604027.2014.934639

Barnes, B. (2001). Practice as collective action. In Karin Knorr Cetina, Theodore R. Schatzki, & Eike von Savigny (Eds.), *The Practice Turn in Contemporary Theory*. pp. 233–247 Routledge.

Barry, A., & Born, G. (Eds.). (2013). *Interdisciplinarity: Reconfigurations of the Social and Natural Sciences*. Routledge.

Barry, A., Born, G., & Weszkalnys, G. (2008). Logics of interdisciplinarity. *Economy and Society*, 37(1), 20–49. https://doi.org/10.1080/03085140701760841

Born, G., & Barry, A. (2010). Art-science. *Journal of Cultural Economy*, 3(1), 103–119. https://doi.org/10.1080/17530351003617610

Boulez, P. (1977). Technology and the Composer. *The Times Literary Supplement*, 3921, 570–571.

Bruce, A., Lyall, C., Tait, J., & Williams, R. (2004). Interdisciplinary integration in Europe: The case of the Fifth Framework programme. *Transdisciplinarity*, 36(4), 457–470. https://doi.org/10.1016/j.futures.2003.10.003

Candy, L., & Edmonds, E. (2018). Practice-based research in the creative arts: Foundations and futures from the front line. *Leonardo*, 51(1), 63–69. https://doi.org/10.1162/LEON_a_01471

Candy, L., Edmonds, E. A., & Poltronieri, F. A. (2002). *Explorations in Art and Technology*. Springer.

Century, M. (1999). *Pathways to Innovation in Digital Culture*. Centre for Research on Canadian Cultural Industries and Institutions, McGill University.

Cetina, K. K. (1991). Epistemic cultures: Forms of reason in science. *History of Political Economy*, 23(1), 105–122. https://doi.org/10.1215/00182702-23-1-105

Cetina, K. K. (1995). Laboratory studies: The cultural approach to the study of science. In Sheila Jasanoff, Gerald E. Markle, James C. Peterson & Trevor Pinch (Eds.), *Handbook of Science and Technology Studies*. SAGE Publications, Inc. https://doi.org/10.4135/9781412990127

Cetina, K. K. (1999). *Epistemic Cultures: How the Sciences Make Knowledge*. Harvard University Press.

Cetina, K. K. (2007). Culture in global knowledge societies: Knowledge cultures and epistemic cultures. *Interdisciplinary Science Reviews*, 32(4), 361–375. https://doi.org/10.1179/030801807X163571

de la Garza, A., & Travis, C. (Eds.). (2019). *The STEAM Revolution: Transdisciplinary Approaches to Science, Technology, Engineering, Arts, Humanities and Mathematics*. Springer International Publishing.

Edmonds, E., & Candy, L. (2010). Relating theory, practice and evaluation in practitioner research. *Leonardo*, 43(5), 470–476. https://doi.org/10.1162/LEON_a_00040

Edwards, D. (2008). *Artscience: Creativity in the Post-Google Generation*. Harvard University Press.

Edwards, D. (2011). *The Lab: Creativity and Culture*. Harvard University Press.

Eldred, S. M. (2016). Art–science collaborations: Change of perspective. *Nature*, *537*(7618), 125–126. https://doi.org/10.1038/nj7618-125a

Felt, U. (2009). Knowing and living in academic research. In Eds. Ulrike Felt (Ed.), *Knowing and Living in Academic Research: Convergences and Heterogeneity in Research Cultures in the European Context*. (pp. 17–39). Institute of Sociology of the Academy of Sciences of the Czech Republic.

Felt, U., & Fochler, M. (2012). Re-ordering epistemic living spaces: On the tacit governance effects of the public communication of science. In S. Rödder, M. Franzen, & P. Weingart (Eds.), *The Sciences' Media Connection –Public Communication and Its Repercussions* (pp. 133–154). Springer Netherlands. https://doi.org/10.1007/978-94-007-2085-5_7

Gamwell, L. (2020). *Exploring the Invisible: Art, Science, and the Spiritual – Revised and Expanded Edition*. Princeton University Press.

Glauser, A. (2010). Formative encounters: Laboratory life and artistic practice. In *Artists-in-Labs Networking in the Margins*. J. Scott (Eds). (pp. 12–22). Springer.

Henchoz, N., Puissant, P.-X., Leal, A. S., Moreira, T., & Vinet, H. (2019). Artist residencies for innovation: Development of a global framework. *ACM SIGGRAPH 2019 Art Gallery*. https://doi.org/10.1145/3306211.3320140

Heylighen, F., & Petrović, K. (2020). Foundations of artscience: Formulating the problem. *Foundations of Science*. https://doi.org/10.1007/s10699-020-09660-6

Holcomb, Z. C. (2017). *Fundamentals of Descriptive Statistics*. Routledge.

Kastenhofer, K. (2007). CONVERGING EPISTEMIC CULTURES? *Innovation: The European Journal of Social Science Research*, *20*(4), 359–373. https://doi.org/10.1080/13511610701767908

Klein, J. T. (2010). A taxonomy of interdisciplinarity. In Frodeman, R., Klein, J. T., & Mitcham, C. (Eds.), *The Oxford Handbook of Interdisciplinarity*. (pp. 15–30). Oxford University Press.

King, B. A. (2020). Space Art + Space Science: A polymathic paradigm shift in the art/science dialogue. *OpenUCT*. http://hdl.handle.net/11427/32739

Latour, B. (1998). From the world of science to the world of research? *Science*, *280*(5361), 208. https://doi.org/10.1126/science.280.5361.20

Neuman, W. L. (2014). *Social Research Methods: Qualitative and Quantitative Approaches*. Pearson.

Nicolescu, B. (2014). Methodology of transdisciplinarity. *World Futures*, *70*(3–4), 186–199. https://doi.org/10.1080/02604027.2014.934631

Paterson, S. K., Le Tissier, M., Whyte, H., Robinson, L. B., Thielking, K., Ingram, M., & McCord, J. (2020). Examining the potential of art-science collaborations in the Anthropocene: A case study of catching a wave. *Frontiers in Marine Science*, *7*, 340. Https://doi.org/10.3389/fmars.2020.00340

Reinsborough, M. (2020). Art-science collaboration in an EPSRC/BBSRC-funded synthetic biology UK research centre. *NanoEthics*, *14*(1), 93–111. https://doi.org/10.1007/s11569-020-00367-3

Rock, J., & Howard, S. (2018). Legitimizing boundary crossing for the average scientist: Two cases acknowledging how arts practice informs science. *Leonardo*, *52*(3), 305–308. https://doi.org/10.1162/leon_a_01637

Schnugg, C. (2019a). Building up the basics: An introduction to artscience collaboration. In C. Schnugg (Ed.), *Creating ArtScience Collaboration: Bringing Value to Organizations* (pp. 1–12). Springer International Publishing. https://doi.org/10.1007/978-3-030-04549-4_1

Schnugg, C. (2019b). *Creating ArtScience Collaboration: Bringing Value to Organizations.* Palgrave MacMillan.

Schnugg, C., & Song, B. (2020). An organizational perspective on artscience collaboration: Opportunities and challenges of platforms to collaborate with artists. *Journal of Open Innovation: Technology, Market, and Complexity, 6*(1), 6.

Scott, J. (2010). Introduction: Networking is both an art and a science! In Jill Scott (Ed.), *Artists-in-Labs: Networking in the Margins.* Springer.

Smith, P. H. (2006). Art, science, and visual culture in early modern Europe. *Isis, 97*(1), 83–100. https://doi.org/10.1086/501102

Snow, C. P. (1959). *The Two Cultures and the Scientific Revolution.* The Syndics of the Cambridge University Press.

Snow, C. P. (Ed.). (1963). The two cultures: A second look. In *The Two Cultures* (pp. 53–100). Cambridge University Press; Cambridge Core. https://doi.org/10.1017/CBO9781139196949.006

Sue, V. M. & Ritter, L. A. (2012). *Conducting Online Surveys.* Sage.

Van Heur, B. (2010). The built environment of higher education and research: Architecture and the expectation of innovation. *Geography Compass, 4*(12), 1713–1724. https://doi.org/10.1111/j.1749-8198.2010.00408.x

von der Leyen, U. (2020). *A New European Bauhaus: Op-ed Article by Ursula von der Leyen, President of the European Commission.* European Commission. https://ec.europa.eu/commission/presscorner/detail/en/AC_20_1916

Wilson, S. (2002). *Information Arts: Intersections of Art, Science and Technology.* MIT Press.

14
MAKING AND TAKING TIME

Work, funding, and assessment infrastructures in inter- and trans-disciplinary research

Ulrike Felt

Introduction

On 4 February 2020, the renowned journal *Nature* published in their news blog a contribution entitled, "What are fake interdisciplinary collaborations and why do they occur?" (Dai, 2020). This question spells out an often only tacitly acknowledged phenomenon: while the list of co-authors on a publication might imply interdisciplinary collaboration, "no knowledge integration occurs", and researchers actually simply "end up working on their individual and mono-disciplinary research separately" (Dai, 2020). The contribution thus points at a tension. Policymakers on the European and national levels, funding agencies, and many academic institutions increasingly call for more inter- and trans-disciplinary research (IDR/TDR), in order to address complex societal challenges, and have even instituted often normatively defined new funding lines (see, e.g., Vienni Baptista et al., 2020). However, simultaneously, we also have dense empirical evidence that many key features of the academic system – such as career structures, evaluation schemes, and reward structures – have not adapted to accommodate multiple IDR/TDR realities. As a result, exhortations to work across disciplinary boundaries (interdisciplinarity) or to integrate societal actors into research (transdisciplinarity) are unevenly distributed, differing by fields, institutions, funding agencies, and countries. We thus witness the creation of multiple, situated, and often only temporally available "knowing spaces", which "set more or less permeable boundaries to the possible and the accessible" (Law, 2017, p. 47). These spaces are framed by locally specific historical developments as well as wider contemporary imaginaries of the university and its place in society. Thus, while international research and teaching systems seem to converge toward neoliberal models of academic governance, we also witness important divergences and local specificities (Felt, 2009).

DOI: 10.4324/9781003129424-17

This chapter focuses on discrepancies between visions and realities in IDR/TDR, specifically on the role of temporal imaginaries, structures, and practices prevalent in contemporary academia. It draws our attention to how historical and geographical contexts shape institutional possibilities, to how the needs of IDR/TDR potentially clash with dominant temporal orders, and, finally, to points for necessary rearrangements of contemporary academia to make space for them. My analysis thus joins a growing body of literature, which critically investigates temporal regimes that govern contemporary research and higher education (e.g., Gibbs et al., 2015; Felt, 2009; Vostal, 2021). The notion of regime aims at capturing how institutions and their leadership, their visions and ideological orientations, aims they define as worth attaining, and policies they put in place come together to bring to life specific temporalities. In doing so, I embrace an actor-centered perspective by analyzing researchers' narratives about IDR/TDR collected in a number of research projects. I am thus investigating narratives dealing with personal and professional challenges, as well as inspirational moments of engaging in such collaborations, epistemic and organizational factors that come to matter in these environments, and ways that institutions open up or close down possibilities and which value regimes they encounter. The stories might differ considerably in detail according to the stage of the career of a researcher, if we speak not only of inter- or trans-disciplinary research, but also moving to different research traditions and fields. However, my analysis will remain on an aggregated level in order to make readers more aware of the importance of embracing a time-sensitive perspective than to show the detailed dynamic of any specific tensions I point at.

A time-sensitive perspective to study inter- and trans-disciplinary research

In his seminal book on *Time Wars*, Jeremy Rifkin (1987) draws attention to the fact that "every culture has its unique set of temporal fingerprints" and that knowing "a people [...] is to know the time values they live by". This is also true for research cultures and research communities. To know them is to know the time values they live by, i.e., to know how time is expressed through diverse arrangements in work, organizations, structures, and the lives of scientists. Moreover, it is of particular salience at a moment in time when we are witnessing a battle involving advocates of speed and efficiency: more specifically, between researchers who have been successfully transformed into competitive "entrepreneurial managers of their own careers, publications, and grant portfolios" (Fochler, 2016, p. 924) and those who stress temporalities of academia need to be brought in line with the needs of researchers. This tension is especially apparent in the IDR/TDR domain. However, as Barbara Adam (1998, p. 9) argues, time often remains invisible for us "work[ing] outside and beyond the reach of our senses". We take time for granted and treat it as a straightforward physical entity that can be managed. Thus, both its multidimensionality and its performativity often escape thorough attention. The temporal regimes governing contemporary academia could thus be compared with an invisible infrastructure that frames ways in which researchers can know and define the kinds of academic lives that they can live. This infrastructure also fosters or hinders creating and sustaining feelings of community and belonging (Felt, 2009; 2017a). Conceptualizing time as a basic infrastructure of any research system draws attention not only to a specific form of political and institutional rationality but also to affective dimensions embedded in and performed through it (Larkin, 2013).

Where do these academic temporalities emerge from? The historian of time, Rinderspacher (1988), points to the role of what he calls "time generators". These are key sites and processes (e.g., evaluative rhythms, steps in careers, work packages in projects) that create binding, standardized, and homogenized temporal requirements and regulations, imposing rhythm and speed on a specific system. Indeed, when investigating more recent academic reforms – for example, regarding funding, assessment processes, and careers – we can observe that each reform also involved crucial temporal re-orderings. Together, these re-timings fundamentally reshape academic "time cultures". As they often remain tacit, they escape closer scrutiny and are rarely subject to questions of responsibility. Indeed, these time generators are key agents in opening up or closing down potential IDR/TDR engagements. The ways in which trajectories and rhythms of academic lives, careers, and projects have to be aligned, implementation of "output per time unit" as a proxy for performance and quality, or asynchronicities between different temporal demands on researchers are but some of the aspects that constitute challenges to IDR/TDR. Embracing a time-sensitive approach is thus a window to a deeper understanding of some of the less visible dynamics fostering or hindering IDR/TDR.

Knowing and living in academic research

To fully understand the role of time in inter- and trans-disciplinary research, two entangled sensitizing concepts underpin analysis and methodological approach in this chapter: *epistemic living spaces* (Felt, 2009) and *narrative infrastructures* (Felt, 2017b). My focus is not so much formal rules and regulations that govern research and teaching in Austrian universities, but more on how researchers perceive their lives in these academic institutions. I thus put researchers' narratives at the center of analysis in order to gain insights into how they make sense of contemporary research environments. This focus means embracing a narrative approach (Czarniawska, 2004) toward time in academic lives to better assess how temporalities matter in IDR/TDR practice. Narratives are key to grasping the constitution of researchers' broader sense of direction and purpose, reconfiguring of individual and institutional identities, and enabling and constraining researchers' actions. "Narrative infrastructures" in particular draws attention to the "network of temporally stabilised narratives through which meanings and values of academic knowledge/work and its relation to society can be articulated, circulated and exchanged" (Felt, 2017b, p. 54). To reiterate, seemingly stable narrative performances of time constitute the ambient discursive environment into which researchers grow, and which, in turn, potentially enables or limits IDR/TDR. These narratives can circulate on the institutional level but are also specific for subcommunities and assume different forms, some future-oriented so encoding hopes and expectations, and others expressing justifications for actions (not) taken and, yet others, voicing goals to be achieved or experienced frustrations.

This definition and the functions of narrative infrastructures are closely tied to the second sensitizing concept – *epistemic living space* (Felt, 2009). It draws attention to the co-productive relation between potential lives in academia and the knowledge that can be produced. The concept sensitizes the analyst to entanglements of institutional rationales, epistemic work, life-course decisions, and wider research and teaching politics. Taking such a perspective then alerts us to how researchers perceive their own room for maneuvering within IDR/TDR, how they coordinate the different demands they are confronted with, how they relate to the, sometimes, contradictory sets of values relevant to their work and identity, and, finally, how all this relates to the constant tacit and explicit evaluations they encounter. IDR/TDR, for example, demands time-intensive engagements with other epistemic environments, which often stand in tension with the expectation to be productive in terms of countable achievements such as publications in top journals. Epistemic living spaces are not fixed but fluid. They differ based on career stage, fields, institutional culture, and the direct work environment, in addition to formal and informal networks that support a researcher (Felt, 2017b). To be sensitive to these different pushes and pulls is especially important when looking into IDR/TDR, as relevant value registers differ and so do work practices and epistemic problems.

Materials and methods

My analysis is situated in the history and current policies of the Austrian university system. In a nutshell, four perspectives are essential. First, in Austria, access to higher education is open. Only proof of successfully completing secondary education is needed: there are no admission examinations for the most part and there are little to no tuition fees depending on the student's nationality. This policy leads to high student numbers and student-teacher ratios that are imbalanced across fields and institutions. Second, while the university finances basic research infrastructure, actual research, and a considerable share of PhDs and post-docs, they must be financed via competitive third-party funding. As a result, the number of early-stage researchers on time-limited, often part-time, contracts has grown disproportionally. This imbalance creates considerable tensions when it comes to IDR/TDR. Third, a number of institutions and funding agencies have launched IDR/TDR program lines highlighting the importance of this knowledge generation practice. The University of Vienna, for example, currently fosters interdisciplinary research through funding of temporary inter-faculty research platforms for four years, and the Austrian funding agency for basic research (FWF) has launched the #ConnectingMinds program supporting trans-disciplinary research in areas "of high current and future social relevance in which possible solutions are sought to complex challenges".[1] Fourth, since the turn of the century, universities have witnessed the growing importance of international competitiveness and research excellence (e.g., measured by European Research Council grants), regular reference to indicators (e.g., publications in high-ranking journals), and the university's place in international rankings, as well as formalization of career procedures including highlighting staff mobility.

However, a broader debate about how these changes have transformed contemporary research cultures has not occurred, including what these conditions mean for who can and who wants to build a career in science, as well as ways that reward systems would need to be adapted to support IDR/TDR. Toward that end, this chapter builds on data gathered from more than 100 interviews, as well as 11 group discussions with 97 researchers in different stages of their careers in the Austrian academic context. Interviews and group discussions took place between 2006 and 2018 as part of three major European and Austrian research projects as well as collaborative work in the research platform "Responsible Research and Innovation in Academic Practice".[2] With one exception, the projects did not explicitly study IDR/TDR, rather, changes in the academic research system more generally. However, the topic of IDR/TDR regularly came up when interviewees reflected on contemporary academic working conditions and on demands to become more open toward societal concerns. Analysis of the interviews yielded dominant clusters of narratives (Czarniawska, 2004) connecting academic temporalities and IDR/TDR. Three of these clusters are discussed in this chapter, exemplifying how researchers narrate, conceptualize, and experience temporalities and how they matter for their work in IDR/TDR projects.

"The project" as key time generator in inter- and trans-disciplinary research

One of the most prominent time generators in contemporary Austrian academia is third-party-funded research projects. The idea that the production of knowledge can be organized into discrete temporal units of time, such as a few years, has become a "blueprint for the way in which whole communities should do science" (Leonelli and Ankeny, 2015, p. 705). It shapes institutional rhythms and lives of researchers. A project is, in the first place, nothing more than an elaborate form of a promise that identifies a relevant problem to be solved, outlines knowledges, experiences, and competencies that are needed, and justifies how much time and resources are required to develop solutions/answers. Lives in science have thus been colonized by "project-related principles, rules, techniques and procedures, aspiring to form a new iron cage of project rationality" (Maylor et al., 2006, p. 664). The project introduces a knowledge/time equivalence (often expressed in person months), supports the idea of maximizing efficiency, and creates an illusion of control (such as defining work packages and deliverables). The project, however, is much more than a clearly delineated unit of funding aiming to answer a specific question. It is a qualitatively new and different form of the social organization of research (e.g., Grabher, 2004).

What, then, does temporal rationality tied to the projectification of research mean for IDR/TDR (e.g., Ylijoki, 2015)? Many interviewees believed IDR/TDR is more time-intensive than classical disciplinary work: including time for building trust, learning each other's languages, and developing a shared thought style (Fleck, 1935/1979) for seeing a problem and developing solutions. Researchers thus spoke of "a different temporal logic", and generally described the research "process as slower", or as a "slow but, very productive, way" of finding solutions for complex problems. They also frequently pondered how much more "time [they] would need to invest" to achieve their goals. This concern is frequently tied to justificatory narratives (Boltanski & Thévenot, 2006) that underline the worth of investing time in socially relevant research and the hope IDR/TDR would assure "a broadening of horizons and an improvement" for research. These observations illustrate additional "registers of worth that [our informants working in IDR/TDR] draw on to inform, orient and justify their actions" (Fochler, 2016, p. 929). Some informants, for instance, underlined their readiness to invest the required time first, hoping a positive impact would become visible later. At the same time, virtually all interviewees believed this ideal stands in stark tension to demands of an output-oriented science system and capitalist logics of accumulation that govern academia (Fochler, 2016; Felt, 2017c). An increasing number of tasks have to be accomplished concurrently despite the limited life cycle of projects – including engaging in collaborative modes of cross-border knowledge production and delivering output in the format and rhythms academic institutions expect and reward. Instead of re-timing research in the case of IDR/TDR projects, researchers testified they had to "squeeze inter- and trans-disciplinary engagements into the already tight schedule".

The tensions time demands create then lead to weighing options, a debate reflected in the following two quotes by researchers working in transdisciplinary projects.

For one:

> if I invest the time I spend in the field with my [non-academic research] partners into method development, probably two or three more publications would have been possible.

Or the other way round, if it were possible to disregard the need for more formal output:

> we could have designed the research process with the community quite differently; with more participation, different participation, more intensive interaction, really thinking together.

210 Ulrike Felt

The phrase "really thinking together" nicely captures the sentiment of the *Nature* news blog cited at the beginning of this chapter – engagement with researchers from other disciplines or with non-scientific partners runs the danger of being conceptualized as an add-on; as "additional work" that in reality often gets confined to very short and specifically defined moments and events that keep time investment under control during a project (Felt et al., 2012).

Of the two remaining temporal narratives, the second project-related one gravitates around the time needed to collectively formulate a research question. Although interdisciplinary researchers describe the collective problem definition as time-intensive yet feasible, in transdisciplinary projects researchers alone typically performed this work. In-depth engagement with non-academic partners was viewed as too time-consuming given chances to receive funding were considered notoriously low. This reluctance was further justified by highlighting the need for a societal problem to be transformed into a scientific problem first in order to be successfully validated within the academic reward system. However, those who hold power to define the problem and render it a taken-for-granted starting point also pre-shape any potential solutions (Jasanoff, 2003).

The third major temporal narrative, in turn, is of epistemic and social fragmentation due to the time-limited character of projectified research. Even if a project team invests time in building a thought collective and developing a corresponding thought style within the project (Fleck, 1935/1979), virtually all interviewees in transdisciplinary projects reported they would not have further collaborative relations with non-academic partners after the project ended. Moreover, they would not have temporal resources to sustain this relational network either before or afterward. This challenge leads not only to a lack of temporal continuity but also to the loss of know-how achieved during a project. Researchers typically move on to the next project and are often already engaging in securing its funding while the first project is still running. Partners outside the academy would also typically remain in their life-worlds. Thus, integration at best would happen only during project time, and at worst never really take place.

Career, socialization, and identity work temporalized

In their reflections on the nature of interdisciplinarity, Barry and Born (2013: 1) reminded us of the core role of disciplinarity: "Disciplines, discipline, disciples". They speak specifically of shared commitment not only to methods, concepts, and practices but, above all, to the aim of ruling out "undisciplined and undisciplinary objects, methods and concepts". Consequently, moving into IDR/TDR is often accompanied by stressing the need to move out of "the comfort zone of my own discipline", as one interviewee called it, and engaging with a different cultural environment. This need then also means getting to know another culture's temporal fingerprints, in the sense of its prevailing temporal imaginaries and orders. This move has often been described as difficult, in particular by younger researchers. It is cast as risky navigation of unknown territories, underscored by statements that life would be easier if they would simply remain "disciplined": in that case, they would know what to expect from a field and anticipate, to a certain degree, their trajectory through space and time, and they would become socialized into the rhythm of disciplinary work and delivery of output.

Compared with IDR/TDR, disciplines are also generally depicted as stable territories with clear internal structures and widely recognized boundaries. They are seen as having a canonical history, traditions, and accompanying myths, as well as having a clear set of core journals and conferences where researchers present their work. Yet, in keeping with this chapter, disciplines as knowledge communities also perform specific "time values" (Rifkin, 1987) researchers have to live by, such as how long one could remain in a specific position, how quickly to publish, or how many published papers would be expected at a specific point in an academic career. Disciplines are perceived as offering a narrative infrastructure (Felt, 2017b), which young scholars can tap into and contribute to, stabilizing it by telling their personal stories about being part of a field. In the context of transdisciplinary research, they also point to the lack of resources available to storify their lives and describe their struggles to identify what could be regarded as an adequate rhythm of knowledge production or what kind of career trajectory they could expect (Felt et al., 2013). Thus, they describe processes of socialization as fragmented, unclear, and always somewhat limited through the temporality of a project that represented the sole institutional attachment for many young researchers. At the same time, socialization is an essential part of learning to engage with specific value repertoires that characterize a field (Fochler et al., 2016), which explains why balancing the complex relation between invested time and expected value are at the core when these young scholars try to figure out who they want to be and how they could describe their emerging identities.

Temporalities, value(s), and evaluation in inter- and trans-disciplinary research work

As we have seen, then, time matters here on many levels. It takes time and extra work to develop and care for attachments to different knowledge communities without knowing if this investment will be rewarded and how long these configurations will last. Furthermore, a clear collective that would define orders of worth to which inter- and trans-disciplinary researchers can subscribe is lacking, as well as which could at least support the hope for a decent career trajectory. In particular, young researchers describe the need to engage in constant positioning work, which demands considerable temporal resources and mental strength. Several questions follow. First, how then can an individual craft an interdisciplinary or transdisciplinary CV that allows one to successfully remain engaged in research? And how is it possible to reconcile values IDR/TDR stands for, such as sensitivity toward societal concerns or readiness to engage with diverse knowledge communities, with evaluation schemes of academic institutions? Both questions open up a related question asked over and over again, even though not always explicitly: Do I simply describe myself as doing IDR/TDR or as being an inter-/trans-disciplinary researcher? While the former is tied to the idea that IDR/TDR is simply a temporarily embraced mode of doing a specific project, the latter points to a long-term commitment to this kind of research.

This invites us to look into the *value ecology* inter- and trans-disciplinary researchers are navigating, i.e., into the multiple, fluid, and situated relationships between values, valuing practices, and identity work, deeply ingrained in research environments our informants are part of, including institutions, labs, groups, funding, and policy discourses. It points to spatio-temporal patterns of research and lives in academia that shape researchers' epistemic living spaces (Felt, 2009), thereby sensitizing us to be attentive to diversity of experiences, justifications, and value orders at work. Researchers actually tap into four different value regimes that are part of the value ecology, all coming with specific temporal imaginaries. On the one hand, they relate to the *academic value regime*, with its ideas of how a career should look, how long each step should take, how many publications can be expected, or how long one should stay in a particular place. At the same time, they nourish self-assessments from the *value regime of science*, which is often related to producing novel insights, no matter the time it takes. Here, value is about long-term and persistent commitments to questions and concerns, as well as to a specific knowledge community. Yet, researchers also encounter the mundane *value regime of research practice* prevalent in everyday life: as a member of a lab, a department, a subfield. These values are expressed through explicit expectations and smaller everyday conversations including feedback on work progress and achievements. Working in IDR/TDR, however, has an additional *societal value regime* related to the ideal of addressing complex real-world problems through cross-border engagements. This value demands different kinds of qualities, such as wanting to get to know different knowledge communities, being open to their concerns and problem perceptions, and understanding their time culture.

Conflicts with regard to the latter *academic value regime* become palpable when inter- and trans-disciplinary researchers tell their stories about how long it takes to produce output that counts in the academic value regime or about concerns that methodological purity ascribed to the *value regime of science* might be compromised if social actors outside the academy produce research input. This concern is then closely tied to questions of how CVs get scrutinized along temporal norms prevalent in academic institutions (Kaltenbrunner et al., 2021). Having been part of many review panels throughout my career, I frequently encountered assessments of the following kind: "for a person x years after the PhD, one can legitimately expect y as an output". Such argumentative strategies of reviewers to comparatively assess the qualifications of a candidate use "time as a judgement device" (Müller, 2021, p. 197). Scientific evaluation processes thus become the locus of generating values (Fochler et al., 2016), making them a key time generator in academia. Being able to craft a CV that meets the temporal expectation then becomes an existential question of whether or not one can have an inter- and trans-disciplinary career. As interdisciplinarity, and even stronger so, transdisciplinarity are ill-supported by preexisting frameworks and well-defined collectives, it becomes harder to assess whether or not the life-course of a person fits situated assessments. While we already witness dissent within disciplines, temporal dimensions of assessment become even fuzzier in inter- and trans-disciplinary work (Lamont, 2009).

Indeed, this fuzziness created considerable tensions between enthusiasm with which young researchers wanted to engage in IDR/TDR because they saw this as a very relevant and caring approach to deal with complex problems and their realization that if they wanted to stay in academia they would have to comply with temporal expectations of disciplined academic structures. The latter pressure then meant prioritizing classical publications over inter- and transdisciplinary engagements (Müller and Kaltenbrunner, 2019). Yet, doing so does not go without consequences. In one transdisciplinary program, we observed the following publication strategy: in higher impact journals, which were generally disciplinarily organized, researchers would publish their findings with hardly any mention of transdisciplinarity, while they would publish their transdisciplinary engagement experiences and less on results in other more interdisciplinary journals, often with lower impact factors.

To summarize, reflections on the temporalization of careers and CVs have opened up the question of how values, evaluations, and temporalities relate to each other. The very idea of opening up research and innovation to a broader range of societal actors and values as well as pluralizing expertise (Nowotny et al., 2001) appears promising; however, if taken seriously, it would demand a radical rethinking of some of the very practices and values that are deeply entrenched in contemporary research cultures. The temporal reflections on careers, socialization, and identity already point to the importance of the nexus time/(e)valuation. While much of the classical valuation and accountability structures are currently focused on publication numbers as the key indicator (Fochler and de Rijcke, 2017), this relates to a specific kind of temporality (Felt, 2017c) that is not welcoming to IDR/TDR.

Concluding remarks

In this chapter, I have argued for the importance of a time-sensitive approach to studying possibilities and limits of inter- and trans-disciplinary research within academic institutions and I have shown how this approach is reflected in researchers' lives. I close with three reflections. First, to return to the initial question, why is it important to look at temporal structures and reflect on transdisciplinarity and interdisciplinarity from this perspective? As prior examples and analysis demonstrated, temporal structures that govern research are rarely made visible but rather constitute a taken-for-granted infrastructure.

Throughout all of the narratives collected from researchers, we saw that they had to perform quite intensive temporal care work to realign their research and their lives with often-contradictory temporal demands in order to create cohesion in an environment that seems fragmented. Yet, a few traces of institutional response to these challenges also appeared. While some special funding schemes supporting IDR/TDR have been created, they remain what I call "island solutions". They are conceptualized as separate from the academic mainland because the different temporalities in these domains are not acknowledged when it comes to career and reward systems. The often-diagnosed emergence of a more problem-driven research (Gibbons et al., 1994; Nowotny et al., 2001) thus cannot develop its full potential as it represents a challenge for individual researchers. Leaving the importance of temporalities unacknowledged reinforces tacitly the territorial imaginary of science (Klein, 2010) as formed by disciplines. This reality means that creating project structures that support IDR/TDR alone will not be sufficient. What is needed is a more profound rethinking of the institutional value ecologies. This goal is much in line with what has been called the paradox of interdisciplinarity (Weingart, 2000; Klein, 2010), which could be easily extended to the transdisciplinary research discussed in this chapter.

Second, it is essential to take the many smaller narratives of researchers and the temporal inconsistencies they encounter seriously. Researchers experience different speeds and rhythms of knowledge communities, be they academic or not. They realize pressure from societal actors to solve a problem while wanting to take the time to develop solutions fitting with quality criteria of science, or they see the value of engagement and the need to produce measurable output. It is, however, critical to attend to these inconsistencies. Certain temporal routines, including the pace and rhythms of developments and institutional responses, are adequate or at least acceptable contributions to creating a feeling of belonging (Edensor, 2006). Therefore, if we want IDR/TDR to flourish and young researchers to engage in the field, making these inconsistencies visible and better aligning different time generators within academic institutions must be the basis for creating attachments and a feeling of community.

Third, as researchers describe their intense time investments needed for "making the transdisciplinary machinery work" as phrased by one interviewee, it is essential to move from focusing so much on project time toward putting process time at the center of institutional considerations (Yliyoki, 2015). While the former is defined by the inherent logic of the project combined with academic expectations, process time draws our attention to the needs and internal logic of research activities. As a focus on the former is already described as problematic for disciplinary research, this emphasis is even more detrimental in IDR/TDR projects, calling for policymakers in universities and funding agencies to not only make proclamations and cast the idea of IDR/TDR into funding programs, but to actually engage with valuation and corresponding evaluation practices that govern the reality of researchers' careers and lives.

To conclude, if the temporal tensions identified in this chapter remain unaddressed, uncertainties and risks related to inter- and trans-disciplinary academic work are made invisible as well. However, these risks and uncertainties are unevenly distributed, and they particularly impact the most vulnerable members of the research community, young scholars who are working in a projectified and highly temporalized academic environment, and in this study, contribute to essential ways that research is produced in Austrian universities. Thus, their epistemic living spaces are under threat. As a result, they often ask the question of whether or not they find them worth inhabiting. If IDR/TDR is to be an attractive option for the next generation of researchers, it is essential to engage in a re-timing of research to make place for realities of inter- and trans-disciplinary work. This means going beyond lip service and allowing different value ecologies to develop with different temporalities that govern contemporary lives in research.

Notes

1 www.fwf.ac.at/en/research-funding/fwf-programmes/connectingminds.
2 These projects were: Knowledge, Institutions and Gender. An East-West Comparative Study (2006–2009, EU/FP6); Living Changes in the Life Sciences (2007–2010; BMWF/GEN-AU/ELSA); Transdisciplinarity as Culture and Practice (2009–2013; BMWF/proVISION).
    Thanks to all who have worked with me on these projects and to the researchers that have given their time and shared their visions. For more information see: http://sts.univie.ac.at/en/research/completed-projects/ and http://rri.univie.ac.at/.

References

Adam, B. (1998) *Timescapes of Modernity. The Environment & Invisible Hazards*. London and New York: Routledge.
Barry, A. and Born, G. (eds) (2013) *Interdisciplinarity: Reconfigurations of the Social and Natural Sciences*. London and New York: Routledge.
Boltanski, L. and Thevenot, L. (2006) *On Justification: Economies of Worth*. Princeton: Princeton University Press.
Czarniawska, B. (2004) *Narratives in Social Science Research*. London: Sage Publications.
Edensor, T. (2006) 'Reconsidering national temporalities: Institutional times, everyday routines, serial spaces and synchronicities', *European Journal of Social Theory*, 9(4), pp. 525–545.
Dai, L. (2020) 'What are fake interdisciplinary collaborations and why do they occur?' https://www.natureindex.com/news-blog/what-are-fake-interdisciplinary-collaborations-and-why-do-they-occur#.XmNoJEurTX8.mailto, accessed 14 June 2020.
Felt, U. (2009) 'Knowing and living in academic research', in Felt, U. (ed.), *Knowing and Living in Academic Research. Convergence and Heterogeneity in Research Cultures in the European Context*. Prague: Academy of Sciences of the Czech Republic, pp. 17–39.
Felt, U. (2017a) 'Of timescapes and knowledgescapes: Retiming research and higher education', in Scott, P., Gallacher, J. and Parry, G. (eds), *New Landscapes and Languages in Higher Education*. Oxford: Oxford University Press, pp. 129–148.
Felt, U. (2017b) '"Response-able practices" or "new bureaucracies of virtue": The challenges of making RRI work in academic environments', in Asveld, L., van Dam-Mieras, R., Swierstra, T., Lavrijssen, S., Linse, K. and van den Hoven, J. (eds),

Responsible Innovation 3: A European Agenda? Cham: Springer International Publishing, pp. 49–68.

Felt, U. (2017c) 'Under the shadow of time: Where indicators and academic values meet', *Engaging Science, Technology, and Society*, 3, p. 53.

Felt, U., Igelsböck, J., Schikowitz, A. and Völker, T. (2012) 'Challenging participation in sustainability research', *International Journal of Deliberative Mechanisms in Science*, 1(1), pp. 4–34.

Felt, U., Igelsböck, J., Schikowitz, A. and Völker, T. (2013) 'Growing into what? The (un-)disciplined socialisation of early stage researchers in transdisciplinary research', *Higher Education*, 65(4), pp. 511–524.

Fleck, L. (1935/1979) *Genesis and Development of a Scientific Fact*. Chicago: The University of Chicago Press.

Fochler, M. (2016) 'Variants of epistemic capitalism: Knowledge production and the accumulation of worth in commercial biotechnology and the academic life sciences', *Science, Technology & Human Values*, 41(5), pp. 922–948.

Fochler, M. and de Rijcke, S. (2017) 'Implicated in the indicator game? An experimental debate', *Engaging Science, Technology, and Society*, 3, pp. 21–40.

Fochler, M., Felt, U. and Müller, R. (2016) 'Unsustainable growth, hyper-competition, and worth in life science research: Narrowing evaluative repertoires in doctoral and postdoctoral scientists' work and lives', *Minerva*, 54(2), pp. 175–200.

Gibbons, M., Limoges, C., Nowotny, H., Schwarzman, S., Scott, P. and Trow, M. (1994) *The New Production of Knowledge: The Dynamics of Science and Research in Contemporary Societies*. London: SAGE.

Gibbs, P., Ylijoki, O.-H., Guzmán-Valenzuela, C. and Barnett, R. (eds) (2015) *Universities in the Flux of Time. An Exploration of Time and Temporality in University Life*. London: Routledge.

Grabher, G. (2004) 'Temporary architectures of learning: Knowledge governance in project ecologies', *Organization Studies*, 25(9), pp. 1491–1514.

Jasanoff, S. (2003) 'Technologies of humility: Citizen participation in governing science', *Minerva*, 41(3), pp. 223–244.

Kaltenbrunner, W., de Rijcke, S., Müller, R. and Burner-Fritsch, I. (2021) 'On the chronopolitics of academic CVs in peer review', in Vostal, F. (ed.), *Inquiring into Academic Timescapes*. Bingley: Emerald Publishing, pp. 249–266.

Klein, J. T. (2010) *Creating Interdisciplinary Campus Cultures. A Model for Strength and Sustainability*. San Francisco: Jossey-Bass.

Larkin, B. (2013) 'The politics and poetics of infrastructure', *Annual Review of Anthropology*, 42(1), pp. 327–343.

Lamont, M. (2009) *How Professors Think. Inside the Curious World of Academic Judgment*. Cambridge, MA: Harvard University Press.

Law, J. (2017) 'STS as method', in Felt, U., Fouché, R., Miller, C. A. and Smith-Doerr, L. (eds), *Handbook of Science and Technology Studies*. Cambridge, MA: MIT Press, pp. 31–58.

Leonelli, S. and Ankeny, R. A. (2015) 'Repertoires: How to transform a project into a research community', *BioScience*, 65(7), pp. 701–708.

Maylor, H., Brady, T., Cooke-Davies, T. and Hodgson, D. (2006) 'From projectification to programmification', *International Journal of Project Management*, 24(8), pp. 663–674.

Müller, R. (2021) 'Time as a judgement device: How time matters when reviewers assess applicants for ERC starting and consolidator grants', in Vostal, F. (ed.), *Inquiring into Academic Timescapes*. Bingley: Emerald Publishing, pp. 197–211.

Müller, R. and Kaltenbrunner, W. (2019) 'Re-disciplining academic careers? Interdisciplinary practice and career development in a Swedish environmental sciences research center', *Minerva*, 57(4), pp. 479–499.

Nowotny, H., Scott, P. and Gibbons, M. (2001) *Re-thinking Science. Knowledge and the Public in an Age of Uncertainty*. Cambridge: Polity Press.

Rifkin, J. (1987) *Time Wars: The Primary Conflict in Human History*. New York: Henry Holt & Co.

Rinderspacher, J. P. (1988) 'Wege der Verzeitlichung', in Henckel, D. (ed.), *Arbeitszeit, Betriebszeit, Freizeit*. Stuttgart: Kohlhammer, pp. 23–66.

Vienni Baptista, B., Fletcher, I., Maryl, M., Wciślik, P., Buchner, A., Lyall, C., Spaapen, J. and Pohl, C. (2020) *Final Report on Understandings of Interdisciplinary and Transdisciplinary Research and Factors of Success and Failure*. doi: 10.5281/zenodo.3824838 (Accessed: 14 June 2021).

Vostal, F. (ed.) (2021) *Inquiring into Academic Timescapes*. Bingley: Emerald Publishing.

Weingart, P. and Stehr, N. (eds) (2000) *Practising Interdisciplinarity*. Toronto: University of Toronto Press.

Ylijoki, O.-H. (2015) 'Conquered by project time? Conflicting temporalities in university research', in Gibbs, P., Ylijoki, O.-H., Guzmán-Valenzuela, C. and Barnett, R. (eds), *Universities in the Flux of Time. An Exploration of Time and Temporality in University Life*. London and New York: Routledge, pp. 94–107.

15
CO-PRODUCTIVE EVALUATION OF INTER- AND TRANS-DISCIPLINARY RESEARCH AND INNOVATION PROJECTS

Jack Spaapen

Introduction

The key concepts that form the title are a starting point for this chapter. Co-productive evaluation simply means that assessment procedures comprise a joint effort between researchers and other participating stakeholders in a given project. Obviously, this collaboration is easier said than done, but it means that such an evaluation cannot be achieved via traditional modes in academia for research evaluation that are top-down and verdict-oriented. New approaches have to be developed that are bottom-up and learning-oriented, characteristics of which appear in the last two sections of this chapter. Some authors make a sharp distinction between inter- and trans-disciplinary projects (Stember, 1991),[1] but in practice, their boundaries can be fluid. In both, more or less pressing issues are addressed that are emerging in current societies and some form of integration takes place between different perspectives and methods of scientific disciplines and/or societal fields. The main difference is that interdisciplinary projects primarily regard academic stakeholders and interests, while transdisciplinary projects include societal partners and issues. In each case, though, it is vital to recognize that mutual knowledge of each other's modes of working and communication is key to attuning different interests and goals of partners and therefore to success. What is needed then is knowledge about collaboration in mixed environments and a common understanding of the kind of innovation participants want.

Together, the two title concepts call for a fundamental change in the way research and innovation projects are set up, conducted, monitored, and evaluated. This imperative has far-reaching consequences for academic institutions and communities and in particular the academic culture of evaluation. In short, institutional changes must be fundamental and second order, replacing competitive modes of organization with collaborative ones in both education and research. Given these consequences, the current societal and policy context of academia calls for an overhaul of current academic structures and culture. In this chapter, I will first regard pressure on academia from the societal context and then response from the research and policy community in universities. Then I will present as an example the way the Netherlands uses a comprehensive national evaluation system that was developed bottom-up from the academic community. Finally, I will argue that an overhaul of the current evaluation systems is necessary to assess inter- and trans-disciplinary research (IDR and TDR) adequately.

Societal context as a pressure cooker

A headline in a Dutch newspaper read: "Not Dzjengis Kahn destroyed old civilization in Central Asia but drought" (*De Volkskrant*, 22 December 2020, p. 29). For a long time, history books held the mythical Mongolian leader responsible for the demise of many people and societies in Asia in the 12th and 13th centuries, but an interdisciplinary study now suggests that drought might be more likely to be responsible for this catastrophe than the ambitious Kahn. Like so many other pieces of new knowledge and important innovations, this finding was based on a collaboration of archeologists, geographers, climate researchers, and other specialists. New insights are not just the result of hard work within a single discipline. They are the consequence of cooperation between different disciplines and are regularly fed by contributions from other academic resources (Syme, 2008).[2] Furthermore, most innovations carry a variety of implications for society and impacts that can be either positive or negative (the latter referred to by Derrick et al., 2018, as "grimpacts"). Such implications need to be researched and evaluated in order to prepare new policy measures. Tony Caro and colleagues refer to such a dynamic network of variegated partners working together on a particular kind of innovation in more or less organized ways as "social innovation ecosystems" (Caro-González et al., 2019)

In such networks, though, some disciplines can be relatively close to each other in subject and methodological approaches (for example, when developing a new curriculum in modern languages for high schools). However, the distance between them can be larger too (for example, new ways of preventing devastating wildfires requiring technical, behavioral, economic, and policy knowledge and expertise). As a result, the complexity of many of today's problems and challenges, including their wide-ranging contingencies, require combining inputs from all fields, including social sciences and arts and humanities, plus knowledge and expertise from society and policy.

The urgency of this need is underscored by the array of questions and problems that emerge from confronting the COVID-19 pandemic. They encompass not only medical and health dimensions but also social, cultural, behavioral, economic, and political questions, as well as their interplay. The year 2020 resembled a pressure cooker in terms of developing a vaccine, but many other questions demand knowledge and expertise from a variety of sources. What goes on in the COVID-19 pressure cooker appears at a somewhat slower pace, but no less urgent, in other areas that present challenges today, including the following: global warming; energy transition; sustainable, safe, and healthy food production; the crisis of democracy; and other concerns summed up in supranational programs such as the UN Sustainable Development Goals (SDG's) and the EU's Grand Societal Challenges. In addition, interdisciplinarity and transdisciplinarity are needed at meso and micro levels of society, for example, in conservation policy for the Great Lakes in the United States (Tyner and Boyer, 2019) and in the architectural design of healthcare buildings (Annemans and Heyligen, 2020).

On the side of society and policy, governments at all aggregation levels are seeking answers to two questions: how to organize multi-stakeholder networks to address large societal challenges in the best possible way, and how to monitor and evaluate progress and results in order to use them in future policy. Examples of government initiatives are widespread. Cities and countries have appointed chief scientific officers (CSOs) to bridge the gap between science and societal demand, and programs have been developed at both the national level (e.g., in the Netherlands, the top-sector policy and the National Science Agenda[3]) and the supranational level (not only the European Grand Societal Challenges and the UN SDGs but also the Intergovernmental Panel on Climate Change – IPCC). Such multi-stakeholder partnerships are inter- and often trans-disciplinary, leading to variegated output of new ideas, products, and services.

In response, traditional procedures of research evaluation centering around bibliographic output and peer review are gradually giving way to more open forms in which societal impact is regarded and broader expertise is used to assess results of research and innovation projects (Debackere et al., 2018). Consequently, universities must adapt their organizational strategy and research policy to this new context including broader and more inclusive allocation and evaluation procedures, even though assessment of multi-stakeholder endeavors is difficult and not well developed yet. As a result, evaluation of societal impact has not yet grown into a mature stage in universities. Moreover, evaluation of inter- and trans-disciplinary research requires an even further step in terms of comprehensiveness and involvement of stakeholders. These institutions have to step out of their academic comfort zone even more. The following section reviews responses of the academic community to developments in the context of society and policy, both at the European level and at the country level of the Netherlands in particular. It is arguably among the countries most advanced in responding to the new societal context, though others are making related efforts.

Gradual response from academia

While inter- and trans-disciplinary research collaboration is gradually becoming part and parcel of the policy and funding context in the 21st century, it is far from unproblematic for academic institutions and their research communities. It is not a substantial part of academic education and training in most universities. The number of funded cooperative endeavors in which various disciplines and/or societal stakeholders are involved is growing,[4] but in many academic institutions it is still a marginal area of attention. Many universities in the world now offer inter- and trans-disciplinary programs or institutes, but only a handful present themselves as fully interdisciplinary institutions for both research and education. Exemplars include Maastricht University in the Netherlands and Shiv Nadar University in Delhi. For most universities, though, the reality is akin to being trapped at the crossroads between the old academic production model based on international competition and evaluation within the scientific community (referred to by Gibbons et al., 1994, as Mode 1 knowledge production) and a new transdisciplinary model (Gibbons et al., 1994, Mode 2). In the latter case, collaboration across disciplines and beyond academia is often met with uncertain rewards and societal impact is difficult to see immediately (Van den Akker and Spaapen, 2017).

In an article in *Times Higher Education*, Zahir Irani, dean at Bradford University in the UK, admonishes that traditional departmental structures are preventing research and education from evolving into the new reality. Apart from departmental rivalries over finances and facilities, he sums up other hindrances:

> Departments make it harder for academics to push boundaries as they struggle to find new intellectual homes for ideas that don't fit neatly into disciplinary boxes. Students lose out too: poorly managed course development across disciplines can lead to a joint degree that is two mealy halves joined together rather than a seamless matrix of ideas and challenges.
>
> *(24 September 2018)*

Irani, though, did cite some progress too in the UK with developing new structures in some universities, and he pointed to the United States where he believes staff are freer to move between departments and interdisciplinary centers. However, he contended overall there is not enough flexibility in most institutional structures.

The European Commission (EC) recognized this problem as well, so initiated in 2018 a call under the umbrella of the Erasmus+ program to develop ideas for "New European Universities". The EC mentions four criteria for these new institutions:[5]

- Include partners from all types of higher education institutions and cover a broad geographic scope across Europe.
- Be based upon a co-envisioned long-term strategy focused on sustainability, excellence, and European values.
- Offer student-centered curricula jointly delivered by inter-university campuses, where diverse student bodies can build their own programs and experience mobility at all levels of study.

- Adopt a challenge-based approach according to which students, academics, and external partners can cooperate in interdisciplinary teams to tackle the biggest challenges facing Europe today.

In addition to the push toward inter- and trans-disciplinary collaboration in these criteria, the EC urges a bottom-up approach for students to develop their own programs, suggesting the EC has less confidence in vested powers in universities to create new structures. Seventeen alliances across Europe are funded under this program. Yet, will this future be interdisciplinary as the dean of Bradford University predicted in his article?

Echoing the old adage that the world has problems and universities have disciplines, universities remain unfit to address the most urgent and complex challenges of today (Wilson, 2009). In a survey for the project "Shaping interdisciplinary research practices in Europe" (SHAPE-ID),[6] principal investigators (PIs) perceived a number of hindrances for inter- and trans-disciplinary research (SHAPE-ID, 2020, p. 15). At the top of the list are career paths, especially for young researchers who feel pressure to adhere to traditional disciplinary norms of publication. Second and third, cognitive differences between partners and academic tribalism make it difficult to be open to others. Fourth and fifth, lack of experience complicates the ability to deal with complex relationships and collaboration. Together, these hindrances show that inter- and trans-disciplinary projects require changes in the reward system and recognition culture. Time is also required for mutual learning. Yet, current funding systems do not as a rule recognize its importance for developing multi-stakeholder relationships. The SHAPE-ID survey further revealed that projects based on partnerships that had time to ripen before getting funded were more likely to be successful. Apart from the time factor, respondents also acknowledged the necessity of enhancing both collaboration and communication between the arts, humanities, and social sciences (AHSS) and natural sciences, technological and engineering fields, mathematics, and medicine (STEMM). Respondents to the survey suggested several strategies to promote better collaboration and integration ranging from informal meetings to regular seminars, working groups, joint publications, and more structured methodologies tailored to each project. While the respondents were a small selection of the European research community, most results overlapped with a comprehensive literature review.

Transdisciplinary collaboration is further hindered by the fact that public organizations such as regional or national governments are also often divided into silos, so universities are not the only type of organization in need of a transition for a better match between knowledge production and societal demand. Interviews in the context of the SHAPE-ID survey showed this match can be improved, for example, via regular personal exchanges, double functions of people in more than one social context, and trading places between academics and stakeholders (SHAPE-ID, 2020, p. 16). But doing so will take time and investment in long-term sustainable networks. As long as universities are trapped at a crossroads between academic competition and societal demand, it will be difficult to change. Change will start with universities rethinking their education and training modalities, research and funding policies, and institutional flexibility to accommodate inter- and trans-disciplinary endeavors. The LERU paper by Van den Akker and Spaapen (2017, p. 3) showed evidence that universities are starting to re-think their position, but practical consequences remain largely unseen in most organizational structures, evaluation procedures, and funding contexts. Hessels and colleagues (2011, p. 558) observed, regarding agricultural research in particular, that, on the one hand, funding in the latter part of the 20th century had shifted toward research aimed at contributing to a more sustainable and competitive agriculture but, on the other hand, performance evaluations based on bibliometric output still prevail in institutional and external funding sources. Performance evaluations are a powerful institution in the research system, influencing decisions by both university managers and external funding sources. A 2018 Technopolis study (Debackere et al., 2018) also documented endurance of performance management in the universities, amplified in the wake of neo-liberal management theories from industry that became popular in the public sector toward the end of the 20th century. The study concluded all 14 European countries that were researched used a performance-based research funding system (PRFS) to allocate money for academic research. While the study noticed the context dependency of these systems, and thus differences in the way countries try to balance scientific performance measurement and societal relevance, it also concluded most of these systems did not adequately succeed to assess the value of research for society. Consequently, the report concluded that given the absence of reliable data and methods, this evaluation can best be done by people. One way of changing the "crossroad" dilemma is for universities to create experimental interactive spaces in which inter- and trans-disciplinary projects can be developed jointly between researchers and stakeholders. This is precisely the idea behind the EU program "New European Universities".[7]

Connecting science and society in the Netherlands: From the bottom-up

The Netherlands does not have a PRFS and was not part of the above-mentioned study, but it is an example of how the challenge of connecting science and society can be addressed in a different way, both at national and institutional levels. As a country having to permanently battle water levels, given a large part of the territory is below sea level, the Netherlands has a long tradition of collaborative arrangements and decision-making. It is generally called the polder model, *polder* being the Dutch word for land regained from the sea. The keywords in this model are consultation, collaboration, and consensus.

The model is applied at all levels of society and in many organizations, evident, for example, in the way climate concerns are currently being addressed via "climate tables" that are discussion platforms, including all relevant stakeholders from society and science. Many collaborative arrangements have been established between the country's 13 universities, and two former presidents of the Dutch Academy of Arts and Sciences, therefore, suggested thinking more broadly in terms of a University of the Netherlands (Van Dijk and Van Saarloos, 2017).

In line with the polder model and cross-university collaboration, in 2012, a new transdisciplinary research and innovation policy was introduced: the top-sector policy.[8] To encourage collaboration between research and industry and the public sector, negotiation tables were organized in nine sectors of society deemed of vital importance for the Dutch economy. These "top sectors" include agriculture, health, water, energy, and the creative industry. The program had a rocky start during its first years, marked by a lot of energy and conflicting ideas in multi-stakeholder meetings. However, it developed over time into regular transdisciplinary public-private partnerships (PPP) where long-term collaboration can evolve. To be sure, there are several downsides to this policy. It came as an unpleasant surprise for the university sector that feared losing its independence because the National Research Council (NWO) was forced to reallocate half of its budget to top-sector applications coming from mixed consortia. As a result, it would no longer be available for disciplinary research. Also, the research community feared that economic interests would overpower other interests such as long-term sustainability (Minkman and Van Buuren, 2019), sadly illustrated by the slogan the minister of Economic Affairs used when introducing the program: "knowledge–skill–cash". To the disadvantage of AHSS, there was only one top sector relevant for fields from AHSS, the creative industry.

As a counterpart of the top-sector policy, the Dutch National Science Agenda (NWA) was introduced in 2015. NWA consists of 25 routes or themes that refer to broad problem areas emanating from an open call to everybody in the Netherlands. Routes or themes are long term (five to ten years) and open to a wide variety of interested societal partners. They address questions around urgent issues, as, for example, circular economy, water, sustainable food production, health, energy transition, art in the 21st century, fundamental research in time and space, living past, and smart livable cities.[9] Both policy initiatives are attempts by the government to break through institutional silos in universities and stimulate transdisciplinary collaboration in order to address societal challenges. A 2017 evaluation of the top-sector policy (Dialogic, 2017, pp. 2–3) concluded that the policy did result in "the 'societalisation' of innovation policy". But it also noted this outcome is "mainly based on the demand from financially strong businesses, [and that] the top-sector approach is still not a panacea for affirming the core importance of (innovative solutions for) societal challenges".

Effects of inter- and trans-disciplinary policy in Europe and beyond

Underlying organizational and cultural changes in faculties and universities have not been researched systematically, but the SHAPE-ID team drew insights from interviews with a number of scholars, university policymakers, and funding officials. The gist of their answers is that efforts of universities to improve support for inter- and trans-disciplinary research are visible in many institutions but are still slowed down by traditional disciplinary interests and funding structures. One researcher said interdisciplinary research is still considered "dangerous for both young researchers and specialist professors" (SHAPE ID, 2020, p. 15). Notably, according to most respondents, conditions at the supranational EU level are more favorable for IDR/TDR than at the institutional level. Most likely, this gap occurs because supranational level policymakers do not have the same institutional responsibilities as their colleagues at national and local levels. Whereas the EU has been working on furthering collaboration via particular missions and societal challenges in subsequent framework programs, and social sciences and humanities (SSH) integration in these programs has been monitored since 2014 (EU DG Research and Innovation, 2018),[10] national schemes in different countries have incorporated them to varying degrees. Some have established substantial financial resources to stimulate inter- and trans-disciplinary research, others have not. Some have created special support mechanisms for AHSS, and stimulated interdisciplinary institutes, others refrain from specific policies.

Reports from the EU also show a growing integration of SSH in the various framework programs, but progress is slow and more for social sciences (especially economics, political science, and business studies) than humanities (EU DG Research and Innovation, 2018, p. 5). To improve the integration of AHSS research into European and other inter- and trans-disciplinary projects, more collaboration between different policy levels is necessary, further attuning research and policy agendas. Interviews with policymakers showed that universities putting time and effort into developing and maintaining relationships with "Brussels" can be successful for AHSS integration. Some have designated senior-level administrators for this task (e.g., Utrecht University), while others operate at a more ad hoc level. The UK is also taking steps toward doing so in its national allocation system, the Research Excellence Framework (REF),[11] requesting university departments to show their connection with societal partners and results of cooperation via impact case studies (see Lyall, in this volume). Other countries such as Canada, Norway, Sweden, and Luxemburg are working on changing national research policy and evaluation systems to incorporate societal challenges along with AHSS integration. And, the French Institute for Agriculture, Food, and Environmental Research (INRAE) is developing ways to assess the value of research for society in broader ways than traditional performance/bibliometric output-oriented systems. Operating in agricultual and food research INRAE has been active in developing new approaches for the interface between science and society.[12] Canada and Luxemburg, in fact, direct special attention to AHSS.[13]

The necessity of a new evaluation culture

Clearly, the growing importance of inter- and trans-disciplinary research and innovation calls for a different kind of university policy, funding, and evaluation. Achieving this goal will not be easy given structural and cultural resistance in academia. In a 2001 editorial, Richard Smith, chief editor of the *British Medical Journal*, when talking about societal challenges and the development of "third stream metrics", deemed it "difficult but necessary". He did so after reading a report from the Dutch Academy of Arts and Sciences on the societal impact of applied health research (KNAW, 2002). It was one of the first attempts to provide a methodology for assessing societal impact in a particular sector, healthcare research. The report mentions four elements for evaluating societal impact:

a. The mission of the research team or the institute.
b. Its performance in relation to that mission.
c. The prospects for the future.
d. Recommendations for adjustments, where appropriate.

The Dutch Academy (KNAW) followed up with reports in several other fields, specifically design and engineering, social sciences, and humanities. All of them were trying to combine scientific and societal relevance into evaluation.[14] The reports also shared a common intellectual orientation to Gibbons et al.'s (1994) Mode 1/Mode 2 theory, and they presented an outline for evaluation methodology that balanced scientific quality and societal relevance. They further suggested suitable quantitative and qualitative indicators and output for both. Many of the indicators for societal relevance regarded different output toward and communication with stakeholders in various sectors.

Since then, in Europe and beyond, numerous studies and policy reports have appeared regarding evaluation systems that include the societal impact of research.[15] Many (experimental) results at both institutional and national levels followed, but in most systems, the accent is still on more traditional bibliometric indicators for scientific quality, not collaboration with stakeholders. Yet, the urgency of addressing societal challenges requires going beyond modes of societal impact evaluation that still look from inside academia outward to effects of work in the outside world. The kind of instruments suggested are often not very different from an impact evaluation in scientific literature, such as citations of academic work in policy documents (Bornmann et al., 2016). Developing more robust measurements for assessing societal impact remains difficult for two main reasons: (i) impact is context dependent and the variation of societal sectors and challenges is large; and (ii) trying to find robust instruments for evaluation the same way as for scientific impact, by collecting large amounts of reliable quantitative data, ignores the fact there are no databases comparable to the Web of Science. It is tempting to refer to the famous words attributed to Einstein: we cannot solve our problems with the same thinking we used when we created them. When Gibbons et al. (1994) developed their distinction between Mode 1 and transdisciplinary Mode 2, they observed robust measurement instruments that help assess the effects of research in broader societal context require novel mechanisms. Mode 2 knowledge production is set in a context quite different from the Mode 1 context, entailing a wide variety of stakeholders with their own expertise, goals, values, and expectations.

Subsequently, Nowotny and colleagues (2001) called the knowledge developed in a wider context "socially robust" in the sense of linking diverse practices, institutions, and actors. Thus, it addresses audiences that are never solely composed of fellow experts, thereby reflecting heterogeneous expectations and modes of understanding in mixed audiences. Nowotny further warned against tensions that go with the "democratisation of expertise", especially on the institutional level where the conception of knowledge and its production is not always ready for the new context of "pluralistic expertise" in which academics operate with partners from policy, society, or industry (Nowotny et al., 2001).[16] The challenge for universities, then, is to combine demands from both Mode 1 and Mode 2 contexts in research and evaluation policy. Researchers will work in Mode 1 or 2 alternatively, sometimes writing an article for a scientific journal, other times collaborating with other individuals inside or outside academia. When it comes to assessing the societal impact of individuals, this variation leads to a problem of attribution, because in collaborative endeavors, results (impact) will always be the product of many different contributions, of a process of co-production. An individual researcher working in Mode 1 can be assessed on his or her impact in the scientific community (e.g., via citation analysis). However, if the researcher works in Mode 2 and is for example part of a team trying to find sustainable energy solutions, it will often be hard to trace the impact back to that individual. That kind of impact is best assessed by looking at the effects of collaboration in a relevant societal context, such as the changing attitude of users or target groups, or at different ways of organizing work or production. In short, the evaluation of societal impact lends itself more for a higher aggregation level than the individual researcher.

Toward a more adequate evaluation of inter- and trans-disciplinary work

The main purpose of this chapter has been to learn how to stimulate and evaluate processes of interaction and communication between stakeholders and innovation projects. One respondent to the SHAPE-ID survey called gathering this kind of knowledge "mapping the ecosystem". It urges participants to learn from each other and improve their collaboration. Unfortunately, most evaluation procedures remain top-down and verdict-oriented with the primary focus on the output of scientific research measured by indicators such as publications in high-impact journals (Debackere et al., 2018). They do not fit inter- and trans-disciplinary research and their societal impact. Moreover, they are not helpful for most fields in social sciences, humanities, and arts or for others such as engineering and design, law, public health, and agricultural and food research. Alternative methods are available but only slowly finding their way into formal procedures. Productive interactions, for example, were introduced a decade ago in the EU SIAMPI project focused on the assessment of the societal impact of research (Spaapen and van Drooge, 2011). It is not product/output-oriented, rather process-oriented and starts with analysis of three types of interactions between academic research and society, revealing the network of stakeholders and offering assessment categories for impact. It also distinguishes three types of interactions: (i) direct interactions via personal contacts; (ii) indirect interactions mediated by carriers such media, exhibitions, artifacts such as websites, prototypes, demonstrations, and designs; and (iii) financial/economic interactions such as economic exchanges between stakeholders and researchers or sharing instruments or facilities.

More generally, the method of productive interactions is to understand processes of interaction and collaboration and to improve the impact of projects under evaluation. It is a bottom-up approach in which all stakeholders can participate, including establishing what information in each of the three categories can be useful for evaluation. Indicators are not fixed in advance, instead decided by the most involved researchers and stakeholders. Stakeholders can also share responsibility for an evaluation committee and report, as well as elaborate suggested improvements. Evaluation thus becomes an integral part of research and innovation instead of a one-time judgment. Similar examples have been developed in various sectors such as development research, health research, urban and regional development, and engineering fields. Participatory impact pathways analysis (PIPA), for instance, is a method for evaluating inter- and trans-disciplinary research that suits the requirements described previously (Van Drooge and Spaapen, 2017). PIPA has two crucial features: involvement of stakeholders from the start of a project, and the joint development of a narrative describing what one wants to achieve, how, and with whom. The narration uses a Theory of Change model, from which stakeholders construct a logical framework as a source for indicators. These indicators enable monitoring a project ex-durante. Instead of looking back to focus on past performance, indicators look forward in the short, intermediate, and distant future.

To conclude, fruitful evaluation of inter- and trans-disciplinary research should be done in a distributed way, as a co-production of all relevant stakeholders, based on a joint narrative focusing on what needs to change, how that can be achieved, and evidence that can support the claim whether quantitative or qualitative. Mutual learning and the development of socially robust knowledge should be its main goals.

Notes

1. Marilyn Stember (1991), for example, distinguishes between intra-, inter-, trans-, cross-, and multi-disciplinary levels of research.
2. Chairing a committee reviewing public health research in the United States, Syme concluded that it was necessary to "transcend our disciplinary silos and consider a much broader set of determinants in a far more complex way than we have so far been able to do".
3. In the Netherlands, the government assigned nine important economic sectors such as agriculture, high tech, chemistry, health and life sciences, and creative industry as top sector. The idea is that in these sectors, science, society, and policy collaborate on the basis of a common research and innovation agenda. Partners show commitment by putting in resources (financial, human, material).
4. It shows, for example, in the CORDIS database of the European Commission's framework programs where the number of funded inter- and trans-disciplinary projects is steadily growing (see report D 2.2 of SHAPE ID, 2020, p. 30)
5. The Erasmus plus program specifically addresses the development of inter- and trans-disciplinary education and training. See https://ec.europa.eu/programmes/erasmus-plus/programme-guide/part-b/three-key-actions/key-action-2/european-universities_en.
6. "Shaping interdisciplinary practices in Europe" (SHAPE-ID) has received funding from the European Union's Horizon 2020 Research and Innovation Programme under grant agreement No. 822705.
7. https://ec.europa.eu/education/education-in-the-eu/european-education-area/european-universities-initiative_en. Under this Erasmus plus program, 17 consortia have been funded to develop ideas and models that bring together a new generation of creative Europeans able to cooperate across languages, borders, and disciplines to address societal challenges and skills shortages faced in Europe.
8. https://www.government.nl/topics/enterprise-and-innovation/encouraging-innovation.
9. https://2.wetenschapsagenda.nl/overzicht-routes/.
10. The integration of social sciences and humanities is monitored via special reports by the Directorate General for Research and Innovation of the European Commission. The latest one appeared in 2019: Integration of Social Sciences and Humanities in Horizon 2020: Participants, Budget and Disciplines – 4th Monitoring report on SSH flagged projects funded in 2017 under the Societal Challenges and Industrial Leadership priorities.
11. https://www.ref.ac.uk/.
12. https://www6.inrae.fr/asirpa_eng/.
13. Approaches to Assessing Impacts in the Humanities and Social Sciences (2017), Canadian Federation for the Humanities and Social Sciences, Ottawa. The University of Luxemburg together with the ESF is currently working on a renewal of their evaluation system for social sciences and humanities. A report is due in the first half of 2021. The Swedish Higher Education Authority (UKA) is finishing a pilot study to renew their institutional evaluation system, pointing out two main assessment areas, "governance and organisation", and "prerequisites", including collaboration and gender equality. It was due in the summer of 2021.
14. The Dutch Academy of Arts and Sciences has been instrumental in developing ideas and instruments for the evaluation of the societal impact of scientific research. The following reports influenced establishment of the national evaluation system Strategy Evaluation Protocol (www.vsnu.nl/files/documenten/Domeinen/Onderzoek/SEP_2021-2027.pdf): KNAW (2005); KNAW (2010a); KNAW (2010b); KNAW (2013).
15. Two comprehensive examples of reviews are conducted by Lutz Bornmann in 2012 and 2013.
16. Nowotny et al. (2001), see, in particular, Chapter 11, which elaborates the transition from reliable knowledge to socially robust knowledge.

References

Akker, W. van den & Spaapen, J. (2017) *Productive Interactions: Societal Impact of Academic Research in the Knowledge Society*, LERU position paper, Brussels.

Annemans, M. & Heyligen, A. (2020) Productive interactions to exchange knowledge in healthcare building design. *Building Research and Information*, 49, 3, 281–293 [published online: 2 May 2020].

Bornmann, L. (2012) Measuring the societal impact of research. *EMBO Reports*, 13, 673–676; published online 10 July 2012.

Bornmann, L. (2013) What is societal impact of research and how can it be assessed? A literature survey. *Journal of the American Society for Information Science and Technology*, 64(2), 217–233.

Bornmann, L., Haunschild, R. & Marx, W. (2016) Policy documents as sources for measuring societal impact: How often is climate change research mentioned in policy-related documents? *Scientometrics*, 109(3), 1477–1495.

Canadian Federation for the Humanities and Social Sciences (2017) *Approaches to Assessing Impacts in the Humanities and Social Sciences*, Federation des Sciences Humaines Canada, Ottawa.

Caro-González, A. & Serra, A. (2019) Towards social innovation ecosystems: From linear pairwise forms of interaction to common purpose-driven networks for shared prosperity. Paper presented at the *5th Global Research Conference: Social Innovation and Socio-Digital Transformation Organised by the European School of Social Innovation (ESSI)*, Dortmund.

Debackere, K., Arnold, E., Sivertsen, G., Spaapen, J. & Sturn, D. (2018) *Performing Based Funding of University Research, Mutual Learning Exercise, Horizon 2020 Policy Support Facility*, Directorate General Research and Innovation, Brussels.

Derrick, G.E., Faria, R., Benneworth, P., Budtz-Petersen, D. & Sivertsen, G. (2018) Towards characterising negative impact: Introducing grimpact. In Costas, R., Franssen, T., & Yegros-Yegros, A. (eds), *Proceedings of the 23rd International Conference on Science and Technology Indicators*. Centre for Science and Technology Studies (CWTS), Leiden University, Leiden.

Dialogic (2017) Evaluation of the topsector policy, management summary [online at www.dialogic.nl].

Dijk, J. van & Saarloos, W. (2017) *The Dutch Polder Model in Science and Research*, KNAW, Amsterdam.

Drooge, L. van & Spaapen, J. Evaluation and monitoring of transdisciplinary collaborations. *Journal of Technology Transfer* DOI 10.1007/s10961-017-9607-7.

EU DG Research & Innovation (2018) *Integration of Social Sciences and Humanities in Horizon 2020: Participants, Budget and Disciplines*, 4th Monitoring report on SSH flagged projects funded in 2017 under the Societal Challenges and Industrial Leadership Priorities, Brussels.

European Commission (2020) Erasmus+ program. https://ec.europa.eu/programmes/erasmus-plus/programme-guide/part-b/three-key-actions/key-action-2/european-universities_en.

Gibbons, M., Limoges, C., Nowotny, H., Schwartzman, S., Scott, P. & Trow, M. (1994) *The New Production of Knowledge: The Dynamics of Science and Research in Contemporary Societies*, SAGE, London.

Hessels, L.K., Grin, J. & Smits, R.E.H.M. (2011) The effects of a changing institutional environment on academic research practices: Three cases from agricultural science *Science and Public Policy*, 38(7), 555–568.

Irani, Z. (2018) The future of the universities is interdisciplinary. *Times Higher Education*. [accessed online 24 September 2018].

KNAW (Royal Netherlands Academy of Arts and Sciences) (2002) *The Societal Impact of Applied Health Research. Towards a Quality Assessment System*, Raad voor de Medische Wetenschap (RMW), Subcommissie Gezondheids(zorg)onderzoek (GZO), Amsterdam.

KNAW (Royal Netherlands Academy of Arts and Sciences) (2005) *Judging Research on Its Merits: An Advisory Report*, The Council for the Humanities and the Social Sciences Council, Amsterdam.

KNAW (Royal Netherlands Academy of Arts and Sciences) (2010a) *Quality Assessment in the Design and Engineering Disciplines. A Systematic Framework*, Amsterdam.

KNAW (Royal Netherlands Academy of Arts and Sciences) (2010b) *Quality Indicators for Research in the Humanities*, Amsterdam.

KNAW (Royal Netherlands Academy of Arts and Sciences) (2013) *Towards a Framework for the Quality Assessment of Social Science Research*, Amsterdam.

Minkman, E. & Buuren, A. van (2019) Branding in policy translation: How the Dutch Delta approach became an international brand. *Environmental Science and Policy*, 96, 114–122.

Nowotny, H., Scott, P. & Gibbons, M. (2001) *Re-Thinking Science: Knowledge and the Public in An Age of Uncertainty*, Wiley, Hoboken.

SHAPE ID (2020) Deliverable 2.2: Report on survey among interdisciplinary and transdisciplinary researchers and post-survey interviews with policy stakeholders. https://www.shapeid.eu/reports/

Smith, R. (2001) Measuring the social impact of research. Difficult but necessary. *BMJ*, 323, 8 September.

Spaapen, J. & Drooge, L. van (2011) Introducing productive interactions for social impact assessment. *Research Evaluation*, 20(3), 211–218.

Stember, M. (1991) Advancing the social sciences through the interdisciplinary enterprise. *Social Science Journal*, 28, 1–14.

Syme, L.S. (2008) The science of team science. Assessing the value of transdisciplinary research. *American Journal of Preventive Medicine*, 2(supplement), S94–S95.

Tyner, E.H. & Boyer, T.A. (2019) Applying best-worst scaling to rank ecosystem and economic benefits of restoration and conservation in the Great Lakes. *Journal of Environmental Management*, 255, 109888 [available online 29 November 2019].

Wilson, G. (2009) The world has problems while universities have disciplines: Universities meeting the challenge of environment through interdisciplinary partnerships. *Journal of the World Universities Forum*, 2(2), 57–62.

16
CONCLUSION

A comparative framework for institutionalizing inter- and trans-disciplinary research and teaching in higher education

Bianca Vienni Baptista, Julie Thompson Klein, and Danilo Streck

Introduction

Institutionalizing interdisciplinarity (ID) and transdisciplinarity (TD) is a dynamic process that requires contextualism to achieve its full potential, as indicated in the Introduction to this book. This aim was our intention four years ago when we first envisioned the book and its importance still holds today. Contexts for both professional and personal lives have changed and even been permanently altered under new circumstances, not the least of which is the global COVID-19 pandemic. Two overarching questions arise: How, then, should institutionalizing proceed in light of this and other challenges? And what do we expect from universities and research centers that aim to foster ID/TD in current times? Even though all contributing authors to this volume have written their chapters under differing lockdown conditions in their respective countries, constraints to institutionalization are similar and influenced by previous conditions. Across contexts, neoliberal and endemic pressures on the scientific system still act as hindrances to achieving the full potential of ID and TD in research and teaching in higher education. Neoliberal policies have long limited and discouraged them by legitimizing individualism and shortening timelines for research and learning (Felt, 2017).

Worldwide privatization of university enrollment and progressive decreases in public funding are among the major factors forcing changes in the structural conditions of universities (Slaughter and Taylor, 2016). Similar and enduring features in different higher education systems affirm they are endemic to higher education, while also affecting relationships between the academy and society (Slaughter and Rhoades, 2004). For that reason, as editors and authors, we argue more attention needs to be paid to how individual protagonists perceive intersections and how different approaches sustain and constrain processes of institutionalizing ID/TD. During 2020 and 2021, universities worldwide implemented rapid changes to adapt lectures and research projects to pandemic lockdowns and confinements. In addition to this urgent crisis, inter- and trans-disciplinary approaches were increasingly aligned with other complex problems, including climate change and social justice. In response, communities and governments across the globe embarked on efforts to respond, including long-term transformations to combat intellectual, bureaucratic, and socio-political inertia. The case studies in this book depicted both successful and unsuccessful implementation in universities and research centers, though few institutions have incorporated a full range of lessons into organizational structures and study programs (Weingart, 2014). Our aim in this concluding chapter is to take a step forward by providing a common framework for tackling continuing and future challenges for institutionalizing ID and TD at intersections of cultures, institutions, and communities.

To begin with, "cultures" are referred here to as broad systems of meanings that structure and are structured by discourse and practices (Hess, 2012). We focus on this intersection because the concept of culture, as D. J. Hess put it:

> draws attention to both explicit and implicit semantic and emotional categories that both shape practices and discourse and are modified by strategy and history; all social action includes a cultural component. Some cultural meanings or systems are obviously specific to a geographical region or social institution, whereas others are broader "imaginaries" (or, as an earlier generation called them, "patterns" and "configurations") that can be found across social fields.
>
> *(2012, p. 177)*

Echoing Hess' recognition of multi-layered meanings of culture, the triad "cultures-institutions-communities" then crosscuts all chapters of this volume. Our understanding of the problem of institutionalizing ID/TD, then, applies a type of cultural analysis that recognizes changes in the underlying systems of meaning and values that emerge in relations between the political field and modern science and technology (Hess, 2011; 2012).

Building upon the authors' previous studies and the literature at large, we further understand inter- and trans-disciplinary institutionalizing processes on two iterative levels: (i) as a policy and (ii) as a practice (Vienni Baptista and Rojas, 2019). Policy is a series of decisions that aim toward a previously established goal in the form of regulations, statutes, and procedures (Palonen, 2003). However, establishing a policy does not guarantee achieving a particular objective or implementing the actions it prescribes. Therefore, we also understand ID/TD as activities that foster and enact related policy and forms of knowledge production. Institutionalization, then, is a composite set of processes by which a policy, a set of activities, or practices attain rule-like status in both thought and action (Palonen, 2013; Louvel, 2021). This definition, in turn, requires examining processes of institutionalization and analyzing how ID/TD are embedded in both policies and practices. In short, they are enacted when they are practiced, exercised, or executed within a particular organizational structure (Douglas, 1986). As the chapters demonstrated, both bottom-up and top-down processes of institution making are taking root in different countries and contexts around the world. Then, a framework is required to provide a sound basis for productive dialogue and mutual learning within and across contexts, avoiding pitfalls of thinking only in terms of simplistic and universalist transfers of knowledge and practices while overcoming fragmentation in the literature. Toward that end, the framework proposed in this concluding chapter is based on empirical evidence, pertinent literature, and insights from case studies. At the same time, it reveals broad tendencies that enable speaking in general terms. By applying a comparative and qualitative approach (Clarke et al., 2015; Charmaz and Mitchell, 2001), the theoretical background that emerges from the framework supports innovative practices, yielding insights that can be applied in future case studies and contexts.

The chapter is based on two premises. First, it revisits the framework for analyzing "campus cultures" Julie Thompson Klein (2010) developed, extended by evidence from new examples and reflections in a broader range of geographical and cultural contexts than her predominantly US- and European-based study. Second, the chapter considers new insights into the nature of interdisciplinarity and transdisciplinarity as social constructs. Universities are crucial to creating structures and spaces for generating epistemological, methodological, and organizational innovations that pave the way to new forms of knowledge production (Bammer et al., 2020; Leahey et al., 2019). Even with differences in context, however, inter- and trans-disciplinary institutions still experience a double identity. They are increasingly legitimized as part of knowledge cultures (Hess, 2011) at universities but also continue to struggle to implement environments for boundary crossing that require "extra" criteria to be seen as "real" institutions. Two final guiding questions follow: How can we capitalize on this double identity to potentially improve research and teaching in higher education? And, how can we capture lessons and encourage trends in such a process? Toward that end, we begin this chapter by briefly presenting methods we used to identify the main dimensions for our framework. We then elaborate on it based on empirical evidence and intersections among epistemic, cultural, and institutional dimensions that guide our understanding of institutionalizing processes. Finally, we draw conclusions for thinking about inter- and trans-disciplinary research and teaching in higher education.

Brief methodological approach

In previous studies, authors of this chapter have investigated processes of institutionalizing ID and TD in different countries and continents, aimed at generating pertinent dimensions of analysis and a corpus of knowledge (Klein, 2010; Vienni

Baptista et al., 2018; Vienni Baptista and Rojas, 2019). Using that corpus, we identified three subthemes previewed in the Introduction as main dimensions of cross-cutting institutionalization processes: (i) epistemic, (ii) cultural, and (iii) institutional. Comparison of case studies in this volume further enabled us to operationalize a set of keywords that constitute foundations of the framework: specifically, interdisciplinarity, transdisciplinarity, and institutionalization, as well as dichotomies of success/failure, change/transformation, space/time, and conditions/indicators. We took into consideration the contextualization of each concept together with relevant intersections (Clarke et al., 2015). Then, in an iterative comparative process, we revisited each case study to identify cross-secting lessons and insights using content analysis (Charmaz and Mitchell, 2001) in a composite of concepts, definitions, processes, and outcomes related to institutionalizing ID/TD (Streck, 2020).

We then complemented this approach with a systematic literature review on the topic of institutionalization (Jahan et al., 2016), including similar models (Hart and Silka, 2020; König et al., 2013), previous studies (Klein and Falk-Krzesinski, 2017; Leahey et al., Lyall, 2019), and policy literature on the topic of institutionalization (GUNi, 2017; OECD, 2020). In addition to these methods, informal exchanges, and discussions informed the framework. In 2021, we tested the framework in an online workshop at the International Transdisciplinarity Conference. Further factoring in insights from additional contributing authors to this volume, we refined dimensions and categories of the framework drawing on the concept of heuristics (Hukkinen and Huutoniemi, 2014). We aimed at building an instrument that can be adapted to different research and educational settings rather than imposing a universal method of a model that ignores local contexts. Broadly speaking, heuristics guide inference and/or judgment in problem-solving and decision-making (Abbot, 2004). Because they are general suggestions, rather than strict formulas (Pohl, 2014), they offer a suitable approach to contextualism.

A framework for institutionalizing inter- and trans-disciplinary research and teaching

This *heuristic comparative* framework synthesizes the main questions and dimensions that need to be taken into account when institutionalizing ID/TD. In doing so, it provides pathways to approach factors acting as negative conditions for institutionalizing, which, in turn, can be identified to transform them into positive ways and sites for change (Vienni Baptista et al., 2020). The framework contributes to growing scholarship on the topic with a tool that can be complemented by future studies. It can be applied at any phase of institutionalizing because it consists of a heuristic, not formulaic, set of dimensions and guiding questions that trigger self-reflective processes in teams (Pohl, 2014). The result is an overview of conditions under which ID/TD are or will be institutionalized, without imposing a normative account of the process. Flexibility and adaptability are their main features, allowing response to conditions that different contexts imprint on their theory and practice.

Four dimensions are entry points to the framework (Figure 16.1):

i. Epistemic: cognitive and conceptual aspects of ID/TD.
ii. Cultural: linkages and intersections between ID and TD as broad systems of meanings that structure and are structured by discourse and practices.
iii. Organizational: the structural context in which institutionalizing processes take place together with communities of practice.
iv. Future potentials and strategies: insights and successful aspects that can be implemented to promote interdisciplinarity and transdisciplinarity in future scenarios.

Figure 16.2 details the factors that hinder or help institutionalizing processes of inter- or trans-disciplinary research and/or teaching. In the next sections, we detail each dimension and factor by offering empirical examples from the cases presented in this book.

Epistemic dimension

The epistemic dimension encompasses four categories: (i) different understandings of ID/TD, (ii) regional distinctions, (iii) methods and tools for research or teaching, and (iv) key problems and obstacles for ID/TD. The interconnectedness of these four categories is evident in all chapters and emerges from institutionalizing processes, influencing types, and levels of integration in research and teaching. As a result, cases are grounded in different understandings that still compete for legitimacy and recognition, sometimes even coexisting with contradicting conceptualizations at the same institution, as Mokiy and Lukyanova demonstrated in Chapter 9. Within the first dimension in particular – (i) understanding – we recognize familiar tensions in the literature revealing institutionalizing processes often get caught in ranging from epistemological to ontological debates. As Lyall put it in Chapter 2:

> well-recognised tensions within institutions appear, ranging from ontological debate on the "validity" of interdisciplinary courses to the disruption of well-established administrative procedures not designed for accommodating interdisciplinary working across faculties.
>
> *(p. 16)*

These discussions, though, have sometimes hindered fruitful advancement, narrowing the heterogeneity of understandings of how to find a space in institutional environments. The cross-dimensional study Vicente and Lucas presented in Chapter 13 revealed that:

Conclusion **237**

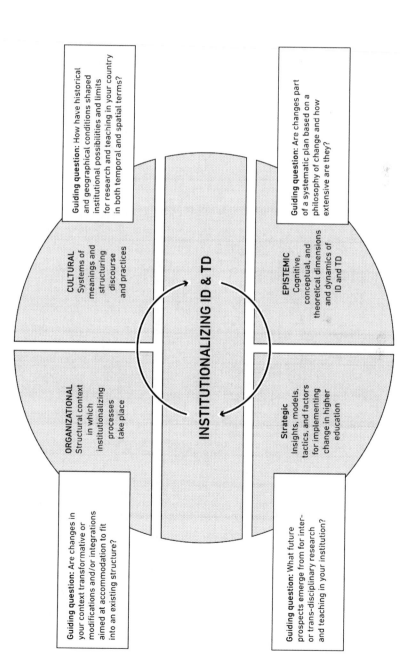

FIGURE 16.1 A heuristic and comparative framework for institutionalizing inter- and trans-disciplinary research and teaching: dimensions for institutionalizing.

238 Bianca Vienni Baptista et al.

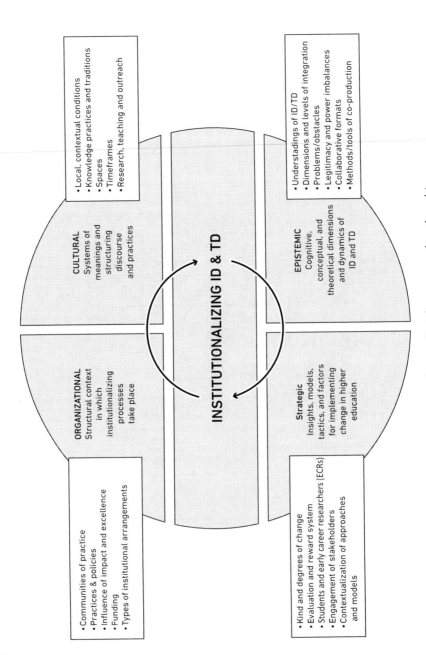

FIGURE 16.2 Factors for institutionalizing inter- and trans-disciplinary research and teaching.

> [Researchers] externalized ontological opposition between the "two cultures" to the modern social organization of education and academic institutions, namely through specialization and departmentalization. They cited both are contributing factors to a cultural divide of arts, science, and technology while considering a more integrated approach is needed to address contemporary societal challenges.
>
> *(pp. 199–200)*

At local and regional levels, differences for producing knowledge, Kondo et al. added in Chapter 12, are driven by differences in understandings in the terms ID/TD. Akua-Sakyiwah, in Chapter 8, also provides a relevant example when stating that these terms,

> cannot be replicated from the global North, where material realities are different from the reality of Africa's environment and sustainability. TD is a Westernized ideology, but its emergent features and integrative approach to co-producing knowledge can be adopted to suit our environmental needs.
>
> *(Akua-Sakyiwah, personal comm., 2020)*

Pearce offered a similar conclusion in Chapter 10, based on the Chinese context. In Chapter 13, Vicente and Lucas added discourses on collaboration in Europe that have often focused on instrumental organizational strategies conducive to institutionalizing ID/TD. Regional distinctions though play a substantial role in countries in which the higher education system, as Holley and Szostak reported in Chapter 6 on Canada and the United States, "has long possessed an ethos of innovation" (p. 72). However, while both countries have been open to interdisciplinary teaching programs and funding, differences still appear in patterns of programming. Geographical differences in case studies documented uneven distribution of resources. Heterogeneous policies also affect the development of inter- and trans-disciplinary institutionalization differently, apparent in Keryan et al.'s Chapter 11; Litre et al.'s Chapter 5; Mokiy and Lukyanova's Chapter 9; and Villa-Soto et al.'s Chapter 4.

Furthermore, differences in disciplinary legitimacy and power imbalances among fields of knowledge need to be taken into consideration. In several chapters, multiple examples of decisions about salary, tenure, and promotion appeared. They are major obstacles for institutionalizing ID/TD, both as a cause and as a consequence of fragile legitimization and consolidation processes of collaborative formats (Klein and Falk-Krzesinski, 2017; Lyall, 2019). Felt also addressed related concerns in Chapter 14 and Villa-Soto et al. in Chapter 4. National catalysts illustrate how networks constitute fruitful spaces for collaboration, shown by the EU-funded European Partnership for an Innovative Campus Unifying Regions (EPICUR) and the International Network for the Science of Team Science (INSciTS) in the United States. As Holley and Szostak also noted in Chapter 6, this latter case demonstrates strong connections with funders and policymakers are essential means of overcoming epistemic barriers. Furthermore, they are not only a concern for scholars. Interdisciplinarity and transdisciplinarity, Holley and Szostak added, have become buzzwords among university administrators, national granting agencies, science-policy bodies, and educational commissions over recent decades in multiple countries. Lyall in Chapter 2 and Villa-Soto et al. in Chapter 4 confirmed this trendline that exhibits a rhetoric reproducing discourse of relevance while implying instrumental use of collaborative practices in research to obtain outcomes tailored to neoliberal ways of understanding higher education systems (Slaughter and Rhoades, 2004).

Cultural dimension

The cultural dimension conveys both symbolic and learned ideas and practices in different communities (Chambers et al., 2021). In addition to temporal and national cultures of science, a third area of variation involves knowledge cultures (Hess, 2011). Co-production of academic and traditional or Indigenous forms of knowledge are, for instance, of increasing relevance in institutionalizing ID/TD (Fam et al., 2018). In Chapter 7, Sebastian et al. analyzed a successful process in which knowledge from local communities and industrial representatives are integrated into projects in Australia.

Both space and time are main categories within this dimension of institutionalizing as well. As Felt argued in Chapter 14, they are contested in the current academic system, making ID/TD more challenging to young researchers:

> The temporal regimes governing contemporary academia could thus be compared with an invisible infrastructure that frames ways in which researchers can know and define the kinds of academic lives that they can live. This infrastructure also fosters or hinders creating and sustaining feelings of community and belonging.
>
> *(p. 206)*

In Chapter 8, Akua-Sakyiwah also asserted timeframes for institutionalizing TD in Ghana to allow identifying complexities when creating appropriate structures or spaces. Timeframes refer to the pace and dynamics in which change is elaborated and finally consolidated within an institution.

Common trends also appeared in regions. In Latin American countries, inter- and trans-disciplinary institutionalizing efforts emerged from re-democratization processes after dictatorship periods, illustrated in Litre et al.'s Chapter 5, and beyond this book in Streck (2021) and Vienni Baptista et al. (2018). When mobilized, societal actors shared interests with scientific actors and created new spaces at universities. For example, Litre et al. reported several universities "being permeable to new socio-environmental agendas that emerged in Brazil and abroad" (Chapter 5, p. 58). Synthesizing lessons from such experiences constitutes a basis for building foundations for new ways to understand and value inter- and trans-disciplinary research (IDR/TDR) at universities, even with differences between disciplines within or among institutions.

Although culture has a substantive role to play in institutionalizing, most transformations and new plans are pragmatic responses to a changing funding landscape that Lyall described in Chapter 2, reducing transformative practices to piecemeal modifications of traditional, discipline-focused structure (p. 19). The result is an inevitable loop that, in the end, is not transformative, rather superficial and instrumental use of ID/TD within institutions (Wallace et al., 2021). Communities of practice in both research and teaching are ideal settings to counter obstacles in higher education. They constitute a privileged setting to build inter- and trans-disciplinary identities, defined as fluid and dynamic formats of "relating" between collectives (Schikowitz, 2021, p. 2261). In this way, ID/TD pose specific challenges for institutionalizing processes that are based on disciplinary teaching and research. Chapters in this book show different dynamics in which micro-level practices are spaces for new ID/TD cultures. Kondo et al., in Chapter 12, revealed that consilience always occurred tacitly and is often driven by individual intellectual curiosity in the form of solo interdisciplinary research, characterized by (1) boundary objects, (2) multifaceted viewpoints, (3) empowerment of early-career researchers (ECRs), (4) scalable organizations, and (5) transition from inter- to trans-disciplinary research. These trends coincide with recent examples of universities that leverage students' perspectives to create pathways toward lasting organizational change in higher education (Kligyte et al., 2021).

Organizational dimension

Chapters in this book have taught us that new spaces are created (and re-created) every time an institutionalizing process occurs, underscoring the centrality of epistemic living spaces, as Vicente and Lucas highlighted in Chapter 13. As Akua-Sakyiwah also exhorted in Chapter 8, "context in which an action, utterance, or expression occurs is crucial to meaning. Yet, while knowledge is dependent on context and practical experience, variability of data is also important" (p. 112). This organizational dimension interrogates how a deeper understanding of these complexities can, at the local level, inform more effective and equitable governance of organizational structures that seek institutionalizing ID/TD.

Relevant categories include: (i) communities of practice, and (ii) aspects set by policy and elaborated in interaction with daily practices. In Chapter 15, Spaapen cited a recent study at the European level revealing that together with the widespread push toward inter- and trans-disciplinary collaboration, the European Commission (EC) urges a bottom-up approach for students to develop their own programs, suggesting perhaps less confidence in vested powers in universities to create new structures. Lyall asserted in Chapter 2 that societal impact and excellence force changes to be implemented quickly in traditional organizational structures that end up trapped at a crossroads between academic competition and societal demand. Spaapen (Chapter 15, p. 223) commented on the challenge of getting past the crossroads:

> change will start with universities rethinking their education and training modalities, research and funding policies, and institutional flexibility to accommodate inter- and trans-disciplinary endeavors.

This dimension is further intertwined with practices that anticipate overcoming obstacles and disincentivizing dynamics coexisting with a top-down level. In the UK, Lyall (Chapter 2, p. 17) reported that persistent use of terms such as "impact" (implying something that is done to someone) and "research users" (rather than "co-producers" of knowledge) indicates the underpinning logic is one of use rather than co-production. The new Horizon Europe research program also affirms that ID and TD have become a requirement in many funding schemes, though most are based on understandings that do not take into consideration specific challenges of local contexts, as Keryan et al. indicated in Chapter 11.

Communities of practice are intrinsically related to institutionalizing processes, as these collectives can thrive in change and often push for transforming the higher education system even though administrations and authorities respond with bureaucratic inertia. Keryan et al. also noted that informal networks and involvement in international collaboration (such as conferences, publications, and projects) constitute means of forming and consolidating inter- and trans-disciplinary communities. Yet, power imbalances are still pervasive and many universities follow international parameters for institutionalizing based on Western strategies inadequate for local conditions. This imbalance also poses new challenges for institutionalizing ID/TD, including adapting external schemes to account for national local agendas (Harris and Holley, 2008). Echoing Akua-Sakyiwah in Chapter 8 (p. 107), "the need for more higher education to address sustainable context-specific solutions is a necessary condition for dealing with complex problems the nation faces". Sebastian et al. in Chapter 7 and Adomßent in Chapter 3 also cited thematically focused integrated programs and recognition of their importance for institutionalizing processes in, respectively, Australia and Germany.

The organizational dimension, then, intersects with the other aspects of our framework. Spaces that allow for intercultural exchanges and timeframes are in constant re-elaboration with knowledge production processes. For example, Sebastian et al. showed in their chapter the possibility of other types of knowledge and Indigenous experience connected to enterprises and industry. Engagement with stakeholders in community, industry, and government gives them – as another category in our framework – a "voice" in research and teaching. Successful lessons include partnerships and shared capacity-building activities, as Adomßent detailed in Chapter 3. However, little is said about the pressure societal actors and even university authorities face in institutionalizing processes to cope with demands from different communities. Sebastian et al. (Chapter 7, p. 103) acknowledged in their case study that "establishing adaptive structures, collaborative practices, and boundary-crossing strategies to enable distributed accountability mechanisms for both industry and academia" is necessary. And, Vicente and Lucas further explained in theirs, fluid modes of research may help bridge key structuring elements of education and academic life, possibly signaling at the organizational level an ongoing disconnect between top-down policy-making and bottom-up aspirations, as well as gaps between legitimated modes of research and modes in search of recognition.

This dimension entails constraints and challenges of funding, which is also a category of analysis identified in the literature. Funding is a main integrative aspect of institutionalizing where expectations need to be aligned with donors. In addition, tensions between STEM (science, technology, engineering, and mathematics) and AHSS (arts, humanities and social sciences) influence this balance (Wallace et al., 2021). These tensions reflect entrenched obstacles to obtaining funding and do not find spaces and times for collaborating with others. Beyond the "what" and the "how" of institutionalizing processes of ID/TD, the "who" raises the question of rights to speak and interrogate underlying assumptions. This understudied topic in the literature usually relates to the discussion on the way in which researchers and/or stakeholders collaborate in research settings (Smolka et al., 2020). In their chapter, Vicente and Lucas showed, when inquiring into individual researchers' guiding epistemic values in the context of their knowledge production and living spaces, entanglements between personal perspectives and structures of research at the micro level of meaning-making can be identified and better understood on the basis of contextualization.

As agents of knowledge, students are usually soft voices in institutionalizing processes as well (Lyall, 2019). Early-career researchers face the most inconsistencies that institutions enact and reproduce in relation to uncertainties and misconceptions on ID/TD (Rogga and Zscheischler, 2021). Inconsistencies urgently demand that evaluation and assessment systems are in line with an institution's legacy. National systems of evaluation and accreditation also exhibited problems at different levels and reproduce inequalities seen at the institutional level. Examples in this book by Lyall in the UK, Litre et al. in Brazil, and Villa-Soto et al. in Mexico revealed common features to disentangle these complexities. Spaapen et al. (2007) also emphasized the need for new dimensions for evaluation processes of ID/TD practices: for example, taking into consideration productive interactions during the research process rather than measuring post-hoc outputs such as scientific articles. Some types of institutional arrangements have also proved to be successful in several of the cases we analyzed. As Sebastian et al. reported in Chapter 7, the Australian boundary-organization format has evolved over time and is engaged in dynamic and collaborative knowledge transfer among science, policy, and practice.

Accounting for micro-experiences in the Ghanian context, in Chapter 8, Akua-Sakyiwah confirmed the need for bottom-up approaches to be proactively supported by institutions. She contended: "institutional engagement is crucial for utilising TD, lest it is sidelined due to a lack of understanding and an over-emphasis on the time–space dichotomy" (p. 117). These examples have called attention to new forms of governance at institutions, allowing for collaborative practices to have a leading role in the current setting of research in Chapter 2, as well as pejorative calls for ID/TD as non-scientific practices, and even "lobbying", raising questions about how expertise is conceived and perceived in inter- and trans-disciplinary settings, as Mokiy and Lukyanova demonstrated in Chapter 9. The main categories that come together in this dimension (i.e., type of institutional structure, funding, internal and external evaluation criteria) are intrinsically related to cultural forms of commitment from universities (Leahey et al., 2019). These entanglements may pave the way for future studies that could compare the epistemic, cultural, and organizational dimensions of institutionalizing processes at large (see Leahey et al., 2019).

Future potentials and strategies

As noted earlier, interdisciplinary and transdisciplinary research and teaching as collaborative modes foster more democratic practices and educational formats that account for shared spaces of action. Given this imperative, institutionalizing requires responding quickly to pressing national and regional problems to consolidate future potentials of ID/TD. Humanists and social scientists, in particular, have urged a more prominent role in confronting societal challenges (Wallace et al., 2021). In their respective chapters, Akua-Sakyiwah, Keryan et al., Kondo et al., and Villa-Soto et al. called attention to transitional moves toward more inter- and trans-disciplinary forms of research that address national problems in their particular contexts. In their chapter, Sebastian et al. further emphasized transformation(s) in universities in the last decade in Australia often emerged in order to justify the need for a transdisciplinary institutionalizing process. Utilized as a learning mechanism, transformation involves profound changes in existing practices or new practices that implement it, an imperative Adomßent reinforced in Chapter 3.

As Lyall cautioned in Chapter 2, however, these challenges contrast with prioritizing impact and excellence in particular research systems that directly influence ID/TD. This understanding of excellence treats impact only as a quantitative indicator, hindering institutionalizing inter- and trans-disciplinary research and teaching. Related tensions were apparent in case studies from different regions, spanning Russia, Ghana, and China. When these and other tensions are overcome, ID/TD become embedded within organizational settings and provide guidance for transformation and change in existing knowledge, allowing more plural institutionalizing processes. Akua-Sakyiwah also endorsed this potential in Chapter 8.

Taken together, potentials for institutionalizing are anchored in common dimensions identified in this concluding chapter at the same time they are directly influenced by understandings in each institution. In Chapter 14, Felt further advised that local and regional approaches do not escape general dynamics of science, policy, and society and depend on timeframes imposed by the logic of productivity measures for collaboration, leading Spaapen in Chapter 15 to call for evaluation processes that seek indicators for integration. Against these pressures, ID/TD appear more as transgressional practices allowing for pluralistic practices to be developed. As beckoned at the outset of this chapter, the delicate balance of dimensions in our framework can counter dynamics that impose challenges to knowledge production at institutions fostered by both bottom-up practices and top-down policies.

Concluding remarks

We conclude this chapter by affirming that inter- and trans-disciplinary efforts are ubiquitous today. Thain (2021, p. 1) captured the far-reaching implications:

> What is at stake at the present time is not just the standing of universities within society and the faith of the general public in academic expertise, it is universities' ability to rise to the challenge of helping to forge a new and newly integrated vision of society in the post-pandemic world.

Yet even though alternatives are at hand and exist in many different contexts, challenges in institutionalizing ID/TD persist. Universities and organizations, as lived and enacted by different societal and scientific actors (Douglas, 1986), have an opportunity to address the urgent problems that confront us, from climate change and pandemics to conflict and inequality. Funders and researchers promote transformation in some contexts but, further echoing Thain (2021), individual and accommodationist efforts are insufficient if methods, networks, and ideas about what constitutes knowledge do not evolve.

Throughout this book, we have called for thinking across intersections among cultures, communities, and institutions. The case studies revealed a rich variety of ways of doing and thinking ID/TD at a time when urgent societal problems are reinforcing demands for responses at epistemological, cultural, and organizational levels. Taken together, they amplify Thain's (2021) exhortation to work across different methodologies and theories on a sustained basis. Each chapter identified dimensions inherent in fostering lasting and effective practices, spanning historical, social, and cultural contexts where knowledge production is situated, with institutional arrangements and conditions for creating and experiencing new ways of doing research and teaching. Our proposed framework aims at contributing to systematizing practices, but it will still require updating and complementing in order to better understand complexities that govern action and cannot be easily quantified in local contexts.

As a result, two final questions arise for further reflection. First, if all strategies collected in this volume became successfully institutionalized, what implications follow for improving ID/TD in higher education? A balance between short-term accommodation and profound transformation of the higher education system will enable a widespread rethinking of how to offer more inclusive and powerful plural answers to current societal challenges. The second question follows: Who should authorize these changes to happen and holds power to do so? Put another way, whose interests are represented and what futures are enabled or disabled? Our framework is not a formula for success. However, it does provide administrators, researchers, educators, students, and perhaps funders and policymakers with an understanding of how to navigate institutionalizing processes. Hence, it is a tool for addressing the main challenges and obstacles that need to be overcome. The task now is to adapt the lessons of this book to new workplaces and collaborations.

References

Abbott, A. (2004). *Methods of Discovery. Heuristics for the Social Sciences.* Contemporary Societies, Jeffrey C. Alexander, Series Editor. New York: Norton & Company.

Bammer, G., O'Rourke, M., O'Connell, D., et al. (2020). "Expertise in research integration and implementation for tackling complex problems: When is it needed, where can it be found and how can it be strengthened?". *Palgrave Communications*, 6, 5. DOI: 10.1057/s41599-019-0380-0

Chambers, C., Brabazon, T., Dumitrescu, I., Davis, L., Bebbington, W., & Moore, A. (2021). "Moving mountains: The reforms that would push academia to new heights". *The Chronicle of Higher Education.* February 18, 2021. Retrieved https://www.timeshighereducation.com/features/moving-mountains-reforms-would-push-academia-new-heights

Charmaz, K., & Mitchell, R. (2001). "Grounded theory in ethnography". In Atkinson, P., Coffey, A., Delamont, S., Lofland, J., & Lofland, L. (eds.), *Handbook of Ethnography*. London: SAGE, pp. 160–174.

Clarke, A.E., Friese, C., & Washburn, R. (eds.). (2015). *Situational Analysis in Practice: Mapping Research with Grounded Theory.* London: Routledge.

Douglas, M. (1986). *How Institutions Think.* The Frank W. Abrams Lectures. New York: Syracuse University Press.

Fam, D., Neuhauser, L., & Gibbs, P. (eds.). (2018). *The Art of Collaborative Research and Collective Learning: Transdisciplinary Theory, Practice and Education.* Dorschet: Springer.

Felt, U. (2017). "Of timescapes and knowledgescapes: Re-timing research and higher education". In P. Scott, J. Gallacher, & G. Parry (eds.), *New Landscapes and Languages of Higher Education.* Oxford: Oxford University Press, pp. 129–148.

Global University Network for Innovation (GUNi). (2017). *Higher Education in the World 6. Towards a Socially Responsible University: Balancing the Global with the Local.* Girona: GUNi.

Hart, D.D., & Silka, L. (2020). "Rebuilding the Ivory Tower: A bottom-up experiment in aligning research with societal needs". *Issues in Science and Technology*, 36, 64–70.

Harris, M., & Holley, K. (2008). "Constructing the interdisciplinary ivory tower: The planning of interdisciplinary spaces on university campuses". *Planning for Higher Education*, 36(3), 34–43.

Hess, D.J. (2011). "Scientific culture". In Neil J. Smelser & Paul B. Bates (eds.), *International Encyclopedia of the Social and Behavioral Sciences*. Oxford: Pergamon, pp. 13724–13727.

Hess, D.J. (2012). "Cultures of science". In Sabine Massen, Mario Kaiser, Martin Reinhart, & Barbara Sutter (eds.), *Handbuch Wissenschaftersoziologie*. Rapperswil: VS Verlag, pp. 177–190.

Hukkinen, J.I., & Huutoniemi, K. (2014). "Heuristics as cognitive tools for pursuing sustainability". In Huutoniemi, K., & Tapio, P. (eds.), *Transdisciplinary Sustainability Studies*. London: Routledge, pp. 177–93.

Jahan, N., Naveed, S., Zeshan, M., Tahir, M. A. (2016). How to Conduct a Systematic Review: A Narrative Literature Review. *Cureus*, 8(11), e864–e864. DOI:10.7759/cureus.864

Klein, J.T. (2010). *Creating Campus Cultures. A Model for Strength and Sustainability*. Washington, DC: Association of American Colleges and Universities.

Klein, J.T., & Falk-Krzesinski, H.J. (2017). "Interdisciplinary and collaborative work: Framing promotion and tenure practices and policies". *Research Policy*, 46(6), 1055–1061. https://doi.org/10.1016/j.respol.2017.03.001.

Kligyte, G., van der Bijl-Brouwer, M., Leslie, J., Key, T., Hooper, B., & Salazar, E. (2021). "A partnership outcome spaces framework for purposeful student-staff partnerships". *Teaching in Higher Education*, Online – early access. https://doi.org/10.1080/13562517.2021.1940924

König, B., Diehl, K., Tscherning, K., & Helming, K. (2013). "A framework for structuring interdisciplinary research management". *Research Policy*, 42(1), 261–272. https://doi.org/10.1016/j.respol.2012.05.006

Leahey, E., Barringer, S.N., & Ring-Ramírez, M. (2019). "Universities' structural commitment to interdisciplinary research". *Scientometrics*, 118, 891–919. https://doi.org/10.1007/s11192-018-2992-3

Louvel, S. (2021). *The Policies and Politics of Interdisciplinary Research: Nanomedicine in France and in the United States*. London: Routledge.

Lyall, C. (2019). *Being an Interdisciplinary Academic. How Institutions Shape University Careers*. London: Palgrave Pivot.

OECD. (2020). "Addressing societal challenges using transdisciplinary research". *OECD Science, Technology and Industry Policy Papers*, No. 8. Paris: OECD Publishing. https://doi.org/10.1787/0ca0ca45-en.

Palonen, K. (2003). "Four Times of Politics: Policy, Polity, Politicking, and Politicization". *Alternatives: Global, Local, Political*, 28(2), 171–186. https://doi.org/10.1177/030437540302800202.

Pohl, C. (2014). "From complexity to solvability: The praxeology of transdisciplinary research". In K. Huutoniemi & P. Tapio (eds.), *Transdisciplinary Sustainability Studies*. London: Routledge, pp. 103–118.

Rogga, S., & Zscheischler, J. (2021). "Opportunities, balancing acts, and challenges - Doing PhDs in transdisciplinary research projects". *Environmental Science & Policy*, 120, 138–144. https://doi.org/10.1016/j.envsci.2021.03.009

Schikowitz, A. (2021). "Chapter 11: Being a 'Good Researcher' in transdisciplinary research: Choreographies of identity work beyond community". In K. Kastenhofer, & S. Molyneux-Hodgson (eds.), *Community and Identity in Contemporary Technosciences*, Sociology of the Sciences Yearbook 31, pp. 225–245 https://doi.org/10.1007/978-3-030-61728-8_11

Slaughter, S., & Rhoades, G. (2004). *Academic Capitalism and the New Economy: Markets, State and Higher Education*. Maryland: John Hopkins University Press.

Slaughter, S., & Taylor, B.J. (2016). "Conclusion. Academic capitalism, stratification, and resistance: Synthesis and future research". In Slaughter, S., & Taylor, B.J. (eds.), *Higher Education, Stratification, and Workforce Development*. London: Springer, pp. 349–360. https://doi.org/10.1007/978-3-319-21512-9_18

Smolka, M., Fisher, E., & Hausstein, A. (2020). "From affect to action: Choices in attending to disconcertment in interdisciplinary collaborations". *Science, Technology, & Human Values*, November 2020. https://doi.org/10.1177/0162243920974088

Spaapen, J., Dijstelbloem, H., & Wamelink, F. (2007). *Evaluating Research in Context. A Method for Comprehensive Research Assessment*. The Hague: Consultative Committee of Sector Councils for Research and Development (COS).

Streck, D.R. (2020). "Pedagogies of participation: A methodological framework for comparative studies". *Global Comparative Education: Journal of the WCCES*, 4(1–2), 35–49.

Streck, D.R. (2021). "Transdisciplinarity as a decolonizing research practice: A Latin American perspective". *Diálogos Latinoamericanos*, 29, 88–100. https://tidsskrift.dk/dialogos/article/view/120252

Thain, M. (2021). "Post-pandemic recovery requires radical interdisciplinarity". *THE World University Rankings*, 18 July 2021. https://www.timeshighereducation.com/blog/post-pandemic-recovery-requires-radical-interdisciplinarity

Vienni Baptista, B., & Rojas-Castro, S. (2019). "Transdisciplinary institutionalization in higher education: A two-level analysis". *Studies in Higher Education*, 45(6), pp. 1075–1092. https://doi.org/10.1080/03075079.2019.1593347

Vienni Baptista, B., Vasen, F., & Villa-Soto, J.C. (2018). "Interdisciplinary centers in Latin American universities: The challenges of institutionalization". *Higher Education Policy* 32, 461–483. https://doi.org/10.1057/s41307-018-0092-x

Vienni Baptista, B., Maryl, M., Wciślik, P., Fletcher, I., Buchner, A., Wallace, D., & Pohl, C. (2020). "Final report on understandings of interdisciplinary and transdisciplinary research and factors of success or failure". *Shaping Interdisciplinary Practices in Europe*. https://doi.org/10.5281/zenodo.3824839

Wallace, D., de Moura Rocha Lima, G., Sessa, C., & Ohlmeyer, J. (2021). "Maximising arts, humanities and social sciences integration in inter- and transdisciplinary research for effective responses to societal challenges". Policy Brief. *Shaping Interdisciplinary Practices in Europe*. https://doi.org/10.5281/zenodo.4442373

Weingart, P. (2014). "Interdisciplinarity and the new governance of universities". In Weingart, P. & Padberg, B. (eds.), *University Experiments in Interdisciplinarity Obstacles and Opportunities*. Bielefeld: Transcript, pp. 151–174.

INDEX

Note: Page numbers in *italics* indicate figures, **bold** indicate tables in the text, and references following "n" refer endnotes.

AASHE *see* Association for the Advancement of Sustainability in Higher Education (AASHE)
AAU *see* Association of American Universities (AAU)
Abe, K. 174
academia 65, 66, 108, 109, 154, 156–158, 160–163, 212, 213, 218, 226; gradual response from 220–223
academic(s) 20, 22, 109, 115, 157, 158, 163, 221, 222, 227; careers 5, 18, 20, 81, 158, 180, 211; community 60, 110, 113, 219, 220; culture 7, 23, 109, 114, 155, 161, 163, 218; departments 187, 192, 197, 198; institutions 124–127, 144, 152, 153, 199, 200, 211–214, 220, 221; knowledge 31, 141, 161; knowledges 206; systems 152–159, 161–163; work 14, 51, 52, 90, 214, 226
accountability 96, 101; mechanism 97; relationships 91; structures 213
accreditation 60, 76, 243; procedures 35
accumulation 209; experience 129; system 154
Adam, B. 205
adaptive learning 96
adequate evaluation: of inter- and trans-disciplinary work 227–228
administration 7, 80, 179, 242
Adomßent, M. 30

Africa 7, 39, 111–113, 115, 118, 169, 179, 239
aggregation 58, 62, 220
agreement 195–199
AHSS *see* arts, humanities, and social sciences (AHSS)
AIS *see* Association for Interdisciplinary Studies (AIS)
AISHE 2.0 *see* Auditing Instrument for Sustainability in Higher Education (AISHE 2.0)
Akker, W. van den 223
Akua-Sakyiwah, B. 5, 8, 239–244
Alianza de Redes de Universidades por la Sustentabilidad y el Ambiente (ARIUSA) 40
Alvarez-Buylla, E. 49
APPEAR *see* Austrian Partnership Programme in Higher Education and Research for Development (APPEAR)
applied disciplines 143
applied health research 226
applied natural sciences 75
applied research: local and national economic impact of 15
ARIUSA *see* Alianza de Redes de Universidades por la Sustentabilidad y el Ambiente (ARIUSA)
Arizona State University (ASU) 78
Armenia: academic systems in transition 153–154; ASPU 156; internal structure

250 Index

of academic system 158–159; practical organization 159–160; societal conditions of governance 160–161; societal role of universities 157–158; transdisciplinarity in academic systems 154–156, *155*
Armenian State Pedagogical University (ASPU) 156
arts, humanities, and social sciences (AHSS) 222, 224–226, 243; disciplines 90; integration 225; research 225
art–science: (re)emergence of a frontier intellectual 200; academic department structure 198, *198*; contemporary societal challenges 198–199, *199*; data analysis 193–194; data collection 193–194; demographic characteristics of survey respondents *194*; educational specialization *197*; educational specialization, impact of 197; epistemic cultures 190–192; in Europe 189–190; institutional design and management 199–200; interactions in 188; interquartile range (IQR) 195; research questions (RQs) 192; sample 193–194; scientists and artists 196–197; two cultures problem 195–196, *196*
ASPU *see* Armenian State Pedagogical University (ASPU)
assessment 13, 18, 21, 43, 48, 126, 128, 130, 213, 220; categories 228; infrastructures 204; procedures 218; processes 206; settings 48; systems 243
Association for Interdisciplinary Studies (AIS) 73, 74; doctoral programs 78; in identifying common challenges and strategies 81; pioneers 73
Association for the Advancement of Sustainability in Higher Education (AASHE) 40
Association of American Universities (AAU) 80
ASU *see* Arizona State University (ASU)
Auditing Instrument for Sustainability in Higher Education (AISHE 2.0) 40
Augsburg, T. 75, 76, 155
Australia 4, 7, 89–91, 94, 102, 240, 242, 244
Australian Research Council 91, 103
Australian Technology Park 93
Australian tertiary education sector 89–91, 93, 103
Austrian Partnership Programme in Higher Education and Research for Development (APPEAR) 156

autonomous non-profit organizations 126, 132, 133
Autonomous University of Queretaro (UAQ) 44, 46; degree programs at 50–51
avant-garde social spaces 58

Bachelor's in Human Development for Sustainability (LDHS) 44–45
Balsiger, J. 162
Bammer, G. 68, 91, 162
Barnett, R. 162
Barry, A. 17, 210
Barth, M. 162
Bergmann, M. 163
Blazquez, N. 46
BO *see* boundary organisation (BO)
Bologna Process 27, 30, 125, 154
Booth, S. A. 32
Born, G. 210
boundary organisation (BO) 89–91, 96, 97, 100–102
Brazil 57–69; (re)fragmenting integration 60–62; graduate education system in 60; interdisciplinary community 67; interdisciplinary pathologies and syndromes 64–66; multi- and inter-disciplinary graduate programs (GPs) in 57; postgraduate system in 58–60; re-democratization 58; traditional peoples and communities in 70n2; traditional populations in 66; universalization *vs.* quality 62–64
Bruce, A. 17
Buitendijk, S. 21
Bursztyn, M. 68

C3 *see* Center for the Sciences of Complexity (C3)
Canada 8, 72–74, 77, 80, 81, 225, 226
CAPES *see* Coordination for the Improvement of Higher Education Personnel (CAPES)
career 18, 77, 81, 82, 205, 206, 208, 210, 212–214; advancement 2; growth 158; paths 35, 82, 222; procedures 208; stage 207; structures 204; trajectory 174, 211
Carew, A. L. 2
Cash, D.W. 112
Caucasus countries: transdisciplinary case study research in 164
CEIICH *see* Center for Interdisciplinary Research in the Sciences and Humanities (CEIICH)

Index 251

Center for Interdisciplinary Research in the Sciences and Humanities (CEIICH) 45, 46, 48–50, 53, 54n6; training programs 46
Center for Sustainable Development (CDS) 57, 66–67, 69; and discipline-based departments 67; research 68; trajectory mirrors 67
Center for the Sciences of Complexity (C3) 45; interdisciplinary research modes 45
Cetina, K. K. 191
chief scientific officers (CSOs) 220
Chilisa, B. 113, 118
China 139–148; contemporary evolution 144–146; historical development 140–144; inter- and trans-disciplinary research 146–148
Chinese: academia 140; context 239; culture 140; enterprises 147; higher education 144; institutes 143, 144, 146; modes 144; tradition 144; universities 144, 145, 147, 148
Chinese Communist Party (CCP) 140, 142, 143
Chowdhury, U. K. 33
Cohen, M. D. 31
communication: networks 128; problems 32; processes 32
communities-of-interest **39**
communities-of-practice **39**
community: engagement 83; impact 78; organisations 103; partners 79; partnerships 98, 101, 103; of scholars 93, 142; support 100
Complementary Studies (CS) 27, 28
Contreras Gomez, L.E. 44, 47
Cooperative Research Centre (CRC) programme 91, 94, 100
Coordination for the Improvement of Higher Education Personnel (CAPES) 60–63, 65, 67, 69; (re)fragmenting integration 60–62, *61*; graduate programs classified in 63; reformulation 67
CORDIS database of the European Commission 229n4
COVID-19 pandemic 2, 13, 23, 79, 82, 90, 114, 116, 119, 219, 220, 232
Crona, B. 90, 91, 96, 97, 101
cross-disciplinary 38; approach 13; courses 60; engagement 79; focus 33; introductory 33; sustainability 34; teaching 34
cultural dimension 240–241

cultures 6, 21, 30–32, 170, 189, 191, 195, 233; analysis 233; anthropologist 179; barriers 161; boundaries 97; changes 2, 145, 225; characteristics 44; and communities 1; contexts 6, 153, 234, 245; factors 3, 44, 145; studies 75, 129, 156
curriculum 51, 73, 74, 107, 113–115, 117, 143, 145; adjustments 116; change 16, 118; development 45, 51, 152, 162, 163; initiatives 78; models 79; transformation 115

data analysis 108, 193, 194, 198
Davidson, C. N. 2
De Rose, K. 112
decision-making processes 153, 158, 160
DeZure, D. 38
disciplinary: approaches 57, 66, 128; backgrounds 22, 66, 67, 69, 156; boundaries 28, 51, 102, 204; knowledge 125, 132, 133; research 15, 83, 214, 224; structures 72, 91, 93, 94
discourses 94, 161, 175, 177, 188, 233, 236, 239
diversity 7, 47, 64, 142, 170, 187, 212
documentary analysis 114
Dutch Academy of Arts and Sciences 224, 226, 229n14
Dutch National Science Agenda (NWA) 224

Economic and Social Research Council (ESRC) **15**, 17
economic development 79, 143, 145, 148
education reform 145
empowerment: of early-career researchers 177, 179, 241
Enlightenment 188
epistemic dimension 236–240
epistemic framework 236
epistemological experience, with institutionalization 4
Europe 7, 14, 189, 192, 193, 221, 222, 229n7; evaluation culture 226–227; inter- and trans-disciplinary policy in 225–226
European Commission (EC) 170, 221, 229n4, 229n110, 241
European Credit Transfer and Accumulation System (ECTS) 154
European Higher Education Area (EHEA) 154
European Network on Higher Education for Sustainable Development (COPERNICUS Alliance) 40

252 Index

evaluation procedures 220, 223, 227
evidence-based policy 17

faculty 35, 36, 74–79, 81, 82, 114–118
Fam, D. 100, 154
Federal University's Restructuring and Expansion Program (REUNI) 62, 64
Felt, U. 4, 9, 187, 191, 239, 240, 245
fetishisation of excellence 20
Fischer, G. 38
flagship programme 91
France 142, 195
Frank, A. 49
Frickel, S. 43, 48, 53, 83
funding 22, 23, 79, 80, 114, 115, 118, 145–148, 210, 243; agencies 43, 204, 207, 214; policies 223, 242
funds 44, 101, 146, 159–160, 168; external 34; governmental 46, 144
future potentials and strategies framework 236

gender equality xx, 229n13
General Education (Gen Ed) requirements, North America 72, 77
Georgia 4, 152–154, 156–158, 160–163; academic systems in transition 153–154; internal structure of academic system 158–159; practical organization 159–160; societal conditions of governance 160–161; societal role of universities 157–158; transdisciplinarity in academic systems 154–156, *155*; TSU 156
Germany 4, 21, 27, 30, 109, 142, 177, 195, 242; Leuphana College 27–29; Leuphana University in 109; scientific and political change in 34
Ghana 107–118; higher institutions in 111–114; Higher National Diploma (HNC) 111; institutionalisation of transdisciplinarity in 108–111; time–space concept 114–118; transdisciplinary research (TDR) 108
Gibbons, M. 103, 226, 227
Gil Antón, M. 44, 47
Global Challenges Research Fund (GCRF) 16
Goldberg, D. T. 2
Graduate Record Examinations (GRE) Board, North America 82
graduation requirements 52
Graff, H. 83
Guston, D.H. 90

Haldane report 14
Hanson, A. 113

Hayhoe, R. 144
HDR *see* higher-degree-by-research (HDR)
Henry, S. 75, 76
Hess, D. J. 233
Hessels, L.K. 223
heuristic (comparative) framework 9, 235, *237*
heuristics 235
higher-degree-by-research (HDR) 92; completions 99; programme 95, 101; student programme 93, 94, 99
higher education 124, 125, 132, 134, 140, 143–145, 148, 232; contexts 38; curriculum 108; institutions 39, 107, 108, 114–116, 124–126, 153, 154; network 125; qualifications 154; regulations 67; research approach 108; for sustainable development 30; systems 68, 72, 143–145, 158, 232, 239, 240, 242
Hiyama, T. 174
Holland, J.H. 112
Holley, K. 78
humanities 28–30, 45, 49, 50, 146, 168, 169, 171, 225, 229n10
hybrid domains 49, 53
hybrid management 91, 101

Indigenous knowledge, research, Peoples 118, 180
individual intellectual curiosity 180, 181, 241
individual learning phases 33
individual practitioners 187, 188, 192
industrial capabilities 111
industry 91–94, 98, 99, 101–103, 147, 148, 223, 224, 242, 243
industry-funded contract research 94, 98, 100, 101
industry-society-science partnerships 91, 103
innovation 15, 145, 152–154, 162, 163, 188, 219, 225; policy 21, 190, 224; projects 218, 220, 227
innovative research activities 124, 125
Institute for Sustainable Futures (ISF) 89, 92–95, 97–103
institutional arrangements 148, 243, 245
institutional changes 6, 8, 16, 19, 34–35, 58, 60, 169, 170, 173, 180, 181
institutional culture 14, 43, 62, 68, 180, 181, 207
institutional development 103, 124, 131

institutional experience, with institutionalization 4
institutional facilities 35–37
institutional structures 8, 15, 16, 23, 52, 57, 79, 101, 124, 221
institutionalization: individual experiences with 3–4
institutions, as mobilizing networks 2
Integrated Classification of Scientific Journals (CIRC) 45
Integrative Graduate Education and Research Traineeship Program (IGERT) 79
intellectual developments 168, 169, 173–175, 177, 180, 181
interdisciplinary, National Science and Technology System 48
interdisciplinary research (IDR) 19, 80–81, 170, 173, 174, 179–180
Interdisciplinary Research Advisory Panel, in UK 13
Interfaculty Coordination Office for General Ecology (IKAÖ) 32
Intergovernmental Panel on Climate Change (IPCC), UN SDGs 220
International Finance Corporation (IFC) 110
ISF *see* Institute for Sustainable Futures (ISF)

Jacobs, J.A. 43, 48, 53, 83
Japan 168–182; business practice 179; center for inter- and trans-disciplinary 168; national inter-university research institute 168; overseas cooperation volunteer 179; societies 180

Keestra, M. 1, 3, 4
Kenya 179
Keryan, T. 152–155, 157, 239, 242, 244
Kirdina, S.G. 127
Klein, J.T. 6, 38, 43, 73, 126, 154, 155, 234
Kleyner, G.B. 128
knowledge co-production 68, 96, 98, 118, 161, 173, 174
knowledge cultures 234, 240
knowledge generation 17, 108, 207
knowledge production 72–74, 109, 112, 113, 188, 190, 208, 211, 221, 222, 233, 234, 242, 243, 245
Kuhn, T. S. 20
Kuzminov, Y.I. 125

Langfeldt, L. 44, 48, 53
Latour, B. 190

leadership 97, 99, 102, 152, 174, 175, 205
Leahey, E. 80, 81
learning 17, 18, 27, 28, 30, 34–39, 90, 141; communities 38, 141; environment 33; for transformation 37–40
legitimacy 43, 68, 80, 103, 236
Leuphana College 27–29, *28*, *29*, 32–39; media(lity)-oriented courses 29; practice-oriented seminars 29; seminars 29; structure and modules of complementary studies at *29*
Leuphana Semester and Complementary Studies *28*
Leuphana Teaching Service 35, *36*
Leuphana University 28, 30, 33, 35, 36
Leuphana's holistic approach *34*
Leuphana's teaching evaluation **37**
Li, J. 144
life sciences 67, 146, 229n3
Lindvig, K. 16
Lowe, P. 14
Lüneburg University: Minor Sustainable Development 33
Lyall, C. 4, 8, 16, 22, 236, 240–244
Lysak, I.V. 128

Mamatov, A.V. 128
March, J. G. 31
Marshall, F. 115
mathematics 47, 49, 50, 90, 200, 222, 243
Meagher, L. 22
media 29, 99, 228
Mexico: auxiliary interdisciplinarity 47; government funds 46; inter-specialties 47; National Autonomous University of Mexico (UNAM) 44, 50; public policies in 43; scientific and technological policy 48, 52, 54n1
Michelsen, G. 30
Miller, C. 91, 100, 101
Minor Sustainable Development 33
Mirsky, E.M. 128
Moore, S. 20

narrative culture 191
National Academies of Sciences 13
National Autonomous University of Mexico (UNAM) 44, 46; degree programs at 50–51
National Organization of Research Development Professionals (NORDP) 80
National Research Council (NWO) 224
National Science and Technology System (SNCyT) 48, 54n5

National Science Foundation (NSF) 81
National System of Researchers (SNI) 44, 52, 54n2; areas 47, 48; criteria 47; evaluation criteria 48; evaluation criteria used by 47–48; knowledge areas 45; members 48; physics 50; researchers 45
natural sciences 28–30, 34, 47, 49, 75, 78, 139, 145, 146, 222
Ndlovu, M. 113
Netherlands 73, 195, 219, 220, 223, 224, 229n3; science and society in 223–224
Network for Transdisciplinary Research (td-net) 14
Nodo de Estudios sobre Interdisciplina and Transdisciplina (Nodo ESIT) 5
non-governmental organizations (NGOs) 59, 164
North America: AASHE 40; academic job market in 82; COVID-19 pandemic in 82; critiques of interdisciplinarity 83–84; financial stringency in 75; general education 76–77; graduate interdisciplinary teaching and degree programs 77–80; interdisciplinary careers 81–83; interdisciplinary research 80–81; undergraduate teaching programs 73–76
Nowotny, H. 6, 115, 132, 213, 227
Nurse, P. 14, 15
NWA *see* Dutch National Science Agenda (NWA)

online questionnaire 193, 200
Organization for Economic Cooperation and Development (OECD) 1, 170, 173, 235
organizational change 30, 32, 78, 241
organizational dimension 241–244
organizational structures 4, 5, 79, 223, 233, 241
Ostwald, J. 38
Ottoline Leyser, Dame 21

paradox 22; of interdisciplinarity 17, 214
Parker, J. 90, 91
participative governance 21, 23
participatory 113, 158, 159; action research 93; discussion formats 158; governance 160, 161; impact pathways analysis 228; innovation 154; processes 152; solutions 69; transformation 118; work 68

participatory impact pathways analysis (PIPA) 228
partnerships 92, 94, 98, 99, 222, 242
Pawlowska, A.E. 110
Pellert, A. 32
Pereira, E. 112
personal experience, with institutionalization 3–4
perspectives 28, 29, 36–38, 112, 116, 187–189, 196, 198, 207
Phillips, D. 3
Phillipson, J. 14
philosophy 6, 49, 129, 130, 133, 142
pluridisciplinary education 54n6
Porus, V.N. 131
practice-oriented educational approaches 39
principal investigators (PIs) 222
professional experience, with institutionalization 3–4
project leaders 169, 174–175, *176*, 178–181
public-private partnerships (PPP) 224

Qualifications Authority Act (SAQA), South Africa 109
quality assurance 35, 101

RAS *see* Russian Academy of Sciences (RAS)
Realising Our Potential: A Strategy for Science, Engineering and Technology (Waldegrave) 14
REF *see* Research Excellence Framework (REF), in UK
reforms 91, 126, 143, 154, 206; efforts 1; undergraduate education 146
Research Excellence Framework (REF), in UK 13, 14, 18–21, 24n7, 225; changes 20; competitive accountability, culture of 21; impact assessment 19; impact case studies 18, 22; looms 13; model of impact 20; rules demand 18
research funding 14, 21, 23, 72, 103, 114, 118, 146
Research Institute for Humanity and Nature (RIHN), Japan 168–171, 174–177, 179–181; boundary objects 178; consilience hypothesis 174; early-career researchers 179; external affiliates of *171*; full research projects (FR) *172*; institutional changes over time 170; institutionalization in 181–182; intellectual development 175, 177, **177**; intellectual development

of **175**; inter- and trans-disciplinary research **173**; interviewed projects **176**; meta-research 170, 173; multifaceted viewpoints 178, 179; projects 175, 181; prospectus booklets 172; research 168; scalable organization 179; semi-structured interviews 174–175, **177**; stage-gate project development system 169–170; timeline of research project **169**; top-down pressures 180–181
Research Unit for Research Use (RURU) 17
Rifkin, J. 205
RIHN *see* Research Institute for Humanity and Nature (RIHN), Japan
Rinderspacher, J. P. 206
Rojas-Castro, S. 7, 109, 155
Romanticism 188
Rural Economy and Land Use (RELU) programme 16–17
Rusinko, C. A. 33, 34
Russell, A. W. 2
Russia 124–133; academic institutes and universities 127–129; autonomous non-profit organizations 132–134; higher education institutions 125; interdisciplinarity in universities 129–130; transdisciplinarity in academic institutions 130–132
Russian Academy of Sciences (RAS) 124; structure of 124

Scholz, R.W. 115, 156
Schriewer, J. 3
Schweisfurth, M. 3
sciences, technological and engineering fields, mathematics, and medicine (STEMM) 222
Scientific and Technological Advisory Forum (FCCT) 46
scientific disciplines 27, 28, 37, 112, 125, 128, 191, 218
scientific knowledge 38, 113, 126, 191
scientific research 130, 132, 175, 177, 228, 229n14
scientific work 47, 49
Scimago Journal and Country Rank 45
self-funding 93, 98, 103
self-learning 4
SHAPE-ID *see* "Shaping interdisciplinary research practices in Europe" (SHAPE-ID)
"Shaping interdisciplinary research practices in Europe" (SHAPE-ID) 17, 222, 229n6

Shevchuk, P. 128
Simon, D. 3
Skills Development Act 109
Smith, K. 18, 20
SNI *see* National System of Researchers (SNI)
Snow, C. P. 44, 187, 189
Social Sciences and Humanities Research Council (SSHRC) 80
Soviet Union *see* Russia
Spaapen, J. 22, 223, 243
Srivastava, S. 110
star model, interdisciplinarity 59, *59*
Stember, M. 229n1
Streck, D. 9, 68, 240
sustainability 32–34, 39, 44, 46, 69; activities 93; concept 31; issues 68; principle 30; project management 52; science programs in Brazil 57, 59, 61, 63, 65, 67, 69
Sustainability Tracking, Assessment and Rating System (STARS) 40
Sustainability with Indigenous Peoples and Traditional Territories (MESPT) 66, 67
sustainable development 30, 32, 38, 57, 59, 61, 108, 162, 163
sustainable university 29–30
Swedish Higher Education Authority (UKA) 229n13
Swilling, M. 108
Szostak, R. 76

Tait, J. 17
Tbilisi State University (TSU) 156
TD-BO *see* transdisciplinary boundary organisation (TD-BO)
Thain, M. 245
Tierney, W. 16
Tietje, O. 156
timeframes 6, 7, 43, 51, 240, 242
time generator: career 210–211; evaluation 211–213; identity work temporalized 210–211; in inter- and transdisciplinary research 208–210; socialization 210–211; temporalities 211–213; value(s) 211–213
time-sensitive perspective: inter- and trans-disciplinary research 205–206
Time Wars (Rifkin, Jeremy) 205
Toombs, W. 16
transdisciplinary boundary organisation (TD-BO) 89–91; adaptive evaluation and reward systems 99; adaptive organisational structures 97; aligning to university goals 98; analytical

model for 94–102; in Australia 91–92; boundary work 101–102; characteristics of 95, **96–97**; collaboration 100; convening 99; cross-boundary orchestration 102; deconstruction 101; distributed accountability 97–98; durable structure 98; hybridisation 100–101; institutional dynamics in 102, 103; ISF's evolution 92–94; legitimate hybrid space 94; mediating 100; practice and function 99; strategy 100; structure and organisation 94; translating 99–100
transdisciplinary research (TDR) 108, 111, 114, 115, 170, 173, 174, 177, 179–181, 204–206, 209; institutionalization 181; process 173; projects 173, 180, 181; research process 170

UAQ *see* Autonomous University of Queretaro (UAQ)
UK Research and Innovation (UKRI) 15; Industrial Strategy Challenge Fund 16
UK's innovation agency (Innovate UK) 15
UNESCO 30
United Kingdom 13–17, 19–23, 221, 242, 243; consultation model 21; discourse 21; funding for interdisciplinary research 22; government 23; government departments 21; interdisciplinary research in 14; perspective 23; productive interactions 22; research 13, 18, 20, 22, 23; research excellence, politicisation of 14; research impact 14; science and innovation policy 21; strategic priorities of 18; thematic teaching programmes 16; transdisciplinary research in 14
United States 72–77, 80–82, 131, 142, 146, 148, 239
University of Bern, Interfaculty Coordination Office for General Ecology (IKAÖ) 32
University of Brasilia (UnB) 57, 66
University of Technology Sydney (UTS) 89, 91–95, 98, 101, 103; city campus 93; faculties 97, 102; planning 98
University of Texas at San Antonio (UTSA) 79
US National Science Foundation's Research Traineeship Program (NRT) 79

Vakhshtayn, V.S. 128
van Breda, J. 108
Van der Zwaan, B. 19
van Drooge, L. 22
Vienni Baptista, B. 7, 43, 109, 126, 152, 155, 161, 204, 240
Villa-Soto, J.C. 46, 48
Vilsmaier, U. 115, 162

Watkins, M.O. 118
Weingart, P. 7
Whewell, William 174
Wickson, F. 2
Wilson, Edward O. 174
World Wide Views project (WWVD) 100

Xinya College 146

Yan, F. 144

Zgambo, O. 113

Printed in the United States
by Baker & Taylor Publisher Services